Western North Carolina: Its Mountains and Its People to 1880

> *I have discovered a Country so delitious, pleasant, and fruitfull, y^t were it cultivated, doubtless it would prove a second Paradise (sic).*
>
> —Henry Woodward,
> circa 1674

Western North Carolina: Its Mountains and Its People to 1880

Ora Blackmun

APPALACHIAN CONSORTIUM PRESS

Boone, North Carolina 28607

The Appalachian Consortium was a non-profit educational organization composed of institutions and agencies located in Southern Appalachia. From 1973 to 2004, its members published pioneering works in Appalachian studies documenting the history and cultural heritage of the region. The Appalachian Consortium Press was the first publisher devoted solely to the region and many of the works it published remain seminal in the field to this day.

With funding from the Andrew W. Mellon Foundation and the National Endowment for the Humanities through the Humanities Open Book Program, Appalachian State University has published new paperback and open access digital editions of works from the Appalachian Consortium Press.

www.collections.library.appstate.edu/appconsortiumbooks

This work is licensed under a Creative Commons BY-NC-ND license. To view a copy of the license, visit http://creativecommons.org/licenses.

Original copyright © 1977 by the Appalachian Consortium Press.

ISBN (pbk.: alk. Paper): 978-1-4696-4136-2
ISBN (ebook): 978-1-4696-4138-6

Distributed by the University of North Carolina Press
www.uncpress.org

Dedicated

to

George Myers Stephens

A Founder of
The Western North Carolina
Historical Association
The Cherokee Historical Association
The Museum of the Cherokee Nation

An Advisor to
The Appalachian Consortium

TABLE OF CONTENTS

	Author's Preface	ix
	Introduction by Cratis Williams	xiii
	Stagecoach Days at Sherrill's Inn	xvi
I	The Land of Mountains	1
II	Eden is Discovered	25
III	Two Races Meet	43
IV	Along the Trading Paths	56
V	Lightnings Flash and Thunders Roll	73
VI	The Lull Between the Storms	88
VII	A New Flag for Western North Carolina	106
VIII	East-West Tug-of-War	125
IX	In Search of Beauty—An Interlude	139
X	With Their Goods and Chattels	152
XI	Weaving a Homespun Pattern of Living	166
XII	Boundaries and Western Leadership	189
XIII	Gold in the Hills and on the Highways	207
XIV	Light and Shade in the Mountains	222
XV	The Crack of Doom in the Mountains	241
XVI	More Government for Western North Carolina	261
XVII	The Lure of the Mountains	284
XVIII	Whigs in the Mountains	306
XIX	War in the Land	328
XX	War Comes to the Hills	343
XXI	The Rebirth of a State	356
XXII	Long is the Night	364
XXIII	Dawn Breaks Over the Mountains	380
	Chapter Notes	400
	Sources	437
	Index	452

AUTHOR'S PREFACE

Some years ago I stood atop a Western North Carolina mountain and looked down upon a boundless and impenetrable sea of motionless white mist. It was, I thought, not unlike the "great void upon the face of the deep." Suddenly, as if at command, a rushing wind swept over the ledge, and the sea of mist began a gentle, undulating motion. As on holy ground, I watched the growing force of the wind sweep the mist into titan waves of white that seemed writhing in the urgency of the first creation.

Suddenly the gray of the sky was broken by a narrow rift and through it a shaft of light sped to touch the tossing sea below me and to open first one path and then others. From these paths arose the solid forms of earth as when the world was new. Before my eyes these forms were clothed with mountains, valleys, and streams, with woods and meadows, all freshly dewed as with Heaven's first rain.

As I left the mountain in great humility of spirit, it came over me that in beauty and majesty these, the mountains of Western North Carolina, had been prepared for the habitation of man. What, I asked myself, had man done to them over the centuries and what had they done to and for the men and women, who for the short spans of their lives, called these mountains home?

To arrive at the answers to my questions I began the absorbing task of research. The Sondley Reference Collection and the North Carolina Collection in the Pack Memorial Library in Asheville furnished a wealth of illuminating and relevant material. Over a period of some ten years, Miss Myra Champion, Miss Ida Padelford, and more recently, Miss Betty Betz, librarians at Pack Memorial Library, were generous in giving me both of their time and of their valuable assistance in securing for me additional material. Miss Elizabeth Shepard, librarian at Warren Wilson College, furnished me with information concerning the excavation of Indian mounds on the campus of that college. To each of these librarians I wish to express my sincere thanks.

Gradually the chain of events making up the shifting pattern of life in the hills became clear. What my sources had revealed I then put into words and sentences and chapters. In the period of time covered (to 1880) that pattern of life was, in truth, a human drama of many scenes and acts performed by many changing characters on a stage arranged by nature itself. Its theme was the interplay of the best and the worst of man's thoughts and deeds, of the noble and the base and of all the gradations between. At its close in 1880 this drama was brightened by the assurance of a new dawn breaking over the ancient hills.

For the publication of this volume I am indebted to George Myers Stephens, who called the attention of the members of the Appalachian Consortium Press to the manuscript. I am also grateful to Mr. Stephens for his encouragement of my efforts and for his share in the selection of the illustrations for the book and for his work on the maps. These maps also reflect the professional skill of Hermon H. Rector. It is hoped that they will prove helpful to readers of *Western North Carolina: Its Mountains and Its People to 1880.*

I sincerely thank F. A. Ketterson, Jr., chairman of the Publications Committee of the Consortium Press and editor for the book. Especially do I appreciate his advice and his locating for my use additional records of the period covered. I thank F. Borden Mace, executive director of the Appalachian Consortium Press, for his careful reading of the manuscript and his evaluation of the text. He has been tireless in his efforts to make the book attractive in appearance and worthy of the high standard set by the Consortium Press. The understanding, help and encouragement given me by both Mr. Mace and Mr. Ketterson have made my work of research and writing a pleasant experience for me.

For the "Introduction" to this volume I am indebted to Dr. Cratis Williams, who graciously took the time from an already busy schedule to prepare a contribution that enhances the book and makes clear its purpose of portraying the events that make up the history of the mountain region prior to the coming of the railroad. He makes clear, too, that while this book is complete in itself, it is at the same time a companion volume to *Western North Carolina Since the Civil War* by Drs. Ina and John Van Noppen.

I deeply appreciate the time given and the helpful comments made by all who read sections of the manuscript. Especially do I thank Dr. Richard W. Iobst of Western Carolina University; Dr. Evelyn Underwood of Mars Hill College; Mrs. Mary Ulmer Chiltoskey of Cherokee; Mrs. Virginia Million of Cherokee; and Paul Rockwell of Asheville.

I feel a deep sense of gratitude toward those who early came into the mountain area and who left records in the forms of letters, diaries, travel sketches, and histories. Their first-hand accounts brought into vivid focus both the land and its people. Of those living in the mountains later I am indebted to all who wrote histories or sketches of their counties. From all of these sources I was able to understand not only the events that took place but also the issues and motives that prompted them.

My hope is that this volume will make a small contribution to the knowledge of the history of this land of mountains I call home.

Ora Blackmun

Asheville, North Carolina
January, 1977

INTRODUCTION

People, whether of a nation or a region, in order to understand their customs and institutions must know how the present forms came to be. One way to gain this knowledge is through the study of history. The history of a region, like its customs and institutions, is constantly being added to; sources of information not available to earlier writers come to light; understandings of past events are seen from new points of view; and the interpretation of the meanings of past events changes. Thus there is a continuing need for historians to study and evaluate and interpret the history of their nation or their region.

John Preston Arthur's *History of Western North Carolina* ended with 1913. Dr. Foster Alexander Sondley's *Western North Carolina* was published in 1930, but it treated mainly the early settlement of the French Broad River Valley. Thus the two most authoritative works dealing with the history of the mountain people of Western North Carolina were published well over a generation ago and one of them was somewhat narrow of scope. This Highland Region needed its history brought up to date. It needed treatment both broad and deep.

The companion volume to this work, *Western North Carolina Since the Civil War* by Dr. Ina Woestermeyer Van Noppen and her husband, the late Dr. John J. Van Noppen, came out in 1973. The Van Noppen book was the end result of twenty years of effort by the Western North Carolina Historical Association, an effort that involved the labor and planning of Dean W. E. Bird of Western Carolina University, Dean Daniel J. Whitener of Appalachian State University, and George Myers Stephens of Asheville. Dean Whitener had planned to write a history of Western North Carolina after his retirement, but, before his untimely death, he had interested the Van Noppens in undertaking the task. President William H. Plemmons at Appalachian State University worked out released faculty time for them and Weldon Williamson of Asheville and Dean Bird were successful in obtaining substantial contributions to an author expense fund for research and travel. When the fund was exhausted, the Van Noppens continued at their own expense to complete the work they had begun nearly ten years prior to its publication.

While the Van Noppens were working on their book, Ora Blackmun arrived from Arkansas to make Asheville her home. Miss Blackmun had recently retired from the English faculty of the University of Central Arkansas. Sometime earlier she spent a year as a researcher for the State Historian of Minnesota, where her forebears had settled during Indian times. She grew up in the Ozark Mountains at Fayetteville, Arkansas, and she spent much time investigating the history of that region. Such a background led her naturally to explore the riches of the Sondley Reference Collection in the Pack Library. Her amazing energy and keen mind took her through much of this source material. She soon found herself writing a voluminous history of this mountain region from early geologic times "for my own satisfaction."

By good fortune, George Myers Stephens, then chairman of the Western North Carolina Historical Association's committee to obtain a new history of the region, learned of Miss Blackmun's manuscript. The manuscript was brought to the attention of F. A. Ketterson, Jr., historian for the Blue Ridge Parkway and chairman of the Publications Committee of the Appalachian Consortium. The Board of Directors of the Consortium, after receiving reports of high praise for the authenticity and artistry of the work, quickly realized that Miss Blackmun's book was the ideal companion to the Van Noppen volume.

Owners of both volumes will note a few years of overlap between the end of the Civil War and the coming of the railroad. Because the earlier and the later periods called for different treatments this overlap served history well. In the recent period life became so varied that such aspects as public education and folklore demanded that the history of several decades be treated in one chapter.

By contrast, the earlier history is clearer for treatments in periods of time. What it meant for the Cherokees to live in an unspoiled land, for pioneers to live in a land of do-without—these are parts of good history writing.

Above all was the meaning of a changed way of life after the railroads came to the mountains. With her gift for taking the long view of an era, Miss Blackmun's final chapter looks forward to what the railroads would do to change life in these landlocked valleys. Landmarks of history are best used as points for charting the future. Ora Blackmun writes with her mind on the future as she did in her history of Asheville's First Presbyterian Church in *A Spire in the Mountains: The Story of 176 Years of a Church and a Town Growing Together, 1794-1969,* which was published in 1970. With the publication of *Western North Carolina: Its Mountains and Its People to 1880,* the people of the Carolina Highlands have a history that will serve the present generation well and will be a guidepost to future generations of historians.

Cratis Williams

Appalachian State University
Boone, North Carolina

Stagecoach Days
at
Sherrill's Inn

The pictures in this set are from wall paintings in the old Sherrill Inn at Hickory Nut Gap. They are the work of Mrs. Elizabeth Cramer McClure, an accomplished artist. After she and her husband, James G. K. McClure, purchased and then restored the hostelry, she began an extensive research of its background and of the history of the region. She was thus able to depict life as it ebbed and flowed about the popular inn during the first half of the nineteenth century.

Mr. and Mrs. James McClure Clarke, present owners of the building and grounds, together with Dr. Reuben A. Holden, President of Warren Wilson College, and the French Broad River chapter of the Garden Club of America, made possible the color section reproducing these pictures for this volume. Mrs. Clarke is the daughter of Mrs. Elizabeth McClure.

This is the view of Sherrill's Inn seen by travelers approaching it from Asheville. At the foot of the long hill the coachman blows his horn to indicate the number of guests so that the Sherrill family might prepare accordingly. Two elegant city guests attempt to kill a rattlesnake while their mountain guide stands ready with a stick in case the gun misses fire. The native wild flowers in the foreground appear in several of the panels.

Small bands of Cherokees sometimes hunted in the Fairview Valley, once a part of their far-flung domain. For protection, white settlers entering the region before 1800 built a small blockhouse, complete with gun ports. This log building still stands beside the Sherrill Inn.

The coach is stuck fast. The feeble attempts made by two young dandies to loosen the wheel are rendered futile by the determination to keep their white breeches unspotted. An elderly gentleman stands aloof to read his paper. A lady and her little girl stroll among the wild flowers. The coachman and his wife on the box await the outcome. This scene must often have been repeated in this red mud country.

Farmers drove their livestock many miles to eastern markets. The passing droves of hogs were offered a choice of chestnuts or acorns at Sherrill's Inn. Applejack was standard for the men. Farmers bringing produce from Polk County to Asheville camped with their covered wagons along the highway just below the Inn.

These people with their scant belongings are moving to some hillside farm. The hardships of life in the mountains are reflected in the strong but pinched face of the mother and in the indomitable spirit of the grandparents trudging by the side of the wagon. The husband looks toward the future with the hope of a better life for his children.

At the arrival of the stagecoach, Mrs. Sherrill descends the steps to greet the travelers. Her husband, Bedford, offers the guests a tray of applejack. A young man at the Inn ignores the coach and its passengers as he introduces a friend to the belle of the hostelry, who is standing near the bee skepts. A neighbor youngster is momentarily absorbed in chasing a chicken. A recent wall crack shows in this picture.

In the stone-paved courtyard back of the Inn a coach could be kept over night. In this yard, too, was the spring house and nearby stood the old fort. In the Inn cooking was done for the guests and the family over an open fire. It was said that at times the ghost of a young lady with long curls and a "sweep-tail" skirt could be seen melting into the fireplace chimney. Her face was always averted.

A detachment of soldiers from Stoneman's forces, coming through Hickory Nut Gap, stopped at the Inn. Sherrill descendants tell of the captain riding his horse onto the porch, demanding a night's lodging. The family had hidden the supply of hams behind the wall boards of the original log room at the end of the house. They had covered the signs of recent carpentry by hanging Mrs. Sherrill's hoop skirts on the wall.

CHAPTER ONE

The Land of Mountains

Western North Carolina is far more than the sum of the state's most westerly counties that make up its area. The Southern Appalachian Mountains extend in lofty and rambling fashion throughout its north-south length and reaching their greatest height, spread themselves in range after range throughout its east-west width. They have set the pattern for all human activity taking place in North Carolina's valleys and on its mountain slopes. Geographically, Western North Carolina differs sharply from the piedmont section of the state to the east and even more sharply from the sand hill and low coastal area that stretches to the Atlantic Ocean. Both geographically and culturally it has been indeed a region set apart, expressing itself in ways peculiarly its own.

From the time a band of wandering, primitive people reached its boundary to the present day, this land of mountains and valleys has been many things to many people. To these first inhabitants it was doubtless a land of refuge from their ever-pursuing enemies. To the Cherokees it has been for many centuries a beloved homeland, worth defending against other Indian invaders and against the constantly encroaching white man. To the adventurous Englishmen it was a challenge, a fair land to be won and occupied. To the botanist it has been a veritable Garden of Eden, offering a wealth of vegetation beyond his fondest dreams. The geologist has found it an open book from which to read the story

JUNE GLENN, JR. PHOTO, *ASHEVILLE CITIZEN-TIMES* COMPANY

This majestic view of Western North Carolina mountains can be seen from the tower on Mt. Mitchell.

CARL McINTOSH PHOTO

The exposed rocks of Grandfather Mountain in Avery County give evidence that this is undoubtedly the world's oldest mountain.

of nature's gargantuan upheavals since the world was young. To the historian it has been the tale of the struggle of men and mountains, the slow and costly experiment of building a way of life suited to the ruggedness that isolates one community from another. And to the engineer it has been the stimulus to prodigious efforts in transportation—the spanning of broad rivers and the tunneling through mountain barriers, the removal of hills and the filling of gorges.

To the industrialist it has been a region of forests and raw material, a land of pure water and abundant man power; and for the mineralogist it has been an area of delight, rich in treasures of mica and feldspar, of pliable clays, of copper and talc, of precious and semi-precious stones. To the hunter and angler it has been a paradise of undergrowth and streams, where deer and bear still follow the ancient water trails and where the clear, cold water, foaming over rocky beds, still yields the finest of nature's game fish.

To the vacationist it has meant relaxation in invigorating air and sunshine, often restored health and vitality, and always the beauty and inspiration of cloud-tipped mountains against a blue sky and of broad, green-clad valleys rimmed in by the hills. To the

APPLACHIAN NATIONAL PARKS ASSOCIATION COLLECTION, N. C. DEPARTMENT OF ARCHIVES AND HISTORY

Rivers, some older than the mountains themselves, have played a role in determining the contour of this land of mountains. Cutting ravines and deepening them into gorges and chasms, the busy rivers have worn down boulders and continue to nibble at the rocks in their beds.

artist it has been a land of cascading waterfalls, of "balds" crowned with the exotic blooms of rhododendron, of range after range fading into a distant blue that defies any brush to capture. And to those who live here by right of pioneer ancestry and to those who have chosen it for their abiding place it is Home, with all of the sacredness that the word implies.

The mountains that dominate Western North Carolina are a part of the great Alleghany chain that stretches from Georgia northeastward through Maine and into eastern Canada, finally hurling themselves into the Atlantic Ocean off the coast of the Gaspe Peninsula. In this great chain the ranges from Virginia to Georgia are known as the Appalachians or Southern Highlands. In Western North Carolina and Eastern Tennessee these massive Highlands achieve their greatest width, varying from about a hundred miles to a hundred and twenty-five, and here they rear their loftiest peaks. Mt. Mitchell, at 6,684 feet, lifts its head above them all, but within the boundaries of North Carolina forty-three

6 / Chapter One

E. DOUGLAS DE PEW PHOTO

The land of mountains is also the land of waterfalls. Whitewater Falls send their spray down the steep mountainside near Sapphire.

mountains have an altitude of more than 6,000 feet and eighty-two others surpass 5,000 feet.[1] Hundreds of lesser peaks rise more than 4,000 feet above sea level. In the Tennessee section of the Great Smokies many additional mountains belong in one of these altitude ranges.

The Blue Ridge Mountain range, a long granite formation which rises abruptly from the Piedmont Plateau in Virginia and terminates in Georgia, marks the eastern boundary of the entire Southern Highlands area. Early unknown English explorers gave these mountains their appropriate name, for a nebulous blue haze surrounds them, deepening late in the day to the soft, dark blue of the night. In addition to their castle-like contours, their ever-changing blue overtones have made them justly extolled in story and song. The western rim of the Southern Highlands is more broken and is formed by the Unaka, the Stone, and the Unicoi ranges. These also form the boundary between Tennessee and North Carolina. It is the Unaka range that rises in the majesty of the Great Smoky Mountains, so named from the grey-blue haze that often surrounds their summits.

In order for readers to visualize this lofty section, writers have repeatedly likened the ranges to a gigantic ladder, with the Blue Ridge as its eastern support and the roughly paralleling Unaka, Stone, and Unicoi ranges as its western support. In the intervening plateau, cross ranges serve as rungs of the ladder. The Balsams, the Snowbird Mountains, the Nantahala Range, the Cowee—all lofty in their own right—are some of these cross bars. Out from both the supports and the rungs shorter mountain spurs extend. The most famous of these is the Black Mountain range in which Mt. Mitchell is the highest of twelve peaks above 6,000 feet above sea level.[2] Between the cross ranges are valleys of varying length and width, each with its own river system.

Man, with his less than pin-point of time, writes and speaks of the "eternal hills." But the expression is, in truth, merely poetic license, for restless nature is unceasingly making and wearing away, remaking and again effacing the contours of this planet man calls the earth. Sometimes the method is one of slow, bit by bit erosion, quietly carried on through eons of time. Again it is one of violence in which cataclysmic forces pummel earth's elements, spew them in liquid form from white-hot craters, or compress and fold and crack them into towering, jagged heights. Western North Carolina over the span of millions upon millions of man-

CARL McINTOSH PHOTO

For untold centuries Table Rock, shown here, has been exposed to the snows of winter and the pelting rains of summer. Yet its granite strength has continued to defy them all.

years has witnessed all of nature's moods and has undergone all of the methods used to alter the earth's surface.

In the cliffs and crags the story of the constant changes that have taken place in the region has been left to be interpreted by those who have the eyes to see. The record, unfolded, explains many mysteries of the present form of the land and the action of its rivers. It makes clear why the Blue Ridge rather than the generally higher Smokies constitutes the divide or watershed between rivers flowing into the Atlantic Ocean and those flowing into the great Mississippi system and through it into the Gulf of Mexico. It explains, too, the wealth of minerals and clays and stones and gems found in the area, and it throws light on the unsurpassed richness of its vegetation.

The underlying rock formations throughout most of the mountain area indicate an antiquity that baffles the imagination of man. More than five hundred million years ago some of the base rocks now visible on mountain sides were originally beds of sand, some in shallow water, some in deep water, but all laid down by long vanished rivers. Some of the base rocks were once flows of steaming lava shot into the air by the force of raging volcanoes. Others were layers of volcanic rock debris carried by the busy streams into the sea.

The sedimentary rocks and the volcanic formations made

CARL McINTOSH PHOTO

The winter storms and the summer rains, aided by the winds that swirl around mountain heights, have battered and split this granite rock on Grandfather Mountain.

from these deposits were later subjected to such tremendous pressure and to such extreme heat during the violent activities of the young world that their very characters were changed or metamorphosed. In their outcroppings today it is not always possible to determine their original natures.[3] Where the distinction between the types is clear cut, the metamorphosed soil sediments of the long ago have given the present mountains their gneisses, schists, and slates, ranging in color from light through dark grey and from greenish grey to black, depending upon other elements embedded in their depths.[4] The volcanic deposits of that ancient geological age, compressed and changed, have produced the granites of the region, predominating in the Blue Ridge range and in the northern half of the plateau stretching from these mountains to the Smokies. They also furnish the family of peridotites that lie in a narrow belt from Clay and Macon to Ashe and Alleghany Counties. This group of igneous formation gives the region its vermiculite, soapstone, olivine, and asbestos.[5]

The rock formations of this most ancient of geological times, changed as they were in character, do not appear in today's outcroppings in either original horizontal strata or solidly in their metamorphosed structures, for the Appalachian region is one of nature's oldest and most complex geological creations. Writhing in the throes of gigantic disturbances, these rocks were upheaved and in the process were bent and twisted and tilted. Into the crevices and fissures thus formed newer deposits were lodged, brought from the soil of distant uplands by the gnawing rivers.

APPLACHIAN NATIONAL PARKS ASSOCIATION COLLECTION, N. C. DEPARTMENT OF ARCHIVES AND HISTORY

Where the gnawing rivers have been powerless to wear down resisting granite walls, mighty cliffs like this one in Hickory Nut Gorge stand as sentinels over the valleys below.

New deposits of lava from spewing volcanoes crept into depressions and cracks, while fragments and powder of igneous rocks were transported by the untiring streams to find resting places in the niches and cuts of the older formations.

This part of the process of enriching the mineral resources of the region nature carried on in what scientists have named the pre-Cambrian period of earth's history. It was a period before living creatures appeared upon the planet or when life forms were too soft in structure to withstand the fierce forces at work in the area. Since these ancient rocks form so large a part of the present Appalachian Mountains, Western North Carolina is noticeably lacking in fossils. Later formations, made during the early

Cambrian period, are found in the Smoky Mountain area and around Grandfather Mountain. They, too, have been metamorphosed, but by a less violent process than was the case with the older rocks. These Cambrian deposits, sedimentary in their original character, furnish shale, sandstone and limestone, together with slate, schist, marble, and quartzite.[6]

Then over the very ancient rocks of the present Western North Carolina crept the waters of a long, narrow sea. Into it flowed the rivers from the east, for a great folding and uplifting of the earth's surface had formed a towering mountain region over the present Piedmont area, a high region that extended beyond the present shore line of the Atlantic Ocean. The busy, tumbling streams of that area nibbled and chiseled the lofty mountains and plateaus in their efforts to wear them down. They deposited their loads of sediment from mountain sides and their fragments of rock and lava from the active volcanoes into the narrow sea. In time that sea was partly or wholly filled with these layers of deposits, and the waters began receding.

Then in the section today called Western North Carolina extreme activity gripped the earth's surface in a terrific shrinking movement. With power beyond human thought, this movement pulled the base rocks of the mountains and land in the southeast, the present Piedmont, forcing them, through a long series of rumbling earthquakes, to push and crowd and slide northwestward.[7] At the same time, land to the northwest was stable or was more gently pulled toward the oncoming mass from the east. The narrow, filled sea was thus squeezed between wedging forces. It became the scene of cataclysmic events. With a force and power in comparison with which man made explosions are mere pop-gun efforts, the pre-Cambrian rock bed of the sea, overlaid with newer deposits, was thrust upward and pushed from both sides. It was crumbled and folded like paper, the ridge at the top creaking and cracking and breaking into countless weird, sharp shapes.

At last the earth attained ease from its internal turmoil and nature lessened its strenuous activities, for jagged and towering, the first Appalachian Mountains had been born. Life had definitely come upon the earth by this time, and the lowly crablike creatures and snails were leaving their shells in the mud that, becoming rock, would entomb these frail houses of earth's early inhabitants. But in the Appalachian region they are rarely found in the rocks of this period, for the violence of folding and tilting and the sliding of the mountain masses ground the tiny shells to powder.[8]

In these new Appalachian Mountains that reared their massive heads to Alpine heights, rivers began cutting ravines and deepening them into gorges and chasms. The sun and the wind and the rain combined their efforts in eroding the lofty peaks, and the intense cold surrounding their summits aided with its ice and snow. As eon after eon slipped into the past, the slow work of erosion went on until the once noble Appalachians were no more. The land where they had stood was a plain, broken only by low hills where now stand the Unaka and Great Smokies.[9] So level did the floor of the plain become that the once swift rivers grew lazy and meandering, wandering in leisurely fashion through their shallow valleys. During the long geological age, there were several periods of more or less gradual uplift, followed by periods of erosion before the region achieved the monotonous level of a plain.

But nature had not yet completed the task of creation in this area, and again the region was greatly uplifted, but this time without folding or twisting or tilting. The result would have been a high plateau except for the work of the rivers. The sluggish streams took on new life and vigor as their decline to sea level increased. So, as the area was elevated, the rivers kept pace with the process, eroding the land at about the same rate as the uplift took place. The river beds straightened and a few rivers, because of new sloping directions, reversed their water flow. Instead of traveling south or east to the sea, they came to follow their old beds north to join rivers that flowed west and, in turn, joined still other streams flowing south and thus into the Gulf of Mexico. Some, joining stronger streams, gave up their waters once and for all, leaving their unused beds to dry and sear in the sun.[10] Still others that were mere rivulets or brooks at the beginning of the uplift grew in length and size as they strenuously worked to cut gorges through the rising mountains to reach lower levels on their way to the sea. The region, then, during the chiseling of the present Appalachian Mountains, saw a general rearrangement of the existing river systems.

Because these streams are older than the present mountain ranges at the western border of North Carolina, those ranges are not a divide, although their general altitude exceeds that of the Blue Ridge. With its hard, granite walls, the Blue Ridge was more impenetrable than the western ranges, and prevented the rivers that developed from cutting passages southeastward through it. The Blue Ridge is, therefore, a true divide, the streams rising to the west of it flowing into the Gulf of Mexico by way of the Ohio and Mississippi Rivers and the streams rising to the east of it flowing into the Atlantic. In Watauga County, near Grandfather Mountain, four rivers have their source, two of which finally empty their waters into the Gulf and two of which empty their waters into the Atlantic. Thus the mountains as they are today in Western North Carolina are largely the result of the never-resting streams gashing through the uplifted plains and forming gorges, wearing down the softer of the formations and leaving the harder rocks to rear their heads in majestic mountains and peaks.[11]

Much erosion has taken place since those long ago days of uplift, for the Appalachians are old mountains, some scholars think they are the world's oldest mountains. In comparison with them, the Rockies are still in an adolescent age. The peaks that once rivaled or possibly surpassed any in the present Rockies have been nibbled away through the thousands of centuries until not a one of them today is above timberline. Many have acquired a rounded, softened appearance, and all have been overlaid with a generous blanket of soil which has become the home of a rich and varied vegetation.

As a result of the many phases of creation employed by nature in these mountains, the Appalachians abound in minerals and rocks, both metallic and non-metallic. Some three hundred kinds of minerals and rocks are accredited to North Carolina,[12] and most of them are to be found in its western counties. Of the non-metallic group, the mountains for untold eons have held their precious loads of mica and feldspar, of clays and sand and gravel, of granite and slate and limestone and marble, of precious and semi-precious stones. These stones are surprisingly diverse and include rubies, sapphires, amethysts, garnets, quartz, emeralds, zircons, even diamonds—all the products of the pressure and heat, the filling in of crevices and fissures in older rocks. In short, they testify to the tremendous processes of nature in its violent activities in Western North Carolina. In 1756, a German engineer by the name of John William Gerard de Brahm, coming into the region to build a fort, wrote more truly than he could know when he recorded in his *Journal:* "This country seems longing for the hand of industry to receive its hidden treasures, which nature has been collecting and toiling since the beginning ready to deliver them up."[13]

Metals in varying amounts have also been among the hidden treasures of the mountains. Gold, silver, and copper the Indians mined and used as ornaments. The gold-greedy soldiers of De Soto

CARL McINTOSH PHOTO

Hoot Owl, an underground mine, yields its treasure of feldspar, one of nature's most useful minerals.

CARL McINTOSH PHOTO

Chalk Mountain mine is one of several open feldspar mines.

prospected for the same metals. For more than a century their sporadic mining attempts probably returned small amounts of gold and silver, for both appear in many places, although for modern purposes, in commercially unprofitable quantities. The gold deposits that gave the state its early title of the "Golden State" and that produced many millions worth of bullion are on the eastern slopes of the Blue Ridge.[14] Copper, however, is in greater amounts in the mountains, principally in Ashe, Jackson, Haywood, and Swain Counties. Also locked in the hidden recesses of the hills is iron, of all minerals the most useful to man, along with lead, zinc, manganese, nickel, titanium (rich in its promise of future uses), and tungsten.[15]

As plant life developed upon the face of the earth, Western North Carolina became the home of those forms adapted to its climate and altitude. In periods of uplift, plant forms requiring warm, humid climates died or gradually moved out of the region to homes more to their liking. Others, thriving in cool, dry climates, moved in. Many such changes and reversals took place over the ageless lapses of time that elevated and wore down and elevated again this little section of the globe. In these changes a few plants were able to adapt themselves to the gradually shifting conditions of altitude and moisture and, in slightly modified forms, stayed in the region.

Then late in time—geologically speaking—masses of ice blanketed the northeastern part of North America and for centuries crept steadily southward in what is now the United States. These ice floes pushed ahead of themselves rocks and boulders, in fact, everything in their paths. At their approach the climate in front of them grew colder and increasingly forbidding, so that both plants and animals beat a slow but constant retreat southward. These Pleistocene successions of great ice sheets did not reach North Carolina although they strongly affected both the flora and the fauna of the Appalachian region.

Creatures and plant forms, yearly seeking new homes to the south, found in the mountains (which were then similar to the present mountains except higher) a climate comparable in coolness to their former northern homes. In their new mountain retreat these visitors settled down at the altitudes best fitted to them individually to live in what harmony they could with the animals and plant forms already in the region, many of which had entered it from areas farther south. The result was a meeting of Alpine and semi-tropical growth with all the graduations in between. At the end of the Pleistocene period, when the unfriendly ice masses receded and a more temperate climate followed them northward, plants sheltered in the Appalachian region of Western North Carolina spread out to repopulate the vast stretches made barren by the grinding force and the arctic air of the ice blankets. When that process had been carried out to the

ELLIOT LYMAN FISHER PHOTO
Rhododendron: Each June the exotic blooms of the rhododendron turn the "balds" and hillsides into fairy gardens. This picture shows a riot of blooms below Mt. Mitchell.

point of providing adequate pasturage and food, the animals sojourning in Western North Carolina likewise returned to their former habitations. But not all of each plant species left the mountains. Some stayed, and their numerous descendants can be seen today in the region. Thus the present Southern Appalachians have a wealth of plant forms unsurpassed in any area of its size in the world and greater than that of the entire continent of Europe. In fact, the area has many plants found in no other section of the United States; some, indeed, not found except in parts of Asia, where conditions have perpetuated the ancient forms.[16]

Of all the mountain plants, the magnificent forests that sweep up the hillsides and cover many of the peaks are the region's crowning glory. In some sections, as in the highest altitudes along the Blue Ridge Parkway, the forests of beech, yellow birch, and yellow buckeye—usually found in moist valleys— are stunted and

HUGH MORTON PHOTO

Upper Left: Western North Carolina is a veritable garden, where some 1,400 flowering plants and shrubs make spring and summer colorful seasons. One of the lovely flowers is the purple fringed orchid shown here; Upper Right: The Pink Moccasin Flower is also called the Pink Lady Slipper; Lower Left: The Huckleberry is a favorite in the mountains; Lower Right: The Osmunda is a very hardy mountain fern.

18 / Chapter One

HUGH MORTON PHOTO
This beautiful picture was taken near Linville.

gnarled, but as much, perhaps, by the force of the winter winds as by the altitude. Along much of this Parkway the trees are mainly oaks, hickories, and maples, interspersed with pine and hemlock. On Mt. Mitchell the present stand of red spruce is one of the finest in the nation.[17] In the Great Smoky Mountains National Park spruce and fir predominate in vast areas of virgin growth. These, with pines and conifers, cover other western ranges, and throughout the entire mountain area tulip trees, yellow birch, yellow buckeye, mountain silver bell, Fraser magnolia, sourwood, Alleghany service berry, pin cherry, and American mountain ash grow in profusion and often attain enormous size.

Both conifers and hardwoods make their homes in these mountains, with more than 140 varieties of trees in the Great Smoky Mountains alone. Many of these are relatives of the migrants from Canada during the ice age. In fact, more than half

APPLACHIAN NATIONAL PARKS ASSOCIATION COLLECTION, N. C. DEPARTMENT OF ARCHIVES AND HISTORY

Summer foliage and sheer rock cliffs combine to bring their beauty to the hills and valleys.

of the woody plants in this area are species of the Canadian zone. Since the mountain climate varies with altitude, most woody plants have been able to find conditions favorable to their growth.[18] This is, of course, true of all the flora of the region so that in traveling from the valleys to the high peaks, one travels through vegetation zones ranging from the latitude of North Carolina to that of central Canada.

This phenomenon of traveling north by climbing a Western North Carolina mountain can, perhaps, best be noticed in May. Starting from a valley where summer has furnished the trees with fully grown foliage and has brought many trees and shrubs and plants into bloom, the climber witnesses the gradual disappearance of the early spring flowers and the shrinkage in size of the leaves of the trees until only leaf buds are visible. Then at higher

20 / Chapter One

HUGH MORTON PHOTO
A fawn on Grandfather Mountain gets acquainted with his forest home.

levels one sees plants and trees still slumbering in their winter quietness, awaiting the touch of warm spring winds and rains to stir them into renewed life.[19]

Even today, after man has wastefully played havoc with much of the timber of the region, in large areas of the Smokies, in the Nantahalas, in the Unicoi and other ranges stands of magnificent virgin timber—like that of the Joyce Kilmer Memorial Forest—give evidence of the glorious growth of trees in the mountains before the white man's advent into Western North Carolina.

While trees are the Applachian region's most common and most magnificent clothing, and certainly the most valuable to man, thousands of other plant forms spring up or nestle closely to the mountain sides and crests and cover the intervening valleys with prodigal abundance. For reasons not understood by scientists, some of the mountain peaks are treeless, even though trees grow on their slopes and on nearby mountain tops. They are, on the whole, well rounded or domed in form and have acquired the descriptive name of balds. They are of two types, depending upon the growth that crowns them.

Some balds are covered with low grasses, used now for pasturage. Whether some ancient forest fire left them denuded and grasses in time crept over the charred area before the forest could regain the summit is not known. The prevailing winds and, during the past century, the pasturing of cattle on them have doubtless combined to help keep them bald. Other treeless balds are covered with dense growths of laurel or rhododendron bushes that sometimes reach considerable heights. These are known as heath balds. On them the growth is often dense and tangled and practically impenetrable. These individual growths are thought to be a comparatively recent development, and it may well be that under favorable conditions trees will attempt to reestablish themselves where perhaps they once lived.[20]

Of the thousands of plant forms in Western North Carolina (and the number reaches 3,600 in the Smoky Mountains) the rhododendron and laurel covering the balds and their relative, the flame azalea, growing both on the balds and on grassy slopes, furnish spring's most spectacular display. But companions of these throughout the section include some 1,400 flowering plants, over 1,700 species of fungi, 330 mosses and liverworts and 230 lichens. From early spring, or even the last winter months, through late autumn, the mountains produce a parade of color, ranging from the vivid yellows and orange of the azaleas[21] and the elusive purple shades of the Catawba rhododendron to the soft, muted tones of the trillium and the breath-taking purity of the rare Shortia or Oconee Bell. In autumn the parade is intensified by the flaunting colors of the trees as their leaves say goodbye with a brave burst of glory.[22]

For untold ages this mountain region has been one of nature's most thickly populated zoos, for the canopy of trees over valleys and hillsides and the rich carpet of undergrowth have furnished ideal coverts for bear and buffalo, deer and panther, and a multitude of smaller creatures. Food has been on every hand, and swift mountain streams, fed by the abundant rainfall blessing the area, have provided reliable sources of water. Western North Carolina was in former times a veritable Garden of Eden where animals were rulers. Animals flourished and multiplied, roaming at will and leaving their hardpacked trails across the mountain gaps and down the valleys to protected drinking spots. The climate, with its short winters and few snows and its long, cool summers, has been kind to animals. Indeed their chief fears, before man's coming into the region, arose from the depredations of one species upon another and from an occasional rock slide or lightning-set fire that swept a mountain side.

HUGH MORTON PHOTO

The mountain region has been one of nature's thickly populated zoos. With trees and undergrowth to serve as coverts and with food on every hand and with streams nearby, the hills have been an animal's paradise. Many species have survived the inroads of man and his gun. Among them is the American black bear. The bears we see here have their home on Grandfather Mountain.

HUGH MORTON PHOTO

The mountain lion once stalked the forests of the North Carolina mountains, but the fearless cat, along with the panther and cougar, is as extinct now as the prehistoric dinosaur.

HUGH MORTON PHOTO

Upper Left: The little Carolina Chickadee sings his cheery notes whenever he lights on a convenient twig or tree limb; Upper Right: The American red squirrel is also called the mountain boomer; Lower Left: These young raccoons find a place to rest on an old rail fence; Lower Right: The ruffed grouse is one of more than 200 species of birds that have found an ideal habitat in the mountains of Western North Carolina.

Even today, after the bows and arrows and guns of men have completely exterminated some forms of North Carolina wild life, such as the buffalo, panther, and elk, and have made vast inroads in the number of small species, and after the remaining animal population has been forced to make room for land-greedy humans, it is estimated that Western North Carolina supports more than fifty kinds of fur bearing animals, in addition to an untold number of insects and invertebrates.[23] Back in the mountain fastnesses the black bear, the white-tailed deer, and the bob-cat live much as they have for thousands of years. But many of the smaller animals such as the oppossums, raccoons, skunks, squirrels, and chipmunks have compromised with man and often share his territory.

Over two hundred kinds of birds have found an ideal habitat in these mountains. Some yearly come from southern countries for the summers; others arrive from northern countries for the winter. Birds of the north and birds of the south meet, then, in Western North Carolina. Many individuals in several species forego the long, hard migratory flights to northern or southern regions and, like the Carolina junco, are content with summer trips to the high mountain altitudes, spending their winters in the lower valleys.[24] All through the year the calls or songs of birds swell from tree tops on mountain sides and in wooded valleys. Every breeze bears a message trilled by the air-borne citizens of the world.

So it is that long before man's appearance, Western North Carolina was prepared for his habitation. Man was to find the climate to his liking. He was to find fish and game. He was to find food and herbs abundant for his needs, and he was to find the materials nature had stored there for the making of his tools. Above all, he was to find an eternal awareness of the mountains—their protection from outside turmoil, their offerings for his use, their challenge to his ingenuity, and their unconquerable strength. They were to make his life hard and isolated and at times narrow. But they were to give him something of their own uprightness and hardiness, a bit of their granite, and the spirit of the freedom-loving winds that sweep their heights. They were to dominate his work and his days until they set the pattern of his life and became for him the "Hills of Home."

CHAPTER TWO

Eden is Discovered

History will never know the day or year when a band of nomadic people wandered into what is now Western North Carolina. These primitive people may have been a family group fleeing from enemies or searching for better hunting grounds. They belonged to one of the tribes or "nations" that resulted from sporadic waves of Asiatic peoples entering America by way of Alaska between eight and ten thousand years ago, perhaps much earlier. By degrees these migrating people traveled south, following a route between the Pacific Ocean and the Rocky Mountains. Some continued into South America. Others skirted the southern tip of the Rocky Mountains and turned eastward across the plains. Many of these crossed the Mississippi River and fanned out in all directions in the eastern part of what is now the United States.[1]

Over the centuries, as family groups increased in size, they developed tribes or "nations." These larger units were loosely bound by ties of family, common racial traits, language, and an ever growing wealth of customs and traditions. The tribes in the east met, fought, and sometimes blended. By modern standards the territory stretching from the Mississippi River to the Atlantic Ocean was sparsely inhabited during the entire period of Native American occupation, both pre-historic and historic. But the tribes, depending upon hunting for food and clothing, required vast hunting grounds. Competition must have become keen and bitter as eastern tribes increased and as more eastward-moving groups crossed the Mississippi River. So it was that on an unrecorded day a band of nomads sought a new home in the present Western North Carolina.

Glimpses of the way of life of some of the pre-historic Indians have been gleaned from artifacts found on the sites of their camps, villages, battlefields, and from their man-made mounds. These mounds, differing in size and shape, dot wide areas of the eastern section of the United States. Leveled by the plows of farmers, many small ones have disappeared, and their treasures have been lost for all time.

In North Carolina, as in other states, mounds have been opened in attempts to piece together the history of the American Indians. In Western North Carolina the earliest explorations were in Burke, Caldwell, and Wilkes Counties. Excavations of both mounds and town sites have been carried on in practically every county west of the Blue Ridge. In addition, extensive work has been done in the old Cherokee country and along the Nolichucky River in Tennessee.[2]

At the excavation site in the Swannanoa valley on land belonging to Warren Wilson College, the oldest culture found furnishes an idea of the first possible human discoverers of Western North Carolina. Their camp was small and probably a temporary one and may have been used over a period of time by wandering family groups. These people were hunters and gatherers. Their homes were crude shelters and their clothing was made from skins. Their spearpoints were fashioned from soapstone as were their cooking pots. Animals killed in the hunt were skinned and the meat roasted over a fire in a pit. Hunters and gatherers like these people roamed over a wide area from Maine to Florida, leaving evidences of their passing throughout much of North Carolina. It is estimated that groups of them were in Western North Carolina at least 10,000 years ago.

The village above the Swannanoa camp clearly showed the cultural development that took place during the thousands of years that separated them. Artifacts found in the last Native American town built on this site, long after the village below was in ruins, are proof of further cultural development. That development was the result of internal improvement and outside influences. The scientists working at the site suggest that this culture is the primary base from which the Middle Cherokee culture developed.[3]

Excavations farther west have provided evidence of a succession of primitive groups or tribes living along the Little Tennessee, the Hiwassee, and other western rivers. The earliest of these people have conveniently been called the Upper Valley People. Numerous man-made pits indicate where their fires were made for cooking the family meals. They made pottery, some of it decorated by pressing the soft clay with fiber cords. In their compact villages they lived in circular houses; they buried their dead in a flexed position. Their tools were crude stone implements.

In time these people were followed by a group with a similar racial background but with slightly different customs. Known to scientists as the Middle Valley People, this second group seems to have lived for a long period of time in eastern Tennessee and the western counties of North Carolina. They lived in family units with their homes strung along rivers and they made pottery that was without cord markings, a fact that indicates they had had no contact with the people they followed. The great number of mussel shells on their home sites and in their refuse heaps points to the fact that they lived partly on mussels and may have come from a coastal area, possibly from the area around the Gulf of Mexico. They were mound-builders and buried their dead in a partly flexed position, one body in a grave but hundreds of graves in a mound.

Following the Middle Valley People, came another tribe, known today as the Hiwassee People. They brought with them a decidedly higher culture than that of the preceding groups. Some of their customs were similar to those of Mexican tribes, indicating an origin far to the south. They lived in villages protected by stockades. Inside the enclosures were rectangular homes made with a framework of saplings set vertically at close intervals in trenches. They built their public buildings on mounds, for they were mound-builders. On one of these mounds was their temple, which may also have served as a community house for tribal business meetings. In it was an eternal fire since they were fire-worshippers. They cord-marked their pottery and also painted some of the earthenware, using a red dye or red on a buff background. No burials made by these people have been found, and it is supposed that they cremated their dead. On plots outside the stockades they raised grain and some vegetables.

These Hiwassee People lived for a long period of time in the area that included the mountain land. They were a part of a wide-spread culture that extended from the Mississippi River to

E. DOUGLAS DE PEW PHOTO

The Judaculla Rock in Jackson County carries a message that for centuries has remained a secret. Its hieroglyphics are the work of some pre-historic tribe or person or of some early Cherokee. Later Cherokees viewed the rock with awe and its markings as the work of Judaculla, a superman or god. A present-day theory is that the inscription on it may depict a battle, possibly between the early Cherokees and their enemies, the Creeks.

Florida. Yet in time, they were forced to make way for a new group, today called the Dallas People. For some time these two tribes seem to have lived in fairly close relationship in their separate villages. They were similar in culture, although the Dallas mounds were oval and their council houses differed slightly from those of the Hiwassee. Yet in the end the Dallas People drove out or absorbed the Hiwassee People.[4]

After this tribe, came the Cherokees, who came with a background of struggle and warfare that had made for them bitter and powerful enemies. Early Cherokee history is necessarily a matter of legends, traditions and myths, of tales of distant lands and heroes and battles told by the wise old men of the tribe to each succeeding generation of braves. Yet from these tales— even with their frequent contradictions and evident interpolations—and from tales current in enemy nations, together with the study of the movements of various native

FROM AN 1890 PHOTOGRAPH IN MOONEY, *MYTHS OF THE CHEROKEES*
This ancient mound at Franklin in Macon County was the site of Nikwasi, for long periods of time the Principal Town of the Middle Cherokees. Donations made by school children and citizens of the county made its preservation possible.

American stocks and of their physical, linguistic, and cultural similarities, the pattern of life of the Cherokees' prehistoric ancestors can be at least partly sketched.[5]

The Cherokees are of Iroquoian origin, a relative nation of the mighty Iroquois.[6] A separation of the two groups came early (perhaps before the crossing of the Mississippi River, but more probably afterward) when the migrants sought a permanent dwelling place. The Iroquois spread north of the Great Lakes and into central New York, while the Cherokees took possession of the vast territory stretching from the Great Lakes to the Ohio River. In time, they entered New York from the south and again came into contact with the Iroquois. The centuries of separation had brought many differences between the two related groups, and although their languages were still similar and their type of arrows still identical, they were now distinct nations. Competing now for the same territory, they developed into bitter enemies.

Also, as the Cherokees advanced east, their struggle with the Delawares intensified. According to their traditions, the state of sporadic warfare existing between the Cherokees and the Delawares dated from the long-past appearance of the latter nation on the west bank of the Mississippi River. From the Cherokees the Delawares had asked permission to cross over and share the vast Cherokee territory. That request had been denied, but the privilege of passing through the country to the eastern lands had been granted. During the undoubtedly slow trek, however, trouble arose between the two groups, at times amounting to a state of war.

When the Cherokees later pushed into the eastern territory, the Delaware settlers were unable to stem the invasion and enlisted the aid of the powerful Iroquois, who were also fully aware of the dangers of Cherokee encroachment. The result was an open war climaxed by a fierce battle near the southern border of Lake Erie in which, despite their fortifications and breastworks, the Cherokees were so soundly defeated that their dream of land in the north and east vanished.

Following this humiliation, they retreated by slow degrees to the Ohio River and down it to the Kanawha. Passing up that, they entered the present West Virginia. Ruins of fortifications of Cherokee design over a rather wide area of that section testify to the opposition they met from nations and tribes in the territory. Because of this opposition and doubtless to gain elbow room, they gradually moved south and west, eventually reaching Western North Carloina, possibly by way of the Holston and Tennessee Rivers.[7]

In the mountain section of Western North Carolina they had an almost impregnable position with a climate favorable for comfortable existence and with abundant food available for the shooting. The Cherokees, as time passed, increased in numbers and in strength, claiming as their hunting grounds regions far distant from their villages strung along the rivers of the present Western North Carolina and Tennessee. In fact, by the time the English speaking people appeared in their territory, they were second only to the Iroquois federation in population and military strength. Their vaguely defined national boundaries included the Appalachian region from the headwaters of the Tennessee into the present Georgia and from the Blue Ridge to the Cumberlands, a tract of some forty thousand square miles which took in all of Western North Carolina, parts of Kentucky, West

Virginia, South Carolina, and the eastern section of Tennessee, together with sections of Alabama and a claim on hunting rights throughout Kentucky.[8]

Protection of their immediate mountain homeland kept the nation at almost constant warfare with surrounding tribes. In addition to their ancient foes, the Delawares and Iroquois, they now counted as enemies the Catawbas east of the Blue Ridge, the Sara, Cheraw, and the Tuscaroras farther to the east and southeast, the Creeks in upper Georgia, the Chickasaws to the west, and the Shawnees wherever wandering bands of that nomadic group appeared. On hunting expeditions to the "Land of Kaintuck," they were always prepared to enter combat with any roaming bands of hunters from still other nations. Thus the Cherokees did their share in making that lovely land "a dark ground and a bloody ground." They were considered in all Indian councils as a powerful nation and a formidable foe.

With their homes favorably located and well protected, the Cherokees thrived and expanded. Their towns and villages sprang up along the rivers and streams in eastern Tennessee, Western North Carolina, northern Georgia, and northwestern South Carolina. The remainder of their vast domain they kept as a hunting preserve. As the years passed, the homeland became geographically divided into three distinct areas, each one developing a dialect and certain individual customs and group traits. The settlements in eastern Georgia and South Carolina made a unit known as the Lower Towns where the language acquired a predominantly rolling "r" sound. The villages along the Tuckaseigee River and along the headwaters of the Little Tennessee, together with those on the Hiwassee and Valley Rivers, became the Middle Towns. There a liquid "l" sound supplanted the rolling "r," making the language spoken the most musical of the Cherokee dialects and the one eventually to become the literary language of the nation.

Farther to the west in Georgia and along the Little Tennessee and Tellico Rivers were the Over Hill Towns where again the "r" sound could be heard. It was in the Over Hill area that the capital, Echota or Chota, was located. It was likewise regarded as a sacred town and was a city of refuge. However, each area had a prominent town, a sort of sub-capital, which also served as a religious center and was therefore a sacred city. Nikwasi, on the site of the present Franklin, North Carolina, was the principal town of the Middle Cherokees. Keowee, on the Tugalo

ASHEVILLE CHAMBER OF COMMERCE

From wood and reeds the early Cherokees fashioned their arrows and the slender darts used in their blow-guns. This craftsman at the Oconaluftee Village in Cherokee is carrying on the centuries-old art.

River in South Carolina, was the largest of the Lower Towns.[9]

The Cherokees lacked the strong propensity for organization that their distant relatives, the Iroquois, displayed, and the three parts of their nation were held together more by tradition, customs, and a common though varying language than by governmental authority. Until they made treaties with the English colonies, they had no official head of the nation although

English colonies, they had no official head of the nation although now and then one individual doubtless wielded a determining influence throughout the territory. Through a council made up of male citizens, each town elected a chief, and most towns had their wise men, whose calm, sage advice carried much weight. In addition, the people were grouped into seven clans with complicated requirements of clan loyalty. James Adair, an early English trader, found them possessing devices of government, religious rites, and moral concepts strikingly like those held and practiced by the ancient Hebrews. Sometimes the nation as a whole determined for or against war, but more often bands of young warriors from a city or clan went on foraging expeditions into enemy country. The use of weapons was a part of each boy's education, and he was eager to prove his prowess by participating in a war or raid.

It was possible, too, for a town or clan or one of the geographical areas to go to war without the consent or aid of other units or the nation as a whole, and there were even periods of bloody intratribal contention. The fates of prominent captives might be decided in council, and a major crime such as shedding blood in a city of refuge would be an affair for authorities to punish. But on the whole, justice (which meant as with the Hebrews of old, "an eye for an eye and a tooth for a tooth") was left to be meted out by the injured person, and revenge was the privilege of the wronged family or clan.[10]

Next to the excitement of war, hunting offered the Cherokee youth satisfyingly thrilling experiences, and children listened wide-eyed to the adventurous tales related by returning hunters. Memorable was the day when a lad was told he might join a party setting out for the far reaches of the Cherokee domain. Each group of hunters was of necessity also a scouting party, ready to give battle to any trespassers found within the considered boundaries of the nation; the hunters brought back to the home councils whatever information could be gleaned concerning the surrounding enemy tribes. Game was abundant, and the Cherokees knew each species, its migratory habits, its breeding grounds, and its lairs. Parties armed with their bows and keen, flint arrows, a supply of darts, and perhaps their surprisingly efficient blow-guns with their poison-tipped, slender arrows, set out from their homes along trails that were well defined near their habitations but which narrowed as they entered denser forests.

EWART M. BALL PHOTO

In the council house at the Oconaluftee Village in Cherokee this maker of masks and designer of feather robes demonstrates the ancient and intricate art of his ancestors.

Some of these trails the Cherokees had made during their era of expansion in the mountain area, but many were ages old, beaten firm by the moccasined feet of prehistoric predecessors in their search for game or enemies. Others were still older, opened through undergrowth and thickets by untold generations of buffalo, deer, bear and other animals whose hooves pounded the soft forest floor into solid highways leading to other coverts or to suitable watering places. Over the centuries these slender, single-file mountain and forest trails became numerous, crossing and criss-crossing the territory, a veritable network of primitive roads giving access to every part of Western North Carolina from the Smokies to the Blue Ridge and on into the lands to the east, north, and south.[11]

Aside from any punitive motive that the hunters might secretly nourish, the aim of the hunting party was the replenishing of the food supply and of material for clothing for the home or clan; for until the white man came with his insatiable greed for pelts, the Cherokees killed only the needed amount of game. Thus the entire nation was able to have both meat and furs in comparative abundance without depleting the wild life that roamed the area.

In fact, the Cherokees had a feeling of respect for all forms of wild life that in some instances, judging from their myths, amounted almost to a feeling of kinship. They gave their clans animal names and bestowed animal titles upon their outstanding warriors as marks of honor. They related animal tales to their children and represented birds and animals in their ceremonial dances. Animals and birds even played leading roles in their stories of creation and of the formation of their mountains. All of that had developed, it would seem, from an ancient animism and animal worship, remnants of which had become woven into the fabric of their religious concepts.[12]

Hunting was, perhaps, for the men an escape from the monotony of daily life. But it was also a necessity, for it furnished the towns with a supply of meat. Aside from game, a goodly portion of the nation's food came from the rivers. From the clear mountain streams the fishermen, expert with their bone fish hooks, could catch a day's supply of fish in a few minutes' angling. In season the women and children gathered a variety of berries, plums, grapes, cherries, persimmons, and nuts from the open glades and the woods. At the proper time they also gathered various herbs, roots, and shrubs to be used for medicines and drinks. Each spring the leaves of many wild plants were picked to be cooked as greens, and the air was then often reeking with the perfume of the ramp, a mighty relative of the onion.

Outside their villages were the fields and gardens. The Cherokees had not yet acquired the concept of individual ownership of land, and the fields were community fields where each household worked its assigned plot. In some instances, however, a family was allotted an additional strip of ground nearer its home on which to raise more food. By the time history unveiled "The Land of the Sky," the Cherokees were producing as good corn and vegetables as could be expected in view of the crudeness of the agricultural implements they had been able to fashion. They grew corn, potatoes, squash, beans, and tobacco, a choice product reserved for use in their ceremonial pipes. From potatoes, from ground nuts, and from dried corn they made breads, which they baked in coals or cooked over their open fires. In big earthen pots they made soups and stews, combining meat and vegetables, often previously dried in the sun. Thus a Cherokee meal could be surprisingly complete and certainly vitamin filled, from soup through fish, meat, and vegetables to berries sweetened with honey taken from a nearby "bee tree." However, accounts left by English traders make it plain that the Cherokee cooks were unhampered by the white man's methods of preparing and serving food.[13]

To these mountain dwellers war was an ever present possibility, a natural result of acquiring and protecting a territory large enough to support a growing population. For protection as well as for social advantages they lived in towns which, by modern standards, were mere villages built along the rivers. Early traders write of them as ranging in size from a cluster of five or six dwellings to some thirty or more houses, although there are records mentioning towns having more than a hundred homes.

Like all Indians, the Cherokees were an outdoor people and spent most of their days in the open. Their houses, used mostly as sleeping quarters, could be adequate without being large. All were constructed from the materials to be had for the gathering. The earliest were simple buildings fashioned by bringing a circle of saplings together at the top and weaving cane gathered from the river banks to these supports. River clay served as a filler and an outer coating for these cane walls. Somewhat more ambitious than these stationary wigwams were the rectangular lodges or cabins built of logs. Here, too, clay served as the needed chinking.

In both types of houses low doors gave entrance into the one-roomed structure and admitted the only light that got inside since there were no windows. The packed earth was the only floor. Sometimes beside a house was a tiny structure with a door so low that one entered it by crawling. This was the "hot house," for here, in the cold weather that came so suddenly in the mountains, a fire burned, and members of the family could enter and enjoy the warmth. The outdoor fires used for cooking and a variety of activities served to offset the chill of frosty mornings and the damp of early evenings.[14]

The largest and most important structure in the village was the council house, which served as an assembly hall and temple, doubtless also as a "man's club." It was accorded an awed respect, for in it burned the sacred fire. In it decisions were made that affected the entire community and projects like the Indian ball games and the ceremonial dances were planned. In it, too, were kept the medicineman's equipment and the paraphernalia used in religious rites. It gained prominence by its position on a mound, made as a temple site centuries earlier by the pre-Cherokee mountain dwellers. At least some of these Cherokee council houses had a symbolic structural form of seven sides, each side representing one of the nation's clans.[15] Furniture both here and in the homes was practically unnecessary, since eating was done out of doors where logs and stumps were plentiful if chairs were desired and since the ground served as a chair in the houses. Buffalo, deer, and bear skins made as good beds as any Cherokee had ever known or imagined.

Like other primitive peoples the Cherokees were necessarily a busy people, for, in addition to keeping the larder supplied through hunting and fishing and farming, whatever was worn or whatever was needed as tools had to be made amd fashioned laboriously by hand. No wonder, then, that during the summer months they reduced the dress problem to a minimum. At this season the men were fully garbed when they wore simple loin cloths of dressed skins. Children up to about ten years of age enjoyed complete freedom from clothes. Girls and women wore simple, knee-length skirts of dressed skins.

More clothing was required for the mountain winters. Robes of buffalo or deerskin were used then by the men, and some were fortunate enough to have squaws who could weave for them warm robes of feathers, slowly gathered from the wild turkeys or other birds during the molting season or when used as food. Beautiful, matched feathers, some of them dyed, were worked into rich ceremonial robes and mantles, often many thousands of soft, tiny feathers being used in a single garment.[16] For shoes, pliable moccasins were made from deerskin. It was no simple task to cure the buffalo, deer, and bear pelts, and it required skill to transform deerskins into the cloth-like buckskin used for clothing and moccasins. Even after the first process had been completed, the garments had yet to be fashioned by sewing with fine, thread-like thongs of leather passed through the eyes of bone needles.[17]

The harvested grain and the gathered offerings of meadows and woods were carried and stored in baskets of varying sizes and shapes. These were made by the women from the river cane and from oak and hickory splints made from saplings, then smoothed and thinned with crude stone or bone implements and made pliable by soaking. The splints or canes were then woven, possibly in the double weave fashion characteristic of the

Cherokee weaving. The women also made the pottery used as pots and pans and the few bowls needed. The process was an ancient one, evolved when the human race was young. Clay from the river banks was formed into coils which were piled one upon another and shaped by skillful hands, then scraped smooth by pieces of sharpened stone or bone, becoming a pot or a bowl or a jar destined to serve many uses. It was carefully fired to withstand heat and to become waterproof.[18]

To the women fell the lot of tilling the fields. Henry Timberlake, visiting the Over Hill Towns in 1761, reported that the "country... is so remarkably fertile, that the women alone do all the laborious tasks of agriculture." The men at certain seasons or on special occasions also did some work in the fields, quite possibly as rituals or as punishment meted out by their chiefs. Martin Schneider, in the Over Hill Towns in 1783, says that at sunrise he saw the chief of Chota calling all the men to work in the fields and that they were not allowed to return until sundown, the women bringing them food during the day. It is perhaps safe to assume that this was an unusual day.[19]

To some extent water travel was available even to these mountain dwellers. They felled giant trees—poplars—by ringing them and leaving them to die so that the felling process could be done easily. It was the same slow method that they had used for centuries to clear forest tracts for cultivation. Then, with a crude stone axe and the use of fire, the log was hollowed out, shaped, and then scraped to the desired thinness and lightness. The result was an efficient watercraft that could easily be transported between streams and that was watertight and capable of carrying several passengers.

The men, too, made the weapons used in war and hunting. Their bows and arrows were similar to those used by other tribes and their flint arrow heads were identical with those made by the Iroquois. In addition they made blow-guns from river cane by removing the pith and making slender, feathered arrows that sped through the tubes with speed and accuracy, sealing the doom of many a small animal and bringing to earth many a bird. Stones of suitable size were also brought into the village by the men and made into a variety of cutting and smoothing tools, while others were gouged out and smoothed to hold the grain and dried seeds and tubers that the women pounded into meal with stone pestles.[20]

By the time the first traders entered Western North Carolina, the Cherokees had long since passed the primitive stage in which they were satisfied with material possessions that were merely utilitarian. They were adding touches of beauty to the objects they made and the garments they wore. The women gathered roots and barks from which they steeped dyes of various rich colors and shades to lend aesthetic touches to their multi-purpose baskets. Sometimes, too, they made simple designs with combs on their pottery, and dyed feathers and even dressed skins gave variety and beauty to their clothes and to their ceremonial robes.

To add to their personal appearance, the women combed their black hair with wooden or bone combs, rubbed it glossy with oil obtained from the abundant sumac, and fashioned it into a knot or club at the back of the head. Ornaments were made for both men and women from shells, sometimes cut into beads, and strung on thin, deerskin thongs or twisted grasses. Bracelets and neck pieces were fashioned from the metals (silver, gold, and the more plentiful copper) they mined in the hills. Additional fineries were now and then brought home by warriors lucky enough to slay enemies wearing them.[21]

Cherokee progress up the culture ladder was also evident in their religion. While traces of earlier beliefs in many spirits that entered both inanimate objects and animals lingered on in their myths, such beliefs had doubtless become to them only half-truths, and the nation had come to believe in a "Great Spirit," maker of all things. Belief in a future life existed, but what was to come to one after death seems not to have been a disturbing thought to them. Their reverence for the Great Spirit and their common prayers for blessings—most of them probably for material forms and immediate needs—were often expressed in religious dances that were beautiful in conception and stately and dignified in execution. Sometimes those participating in the dances were men only, sometimes both men and women, and sometimes women only. One of these women performances witnessed by a white traveler in Chota of the Over Hill Towns lasted for four days. The "foreigner" was not able to learn its purpose.[22]

Cherokee history and literature consisted of tales and myths accumulated over a long past and told and retold to each generation. The custom of absorbing groups and individuals from other tribes greatly enriched the fund of stories but has proved confusing to the modern historian attempting to see in them the trend of actual Cherokee religious beliefs. However, as a whole, the stories reveal vague, racial memories of other lands,

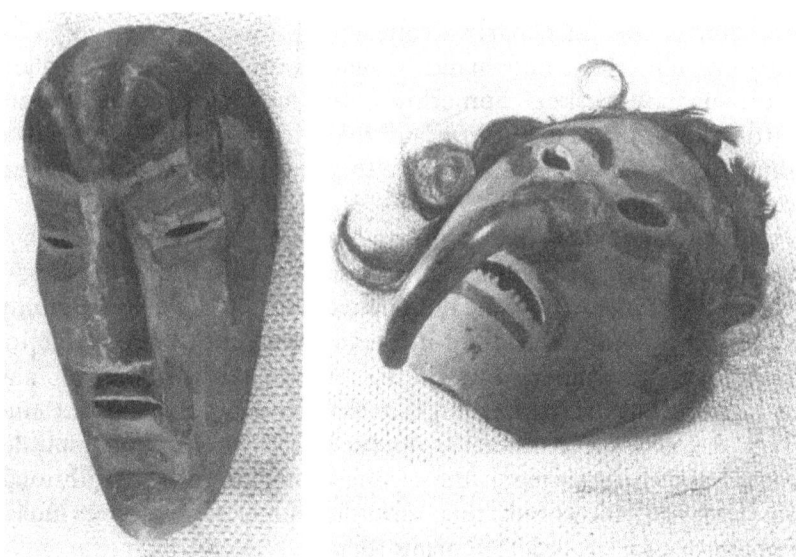

HALL OF HISTORY COLLECTION, N. C. DEPARTMENT OF ARCHIVES AND HISTORY
The Cherokees developed many ritualistic ceremonies through a variety of dance forms. Some depicted battles. Some were religious. Participants often made their meanings vivid by the use of masks. Cherokee masks varied in size, shape, and expressions. Some, like the one with the exaggerated nose, were doubtless designed for humor.

widely separated lands, of pride in heroes, of ancient hates and wars and battles. They reveal, too, the Cherokee's closeness to nature and record his primitive attempt to explain his world and the creatures in it, to fathom the creation of his mountain land, and to account for the strange natural formations. Some of these stories show a surprising tenderness of treatment, while others, like the Judaculla tales, are examples of man's universal love for exaggeration. Many tales also show the Cherokee's sense of humor, and it is entirely possible that groups of the old tales which modern man reads seriously and accepts as the Cherokee's superstition, brought roars of laughter when told evenings around the village fire by an expert storyteller.

As with all primitive peoples, storytelling was a popular form of entertainment, and the old, familiar tales were constant favorites. Then, too, every returning warrior or hunter could be sure of an interested audience as he related his experiences with wild animals or with prowling bands of enemies during the weeks or even months spent in distant regions of Cherokee country. The religious rituals and ceremonies and colorful dances furnished not only an outlet for religious emotion, but also a solemn social satisfaction. In addition, the Cherokees had many games and contests of skill in which individuals, towns, or clans participated.

The outstanding athletic event was their ball game that has survived the inroads of the white man's civilization and today is played yearly in the age-old manner. How it originated no one knows, for its beginning fades into the obscurity of the distant past. It was played by two opposing teams representing two clans. It was—and still is—a rough and tumble tussle with almost no rules, and the players took whatever treatment was given them, returning it with interest if possible. At times of strained relations between two clans, their ball game assumed the form of group combat, and the feelings of the spectators seated or standing on the hillside ran high, while an occasional casualty occurred.[23]

By the time English speaking people discovered the hills of Western North Carolina, the Cherokee nation was a powerful people, happy and contented in their mountain homeland. In fact, so powerful were they that they could call themselves simply, but significantly, *Yunwiya* or *Ani-Yunwiya*, "The People" or "The Principal People." True, other nations had other names for them, designating them as *Rickahockans* or *Rechahecrians*,[24] or more often used a name which the English corrupted into Cherokee. This name, however, the People themselves did not recognize since it had been bestowed by tribes who were enemies.

Several meanings have been given for the word "Cherokee." Dr. Swanton of the Smithsonian Institute suggests that it may be from a Muskogee word meaning "people of a different speech."[25] A somewhat widely accepted meaning is cave or pit. If this origin of the word is accurate, it may have had reference to their mountain homeland. More probably it carried the still smarting sting of their ancient defeat when they depended in vain upon their pit-like trenches and their breastworks to ward off the attack of the Iroquois and the Delawares, a defeat kept alive in the fireside tales and in the jibes of their enemies.

How long it took the Cherokees to achieve the spreading borders of their nation is not known. Nor can it be estimated with any degree of certainty how many centuries passed as they extended their homeland settlements south and east along the Middle rivers and into the present South Carolina and Georgia and into the Over Hill Country. The gradual process of settlement included driving any people they encountered out of the region and absorbing the remnants left. By 1540, when the curtain of antiquity was briefly drawn aside, they had not reached the later Lower Towns section. They had, however, attained more than a foothold in the Middle Towns area along the Valley and Hiwassee Rivers, with an undetermined number of scattered villages. They had a thriving settlement that the Spanish transcribed as Gau-ax-u-le or Guasili, almost certainly on the site of Peachtree Mound, five and a half miles east of the present Murphy. This seems to have been the largest settlement encountered by DeSoto within the present Western North Carolina.[26]

So it was, that as spring came over the mountains in 1540, trailing its robes of flashing color across the hillsides, the Cherokees could look with confidence to the future, and security could be taken for granted.

CHAPTER THREE

Two Races Meet

The serenity of the on-coming spring was shattered on a May morning in 1540 when an Indian runner, spent with his race along the ancient trails, stumbled into a mountain town with news that brought the men of the village hurrying to the council house. To them he poured out his fantastic tale. Stories reaching southern towns, he said, told that men, strange men of pale, ghastly hue and wearing clothes of metal, were traveling westward along the paths from the east. They were many and with them were strange beasts, some bigger than a bear (although not so stockily built), and on these some of the men sat. Others of the animals were small and black, grunting and squealing as they were driven westward.

Through the lands of the nations to the east they had come, for no tribe could withstand them and the sharp, popping thunder that they hurled to slay opposing braves. One thing was certain—they were on the warpath, for they stole or destroyed crops. They were also forcing villagers to join them as "tomemes" or burdeners and as guides from town to town. Soon they would reach the land of the hills. The dire news was sent from scattered village to village, and men, women, and children stopped their tasks and play to listen in wonder, only half believing the outlandish tale, yet not daring to ignore it. Thus was the white man's coming heralded in Western North Carolina.

The previous May, Hernando DeSoto, with a flotilla of seven ships carrying six hundred men, had landed in the proximity of the

CHEROKEE HISTORICAL ASSOCIATION
Indian women patiently gathered feathers which were skillfully used in making a robe that was proudly worn by the head man on ceremonial occasions. Such a feather robe was made for the outdoor drama, Unto These Hills, which is presented each summer at Cherokee.

present Tampa, Florida. As governor of Cuba, he was exercising his official prerogative of exploring and possessing any lands he might discover, together with whatever wealth they might contain. Earlier in the century, he had taken part in the Spanish conquest of Nicaragua and later, with Francisco Pizzaro, shared in the fabulous wealth taken from the proud Incas. Through the simple expedient of breaking their promise, they had killed the Inca ruler and devastated his vast empire of Peru, robbing the temples of their gold and silver. Surely in the mountains of North America, reasoned DeSoto and his Spaniards, similar treasures could be had for the taking.

The army wintered with the Apalachee Indians in northwest Florida and learned of towering hills far to the west where lived many Indians. They learned of gold and silver taken from the

ASHEVILLE CHAMBER OF COMMERCE

DeSoto and his soldiers, clad in plate armor, confront the Cherokee chief, who is wearing his ceremonial regalia. This dramatic event of 1540 is enacted effectively in the outdoor drama **Unto These Hills.**

ground and of a mighty river toward the sunset. So in the spring DeSoto and his men hacked their way through the dense undergrowth of the forests to the Savannah River. After a devious circuit to the north and east, they turned west, and picking up an Indian trail, proceeded northwest. To the awed and frightened Indians through whose lands they passed, they must have seemed like an endless throng as they journeyed single-file or two, three, or four abreast, as the narrow trails allowed.

At the bannered head rode DeSoto himself in his suit of mail, and following him were his three hundred horsemen. Behind them came a like number of footmen and laborers, while bringing up the rear was a herd of some two hundred hogs to insure a food supply. Lastly came more than three hundred captive Indians, burden bearers in chains. Near the vanguard were Indian guides, impressed in each village to conduct the army to the next town. One of these, captured in the present South Carolina, was a woman chief or "princess," Co-fi-tash-e, taken possibly to serve also as a hostage to prevent her people from attacking the invaders.¹ With DeSoto were a few Spanish priests, who entertained the vague hope of converting the Indians along the way, but whose chief duties must have been to hear confessions and to absolve the men from constant sins of atrocities committed upon the hapless Indians, their villages, and their crops. DeSoto appointed one of his men as historian, and the account left by this scribe gives the name Cherokee, the first time it appeared in writing. He had heard it from the tribes to the east and in transcribing it to his alphabet, he spelled it *Chalaque*.² It was left to the French of a later century to write it *Cheraqui* and to the even later English to perpetuate it as *Cherokee*.

In due time the Spaniards reached Western North Carolina, entering from the present Georgia just east of Rabun Gap, and going by way of the present Highlands to Nikwasi on the site of the present Franklin, arriving there on May 26. In this region they came for the first time upon a tributary of the Mississippi River. In addition to the official record kept by Roderigo Ranjel, a short account was written by Louis Hernandez de Biedma. A third was written by "a gentleman of Elvas," probably Alvaro Fernandez. Later a fourth one was written by Garcilasco de la Vega, who got his material from what was told him by a member of the expedition. As a result, various routes have been given by historians.

In 1936 Congress created a seven-member DeSoto Expedition Commission to determine from the original sources available the Spanish line of march from the coast of Florida to the Mississippi River and the route of return. This Commission, with Dr. John R. Swanton of the Smithsonian Institution as chairman, made use of the four accounts together with a map which the expedition had worked out. The Commission submitted its detailed report in 1939. With this as a guide, the North Carolina Department of Archives and History marked the one hundred mile journey through the state's western counties as it was traveled by DeSoto and his men.³

The mountain Indians treated their unwelcome guests with a kindness and respect that must have been wisely considered the better part of valor. Too, they must have been secretly elated and amused that it was in their territory that the captive "princess" made her escape, taking with her the priceless collection of pearls entrusted to her care and leaving the "foreigners" without a guide. From Nikwasi DeSoto pushed on over the mountains to the headwaters of the Hiwassee River, to the site of the present

Hayesville, and from there to the earlier mentioned Cherokee village of Gau-ax-u-le, probably near the present Murphy. This village, possibly like others along the route, he found partly deserted, for many terrified Cherokees had fled to the safety of the hills.

Here at Gau-ax-u-le, if not earlier at Nikwasi, the impressive army was received by the Cherokees, who dared not refuse the demands for supplies of food for both men and horses issued by the uninvited visitors. Among the provisions given to the Spanish were little "dogs that do not bark." It has been suggested that these animals might have been oppossums, as unfamiliar to the Europeans as horses and hogs were to the Cherokees. Perhaps two days later DeSoto forged ahead to the site of the present Murphy and some fifteen miles farther northwestward into the present Polk County, Tennessee. From one of the villages he had sent out exploring parties in search of gold and silver. The men are reported to have returned with copper, possibly from the mines later known as the Ducktown mines.[4]

The uneasy Cherokees seem to have told the Spaniards only what was necessary and doubtless held out hopes for more success in discovering the coveted gold farther west, much farther west. Indeed, it must have been with relief that the Cherokee hosts saw the long procession of strange men and beasts disappearing into the land of their enemies toward the sunset. As they resumed their normal summer activities, they could not know that the security of their race was gone, that never again would the mountain Redmen be free from the ever-darkening and lengthening shadow of conquest and subjugation by an alien people. They could not foresee that their mountain land was to become a battleground for opposing nations of these Pale Faces in a bitter struggle for the possession of the continent.

Twenty-seven years later Juan Pardo, an officer in charge of the Spanish fort on Port Royal Island, led an expedition organized by Florida's governor, Pedro Menendez de Aviles, into the Indian country where a fort or two had been built east of the Blue Ridge. With the discovery of gold and silver as his objective, Pardo led his forces from one of these forts into Western North Carolina, following approximately the route taken in 1540 by DeSoto. Even more demanding and ruthless than his predecessor, Pardo left death and destruction and terror in his wake.

His men were moderately successful in their prospecting, locating limited amounts of gold and silver. For the next 125 years groups of Spaniards sporadically carried on mining operations both east and west of the Blue Ridge. A few of their shafts, tools, and coin dies have been found, but for obvious reasons they kept their mining activities a guarded secret; reports of their presence, however, reached the Cherokees and other tribes so that the first English explorers to the region were told of "white, bearded men," trespassers on Indian territory.[5]

At this time on a distant island, even more important events were taking place, events that were destined to upset the pattern of living developed over the ages in the Western North Carolina mountains. About the same time as Pardo's expedition, England came to feel that if the Spanish in the south and the French in the north along the St. Lawrence River were to be checked in their greed for American possessions, the time had arrived to plant colonies on the vast English claims. These claims stretched from Florida northward to the Dutch and French territories and from the Atlantic Ocean westward to the Pacific or South Sea. Accordingly, on March 24, 1584, Queen Elizabeth granted to her courtier, Sir Walter Raleigh, a patent for "discovering and planting of new lands and Countries [sic]" throughout the English area unsettled by "Christian nations." The patent was good for six years and Raleigh set about his planting of settlers upon the land he called Virginia.[6]

In 1585 his first colonizing expedition landed on Roanoke Island on the North Carolina coast and built a palisaded village. But practically all the discouraged settlers returned to England on Sir Francis Drake's ships which put into harbor in 1586. In 1587 Raleigh sent a second expedition directed by John White. The mystery surrounding the fate of this little band of men, women, and children has never been solved. But its disappearance meant failure for Raleigh and his patent lapsed. Yet a beginning had been made. James I, breaking the extensive territory into two sections with a buffer zone of a hundred miles between, granted a patent to a company organized as the London Company, which in 1607 established a tiny settlement named Jamestown on the James River.

To this tiny, struggling settlement reports of western mountains were made by the surrounding Indians. John Smith, during his stormy year in the colony, learned from Powhatan that far to the west were "mightie Mountaines [sic]." Some thirty-five years later, in the 1640's, Governor William Berkeley learned that to the west was "a huge mountain within five days journey, and at the foot thereof great Rivers that run into a Great Sea, to which people come in ships [sic]."[7] This report convinced Berkeley that what is now Western North Carolina bordered the South Sea and so was the long-sought passage to India.

Enthusiastically Berkeley planned an expedition into the region with the two-fold purpose of locating the passage and of discovering gold and silver as he knew the Spanish had done. But, he wrote, he was hindered by "Unusual and continuous Raynes [sic]." The colony over which he ruled required much attention, and he became deeply involved in matters of politics until the years had sped by and he came to know that he would never make the journey himself. In 1649, however, the Virginia General Assembly offered grants of land and mining rights to persons discovering new territory and minerals in the uncharted area. There is no record of anyone taking advantage of this offer.

But Governor Berkeley could not forget his dream, and in 1670 he equipped and sent out an explorer, a German physician named John Lederer. With him were several aides and guides. But when at the end of a few days, these men became frightened and turned back, Lederer went on with only one Indian guide and companion. In time he reached the eastern fringe of the Cherokee country and may have been the first Englishman to see the eastern slopes of the Blue Ridge. But he did not cross them. He learned, however, that over these mountains lived the Rickahockans, or Cherokees, whose land was "great waves." He was told also of bearded white men not far distant. These men he thought to be Spaniards, and the waves he interpreted to be those of the South Sea, confirming Berkeley's belief that in this direction lay the passage to India. He could get no information about gold or silver but was told that from the mountains the Indians got a substance with which they painted their faces.[8]

During the year of Lederer's trip, another physician made the first of several journeys into the Indian country. He was Henry Woodward, a young Englishman lately come from England, who had thrown in his lot with the settlers on the Ashley River. It was a tiny settlement that was to become known as Charles Town and that was to have a direct effect upon Western North Carolina. What Henry Woodward's reasons were for risking his life in the Indian country he does not say, but he may have had several. He was young. There was the thrill of new adventure and doubtless the hope of finding gold, for he was sure to have heard of the Spanish gold expeditions. And judging form the records he left, there seems to have been a genuine interest in the native settlers and a concern for the future possibilities of land.

It was largely due to the good will toward the English which he was able to build up in the tribes and nations he visited that the colony of South Carolina was able later to secure trade treaties. Among those nations willing to make such agreements were the Cherokees, or *Chorkees* as Woodward spelled the name. With the delight of a true explorer, Woodward viewed the "brave, new world" through which he passed and wrote enthusiastically to an English friend, "I have discovered a Country so delitious, pleasant, and fruitfull, y$_t$ were it cultivated, doubtless it would prove a second Paradise [sic]."[9]

The motive that brought the earliest known travelers into Western North Carolina was trade with the Indians. From the time that frightened Indians watched from behind protecting trees as the pale, grotesquely garbed Englishmen landed on American shores, the Indians and the colonists were engaged in a struggle for a continent—a struggle that was to last some 250 years. Yet during the first hundred of those years each race became increasingly dependent upon the other for trade. At first, the Indians brought their furs and pelts on the backs of runners called burdeners to the white man's towns and villages. In the same manner they took back to their own villages the superior tools of the white man, guns and ammunition, cloth and trinkets.

But some of the tribes were constantly shifting their living places, and as time went on others became increasingly adverse to going to the white settlements. Many Virginia merchants then found it profitable to devote their entire time to the Indian trade since they could sell the furs to good advantage on the English markets. Thus they began the practice of supplying white traders with goods and sending them into the Indian territory over the age-old trails, now firmly packed into trading paths by the bare or moccasined feet of hundreds of burdeners. These men heard of tribes farther to the west, and so the lure of profits enticed traders into the Cherokee country of Western North Carolina.

In 1673 General Abraham Wood, a prominent Indian trader in charge of Fort Henry near the present Petersburg, Virginia, employed James Needham, a young Englishman who had recently come from the mother country to Charles Town where he had built his home. Needham was to go into the unknown territory and "explore beyond the mountains" and to chart the rivers. General Wood furnished him with supplies and horses, eight Indian guides, and one of his own servants, possibly an indentured laborer, Gabriel Arthur, as a companion. Needham was an able, promising young man, apparently eager to make the exploration. The little party followed the trading path westward to the Yadkin River, which they followed southward, possibly into the Catawba country east of the Blue Ridge.

At some undetermined point they turned west and crossed the range. Three possible routes have been traced by historians. The men may have veered west from the Yadkin, entering Western North Carolina along the same path that was later used by Daniel Boone. In that case, they would have crossed the site of the present Boone and picked up one of two trails leading to the Watauga River and then on to the Over Hill Towns on the Little Tennessee River.[10] They may have gone farther south in the Catawba country, however, and selected a crossing at Swannanoa Gap where an ancient trail led over the mountains. In so doing, they would have passed through the southern part of the present Asheville and, picking up a trail from there, traveled west to the present Canton and Pigeon River. A trail there would have led them west to the Middle Cherokee Towns and on to the Over Hill Towns. Again, they may have continued in a southerly direction until they turned west by way of Hickory Nut Gap, passing through the present Henderson County, going up the French Broad to Hominy Creek and along it (over land now occupied by the Enka Corporation Plant) to the Pigeon River and west to the Middle and Over Hill Towns.[11]

By whatever route they traveled, they were in one of the Indian towns by mid-summer. The Indians of this village had never seen a white man, and they gazed in wonder at these washed-out specimens of the human race and with even more amazement at the strange beast they had brought with them. They made the men tie the one horse that had withstood the rigors of the trip to a stake in the center of the village so that all might gaze at the freak of nature.

After exploring for several months Needham returned to Fort Henry, taking several Cherokees with him and leaving Arthur as a hostage charged with the responsibility of learning the Cherokee language and of fostering good relations between the Cherokees and the English. Needham and his party reached the fort and, getting fresh supplies, set out again for the mountains. But he did not arrive at his destination. One of the Indians, nicknamed John by the whites, may have had misgivings about this friendship with the white men and he killed Needham on a lonely stretch of the trade route, taking the horse and what goods he could. He charged his Cherokee companions to see that the same fate was meted out to Arthur. Back in their village, the Indians set about carrying out those orders. They tied Arthur to a stake and piled brush around him. Then two Westoe slaves began to strike a fire. At that dramatic moment the chief arrived, saw what was happening, and in anger shot the slaves and took Arthur for his own personal slave. He seemed to have treated the young man as his son.

With a hunting party, Arthur was taken by the chief into Kentucky and was thus probably the first Englishman to see the famous "Land of Kaintuck." He was later taken through South Carolina and the Lower Towns of the Cherokee to eastern South Carolina on a raiding expedition against enemy tribes. On another occasion he was a member of a revenge party sent into Florida. Among his various experiences was also that of being captured by a band of Shawnees. But Arthur had by this time learned much about Indians and was able to gain the good will of his captors, who set him free and put him on the trading path back to the Over Hill Towns.

It was a year before he could get the consent of the chief to return home. Then the chief announced that he would accompany the white man to Virginia. After a series of hairbreadth escapes from raiding parties of unfriendly Indians during which the two were separated, both reached Fort Henry. There Arthur related his experiences to General Wood, who reported them to his superiors.[12] That record is disappointingly meager, for the journal that Needham kept was lost. It is safe to assume that Arthur could not read or write, and little came of this expedition into the mountains. It was almost twenty years before other Englishmen are known to have entered Western North Carolina.

Preceding and during this quiet interlude events were taking place in England and along the American coast that insured trade with the Cherokees—trade agreements which General Wood had complained received no encouragement from his superiors and for which young Needham had given his life. In 1629 the King of England, Charles I, with bland unconcern for the Indians, gave the entire Cherokee nation, with the exception of some hunting grounds to the north, to a friend. This grant was issued to Sir

Robert Heath, the attorney-general, and it conveyed to him a vast tract lying between the thirty-first and thirty-sixth degrees of latitude and stretching westward from the Atlantic Ocean "so farre as the Continent extends itselfe[sic]."

Thus the Heath grant was between the territory of the London Company's tract, to which the once over-all name of Virginia had by now been limited, southward toward Florida. In its westward sweep it included practically all of present North Carolina. Through this gift, Heath became one of the most extensive land owners of all times. In return for this royal favor, he was to plant settlers in the new colony, which in the charter was named Carolina or Carolana, honoring Charles by using the Latinized form of his name. But Heath brought no colonists from England to his rambling estate, and shortly after 1660 the grant was declared void. Fortunately for the peace of mind of the Cherokees, they never learned of this kingly grant, but the ghost of this gift later arose to haunt and harry the British government and was not quieted until 1769.[13]

The idea of forming a new colony was not easily crushed. The newly crowned Charles II, searching for a suitable, yet inexpensive method of rewarding his friends active in restoring him to the English throne, bethought of this vast American territory. Accordingly in 1663 he presented the former Heath tract to eight of his Lords. They were to be known as Proprietors of the region and were to make settlements, select governors, establish a nobility, and, aided by an assembly of elected colonists, otherwise rule the colony. The proprietors were to be answerable to the Committee of Trade and Plantations which was set up in England under the King and Council. Almost at once the Proprietors found that they wanted more land and presented their reasons for an extention of the grant.

From 1609, when John Smith sent a search party from Jamestown into the territory to the south, hoping to locate Raleigh's vanished colonists, Virginia trappers had been going into the region west of Albemarle Sound. They had been followed by occasional private traders and now and then by a company of soldiers sent to avenge Indian attacks on Virginia settlements. Just when the first Englishman decided to remain in this land is not known, but by 1648 a few had acquired land from the Indians along the Chowan River. From time to time other hardy pioneers trekked into the region and settled around Albemarle Sound. By 1663 there was an unrecorded number of these settlers, but a large enough group existed to attract attention to the area now called

Albemarle. The northern boundary of the 1663 grant passed south of these tiny settlements and left them isolated since they did not come within the Virginia boundaries. Therefore, in 1665 Charles II, by means of another grant to the eight Proprietors, extended the northern boundary of their lands by half a degree latitude and the southern boundary by two degrees. Thus was the colony of Carolina established and the way paved for its mountain section to be opened to the white man.[14]

The coast of the northern section of Carolina offered few harbors suitable for populating the colony with English immigrants. In 1667 a settlement was made on the Cape Fear River but was shortly afterward abandoned.[15] However, in 1670, a band of English colonists formed a little settlement on the Ashley River in the southern half of the colony. Almost from the first the village grew, and in 1679 it was moved to the peninsula between the Ashley and Cooper Rivers and named Charles Town. With its harbor unhampered by the reefs which discouraged mariners from landing along the coast farther north, this settlement grew and became the chief Carolina port of entry for English ships. Relatives and friends of the settlers arrived on every vessel, and ambitious young men, some of them younger sons in families of wealth and estate, came to cast their lots with the forward-looking colonists. Soon there was a pleasing bustle of activity and an infectious spirit of optimism in the village.

With the earlier Jamestown experiences to guide them, the colonists set about adjusting themselves and their way of life to the conditions of an American frontier. They enlisted the aid of friendly Indians in learning to cultivate tobacco on the extensive holdings they cleared along the Ashley and Cooper Rivers. Then they looked about for other crops and products that could be marketed in the mother country in exchange for English goods needed for a degree of convenience and comfort in their new homes. Like all of the earliest settlements, Charles Town was surrounded on three sides by Indian tribes, and the safety of the village and plantations depended upon gaining and maintaining friendly relations with these natives. Happily, they discovered that could be accomplished at a handsome profit, and from the first, trade with the Indians became an important business. So flourishing did the town become that it was designated as the capital of the colony of Carolina in 1691 (or more accurately, perhaps, as the home of the governor appointed by the Proprietors).

Previous to 1670, the elected General Assembly of Carolina,

first convened in 1665, met in the district called Albemarle where the first settlements in the vast new colony were steadily if slowly growing, largely through newcomers from Virginia. In this area, too, the first colonial governor, William Drummond, resided as did several of his successors. Taking his title from the region, each was called the Governor of Albemarle. The proprietors hoped as soon as practicable to break their territory into three counties, Albemarle in the north, Clarenden in the Cape Fear area, and Craven in the south. They apparently did not take the shore line into consideration and seemed to anticipate a gradual growth from north to south. Instead, the first attempts at settlement in the center region failed and Charles Town became the second settlement.[16]

With one assembly for the two widely separated groups of colonists, problems of a physical nature arose, for it proved almost impossible for assembly members in one area to attend sessions of the General Assembly held in the other. To alleviate this situation, after 1691 separate assemblies were established and Governor Philip Ludwell was told that "If you find it needfull you our governor are hereby empowered to appoint a Deputy Governor of North Carolina[sic]."[17] Governor Ludwell did, indeed, find this "needfull," and several deputies served in Albemarle during the following years. These officers were directly responsible to the appointed governor rather than to the Proprietors.

The title North Carolina used in the permission given by the Proprietors was unofficial, but had been locally in use for some years. By 1700 it was appearing in reports and accounts recorded by colonial writers. In 1710 Edward Hyde, deputy governor, was chosen by the Proprietors as full governor of North Carolina although he did not receive this title until 1712. For that reason one of these dates has usually been given as the date of the separation of the two parts of the colony into North and South Carolina. But in either case both areas made up the colony of Carolina until 1729 when the Proprietors, with the exception of the heirs of Lord Carteret, sold their territorial rights to the English government and the colony became a royal colony. Then one of the first official changes to be made was the separation of the territory into the two distinct colonies of North and South Carolina.

Thus the mountain section, which had been a part of Carolina, now became a part of North Carolina. Nonetheless, for many years before and after that separation Western North Carolina was influenced not by the laws or government of its own colony, but by the government of South Carolina.

CHAPTER FOUR

Along the Trading Paths

By the time General Wood sent James Needham and Gabriel Arthur across the Blue Ridge, Virginia merchants and traders were carrying on a thriving trade with the Catawba Indians in Carolina, just east of the mountains. With the way now opened by the travels of Dr. Henry Woodward, accompanied on one of his journeys by young Needham, Charles Town took steps to link the tribes to the south and east of the Catawbas in bonds of friendship and trade with the southern port. Accordingly, trade treaties were made in which, for a promise of protection against their enemies, tribal chiefs agreed to funnel their furs and pelts to Charles Town and to allow only Carolina traders in their territory.

In 1684 such a treaty was signed with the marks made by eight chiefs of the Lower Towns,[1] thus determining future trade relations between the Cherokees and Charles Town. To strengthen these new relations and to cast about for gold deposits, James Moore, later to be governor of Carolina, and Maurice Matthews made a trip of good will into the Lower Cherokee country. However, hearing of mining operations being carried on by the Spaniards just twenty miles away from an Indian village, they decided that it would not be expedient to go into the mountain section of the Cherokee nation.[2]

The Indians living in the Middle and Over Hill Towns learned of the white man's goods that could be had for making little marks on a white man's piece of paper. They learned, too, that such

Along the Trading Paths / 57

ASHEVILLE CHAMBER OF COMMERCE

English traders in the 1700's brought glass beads into the Indian country. Shell ornaments were then discarded, and women fashioned the colorful beads into many forms of adornment. This woman at the Oconaluftee Village at Cherokee is carrying on the tradition of her ancestors.

marks might bring the white man's aid against their enemies. In 1693, therefore, a group of Cherokees, including several mountain chiefs, appeared in Charles Town with a request for protection against eastern tribes attacking the eastern border of the Cherokee nation. Some sort of promise seems to have been given to the chiefs, although with no official sanction, and there is no evidence that any active help was extended to the Cherokees at that time. A basis for a trade treaty had been laid, however, and shortly afterward Cherokee chiefs representing all sections of the nation signed a trade treaty with South Carolina.[3]

About this time the colony took the first step in transferring lucrative trade with the Indians from the control of private individuals to the colony itself. This process was fully justified in view of the fact that in 1703 the estimated population of all Carolina numbered not more than four thousand white men, women, and children, with perhaps only about eight hundred available for military duty.[4] Traders dealing with the Indians and going into their territories wielded immense influence with the tribes and their leaders. They could, if they were unscrupulous in their dealings or imprudent in their words, endanger every white settlement.

In 1707, then, South Carolina began its task of assuming full control of this important trade by establishing a nine-member Board of Commissioners of Indian Affairs,[5] later reduced to five members. It also appointed for each tribe a Factor or Superintendent, who was to spend at least ten months of each year in the Indian country as supervisor of the trade and traders already in the area and of those appointed as his aides.[6] The first Factor to the Cherokees was Colonel Theopholus Hastings. He made his home on the Tugalo River in the Lower Towns, and was paid two hundred pounds a year, a salary later increased to three hundred pounds. He was given two aides, John Sharpe and Sam Muckleroy, but later asked for and got more men. He served until the end of December, 1717, when he was transferred to the Creeks.[7]

Another step toward trade with the Indians was taken with the building of Fort Moore on the Savannah River near the site of the present Augusta, Georgia, in 1716. It was both an armed fort and a trading post, and under an agreement with the Cherokees (a treaty which had been worked out by James Moore and the Cherokee representative, Charite Hayge), South Carolina was to transport goods from Charles Town to the fort, while the Indians were to make new trading paths connecting the fort with their old trails. They were to furnish burdeners to bring furs bought by the traders and the agent to the fort. In addition, the Indians were to carry back to the traders the coveted manufactured articles brought from Charles Town by slow river transportation, by hired Indian burdeners, or by pack horses over a land route often made dangerous by roving bands of unfriendly tribes.[8]

On July 18, 1716, the Board of Commissioners ordered that "the twenty-one Burdeners, that brought down the bever be paid for that service and for carrying the Goods which we are to send by them to our Factor at the Charikees each, one Yard and a Half of blew Duffields for matchcoats, and a quarter Yard Strouds, for Flaps [sic]."[9] As time went on, the burdeners were endangered by marauding bands that attacked the slowly moving human caravan. Often the result was loss of goods and occasionally loss of life. The fort was opened in March, 1716, and by the end of that year some ten thousand dollars worth of goods had been brought there from Charles Town. During 1717 fine furs carried to the fort on the backs of ninety-one burdeners from Western North Carolina brought almost fifteen hundred pounds sterling to the English.[10]

The demand for the white man's goods rose rapidly in Western North Carolina. Cherokee hunters and trappers exchanged their furs for manufactured goods at a bartering ratio worked out under the terms of the treaty by the Board of Commissioners. A Cherokee purchaser paid 35 skins for a gun, 16 for a blanket, 30 for a broadcloth coat (provided it was laced), 14 for a callico petticoat for his wife, and 2 for a red girdle for himself. Mirrors and teakettles were soon in such demand in the mountain country that traders were allowed to charge whatever they could get. Even at the high prices some traders asked, the demand exceeded the supply.[11]

Cherokee chiefs were soon complaining to the Factor and the Board of Commissioners of the hardships endured by their burdeners on the long trip to the fort. A few Virginia traders were in the area east of the Blue Ridge doing business with pack horses, and the chiefs asked for a similar arrangement with South Carolina. Feeling that it was unsafe to send pack horse trains into the mountains, the Board at first refused the chiefs' requests. By 1718, after several Cherokee burdeners met death on the trading path, the petitions became too insistent to be longer denied, and the Board yielded.

The entire trading regulations were then revised. Under the new order, the colony licensed traders for a fee of eight pounds per year and the posting of a bond of a hundred pounds currency, later raised to two hundred. Traders were given credit at the fort. There they purchased a supply of goods to be transported to the Indian country, at first partly by burdeners, but as soon as they could procure horses, entirely by pack train. Then the trails were widened where necessary into trading paths over which heavily-laden horses could take the wares into the chief Cherokee towns, where, from the storehouses, traders could distribute them throughout the nation.[12] The earliest of these pack trains made use of the old trail from the Lower Towns to the Middle Towns. It was the trail, perhaps older than the towns themselves, traveled a century and a half earlier by DeSoto and his Spaniards.[13]

The stout little ponies used for this work would carry from 150 to 200 pounds each and, over favorable terrain and with good forage, could travel twenty miles a day. Over the narrow, rugged, densely forested mountain sections the progress of the trains was much slower. John William Gerard deBrahm, transporting supplies for the building of Fort Loudon in 1756, reported that in the mountains six miles was sometimes a day's journey.¹⁴ William Byrd, writing in 1728, mentions seeing a pack train of a hundred horses and fifteen men going south on the trading path from Virginia to the Catawba country.¹⁵ As the demands for goods increased, these trains became longer, and James Adair tells of seeing a train consisting of 360 horses leaving from a South Carolina fort and heading for the Chickasaw country.¹⁶

The horses were in the charge of drivers, each of whom had one or more helpers, usually boys. Each driver was in charge of a section of the train, often destined for a particular trader. At the command of a leading driver, the train started, the horses going in single file, while the drivers cracked long, leather whips to get their charges in line. Each horse wore a bell, and as the snake-like procession jogged along a comparatively smooth stretch of the trading path, the discordant jangling of the bells made a fitting accompaniment for the men's coarse shouts.

Continuing its trading plans, South Carolina built the second of its western forts in 1718. It was Fort Congaree on the Congaree River near the present Columbia, and it greatly shortened the distance from a supply station to Western North Carolina. As time went on, privately constructed forts appeared, some of which, like Gowdy's at Ninety-Six, were also trading posts and aided in the rapid transportation of goods into the mountain section. From Gowdy's a path extended through the present Spartanburg area, entering the mountains near the present Tryon and going westward to the Middle Towns.¹⁷ The fort nearest to the mountain Cherokees was Fort Prince George, built opposite the town of Keowee in the Lower Cherokee section. But it was a much later one constructed in 1753 that was destined to play a far grimmer role in the affairs of the Cherokees than that of supplying them with goods.

The first generation of traders going into Western North Carolina became almost a race unto themselves. Those arriving before South Carolina made the Indian trade a colonial monopoly, purchased their goods from eastern merchants, set their own prices, and got what they could on the Charles Town market for their furs. After the appointment of a Factor, traders were assigned stations, received their supplies from the fort, and were required to observe the price list sent by the Board. In receiving their licenses from South Carolina, they assumed the duty of promoting peace and good will between the races, of being fair and honest in all their dealings with the Cherokees, of not selling firearms to enemies of the Cherokees, of buying no Cherokee slaves, and of letting no whiskey come into their territory.

Both the traders' lives and their livelihood were under the supervision of the Factor. Of necessity these men isolated themselves from their own race, making their homes in Cherokee villages. They learned about the Cherokees and the Cherokee language. Although they never forgot that they were white men and remained loyal to the colony and to England in all cases of trouble, they adopted enough of the Cherokee customs and manners to make life in Western North Carolina livable and at times very pleasant. Practically without exception, they married Cherokee women.

In this way the traders played a unique role in the affairs of the colony. They were in fact, interpreters for both races. To the Cherokees they represented South Carolina and, indeed, all Englishmen (at first, doubtless, all white men). To the Board of Commissioners and to the Factors they furnished needed information concerning the Cherokees and their attitudes. They also reported on the activities of the French, both west of the Cherokee nation and within it. They were thus able to advise the home colony on its Indian policy.

After 1750 the tension between the colony and the Cherokees made future trouble seem certain. The early traders, now old in years and in service, pleaded with the Board of Commissioners, the Legislature, and Governor Glenn for a course of action that they felt would lead to a restoration of the friendly relations existing from 1716 to about 1743. Those were the years of closest contact and good will between the races and the period during which trade flourished, a trade bringing to South Carolina an annual harvest of 200,000 furs.[18]

Some of these men had come into Western North Carolina as private traders, identifying themselves for the rest of their lives with the Cherokees. Cornelius Dougherty is accredited by most historians as being the first, going into the territory from Virginia in 1690. That date may be too early, and it is possible that Robert Bunning preceded him, if Dougherty was accurate in a statement implying that.[19] In any case, these two traders were joined by James Beamer, Ludovick Grant, and other men with a desire to carry out the responsibilities of their positions. Still later others came, as did James Adair, and as new trading paths were opened from newly built forts, others, like Richard

Pearis from Tryon, arrived to serve the Indians.[20]

Now and then traders from Virginia and later from Georgia also entered Western North Carolina, purchasing licenses from South Carolina for the privilege of trading with the Cherokees. William Byrd voiced the opinion of many of his fellow Virginians when he bitterly complained of the license requirement and of the fact that the traders from his colony had to make the long trip to South Carolina to secure the permits.[21] With some exceptions that were deeply regretted by the Factor and the other traders, this first generation of white men dealing directly with the Cherokees lived up to their obligations and gained the respect and confidence of the Indians.

The type of man attracted to the out-door life of a trader and to the Cherokee life style could not be expected to be interested in the art of writing. But with the goods sent to the "Factor at the Charikees [sic]" went writing paper and ink powder. He sent reports and wrote letters to the Board of Commissioners, while traders wrote letters when the occasion arose.[22] One trader, however, had both the desire and the ability to leave a record of the Cherokee nation as he had come to know it, and to his *History of The American Indians* today's historian owes a debt of gratitude. This author was James Adair, one of the most influential of the traders. He was Irish, a member of the powerful Fitzgerald family, Adair—or Adare—being the name of the ancient family estate. He was a younger son and arrived in Charles Town in 1735.

Deeply interested in the surrounding Indian tribes, Adair seems to have taken up trading almost at once and in 1736 entered Western North Carolina. With a background of learning and culture, he was by nature forthright and honest and had a genuine respect for the Cherokees. From their chiefs and headmen, who became his friends, he was able to learn their traditions and myths, their forms of government, and their moral and religious beliefs and practices. For the rest of his life he was a staunch supporter of the Cherokees, even though he fought them when they joined the French in the bloody struggle known as the French and Indian War.[23]

In 1721 chiefs from Western North Carolina joined a group of Indian delegates representing thirty-seven villages at a council called by Governor Francis Nicholson of Charles Town in South Carolina. There they signed a new treaty in which new regulations governing trade were agreed upon as needed to curb evils arising with the expansion of trade. Pressed by the colonial government, the Indians also agreed to determine a definite boundary line, clarifying the eastern limit of their country. By this treaty the Indians lost a goodly strip of hunting territory to the whites, but the lost land was farther east than any portion of Western North Carolina. At this same meeting the Cherokees approved the presence of the Factor, his aides, and white traders in their lands and agreed to elect one of their headmen as nominal head of and spokesman for the entire Cherokee nation. A chief with the unpronounceable name of Wrosetasatow was elected to this honor, becoming the first Cherokee in all the long history of the race to rule over the entire nation.[24]

During the entire trading period, despite treaty safeguards, it took the combined efforts of trader, Commissioners, and loyal chiefs to maintain a spirit of good will conducive to carrying on trade to the mutual satisfaction of the races. In 1725, in answer to letters of appeal and protest, the Board of Commissioners sent Colonel George Chicken, a member of that Board, into the Cherokee nation to report on conditions. Colonel Chicken, familiar with Indians and Indian affairs, made a thorough inspection. In his report he recommended the revoking of some licenses, gave the names of certain traders operating without licenses from South Carolina, and asked that several traders be put on probation of good behavior.

From Keowee in the Lower Towns to Great Tellico in the Over Hill Towns he went, talking to the chiefs, hearing their complaints, and telling them of the complaints lodged against their people. His presence, tact, and diplomacy accomplished much, and the renewed loyalty of the Cherokee was reflected in an increase in trade with South Carolina. There followed several years of harmony between the races.[25]

Forces were at work in Western North Carolina, however, that brought concern to thoughtful traders and chiefs alike. Some of these forces were inherent in the business of trading itself. By 1730, the demand for the white man's goods was coming from every Cherokee village, however remote. Guns, hoes and axes, knives and hatchets, blankets and cloth, pots and pans had become necessities, and the Cherokees were gradually adopting parts of the white man's dress. This swelling trade meant that more drivers and their helpers were needed to man the ever-lengthening trains and that more traders and their aides must live in the Cherokee nation.

These factors, in turn, meant that South Carolina, in its attempt to meet the demand, was forced to issue licenses to traders without too fine a regard for their abilities or their moral characters. In time, drivers and their helpers were hired whose only recommendation was that they were willing to make trips for the money offered. Every year increased the number of white men heading westward along the trading paths into Western North Carolina. They were now men of assorted abilities and business ethics. The inevitable result was the gradual lowering of the earlier high standards of trading and the slow growth of unscrupulous practices.

Unsavory dealings were not, of course, confined to the whites. Cherokees sometimes pilfered or openly robbed a pack train, and those working with the trains often demanded their pay at the beginning of the trip only to desert it along the way. Indian trappers and hunters, too, shirked in the slow process of preparing their furs; yet they asked as much for their inferior products as traders were giving for perfect furs. There were even times when traders complained that the Cherokees refused to bring them any furs.[26]

The situation was further complicated by the growing influence of the French in Western North Carolina. Even in 1725 Colonel Chicken had found that influence rather strong in the Middle Towns. Because of the explorations in the sixteenth century of John Verrazzano along the Atlantic coast and those of Jacques Cartier farther north, France had laid claim to much of the North American continent. Early in the following century there were French settlements along the St. Lawrence River. Checked in their southward advance along the Atlantic coast by the English claims and by the Spanish occupation of Florida, the French explored lands south of the Great Lakes and the regions farther west.

French trappers and missionaries roamed over a wide territory. On one of his trips Jean Nicolet discovered the upper Mississippi River and explored the area around it. Sieur de la Salle, on his exploratory travels, discovered the Ohio River. In 1673, the very year that Needham and Arthur made an English contact with the Cherokees of Western North Carolina, Louis Joliet and Jacques Marquette were drifting down the Mississippi to the west of them (actually in territory covered by the Carolina grant which extended to the Pacific Ocean.) Nine years later at the mouth of the Mississippi River, La Salle took possession in the name of France of that mighty stream together with all territory drained by its tributaries, a region so vast as to be beyond the imagination of the colonists of any nation.

All of Western North Carolina lying west of the Blue Ridge was included in this French claim. With a definite claim now established, France allowed her trappers and missionaries to roam at will in any or all sections of the area, and in time these men came into contact with all of the tribes and nations occupying land east of the Mississippi River. The next step was to establish trade relations with as many of the tribes as possible. With their ability to learn the various Indian languages, to take up Indian ways of living, and to ingratiate themselves into the favor of chiefs and headmen, the French were soon sending traders into many of the Indian territories.

In order to protect their trading interests and to maintain their claims to the region, the French government gave commands for the building of forts, and one by one a string of military and trading posts arose, extending from the present Erie, Pennsylvania, southwestward to the newly established Mobile, Alabama. In 1714 Fort Toulouse was erected near what is now Montgomery, Alabama. From it the French could and did transport goods into Western North Carolina. By 1730 French traders were appearing in the mountains in alarming numbers.

These French traders, like the English, were there on claims of their government and had come to stay. Simply by virtue of their location—a location that had served them well in the past—the Cherokees now became the pawns of two opposing white governments. They were swayed by promises or considerations shown first by one and then the other of these foreign nations. There followed, after 1730, a period of continuous fluctuation on the part of the Cherokees, a period of great bitterness toward one or the other of the encroaching peoples, a period of alliances and treaties made only to be broken, a period of utter bewilderment and confusion. All of these shifting moods brought sharp upward or equally sharp downward swings in the trade with South Carolina.

Unlike practically all other frontier regions in America, Western North Carolina was never out of touch with the more populous and settled sections in the East until after the Revolutionary War. The Indian trade kept open a constant and active line of communication with Charles Town and through it with England itself. But like all other frontier regions, Western North Carolina attracted colorful characters and had its quota of men coming into the mountains for exploitation and adventure

66 / *Chapter Four*

THE SMITHSONIAN INSTITUTION

These native Americans were taken to London in 1730 by Sir Alexander Cuming. There they created a sensation. Dressed in the latest English style, they were presented to King George II. As a token of the loyalty of their people, they gave him an oppossum "crown," four enemy scalps, and five feathers. The youngest of the group was Attakullakulla, who became the greatest of all Cherokee chiefs.

along with its share of dreamers aquiver with grandiose schemes of accomplishment. In this category is Sir Alexander Cuming.

As an English lawyer, Cuming had come to Charles Town on a trip involving banking business and had stayed to indulge in several business ventures of his own. He was always alert to the call of opportunity. It had become evident by 1730 that the salutary effects of Colonel Chicken's visit to the Cherokees were wearing thin, and there was a possibility of the nation making an alliance with the Creeks and the French. The Board of Commissioners then accepted Cuming's offer to go into Western North Carolina as a self-appointed ambassador of the King of England.

In late March, accompanied by Colonel Chicken and several traders, he entered the mountains from the Lower Towns. Stopping briefly at Nikwasi on March 26 to order all chiefs and headmen of the nation to assemble there by April 3, Cuming passed on over the spring-clad hills to the villages on the Tellico and Little Tennessee Rivers. Along the way he made friends with Cherokee chiefs and gathered strange flowers and specimens of rock to take back to England. As he turned east again, his retinue steadily increased until it must have resembled a primitive caricature of an Elizabethan procession; Indians of all ranks joined him to form a long queue winding over the rough, tortuous trading path to Nikwasi.

The Cherokees were eager to witness the colorful ceremonies that they knew would take place. But the traders were filled with misgivings as they recalled what had transpired at Keowee, where Cuming had arrived on March 23 and, without benefit of invitation but armed with pistols, had boldly walked into the council house containing some three hundred Cherokees in conference. For this arrogant display of bad manners and unpardonable breach of Indian etiquette, Ludovick Grant, a veteran trader, had later upbraided Cuming and had learned with horror that the Englishman had planned to fire the building and to guard the entrance against escape if the Indians resented his intrusion. Of this detail, however, the Cherokees were happily unaware. They were also unaware of the scheme that Cuming may have had even then of planting a colony of perhaps a million unwanted European Jews on a vast tract of land in their territory.

At the village of Joree the procession was met by both Indian and white dignitaries, including traders, and escorted the few miles into the awaiting Nikwasi and to the council house, where a two-day celebration was begun. That night the gleeful Cuming recorded in his *Journal*, "This was a Day of Solemnity, the greatest that ever was seen in the Country [sic]." One feature of the ceremonies was the impressive rites by which Moytoy of Great Tellico was raised from the rank of chief to that of headman. As Moytoy was crowned with a red dyed oppossum cap, symbol of his new authority over his fellow Cherokees, Cuming's imagination reached out for a use to which he might put the ritual. He found it.[27]

After the crowning of Moytoy and the slow progress of the peace pipe from one to another of the three hundred assembled in the council house, the moment for which Cuming had made the long trip came. In a pompous speech he brought the greetings and love of King George to these, his loyal subjects, and he climaxed his words by proposing a toast to the great English Overlord of the Cherokees. He suggested that, to show their allegiance, they kneel before him, the king's representative. A tense moment followed during which every white man present except the eloquent Cuming felt sure that nothing short of a riot could ensue. The Cherokees were a proud people. Never, in all their long history, had they acknowledged allegiance to any foreign country. In all their relation with the colonial governments they had conferred and made treaties as an independent nation dealing with foreign nations.

Perhaps it was the personal charm, together with the sheer audacity of the speaker that hypnotized the chiefs. At any rate, they came forward, knelt before Cuming, the self-appointed ambassador, and (with good whiskey of the white man) drank a toast to "their" king. Cuming then suggested that they present him with the oppossum cap lately used in their ceremony, in order that he in turn might present it to King George as a token of Cherokee acknowledgment of the English ruler as their king. Again the chiefs agreed. But Cuming went still farther. He requested that he be allowed to select several prominent Cherokees to accompany him on a forthcoming trip to England so that they might present the crown to King George in person. Once more they agreed. Perhaps in making his *Journal* entry, Cuming had been right, after all. Certainly for the Cherokees it was a "Day of Solemnity," and surely nothing comparable to it had ever taken place in Western North Carolina.[28]

Cuming selected six men, a seventh joined him in Charles Town, and with the Cherokee party he set sail for England on the man-of-war Fox, arriving at Dover on June 6. In London, where they were entertained at the expense of the government, these Cherokees from the Carolina mountains created something of a sensation. They were taken to see places of interest with stress on the military and naval might of the island country, and they were the guests of prominent Englishmen, even posing for their group portrait. But the high point of the sojourn came when, dressed in the "civilized habit" of knee breeches, lace-and ruffle-trimmed shirts, white stockings, and shoes adorned with silver buckles, they were presented to his Majesty, King George II.[29] Attakullakulla, the youngest of the group and later to be an outstanding chief, made a speech to the king and either he or Cuming himself presented the English ruler with the oppossum crown, four enemy scalps, and five eagle feathers as symbols of Cherokee loyalty.

What the king thought of his self-appointed "Ambassador to

the Cherokees" is not recorded. But letters of complaint about Sir Alexander Cuming's business dealings in Charles Town reached London during this time, and the Cherokee delegation was taken from his supervision and placed under the sponsorship of Governor Robert Johnson of South Carolina, who was in the English capital on business, and under Sir William Keith of Pennsylvania. For two months the Indians were in England since they were not allowed to leave the country until a treaty had been drawn up by the Board of Trade.

On this paper, known as the Treaty of Whitehall, the Cherokees put their marks and in so doing acknowledged the English government as virtual owners of their vast domain and the English king as their ruler. They agreed to fight with the English against any or all English enemies in America, to trade only with the English, to allow only the English to build forts and to "plant corn" in their territory, to return all runaway slaves to the English, to allow crimes against the English to be tried in English courts, and to notify the English of all trespassers of other nationalities entering the Cherokee country.[30]

Back in their own land, neither these delegates nor the Cherokee nation made any attempt to abide by this treaty. It seems evident that not a one of the signers understood the significance of making his small cross on the white man's piece of paper. It is certain that the group had not been given the authority by an Indian council to make treaties or to give promises in the name of their nation. For some years, however, the Cherokees swayed again to the English, and trade with South Carolina increased. All of this may well have been the result, not so much of the treaty to which the English tried to hold the Indians, as of Cuming's spectacular trip and the exciting visit of the chiefs in London.

But the French to the west, bent on making good their claim to Western North Carolina, had no intention of permitting this new Cherokee-English era of good will to endure. In 1736, just six years after Cuming's visit, they sent into the region a man whose influence and grandiose schemes presented the gravest threat to English trade and prestige yet felt. He was a shrewd, shriveled, little German, calling himself Christian Priber (although that may not have been the name by which he had been christened some thirty-five or forty years earlier). He was charged with the duty of winning both Indian trade and Cherokee loyalty from the

English to the French.

No better choice of a spy could have been made. Entering the Over Hills section, he soon added a fluent use of the Cherokee language to his long list of speaking languages which included French, German, Spanish, Latin, and English. He adopted Indian dress and the Cherokee manner of painting his body and face, and he married a young Cherokee woman. In a short time he succeeded in speaking, in looking and in living like a Cherokee. As a result, his power in the Over Hills area was solidly established.

Priber had entered the Cherokee country for reasons undreamed of by either the English or the French. His schemes included nothing short of a vast Indian empire or confederacy made up of all the tribes and nations living between the Blue Ridge and the Mississippi River. The Cherokee nation was to form the nucleus of this far-flung dominion. During a period of expediency, he planned to ally with the French, but when the time was ripe, anticipated throwing off all foreign control, thus hastening the day he foresaw when "European nations will have a very small footing on this continent."

Priber's first step in forming the empire was to select a capital, and as a temporary one he chose Great Tellico where he made his home. There in a colorful ceremony he crowned Moytoy, raised to the position of headman at the time of Cuming's visit, as Emperor to rule over the many nations. Then he had himself appointed His Imperial Majesty's Principal Secretary. Under that title he wrote arrogant and demanding letters to the colonial governments, and when his requests were summarily refused, as he knew they would be, he used the replies as propaganda against the English. It was then comparatively easy to arouse in the Cherokees a feeling for the importance of their position and hence to make them aware of their bargaining power in the English-French struggle.

The resulting unfriendliness toward the English and the rapid decline in English trade alarmed the traders, and South Carolina at length sent Colonel Joseph Fox and two aides to Great Tellico to arrest Priber.[31] Priber received the officers cordially and freely admitted that he was working out an alliance between the Cherokees and the French at New Orleans. He also revealed his hopes to bring into the Indian nation some qualified Frenchmen to teach the art of ammunition making. He must have been secretly amused at this naive gesture on the part of South Carolina, knowing himself far too intrenched with the Cherokees to be in danger from the three English officers. To their chagrin, Colonel Fox and his men found themselves being politely conducted out of the Over Hills section by Priber's men.

As his *Journal* shows, Priber was meantime laying the foundation for his Indian empire. He drew up elaborate plans for a worthy capital which would be called Cusseta to be built in the present Georgia. It would have a communal form of government and would be a city of refuge, welcoming the oppressed of Europe, those fleeing from justice, runaway slaves, in fact, any one wishing a haven from political or personal storms. Trial marriages would be allowed, even encouraged, and children would be the wards of the state. Property ownership would be, as already with the Indians, a privilege of the community. Laws were to be few, and the only crimes recognized in this city would be an act of murder actually committed within it and laziness.

By 1743 Priber apparently felt that the time had come for further developments in his plan, and with several Indian guides he set out for Mobile, intending to stop enroute at the French fort of Toulouse. But before he reached this first goal, he was captured by the English and taken to Frederica in the new colony of Georgia. There he was held a prisoner until General James Oglethorpe's return from his campaign against the Spanish in Florida. Both General Oglethorpe and the English soldiers were deeply impressed by the charm, learning, and quiet courage of this ugly, odd, little man.

On his person they found the manuscripts giving in detail the plans for organizing the empire and the detailed plan of his capital city. When they pointed out to him that this whole scheme was treason from the angle of both the French and the English, his reply hinted at a well organized group of which he was only one. Priber implied that, regardless of his fate, the work would be taken up by others.[32] That there may have been some truth in this is evident from the fact that he apparently intended to publish his plans in Paris and to procure from there and from other European cities and countries financial aid for the project.

Before the English brought Christian Priber to trial, however, he sickened and died; and the dream of a vast Indian empire died with him, although the English were never able to offset his influence in the Over Hills area. His work and influence there may have been a strong factor in the Cherokees of this section joining the French some years later in the conflict known as the French and Indian War. More immediate results were the frequent attacks on Englishmen and the burning of scattered English villages on the fringe of the Cherokee country. Historians have differed in their opinions of this extraordinary spy and schemer. How much personal ambition entered into his plans can not be determined. He claimed to have a genuine love for the Cherokees, in fact, for all Indians and insisted that his aim was to serve the interest of the Indians against white aggression. In that, too, there seems to have been at least a kernel of truth, for at the time he was arrested, he was carrying the manuscript of a Cherokee dictionary which he had written and doubtless intended to publish in Paris. Certain it is that English traders, while they feared his influence and struggled to keep the Cherokees loyal to the English, acknowledged Priber's brilliant mind and great learning and ability. One of these traders, James Adair actually kept up a personal correspondence over a period of several years with the German in the pay of France.[33]

The removal of Christian Priber from the scene temporarily relieved but did not solve the complicated problems of the English in their relations with the Cherokees of Western North Carolina. By the middle of the century many forces were being woven into the dark fabric of contention and warfare. The clouds over the mountains were threatening a deluge and gathering their thunderbolts of fire and carnage.

CHAPTER FIVE

Lightnings Flash and Thunders Roll

After 1743 South Carolina's trade with the mountain Cherokees was carried on with constantly increasing friction between the two races. Part of the growing difficulties arose from sources that the colony could not control, but much of the trouble was due to general mismanagement in Charles Town. Virginia and Virginia traders had been resentful of South Carolina's grip on the Cherokee trade. When William Byrd voiced that resentment in 1728, he said that the colony of Virginia had been trading with the Cherokees for eighty years.[1] That seems hardly possible except as some hunting bands of Cherokees may have come by chance to eastern settlements. Yet it was a Virginia trader, Abraham Wood, who had envisioned the possibility of trade with the mountain nation and who had made possible the first contact with it.

    In the eighteenth century, however, two restraining factors had kept Virginia traders from what they considered their fair share of the lucrative Cherokee trade. One was the inconvenience of obtaining licenses from South Carolina. The other was the contour of the land over which they had to transport their goods from the supply stations to the Over Hill Towns. From Charles Town the trading routes were over fairly open country along broad rivers and traders did not meet the difficulties of mountain trails until comparatively close to their destination in Western North Carolina. This was not the case with Virginia traders. Shortly after leaving their supply stations, they found themselves in a mountainous region where the paths were winding and often tortuous. The discomforts increased when they had to cross the precipitous Blue Ridge. The shortest route, directly west from the upper Yadkin River across what is now Watauga County and on to the Indian towns, made far too strenuous a trip to be undertaken by traders with loaded pack horses. In fact, as late as 1766, when James Smith and his Negro companion left a Kentucky-bound party and traveled eastward from the Tennessee River to settlements on the Yadkin River, the colonists there could scarcely credit Smith's story, declaring that they had never known of any one coming directly over the mountains by that route.[2]

Virginia traders had to travel farther south, therefore, crossing the Blue Ridge at Swannanoa Gap or at Hickory Nut Gap. Even then they had a long mountain trip before reaching the villages of the Cherokees. Frequently because of that fact, they continued south on the east side of the Blue Ridge until they made connection with the route passing through Keowee of the Lower Towns. There they sold their wares or took the trail through Rabun Gap into the mountain section, although this meant, after 1733, the purchasing of a license from Georgia as well as from South Carolina. It is no wonder then, that in 1725 Colonel George Chicken reported having seen not more than three Virginia traders in Western North Carolina.

The physical hardships endured by Virginia traders were overcome, however, when in 1740 Stephen Holstein, a hunter from their colony, crossed the Blue Ridge farther north and west of the Yadkin River and discovered the river that is now known by his name modified into Holston. Explorers then found that it connected with the Tennessee and thereby with the Over Hill Towns. Consequently, a shorter and more convenient trade route was soon in operation from Virginia to the Cherokee villages.[3] In 1751 a group of chiefs, throughly disgruntled at the treatment they were receiving from South Carolina, went to Williamsburg, seeking a formal trade treaty with Virginia. In spite of the immediate and vigorous protests of South Carolina's Governor James Glenn, Virginia, under the governorship of Robert Dinwiddie, openly laid claim to its share of the Cherokee trade. He allowed its traders to enter Western North Carolina without licenses from South Carolina.[4]

One of the Cherokee grievances was the fact that South Carolina was allowing its traders to deal with the Creeks and other Indian tribes to the west who were Cherokee enemies and with whom at times they were engaged in actual warfare.[5] These grievances were deeply felt in the Lower Towns, which were almost constantly at war with the Creeks. The resulting petty annoyances perpetrated against the English culminated in 1751 in an act of sabotage that threatened open war with the English. Spurred on by inflamed Indians from Keowee, Middle Town Cherokees looted the English storehouse at Stekoa on the Tuckaseigee River, on the site of the present Whittier.

The rumor spread that a trader, Barnard Hughes, and three other white men had been slain and that all English traders were to be killed. Traders from the entire section fled to the safety of English forts. The rumors proved untrue, and the English, with the aid of Old Hopp, the revered Cherokee chief, succeeded in regaining most of the stolen goods. But conscientious traders could read in this incident the writing on the wall. Ludovick Grant, James Beamer, Cornelius Dougherty, and Robert Bunning all sent formal statements to Governor Glenn, pointing out the explosive conditions prevailing, citing abuses perpetrated by English traders, calling attention to the ever-strengthening French influence, and pleading for a firm and just course of action on the part of South Carolina.[6]

As a result, in 1753 Governor Glenn held a council with Cherokee Chiefs. The Indians demanded more guns and ammunition to fight the Creeks and a cessation of all English trade with their enemies. They also wanted forts built for their protection against western tribes and the French. A compromise was reached by which Governor Glenn promised the forts in exchange for a promise of peace between the Cherokees and Creeks. In compliance with its promise, South Carolina built a fort across the river from Keowee, which was named Fort Prince George.[7]

Two years later still another treaty between South Carolina and the Cherokees was signed when representatives from both groups, including Governor Glenn himself and Old Hopp, met at Saluda Old Town, some twenty miles west of the present Columbia, South Carolina. By affixing their marks to this document, the Cherokees agreed to an eastern boundary of their territory that would run between the present cities of Spartanburg and Greenville, South Carolina, thus ceding to the

TENNESSEE VALLEY AUTHORITY

Fort Loudon: The English, at the request of the Over Hill Cherokees, built this fort on the Little Tennessee River for protection against the French. The cannons were brought over the mountains on the backs of stout little ponies. The Cherokees, angered at the actions of the English shortly afterward, burned the fort in 1760. This picture shows an ancient cannon and the restored stockade.

colony a vast stretch of land, none of which was in Western North Carolina. In return, the colony agreed to certain trading reforms and again promised a fort for the Cherokees in the Over Hill country.[8]

Dilatory in carrying out the renewed promise of an Over Hill fort, the colony took no action until rumors reached Charles Town that the French were planning to erect a fort on the Hiwassee River. In 1756 Fort Prince George, which had been built in 1753 only to be allowed to fall into ruins, was renovated and steps were taken to construct the promised fort. A site was selected by the Cherokees on the Little Tennessee River near the mouth of the Tellico River, six miles from Chota, the city of refuge.

Then to Western North Carolina came its first architect-engineer. John William Gerard de Brahm, a German, had earlier pleased the colony with the ramparts he had constructed for Charles Town.[9] At first he refused to undertake the enormous task of getting needed supplies and arms over the narrow trails leading into the mountain section, even though he was offered three hundred men and five thousand pounds sterling for the project. He accepted the mission when John Elliott, an able trader, assumed the burden of transporting the materials from Fort Prince George to the Tennessee River site.

In his *Journal* de Brahm described that job of transportation, the most difficult so far undertaken in the mountain country. The cannons presented the gravest problems. They were poised crossways over the backs of the pack horses and lashed to the bodies of the animals with belts. Occasionally, in fact, distressingly often, one end of a projecting cannon would catch on a tree and become twisted, throwing the horse and breaking its back or neck. Over the rugged trails six miles proved to be a day's journey.[10]

On a location superior to the one selected by the Cherokees de Brahm constructed a fort in the form of a rhombus. Captain Raymond Demere came from Fort Prince George and was placed in command of the forces at the new fort, so far the most westerly of all those built by the English. It was named Loudon, in honor of John Campbell, Earl of Loudon, who had recently arrived in America to become governor of Virginia and commander-in-chief of all British troops in the English colonies. Following a disagreement with Demere, de Brahm left Western North Carolina before the fort was completed and the work was finished by Demere. Thus the engineer-architect became known among the Indians by the title bestowed upon him by Old Hopp, "The Warrior Who Ran Away In The Night."[11]

Even with their long desired fort a reality, the Cherokees could not remain on amiable terms with the English. The Indians and the whites—both the English and the French—were caught in an eddying whirlpool of conflict that was international in scope. Even had they so desired, they perhaps could not have stemmed the tide of war in this remote frontier so far from the warring European countries that had declared it. Locally, however, the English were largely responsible for the nagging irritations that eventually sparked open warfare and drove the Cherokees into the French camp.

Much of the blame was attached to Charles Town itself. During the years since the Indian trade had been taken over by the colonial government, the port city and the colony had grown and prospered. Other industries, especially rice and tobacco raising, had come to exceed Indian trade in importance as broad plantations along the rivers were cleared and cultivated.

Decreased interest in trading with the western tribes resulted, and contact with the Indians lost its adventurous appeal for men of ability, judgment, and character. Instead of going into the Indian trading as many of their predecessors had done, newcomers were now taking up other occupations, as were also the young men reared in the colony. Then, too, a new generation of men had come into political control of South Carolina with ambitions along many lines other than the colony's relationship with Indian tribes and nations.

As the fear of Indian attacks on coastal settlements vanished, the securing of added territory and the desire to make money became the chief motives in all colonial dealings with the natives. The Commission of Indian Affairs failed to function, and when a Superintendent of Indian Affairs was now and then appointed, he was no longer required to spend most of his time in Indian country. Any and all persons asking for trading licenses received them, and there was scant supervision of their lives and business methods. Complaints from older traders and from Cherokee leaders got little attention in Charles Town. Finally there came a time when Old Hopp, nominal head of the Cherokee nation, said sadly, "Charles Town is a place where nothing but lies come from.[12]"

Traders within the Cherokee territory kept the turmoil at the boiling point. Two reasons had been given by South Carolina for taking over control of the Indian trade: to correct the abuses arising in connection with private trading and to introduce Christianity among the natives. Over the long years this latter motive had been a dead letter. No attempt had ever been made by the colony to send or to sanction missionaries in the Cherokee country. The only knowledge gained by the Indians of the white man's Christianity had come through their contact with traders. During the first years of the trading arrangement, with its rather close supervision, that contact had been comparatively wholesome, and the Cherokees had respected many of the traders and had even at times protected them. But by 1755 the English traders in Western North Carolina were, with many exceptions, a motley crew, bent on making money by whatever methods presented themselves.

Henry Timberlake, in his notes on conditions he found in the Over Hill Towns in 1761, states that on most of their wares the traders were making five or six hundred per cent profit, although he thought that they doubtless lost on some items. Diluted whiskey, which sold at the same high price of the pure product, increased in volume each year. Before 1755 the vicious system of selling on credit under a plan that held relatives responsible for a Cherokee's debts had been firmly established so that hundreds of Cherokees, now dependent upon English goods, were hopelessly involved in debt and found themselves and their families at the mercy of unscrupulous traders.[13]

It seems almost a miracle that influential Cherokee leaders like Old Hopp, Attakullakulla, and Ostenaco should remain friends of the English; yet these and other leaders were unable to control their own people. A new generation of Cherokees had arisen, young braves softened by the labor-saving devices of the white man and corrupted by their contact with the conscienceless traders whom they came to hate. Bands of these young Indians, on pretext of hunting or of going on war raids against enemy tribes, pillaged the small, white settlements east of the Blue Ridge and stole horses and whatever else they could lay hands to. With no respect or regard for each other, hotheads of both races were quick to avenge real or fancied wrongs, rushing into rash actions that were sure to have far-reaching repercussions.[14]

In 1757 the colony of North Carolina, within whose territory the mountain section of the Cherokee nation lay, passed its first law affecting that region. The division in 1710 of Carolina into North and South sections, each with its own governor and assembly, was later made official; yet, until 1750 North Carolina had been in no way able to assume any of the trade with its western Indians. Following the early settlements on Albemarle Sound, groups of Europeans had made small settlements along the Pamlico, Neuse, and Cape Fear Rivers. Later migrations had brought settlers into the piedmont region. But not until past the middle of the eighteenth century had white men reached the Blue Ridge with plans for making settlements. Then for the first time citizens of North Carolina were in danger of raiding parties of Catawbas and Cherokees.

In 1756, Virginia had asked to join South Carolina in the building of Fort Loudon, but the Cherokees wanted each colony to construct a fort. Virginia built a small fortification, therefore, near the ancient capital of Echota, but it was never garrisoned.[15] At the same time North Carolina took steps to protect the Catawbas east of the Blue Ridge from the ever-raiding Cherokees by building a fort, thus strengthening the colony's relationship with the Catawbas and safeguarding the westward moving settlers. Later, for protection against both the Catawbas and the Cherokees, settlers just east of the Blue Ridge built Fort Davidson, on the site of the present Old Fort.

During the far-flung ramifications of the French and English conflict, the attention of King George was called to the mounting tension at their meeting point in the wilds of Western North Carolina. He removed all Cherokee affairs from the control of the Board of Trade, placing them directly under the supervision of the Crown. This brought an end to South Carolina's monopoly of the Cherokee trade. Edmund Atkins was then named as Superintendent of Indian Affairs in 1757, and in December of that year the colony of North Carolina passed a law putting all trade with the Catawbas and Cherokees within its borders wholly under the supervision of Atkins and his successors. The new law gave these men complete power to enforce their authority. For the first time North Carolina took legislative cognizance of the western portion of her territory. Upon the death of Atkins in 1763, Captain John Stuart was named to succeed him and held his position until after the Revolutionary War.[16]

This attempt at centralizing the Indian program came too late to save Western North Carolina from becoming a bloody battleground, and if James Adair is to be taken as an authority on conditions of the period, Atkins was inexcusably delinquent in putting a constructive program into action. In spite of pleas from Cherokee chiefs, Atkins did not go into the territory for a year. In the interval, according to Adair, the French were steadily gaining converts to their cause among the Cherokees. In fact, Adair summed up the situation by declaring that the English forced the Cherokees to become enemies through a long chain of wrong measures that proved costly both to the English and to the Indians.[17]

Two unfortunate incidents touched off the spark that enkindled the raging fires of horror known as the Cherokee War, one phase of the wide-spread French and Indian War. The details of one of these incidents are not too clear since the episode was reported to both Indians and whites by the excited, prejudiced participants. This much seems clear. Some Cherokees returning from Virginia to their Over Hill Towns, losing some of their horses, replaced the animals by stealing those belonging to a band of Virginia frontiersmen coming back from western Virginia where they (and possibly the Cherokees) had been engaged in war activities. The white men were quick to retaliate, and a skirmish ensued during which some Cherokees were slain and others taken prisoners. This episode aroused the already French-inflamed faction of the Cherokees, and they replied to the insult by laying seige to Fort Loudon and its English garrison.[18]

The way for this action had been well paved by the operations of the Chevalier Christian De Lantagnac, a Frenchman appointed by the governor of Louisiana as liaison officer to the Cherokees. His base was Fort Toulouse, but he seems to have spent much time in the Over Hill Towns, possibly as a trader. There his propaganda had been successful enough to worry the Cherokee leader and Great Warrior, Ostenaco (known as Judd's Friend) and to alarm Captain Paul Demere, who had succeeded his brother as officer in command at Fort Loudon. Lantagnac's efforts also caused the French governor to report to Paris that the Cherokees had been won to the French cause.[19]

The second incident was a shocking example of South Carolina's mismanagement of its Indian affairs. Cherokee retaliation after the previous incident had included the murder of two soldiers and a trader at Fort Loudon in 1759. Governor William Lyttelton, who had replaced Governor Glenn, demanded that the Cherokees surrender those guilty of the crime. The Indian answer was to lay siege in September to Fort Prince George. To Lieutenant Cotymore, in charge of this fort, this act signaled the beginning of an Indian uprising. His spies had earlier brought him rumors that the Cherokees had entered into an agreement with the Creeks to join in a general attack against the English as soon as the Creeks began hostilities by killing all English traders within their nation. Learning of the siege, the Council at Charles Town advised an immediate declaration of war. This action was delayed when in October a large delegation of Cherokees, headed by outstanding leaders, went to Charles Town in an attempt to prevent a conflict and to ask for additional ammunition.

The Council then advised the new governor, inexperienced in Indian affairs, to hold a specified number of the delegates as hostages until the murderers of the white men were turned over for punishment. Governor Lyttelton, however, suggested going to the relief of Fort Prince George with an impressive number of troops, and this plan was adopted. Accordingly, Lyttelton refused to make any treaty or agreement with the Cherokee delegation. At a meeting with the Indians he announced his intentions of going to the fort on the Keowee unless the Cherokees surrendered the murderers. At the same time, he promised the delegates safe return to their nation. It was thus an unpardonable breach of good faith when, a few days later as the Indians were on their way home, they were taken into custody and held as hostages, being later taken to Fort Prince George.[20]

With an army of approximately fifteen hundred, Governor Lyttelton reached Fort Prince George on December 19, 1759. In the year that had followed since South Carolina had paid the Cherokee nation an indemnity for the murders, earlier mentioned, of their warriors returning from Virginia, twenty-four Englishmen had been victims of the Cherokees.[21] The governor now demanded twenty-four Indians for execution as the price for releasing the three Cherokee peace leaders being held at Fort Prince George—Oconostota, who had headed the delegation to Charles Town, Ostenaco, and Fiftoe of Keowee. Largely through the efforts of the Cherokee peacemaker and friend of the English, Attakullakulla, a compromise was worked out by which several unfortunate braves were substituted for the three leaders, who were liberated. Three, and shortly afterward the fourth, of the participants in the Fort Loudon siege were then turned over to the English, and the Cherokees agreed to twenty-two of their men being held at the fort as hostages until the remaining guilty Cherokees were turned over to the English. In view of an outbreak of smallpox that threatened widespread desertion from his army, Governor Lyttelton then led his troops back to Charles Town.[22]

As might be expected, this agreement was unsatisfactory to the Cherokees, and the insult to their delegates on an avowed peace mission rankled in the hearts of men in all sections of their nation. The growing hatred of the English was fanned by the propaganda of the French, and on January 19, 1760, some English traders in the Cherokee country—reports reaching English officials said twenty-four—were murdered and all Englishmen in the territory fled for their lives to the hills. Fort Prince George was again besieged, and the aroused Cherokees began attacks on small white settlements on the South Carolina and Georgia frontiers. On February 16, Lieutenant Cotymore, who was roundly hated by the Indians, was enticed from the fort on a pretext of truce and shot from ambush. Inside the fort, officers were at once ordered to put hostages in chains. When the first captive approached and stabbed the officer, the English soldiers fell upon the group of hapless Indians, brutally slaughtering every one of them. This atrocity crystalized anti-English sentiment in the Cherokee nation and united all sections. The war was on.[23]

Immediately white settlements along the Yadkin and Catawba Rivers were attacked by bands of incensed Cherokees led by the recently liberated Oconostota. All of this was a matter for the king's government, and in June a revenge army made up of Highlanders and colonial volunteers under command of Colonel Archibald Montgomery arrived at Fort Prince George. They succeeded in raising the siege and then moved on to nearby Keowee, capital of the Lower Cherokees, and burned it. From there they went systematically through that section of the Indian nation, burning towns, destroying all crops, grain stores, and orchards, and forcing frightened women and children to flee into the mountains. When the scorched earth policy had been carried to its completion, Colonel Montgomery sent word to the Middle Towns to surrender. They refused, and he and his troops proceeded over the mountain pass. After carrying out his mission in this area, he planned to go to the aid of the besieged Fort Loudon on the Little Tennessee River.

In this attempt he failed, for the Cherokees had assembled a large force and met Montgomery's army at Echoee, a few miles from Nikwasi. There, on June 27, a bitter battle was fought, during which twenty Englishmen were killed and seventy-six wounded. The Cherokee losses are not known. Although the Cherokees withdrew, the English were compelled to retreat, returning to Fort Prince George.[24] This left the besieged garrison at Fort Loudon with no hope of aid, and it was forced to surrender or starve. Captain Demere capitulated on August 8, 1760. Under the terms of surrender, the garrison was to be allowed to leave the mountain country unmolested and with sufficient arms and ammunition to ensure a safe journey to Fort Prince George. The English, in turn, were to leave all their stored arms and ammunition in the fallen fort.

As the retreating Englishmen, two hundred strong, wound along the Tellico Creek, they were suddenly attacked about ten miles form the fort by the victorious Cherokees, who shot Captain Demere and twenty-nine of his men, taking the others prisoners. These soldiers, with the exception of John Stuart, who was allowed to escape, were later ransomed by the English. The occasion for this violence was the fact that the Cherokees, inspecting the deserted fort, had discovered that ten bags of powder and a quantity of cannon balls had been hidden under the floor and that other small arms and ammunition had been thrown into the river by the departing soldiers. Furious over the white man's perfidy, the Cherokees had rushed to avenge it. They later burned the fort.[25]

As news of this atrocity spread eastward, resentment against the Cherokees flamed up throughout Virginia, North Carolina, and South Carolina. The colonists and British army planned a convincing answer to this massacre and to Colonel Montgomery's defeat in the form of an army of sufficient size to quell the Cherokee uprising once and for all. No attention was paid to Ostenaco's rather pathetic attempt at avoiding further warfare made at Niwasi in September when the English flag was raised over a group of Cherokees gathered there prepared to express loyalty to the English.

Each colony organized its militia and received volunteers to join the British forces placed under the command of Lieutenant-Colonel James Grant. The Virginia troops, commanded by Colonel William Byrd III, marched westward to the Holston River. When Byrd found it necessary to return east, he left his men in the charge of Colonel Adam Stephen. Stephen stationed the Virginia sector of the army on the Long Island in the Holston River, site of the present Kingsport, Tennessee, some 140 miles from the Cherokee Over Hill Towns. There they constructed a fort which would serve as a border protection, as a base of supplies, and as a point of attack upon the Over Hill Indians.

South Carolina's force of seasoned Indian fighters under Colonel Thomas Middleton and North Carolina's volunteers under Colonel Hugh Waddell joined the British forces moving west from Charles Town. That force was composed of regulars, many of whom were Scottish Highland troops, and all were experienced in border warfare. Indian warriors from tribes that were century-old enemies of the Cherokees formed one unit in the campaign. Catawbas from North Carolina, Mohawks from New York, and Chickasaws recruited from Georgia by James Adair were put under the command of Captain Quentin Kennedy. Altogether, the colonies furnished about half of Grant's army of three thousand men, a number in contrast with the two thousand led by Montgomery the previous year.

On May 21, 1761, this army, the largest yet sent into the district, had traveled three hundred miles from Charles Town along the old trading path and had arrived at Fort Prince George. There the peacemaker, Attakullakulla, brought renewed peace overtures. They were rejected by Grant in view of orders given by

Lord Jeffrey Amherst, Commander-in-Chief of the British forces in America at the time. Grant had been instructed to punish the Cherokees throughly before making any terms of peace. On June 7, therefore, the army started for the Middle Towns.

Entering the mountains by way of the trading path from Keowee, the forces stretched in single file for a distance of some two miles as they wound along the narrow, tree-lined trail. In addition to the soldiers, there were six hundred pack horses laden with the officers' baggage, stores of ammunition, and a thirty day supply of flour for the army. There was, also, a sizable herd of beef cattle. All the animals were in the charge of rangers and herders. As Grant had expected, the Cherokees, from six hundred to a thousand strong, attacked the moving army as it passed through a gorge. But by detailing added troops to protect the pack trains from serious threat of being cut off and by ordering certain troops to keep up a steady volume of shots into the woods where the attacking Indians lurked, Grant succeeded in keeping the men advancing to an open plain.

There, in spite of the constant fire of the Cherokees, he was able to get his forces across the ford of the Little Tennessee River and to defend his position through several hours of sharp fighting. The Indians finally suffered such a casualty toll that they retreated. Grant lost ten men and found that fifty-three others had been wounded, one of them dying later. Thus, just short of a year after Montgomery's defeat, this so called second battle of Echoee (actually fought a short distance from the scene of the first encounter) was ended. After burying the dead, Grant's troops marched on into the village of Echoee.

News of the immense size of Grant's army and of the heavy loss of life suffered by the Cherokees preceded them, and they found the village deserted. They destroyed it. Without resting the troops continued in the darkness to Nikwasi, destroying the deserted village of Tassee on the way. At Nikwasi the tired army rested several days. Then there began a thorough destruction of towns, crops, gardens, and orchards, all of which had been deserted by the frightened Indians, who had fled into the hills. Passing through the country, Grant and his forces encountered almost no opposition. The only casualties occurred when some Cherokee sniper succeeded in killing a sentry or two. On this punitive campaign the British forces traversed the most difficult terrain yet crossed by a British army when, with a detachment of fifteen hundred men, Grant passed over the wild, pathless Cowee range in the darkness and rain to reach the towns scattered along the banks of the Tuckaseigee River. Wherever he went, the pattern of total destruction took form until the villages of the Middle Towns were mere heaps of ashes; the farms became ghosts of burned and broken trees and scorched fields.[26]

The British Army was not without its losses. By the time that Grant got back to his temporary base, he found that three hundred of his men were ill and that one thousand more were without shoes after their long marches over the rocky mountains. Grant sent a detachment to the most westerly of the Middle Towns to prevent the Cherokees there from joining the Over Hill warriors in an attack on the Virginia troops and then led his men back to Fort Prince George. He had been in Western North Carolina a little more than a month and as a result, fifteen towns of the Cherokees had been burned and fifteen hundred acres of growing crops destroyed, while an estimated five thousand Cherokees had been driven into the hills to survive as best they could. In a little short of a year, Montgomery's defeat had been avenged with ample interest.

The widespread devastation, together with the presence of British troops at the site of the present Murphy, deterred the Over Hill Cherokees from putting into action any plans they may have had for attacking the Virginia contingent on the Long Island of the Holston. In early autumn, therefore, a delegation led by Old Hopp and made up of other chiefs and four hundred of his people arrived at the fort to sue for peace. By November 19 the terms were ready, and a cessation of war was granted to the Over Hill Indians. Once more Attakullakulla led a delegation representing the entire nation to Fort Prince George where terms of surrender and peace were drawn up. That segment of the French and Indian War known as the Cherokee War came to a close.[27]

Broken in spirit and with hundreds of its young warriors dead, the Cherokee nation faced the task of rebuilding homes before a winter that could well bring starvation and disease. The Principal People were never to recover wholly from this national disaster. The Indian trade was completely disrupted, and the people were without needed supplies and without money. Nor could they fall back on the French, upon whom so many of them had pinned their faith. The French had had a large part in provoking the war and had aided the Cherokees, perhaps, as some of the English soldiers felt, even joining in their battles. But in the Cherokee defeat, the French had also met defeat. Their mother country and their colonial empire had fared badly in other sectors of the long battle line that stretched from Canada to the Gulf of Mexico. Their bastions of defense had fallen like ten pins before the steady fire of the British forces.

In 1758 the French fort at Louisburg had fallen as had the Fort Frontenac and Fort Dusquesne. The next year Montcalm and his French army were defeated by General James Wolfe, bringing Quebec into the hands of the English. Fort Ticonderoga and Crown Point were then given up, and Montreal surrendered in 1760. By the time the Cherokee War was over, the dream of a vast French empire in the New World had vanished, and a treaty of peace between France and victorious England was signed in 1763. Through it England gained the French possessions in Canada and forced the French to relinquish their claims to land east of the Mississippi River. French traders in the Cherokee country packed their wares, ceased their propaganda, and silently betook themselves away from the councils of the Indians and out of the Cherokee villages. As a permanent reminder of their old claims to Western North Carolina, they left only the adjective *French* attached to the Broad River west of the Blue Ridge.[28]

CHAPTER SIX

The Lull Between the Storms

No Cherokee population statistics were available until well into the nineteenth century, but from time to time South Carolina officials and white traders made estimates of the number of people, especially warriors, living within the boundaries of the Cherokee nation. In 1715 Governor Robert Johnson reported to the Proprietors that there were perhaps nine thousand Cherokees trading with his colony and that the nation had eleven towns in the Lower area, thirty in the Middle settlement, and nineteen in the Over Hill area. William Byrd in his *History of the Dividing Line* gave the number of towns as sixty-two and thought that there might be four thousand warriors.[1] In 1735 traders estimated the population at seventeen thousand and gave the number of towns as sixty-four. In 1738, however, small-pox reached Charles Town by a European ship and was unwittingly carried to the Cherokee country by trading caravans. The rapidly-working disease swept unchecked over the Indian nation. By the spring of 1739 every home was mourning its dead, and not more than half the people were left to till the fields and furnish the pelts and furs wanted by the white traders. By the middle of the century the population had greatly risen but was still apparently far below the 1735 figure. When the Cherokee War broke out, traders estimated that the Cherokees could muster not more than twenty-three hundred warriors.[2] How many defenders were slain in the raids by Montgomery and Grant and how many men, women, and children died in the starving times that followed is not known, but the number must have been large.

During the trading period, Cherokee villages varied greatly in size, many of them being merely clusters of five or six houses with their outlying fields and gardens. In fact, no town approximated the status of a city. No record left in pre-Revolutionary accounts credits Echota with more than thirty houses, although mention is made of a Lower Cherokee town of some five hundred dwellings.[3] Over the years towns were destroyed by accidents, by inter-tribal conflicts, and by the whites. Some of them were rebuilt, but others were not.

Now and then new towns were erected as was the case in the Middle settlements when refugees from the Lower Towns fled there after Montgomery's raid. Then, too, the importance of towns changed, some losing their prestige to others. For example, Great Tellico, during the time that Priber lived in it, superseded Echota, although the latter remained the city of refuge. Also for a period of time the capital of the Middle Towns seems to have shifted from Nikwasi to Joree, a few miles away. When the peace treaties were signed in 1761, ending the Cherokee War, only nineteen or twenty Over Hill Towns remained.[4]

When Old Hopp sued for peace at the fort on the Long Island of the Holston River, some four hundred Cherokees were with him. After the signing of the armistice, he requested that an English officer be sent with the delegations to their towns in order to explain the terms of peace and to receive the pledge of loyalty from his people. Colonel Stephen felt he could ask no officer to undertake a task so far beyond the call of duty as a journey into the strongly pro-French towns might well prove to be. Henry Timberlake, a young Virginian who had helped to draw up the terms of the treaty, volunteered to make the trip. He refused, however, to join the Cherokees and with one companion made the one hundred and forty mile, adventure-packed journey to the Indian capital. From there he went to town after town, smoking innumerable peace pipes, being entertained with Indian dances and games, and feasting on the choicest meats of the hunt and the best of the stored vegetables. In the council houses he received protestations of Cherokee loyalty, and he, in turn, expressed the good will of the English and the hope of long peace between the races.[5]

Timberlake became deeply interested in these people and learned what he could of their customs and ways of life, of their beliefs and religious life. He made observations on the land and its possibilities. He felt that in their thinking and basic manner of living the Cherokees, even after fifty years of trading with the whites, had absorbed little if any of the white man's civilization. They had, Timberlake said, adapted some of the white man's wares to their needs, and he saw that they had some European vegetables in their gardens and some European fruit trees in their orchards. He was pleased with the fine breeds of horses and the fine droves of hogs he observed, although he noticed that there were no sheep or cattle. Both men and women, he found, were adopting the white man's dress, and the women had learned to sew. In spite of the fact that the young Virginian was constantly on the alert as a hostage, he was drawn to the Cherokees and freely and sincerely gave them his friendship.[6]

Timberlake was called upon to test that friendship in an unexpected manner. When at last he was allowed to return to Williamsburg, taking with him about thirty white prisoners held by the Indians during the war, the Great Warrior of the Over Hill Towns, Ostenaco, announced that he would accompany the white men. Joining the party were also a hundred and sixty uninvited warriors. In Williamsburg, Ostenaco saw a portrait of King George and suddenly decided that he must go to England and personally express the Cherokee loyalty. When he could not be dissuaded, Governor Fauquier detailed Henry Timberlake to conduct the Great Warrior and two of his Indian companions to the English capital.

Like the chiefs taken to London by Sir Alexander Cuming thirty years earlier, these Cherokees made a sensation in the capital city. Among their noted visitors were Sir Joshua Reynolds, who painted a portrait of Ostenaco, and Oliver Goldsmith, who wrote an account of these American aborigines in his *Animated Nature*. Sir Alexander, who was languishing in a debtors' prison, was given a parole to act, as best he could, as interpreter for the Warrior. The Cherokees were given an audience with King George, and Ostenaco made a speech. He doubtless experienced some difficulty in maintaining his native dignity and poise in the English garb he wore, the latest word in ruffles and silks. The Indian holiday seems to have been a delightful affair, thoroughly enjoyed by the Britishers and the Cherokees, in fact, by all save Timberlake. He had personally paid all the expenses and was never able to gain complete reimbursement from the Board of Trade.[7]

With the close of the French and Indian War in 1763,

representatives of Virginia, Georgia, and North and South Carolina met with a group of Cherokee chiefs and explained to them the terms of the peace treaty. A royal proclamation that same year restrained the whites in the two Carolinas from entering or taking up land west of the Blue Ridge, that is, west of the headwaters of streams flowing into the Atlantic Ocean. By this means the king hoped to avoid further border conflicts. The Cherokees were, of course, in no position to bargain to their own advantage. Also that year the native Americans signed a treaty ceding to South Carolina approximately one hundred square miles of their land in that colony, pushing their eastern boundary west to a line running north and south through the colony from a point on the Savannah River and passing near the present Greenville, on to the North Carolina line.[8] Unaffected by the king's proclamation, Virginia gained by a forced treaty all Cherokee lands within the present state of Virginia and West Virginia in 1770 and in 1772 won from the Cherokees all lands east of the Kentucky River.[9]

The Cherokees, scarred by memories of the recent war and fearing the encroachment of the whites, asked for a clearly stated eastern boundary line in the two Carolinas. That request was granted, and by royal order in 1767 North Carolina's Governor William Tryon, accompanied by two surveyors, two regiments of militia, and sixteen servants and aides, made the trip to the Cherokee country.[10] The new South Carolina-Cherokee line was surveyed and a line run from it into North Carolina. But to survey the wild terrain of the Blue Ridge was an impossible feat.

Both Cherokees and whites agreed to a line declared from Tryon Mountain, passing near the present town of Tryon and following the crest of the Blue Ridge in a northeasterly direction to the mines of Colonel Chiswell in Virginia. The Board of Trade also agreed to this arrangement. While later surveys showed that such a line would not pass the designated site in Virginia, the crest of the range provided a boundary sufficiently clear to both races. The Cherokees were to stay west of that line; the whites were to stay east of it. The present Blue Ridge Parkway, along stretches of its North Carolina length, follows that old line of demarcation.[11]

But there were loopholes in this agreement. In the first place, the line did not apply to Virginia. In the second place, it was possible that it would not govern the Lord Granville tract that crossed the Blue Ridge Mountains in the northern part of North Carolina. And in the third place, white men had already looked upon the fair mountain land with covetous eyes, and spirals of blue smoke were already rising skyward from scattered cabins dangerously close to the Blue Ridge. South Carolina traders had entered the Cherokee country under treaty arrangements and could in no way be called settlers, although many of them remained in the territory for the rest of their lives. Even though they married Cherokee women and their children were Cherokees, their status remained that of visitors or sojourners. They had no desire to own land, but they adopted the native American way of life, becoming a part of the Cherokee community.

How early daring hunters and trappers, with only their wits and their guns to protect them from the natives, crept warily over the mountains will never be known, for they were not the type of men to write of their deeds. But like the traders, they were not settlers and had no interest in owning the land they saw beyond the Blue Ridge. Even before Governor Tryon's line was drawn, a few hardy settlers east of the mountains had begun the practice of taking their cattle over the ranges to the meadows beyond for summer forage. For convenience, some of them had built tiny log shelters. But these men, too, had no intention of settling in this region, and when pasturing days were over, they took their way back over the hills to their cabins to the east.[12]

But there were other men coming into the Cherokee country on other missions who pictured the land as it might be under the tillage of white settlers. As early as 1670-1674, Dr. Henry Woodward had seen the western country as a "second Paradise" beckoning to Englishmen with the vision and the courage to enter it. The dashing Sir Alexander Cuming conjured up in his mind the picture of Zion, its Jewish inhabitants dwelling in the midst of the Cherokee Philistines. Apparently he also had visions of permanent English occupants, for with a view to future mining, he took back to England specimens of rocks and "iron stone."

A quarter of a century later the engineer de Brahm uttered a surprisingly accurate prophecy of this land's future when he wrote: "Should this country once come into the hands of the Europeans, they may with propriety call it the American Canaan, for it will fully answer their industry, and all methods of European culture, and so as well for European produce (the rice only excepted) for provisions of all kinds; indigo, silk, cotton, hamp [sic] flax, oil, wine; be it for raising stocks of horses, cattle, sheep, goats, and hogs; be it for metals, minerals, fossils, and stones, or be it for manufacturys [sic] of all kinds. This country seems longing for the hands of industry to receive its hidden treasures, which nature has been collecting and toiling since the beginning ready to deliver them up."[13] In 1752 an exploring party had actually entered Western North Carolina with the aim of selecting a tract of land upon which to settle a colony. The Cherokees were fully justified in wanting a line drawn, past which the white man would not be allowed to "plant corn."

In the years immediately preceding the Revolutionary War, the population of North Carolina increased with amazing rapidity. In fact, between 1759 and 1771 it practically doubled.[14] Political upheavals and religious persecutions in various European countries brought many thousands of immigrants to America. From the German Palatine provinces individuals and organized religious groups arrived in Philadelphia to join German settlements established earlier. They became known as the "Pennsylvania Dutch." Although fewer in number than the Germans, many Swiss also landed at the Pennsylvania port city, and there was a rather steady stream of Irish and a few French Huguenots.

Two waves of migrating Scottish settlers likewise swelled the tide of incoming Europeans. These newcomers sought both religious and political freedom in the New World. One wave brought men, women, and children from northern Ireland, where Scottish settlements had been made more than a century before in six counties of Ulster. The political and economic disorders were generated by two acts of Parliament. The Woolens Act of 1699 restricted the sale of Ulster woolens and linens to markets in England and Wales, thus destroying the woolen industry in Ulster. The Test Act of 1704 was an attempt to coerce Ulster Presbyterians (followers of John Knox) into adhering to the Anglican Church. Both of these acts resulted in an uprising that gave North Carolina a goodly share of its population by the time of the Revolutionary War.

These Scotch-Irish arrived in America by way of Philadelphia and Charles Town, or Charleston as the southern port was now frequently called. From Scotland itself came the other wave of immigrants, made up of both Highlanders and Lowlanders, most of whom had taken part in the abortive attempt of "Bonnie" Prince Charles to regain the English throne and reinstate the Stuart rule. After the decisive defeat of the Prince's Scottish forces at Culloden Moor in 1746, many participants, forced to take the stringent oath of allegiance to the English king, were glad to put as

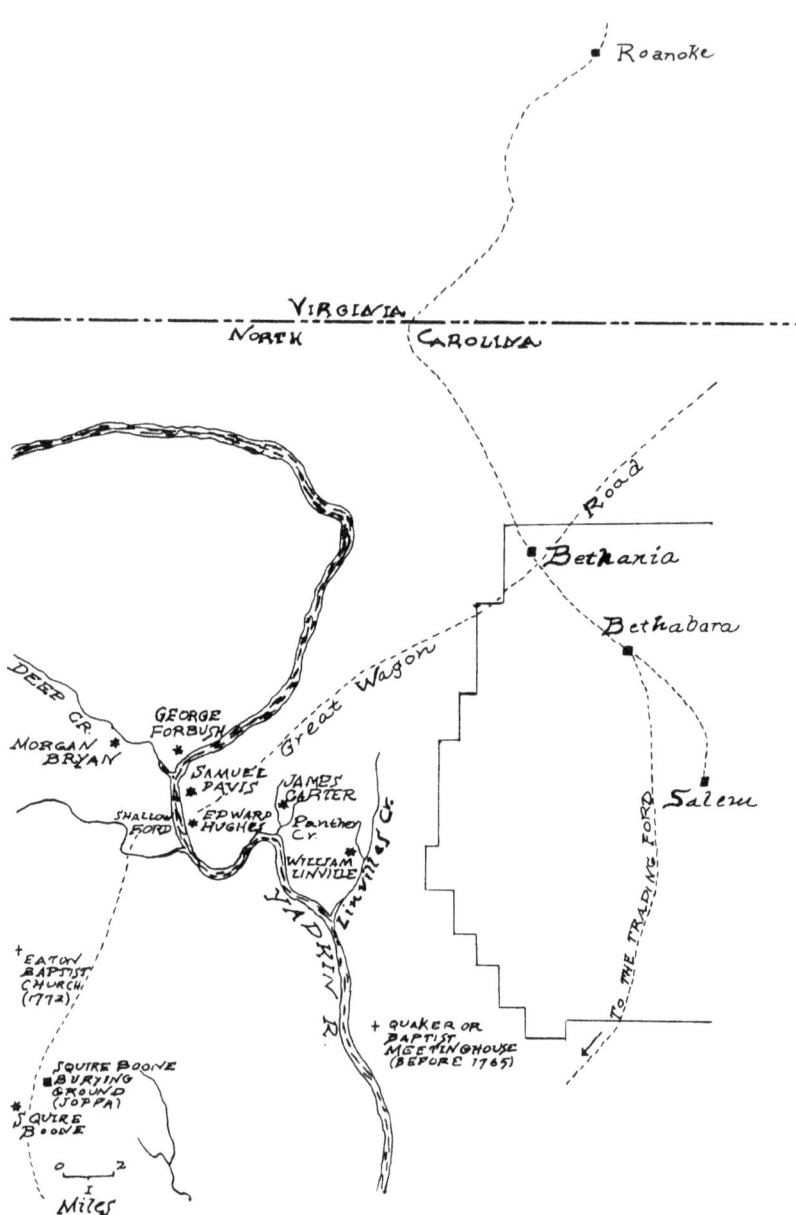

PUBLISHED BY THE UNIVERSITY OF NORTH CAROLINA PRESS, 1964

The Bryan Settlement and Squire Boone Home, 1747-1773: Before 1750 people were entering the Yadkin valley by way of this Great Wagon Road from Pennsylvania. Among those early settlers were Bishop Augustus Gottlieb Spangenberg's group of Moravians (1753) and the parents of Daniel Boone (1750).

many miles as possible between themselves and the British crown. At the orders of the English government, therefore, they came to the colonies to start life anew.

Many of these immigrants, in view of the oath they had taken, became Tories during the Revolutionary War. For the most part, they settled along the Cape Fear and other rivers in the eastern part of the colony; some of them found their way into the piedmont. But the Scotch-Irish who came to dominate the "back country" had taken no such oath, and their resentment against English restraint and decrees made them ardent exponents of both political and religious freedom. They became leaders in the movement that led to the struggle to win freedom and separation from the mother country.[15]

After 1740 immigrants of all nationalities found that both Pennsylvania and eastern South Carolina were fairly well settled, with the best lands taken up by earlier arrivals. Then, too, the gathering conflict with the French opened Pennsylvania's western border to Indian and French guerrilla warfare. Thus the newcomers streamed westward. Those coming to South Carolina followed the old trading paths to the west, settling south and east of the Catawba lands or, turning north into North Carolina, settled along the Pee Dee and Catawba Rivers and their tributaries. The German, Swiss, Welsh, Irish, and Scotch-Irish arriving at Philadelphia, followed an old Indian trail to the Shenandoah valley in Virginia. They traveled along its length and, crossing the mountains, reached the Dan River from whence they crossed to the Yadkin valley and continued south to the land east of the Catawba River. This "Pennsylvania Road" was a harsh, unfriendly, tortuous, narrow trail, but over it, with their meager belongings, came most of the families making up the settlements in the piedmont and western sections of North Carolina.[16]

As early as 1740 daring settlers had begun the community that was to grow into Charlotte, while others that followed during the next few years took up land in the present Burke and Rutherford Counties. It was to gain the good will of the Catawba Indians and to protect these westward moving settlements that North Carolina in 1757 built a fort east of the Blue Ridge. Even so, during the Cherokee War these tiny villages were in constant danger of raids, and occasionally a settler lost his life.

When in 1729 the English Crown had purchased the Carolina shares from the Proprietors or their heirs, Lord George Carteret's heir had refused to sell and had been given his eighth of the vast territory from the Virginia boundary southward for a distance of sixty miles and stretching, as granted in the 1663 charter, from the Atlantic Ocean to the South Sea. By 1750 this strip of land, with two thirds of the colony's population, was held by John, Earl of Granville, and was known as the Granville Tract. Lord Granville's agent set up a land office in Edenton to sell tracts of land in the area to incoming settlers.[17]

To this office in 1752 went Bishop August Gottlieb Spangenberg of Pennsylvania with a party of six "Brethern" and was granted by Francis Corbin, the agent, a huge area in the "back country" of North Carolina. The land was to be selected by Spangenberg and surveyed by the men accompanying him on an exploring trip into the region. This property was being purchased in the interest of a group of Protestants, Germans of the Moravian faith. They had come to Pennsylvania to colonize but had found there no suitable tract large enough to serve their purpose. Bishop Spangenberg, leader of their faith in America, hoped now to locate land farther west where a colony might be settled to carry out the religious beliefs and practices of the group and to engage, if possible, in missionary activities among the Indians.

The little party started westward but because of illness two of the men were forced to drop out, being left at the homes of friends in Pennsylvania. The remaining four (Spangenberg, a surveyor, and two guides) followed early trails and roads, which brought them after a strenuous trip into the Yadkin valley. From this trail they branched off on Indian trails and then onto the even narrower buffalo trails in search of land. They stopped long enough to make surveys around the present Hickory and Morganton areas. They continued their journey by traveling north and west and on a day in early December found themselves lost in the rugged Blue Ridge range. After the loss of a horse on the pathless, precipitous hills and after chopping their way out of laurel and rhododendron thickets, they came to a valley, open and beautiful, in which three creeks united. There, Bishop Spangenberg felt, would be an ideal place for an Indian mission. The Moravians were looking at the valley in the present Watauga County where today the city of Boone stands near those three forks of the stream. In spite of the inviting valley, the country did not appeal to the Bishop as a place to settle his colony, for, as he wrote, "The western part of North Carolina is all hills and valleys and that pours the water together."[18]

The Lull Between the Storms / 97

COURTESY OF DR. INA W. VAN NOPPEN

Daniel Boone: Boone was born in Pennsylvania in 1735 but lived for 26 years in North Carolina. He won fame as a hunter, an explorer, as a scout for the Richard Henderson Company, and as a trail blazer. With a crew of men he hacked out the Wilderness Road to Kentucky. Over it the Henderson Party traveled. This likeness of him at 80 is a copy of the only portrait ever painted of him.

Unfortunately for the travelers, Western North Carolina gave them an unfriendly welcome in the form of a blinding snow storm. So it was with decided relief that a few days later they chanced to meet and join with three hunters returning to the

PHOTO BY BARBARA GREENBERG, FOR THE APPALACHIAN CONSORTIUM

Daniel Boone's Trail from North Carolina to Kentucky, 1769. Marked by N. C. Daughters of The American Revolution: The rock on which the plaque is mounted was hauled from Rich Mountain Gap (circa 1905) by Cicero Greer and Lewis Bryant of Boone to its present site in the yard of Mr. and Mrs. Howard T. Greer in Zionville in Watauga County.

Yadkin across the mountains. Back in the land of the Yadkin Spangenberg's party surveyed a tract of land ten miles wide and eleven miles long and gave it the name Wachovia, a word meaning meadow and stream. The tract was approved by Granville's agent, and an additional tract was later arranged for, making the Moravian grant approximately 100,000 acres. There in 1753 a party of the "Brethern," having accomplished the incredible feat of bringing with them a wagon over the Pennsylvania Road, began their central village, Bethabara. This palisaded town proved to be a haven of refuge to the scattered families east of the Blue Ridge during the frightening days of the Cherokee War.[19]

Although the hunters and cattlemen were not themselves settlers in Western North Carolina, they furnished glowing accounts of fertile valleys beyond the Blue Ridge to land-seeking men streaming along the Pennsylvania Road into the Yadkin valley. Several of these hunters and trappers became guides for exploring parties looking for suitable homesites. The most famous of these was Daniel Boone. His parents had been among the earlier immigrants from Pennsylvania, settling in the Yadkin section where in the present town of Mocksville, a marker designates the site of his father's cabin.

Young Daniel grew up on the frontier and at an early age was now and then crossing the mountains into the same valley viewed by Bishop Spangenberg. There, on occasion, he is reputed to have made use of a shelter cabin for herders built by Benjamin Howard. The site of that cabin is today marked by a plaque on the campus of Appalachian State University. Throughout this section Boone hunted and trapped and explored until by 1767 he was familiar not only with the best trails in the present eastern Tennessee, but also with those running on west into the "Land of Kaintuck." In fact, he had by that date conducted a party into that western land.[20]

Back at his home—now a cabin near the Blue Ridge in the present Wilkes County—Boone's knowledge of lands and trails beyond the mountains won him a local reputation. In 1761 he was asked to guide a party of hunters from Virginia into the eastern part of the present Tennessee, which was then a part of Western North Carolina. In 1769 a hunter named John Finley asked Boone to conduct an exploring party from Virginia into the Kentucky country, where a site was selected for a village to be known as Walker's Settlement. Along the route the men selected farm sites for their friends back east under an open grant for 120,000 acres from the colony of Virginia. Some of the locations chosen were actually within the colony of North Carolina, but no settlements were made at that time.[21]

Colonel Byrd's troops in 1761 had passed through a part of North Carolina's western lands on their way to quell the Cherokee uprising, and some of the officers and soldiers, during their stay on the Long Island of the Holston, saw the possibilities for future settlement in the western valleys. At the end of the French and Indian War with the danger of Cherokee raids supposedly over, pioneer families from east of the Blue Ridge and many arriving from Virginia and Pennsylvania took their belongings over the mountains, selecting land and building their cabins on the upper Holston, Watauga, and Nolichucky Rivers.

These scattered pioneers had received grants from Virginia. The earliest came perhaps in 1769 and were joined in the following three years by hundreds of others seeking cheap land and elbow

SOUTHERN APPLACHIAN HISTORICAL ASSOCIATION

Daniel Boone hoists a bear in an exciting scene from the historic outdoor drama, **Horn in the West,** *which has been performed for 25 consecutive years in Boone, North Carolina.*

room. Soon the smoke of home fires could be seen up and down the fertile valleys. The increasing numbers pushed the settlers south and east, and one of them, running a surveying line, discovered that many had claimed and were clearing land in North Carolina and were therefore outside the protection of Virginia. William Boen (or Bean) is said to have been the first of those settling that area.[22] To insure a degree of safety the settlers made a temporary agreement with the Cherokees by which they were granted settlement rights, and they notified the North Carolina government. The new North Carolina settlement came to be known as the Watauga Settlements, extending over a considerable area in the present Tennessee and along the Watauga River in what is today Watauga County, North Carolina. They were the first permanent white settlements in Western North Carolina.

Among the hundreds who came to make their homes in the newly opened area were a surprisingly large number of able men with courage and vision. They were willing, even eager, to work hard in order that they might create in this wilderness a home for themselves and their children. But they were intolerant of restrictions and demanded a just share in their political organizations and freedom in their religious thinking. Out of this number, two gradually assumed leadership, expressing in their words and actions the finest and best of the pioneer spirit that was common to all.

One of these was James Robertson, who arrived early in 1770. He was a self-taught North Carolinian whose sheer ability and impressive personality insured him immediate recognition by the other settlers. He was by his very nature a pioneer, and others caught the enthusiasm for the sentiments that he genuinely felt and expressed. In fact, after a year in the section, he returned east and led a party of sixteen families to the area. He was to prove a tower of strength to these western settlers in the trying years ahead.[23]

The second of these leaders was the educated Virginian, John Sevier. Handsome, courtly in manner, and military in bearing, he was able to adapt himself with poise and tact to any situation. He understood men, and his unerring judgment, far-seeing plans, and sound principles made him the most outstanding and influential of all the Watauga settlers and one of America's greatest pioneers. Without his leadership the story of the scattered Watauga Settlements in the following eight or ten years might well have been a sad, deeply tragic page in the history of Western North Carolina.[24]

In the summer and fall of 1771 and throughout the next year, men from the piedmont section of North Carolina, many of them earlier settlers or sons of settlers there, arrived in the Watauga Settlements to take up a new life in a territory where they hoped to find economic security and justice, together with freedom from the oppressions of the colonial government. They were the Regulators who were defeated at the Battle of Alamance and were fleeing west to avoid taking an oath of allegiance to the king's colonial government. The experience through which they had just passed still rankled in their hearts.

The Germans, Irish, and Scotch-Irish, together with a sprinkling of English, who had made settlements on the choice river lands in the piedmont section of the colony, had brought with them a distrust of government and bitter memories of the intolerance and injustice that had caused them to leave the lands of their birth and ancestors. In North Carolina they sought freedom along many lines. They found themselves, however, a long distance from the seat of the colony's government; moreover, this area, especially after 1750, grew with such rapid strides that the western representation in the colonial Assembly was increasingly out of proportion to its population. The western delegates, constantly urging reapportionment, always met with failure because of the controlling votes of delegates from the older and more stable section of the colony, who intended to keep a firm grip on the legislative policies of the government.

To add to the general aggravation of the westerners, they found themselves the economically poor section of the colony; yet because of their rapid growth in population, they were furnishing a large share of the colony's taxes. They came to feel that the chief—perhaps the only—interest of the government in them was the amount of taxes that could be raised in their settlements, a goodly portion of which was spent in eastern communities. Deepening their resentment was the unjust system of their courts. Both civil and criminal cases considered important were tried in the east, a regulation that brought bitter complaints from the Western North Carolina and piedmont settlers. As an added grievance, they were forced to support the Anglican Church although they were, for the most part, Protestants.[25]

Whatever ties these newcomers from Europe might have developed with the colonists along the coast were prevented by the extremely meager means of communication between the two sections. People in the "back country" were forced to rely upon themselves for protection and for the solutions to their local problems. The result was a growing spirit of independence that led to opposition to the eastern delegates and to the often ill-chosen administrative officers which the Crown sent into their area. At last these western discontents organized, calling themselves Regulators. They issued a series of "Advertisements" calling for reforms of stated abuses, held several large mass meetings, and petitioned Governor Tryon to correct certain flagrant injustices.

No redress was forthcoming from the Governor, Assembly, or courts, and the rapidly growing Regulator organization made plans to take affairs into its own hands. A crown officer (one Colonel Lynch, sent into the area to collect special taxes levied to pay for Tryon's "Palace") was hanged, and rumors that the Regulators were planning an armed attack against New Bern caused Tryon to order out the militia.²⁶ Under Hugh Waddell, the troops marched west where a pitched battle took place on May 16, 1771, at Alamance. The poorly-equipped and untrained Regulators, no match for the disciplined militia, were defeated and forced to take an oath of allegiance.²⁷

The Regulator movement, arising out of geographic conditions and pioneer economic problems, was pitted against a comparatively stable eastern society and English colonial policy. It left its scars in the hearts of the piedmont settlers that did not completely disappear until the colonists of all sections of the state were united in a common struggle against England itself. The spirit of the Regulators was to crop up again during the long process of welding North Carolina into a state, but the immediate result of the Battle of Alamance was the westward movement of many of the Regulators, who, rather than take the required oath, fled across the mountains to join the Watauga settlers.

During the era of Indian trade with South Carolina, a comparatively easy and continuous contact with the eastern ports was enjoyed by traders in the Cherokee villages. That contact did not exist for the pioneers in the Watauga Settlements. In fact, it was not to exist in any part of Western North Carolina later opened to white settlers. Roads and trails leading from the coastal areas of North Carolina westward to the mountains were poor and often circuitous. Men finding it necessary to travel to the capital took the Pennsylvania Road to Virginia and at some trading path in the east turned into North Carolina. An alternate route went to Charleston by way of the old trading path from Tennessee that ran east of the Blue Ridge into the Spartanburg area, linking with the Great Path to Charleston. At Charleston a boat could be taken to some North Carolina port.

Realizing, then, their isolation from the North Carolina government, representatives from the scattered Watauga Settlements met early in 1772 and drew up a document that they called the Articles of the Watauga Association. The document has not survived. Existing references to it, however, reveal that although formal independence was not declared, it established a real and impressive informal independence. It provided for a Court of five elected Commissioners, a clerk of the Court, and a sheriff. It recognized no higher authority and it authorized the raising and directing of its own militia and the power to negotiate with the Indians, British agents, and the colonies of North Carolina and Virginia.

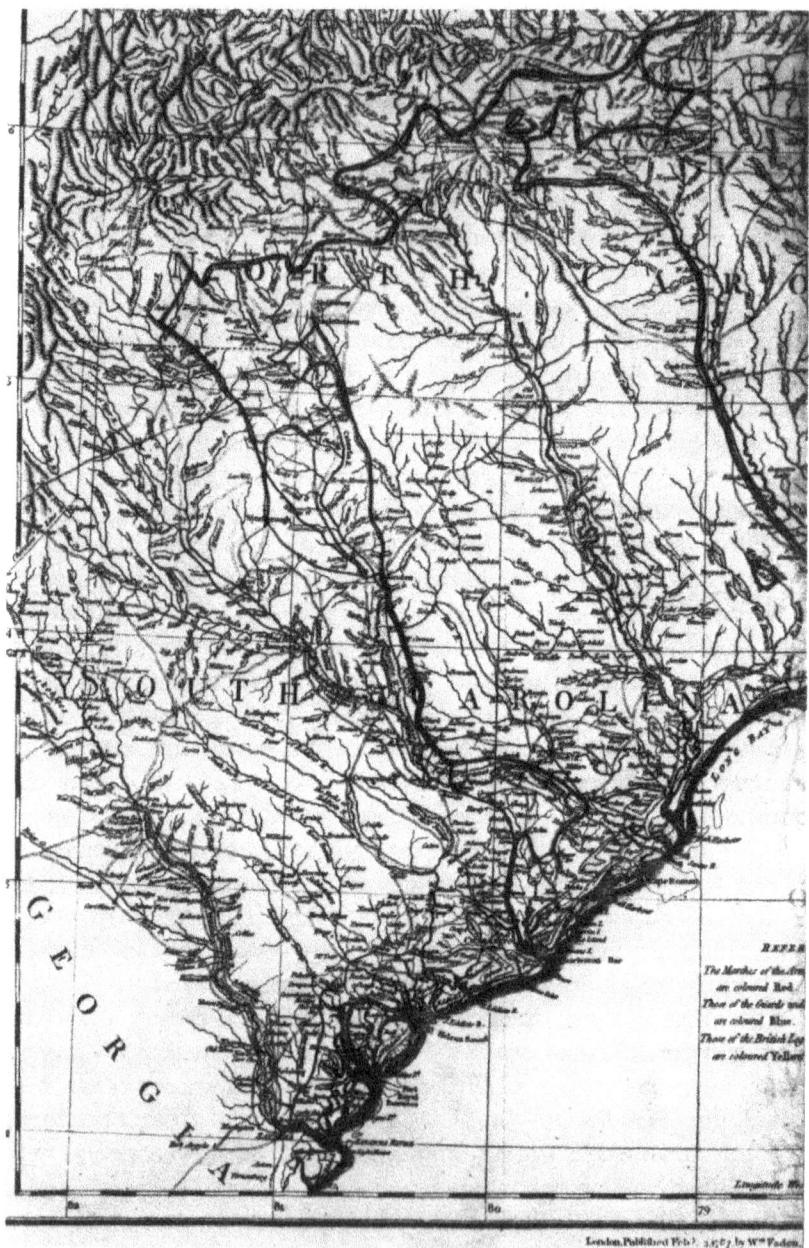

The injustices and political, economic, and religious oppressions suffered in their European home countries and again in the piedmont of North Carolina had taught these settlers much. A group of sturdy pioneers, able and far-sighted men, learned to

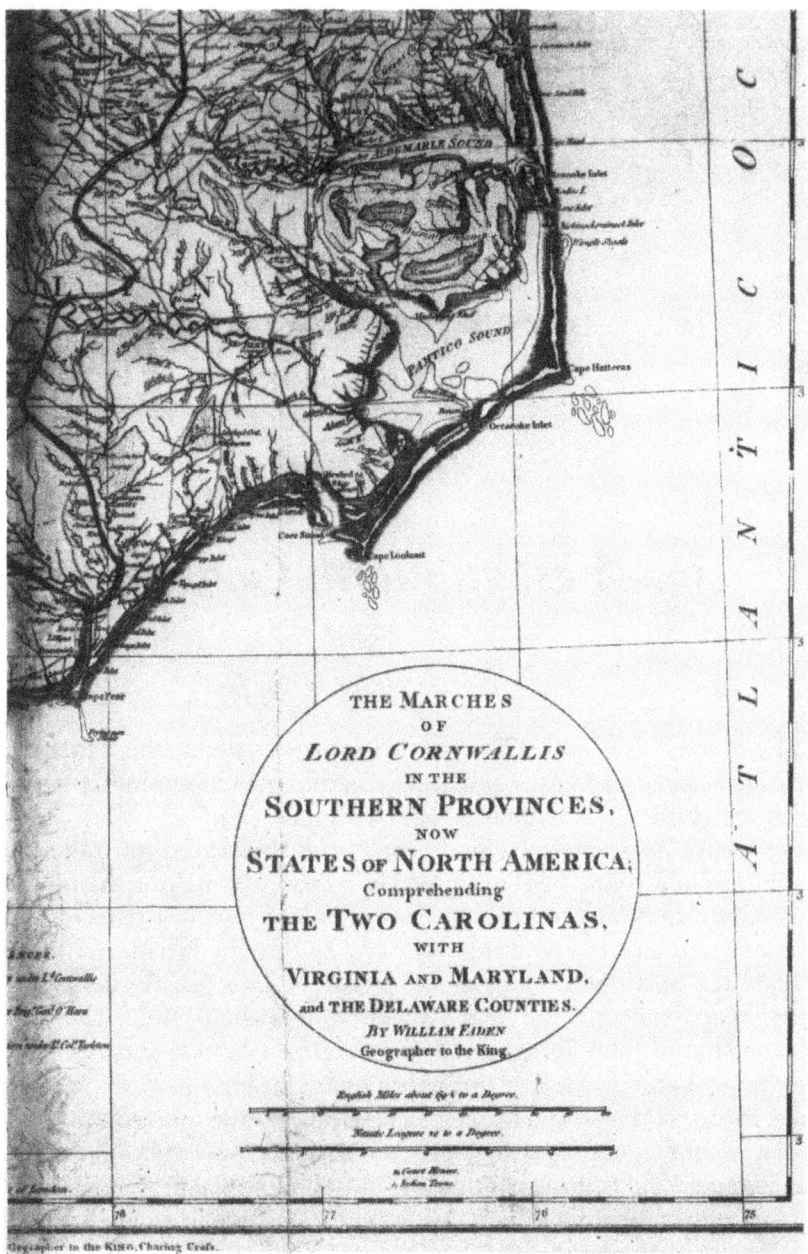

prize freedom above all things, and they now had a determination to build a community in which justice and equality might rule. The result was Western North Carolina's first constitution. Democracy had come to the mountains.

CHAPTER SEVEN

A New Flag for Western North Carolina

Between 1771 and 1776 the settlements along the Holston, Nolichucky, and Watauga Rivers steadily grew as colonists from central North Carolina, from Virginia, and families from Germany, Scotland, Ireland, and Wales arrived to take up holdings and to adapt themselves to a new way of life. Although the Cherokees viewed this spreading colony with distrust and at times with alarm, the temporary treaty they had made with the Watauga Settlements remained in force. This was largely due, perhaps, to the militia that had been organized under the able leadership of John Sevier and Isaac Shelby. The native Americans were probably further intimidated by the brave show of strength displayed by the colonists in the palisades thrown up around their villages and in the forts they erected. In addition, every Cherokee recognized the fighting ability of "Nolichucky Jack" Sevier.

North Carolina, busy with the distressing events of a gathering war, could not take—at least did not take—any steps to make the agreement with the Cherokees permanent. The pioneers were left to their own devices and continued to control their own affairs, becoming the first colonists to isolate themselves from the older, more stable seacoast areas of their colony.

The Western North Carolina settlers were, in these years,

practically unaffected by the chain of events taking place along the Atlantic. From newcomers and from their own men returning from infrequent trips to eastern ports for supplies or for a meeting of the General Assembly they learned of the passage of the Stamp Act in 1765; and news also arrived of the subsequent taxes levied by the English government upon the colonies, including the hated tax on tea. They heard, too, of the active opposition in North Carolina to all these acts and of rumors that other colonies were likewise bitterly protesting the English measures. In 1774 people of the mountains were informed that aroused citizens had taken the reins of government from Governor Josiah Martin, who had later fled to the safety of an English vessel, and had set up the Provincial Congress of North Carolina. They also learned that in September representatives from all the colonies had met in a Continental Congress in Philadelphia to which North Carolina had sent three men.

But the news of all these events reached the settlements west of the Blue Ridge weeks—more often months—after they had occurred and must have seemed to the pioneers unrelated to their own immediate problems. Without doubt many among them felt a sense of relief that they and their families were well away from the scenes of turmoil. In 1775, however, came news that made every pioneer aware that even the mountain settlements were to have a part in the oncoming struggle with the mother country. Before the Second Continental Congress was to meet in May, a battle was fought at Lexington on April 19 at which the hastily gathered Massachusetts militia forced Major John Pitcairn's British troops to retreat to Boston. American blood had been shed by the king's soldiers! It took no crystal ball for the West as well as the East to read the future. War was inevitable.

Even before receiving news of this battle, the men of the "Back Country" went into action. Thomas Polk, commander of the Mecklenburg Council of Safety, issued a call for two delegates from each county unit to meet at the courthouse in Charlotte on May 19. These delegates were accompanied by approximately half of the men of the county. During the meeting word of the Battle of Lexington reached the village. In the fervor of patriotism aroused by the news, a committee was reportedly appointed to draw up a statement embodying the sentiments of the delegates, a copy of which was to be sent by horseman to the Second Continental Congress in session at Philadelphia. Much controversy has raged around this document since it was never read in the Continental Congress, and the original one was lost in 1794 when the home of John McKnitt Alexander, Secretary of the Assembly, was destroyed by fire. It was rewritten from memory in 1800, twenty-five years after the Mecklenburg meeting.[1]

If the facts recorded in this 1800 document are accurate, the original contained the first declaration of independence from England to be penned by American colonists. The belief that it did contain such a declaration was widespread, and May 20, 1775, became known as Mecklenburg Day. In 1861 that date was put on the North Carolina flag. Whatever may have been presented and approved by a majority of the delegates on that May 20 will never definitely be known although a set of "Resolves" was drawn up and adopted on May 31. These "Resolves" appeared in June in *The North Carolina Gazette*, in *The Cape Fear Mercury,* and in *The South Carolina Gazette and Country Journal.* Thus, although the original copy was also destroyed in the Alexander fire, the contents of the "Resolves" have survived. They declared all commissions issued by the king "null and void" and any person accepting an office under the crown an "enemy to his country."[2]

In the first year of the war a few men shouldered their small-bore rifles and left the mountains and "back country" to join the American forces as volunteers. Since the scenes of combat were distant, their number was small and almost from the outbreak of the conflict it became evident that the western settlements would have all they could manage with their own problems. Many of the settlers had but recently come from Europe, and the influx into the region had been too rapid for assimilation into the social pattern that was shaping up in the area. Finding in the colony greater freedom than they had enjoyed in their home countries, many felt that the uprising against England was unjustifiable and so took a stand as Loyalists. They were joined in their attitudes by the region's Scottish veterans of Culloden Field, who, thirty years earlier, had suffered from the might of England's power and were bound to English loyalty by the strongest of allegiance oaths. Many Regulators, too, remained true to the oath of allegiance they had been forced to make after the Battle of Alamance.[3]

On the other hand, there were settlers of longer standing in their communities as well as newcomers who, like the Scotch-Irish, had brought with them grievances against England and who had taken no oath. Both factions took up the cause of freedom and independence. Throughout Western North Carolina, as in other parts of the colony, neighbor was often lined up against neighbor. In addition, there was in all the western settlements a sprinkling of adventurers and opportunists, rough characters prepared to take either side as expediency dictated. From them came a trouble-making element that stole horses and cattle and that pilfered and plundered individual settlements and villages.[4]

The Cherokees, too, became embroiled in the conflict. Their resentment against the encroaching white man yearly increased as they were forced by treaties they dared not refuse to give up their hunting grounds piecemeal. Under Colonel Evan Shelby, volunteers of western settlers joined the Virginia militia in 1774 in the campaign that, over the protests of the Cherokees, won for that colony the land between the Kentucky and Cumberland Rivers through the Henderson Purchase. Richard Henderson, a North Carolina lawyer, had become the promoter for Boone's plan to settle Kentucky, and with several other men he formed the Transylvania Company to colonize the west and create a fourteenth colony.

The treaty with the Cherokees, signed on March 17, 1775, at Sycamore Shoals on the Watauga River, ceded to the newly formed company twenty million acres of land. In payment the Cherokees received approximately ten thousand pounds' worth of goods. The colonial governors of Virginia and North Carolina declared this Henderson Treaty "null and void," but neither colony did anything to halt migration into the acquired lands. The Cherokee chief, Oconostota, is said to have remarked, "The land beyond the mountains is a dark ground, a bloody ground." No longer did the Cherokees have any claim to lands north of the present Tennessee.[5]

After the French and Indian War the Cherokee trade with the colonists had been revived but amounted to only a trickle of its former volume. It was no longer highly profitable and was kept up by the whites largely as a means of gaining the good will of the Indians, for other industries were engaging the energies of both South and North Carolina. Moreover, after seventy years of widespread and continuous commercial hunting, all forms of game in the mountains were practically depleted. The Cherokees were now a poor people, but a people with wants and tastes cultivated by their trade with the white man and now with small chance of satisfying those wants. That small chance grew less with each loss of territory.

With the outbreak of hostilities, England, through its agents and through Tories in the region, spread propaganda among the Cherokees. Loyalists and English agents pointed out to the Indians that as recently as 1763 England had proved its power and might by defeating France, and the propagandists reminded the Cherokees of Montgomery's and Grant's raids in their territory. All too well did the listeners recall the destruction of their homes and towns and crops, and the native Americans logically concluded that in any struggle against England the colonists would be destined to be defeated. Their logic fitted in neatly with their desire to be rid of the settlers in Western North Carolina and Virginia, and the Cherokees allied themselves with the English. For encouragement England provided them with guns and ammunition and offered bounties for the scalps of settlers.[6] For a second time the Cherokees were drawn into an international conflict not of their making, and for the second time they had chosen the wrong side.

Cherokee warriors went on the warpath in June, 1776, planning a war of extermination. At first their raids were scattered and light, but by July they were striking at isolated farms and small villages in Georgia, where they brought panic to the settlers. Widespread attacks were also made on the whites along the Broad and Catawba Rivers east of the Blue Ridge in both North and South Carolina. In several instances they wantonly killed entire families. Women and children fled for safety to the fort built at the present Old Fort as terror spread throughout the region.[7]

The Indians then crossed the mountains for a surprise attack on the settlements west of the Blue Ridge. But here they were repulsed, for the pioneers had been warned of the impending raid by the Cherokee Beloved Woman, Nancy Ward, the daughter of a white trader and a Cherokee mother, who was a friend of the settlers but was respected and revered by her people. Yet there was some loss of life in these settlements, for now and then some one would be caught outside a fort and become the target of a brave's gun. Throughout Western North Carolina the fear of Indian attacks spread. No one was safe as marauding bands of white desperadoes joined the Indians in their raids.[8]

It was during these tense days that leaders of the Watauga Settlements, aware of the immediate need to protect their part of North Carolina, met in convention and on July 5 drew up a petition addressed to the Provincial Congress, asking to be recognized as a part of North Carolina and to be called the Washington District. This document, signed by 113 landowners, was taken to the Provincial Congress by two representatives at the convention, John Carter and George Russell. There the men were received and were instructed to send five elected respresentatives from their district to the Congress at its next meeting in Halifax. This was done, and John Carter, John Sevier, John Haile, Charles Robertson, and Jacob Womack were elected. Jacob Womack did not report at the Congress and John Sevier arrived at Halifax late; however, the others were present at the opening of the session, and by a vote of 153 to 1, all four were seated in North Carolina's war time legislative body.

As representatives of the district officially named Washington County and given the boundaries of the present state of Tennessee, the men from beyond the Blue Ridge took part in drawing up the Constitution of 1776 by which the colony of North Carolina became the state of North Carolina. At the same session the Congress took steps to organize a county government for the western area, the first area of any of the colonies to be named officially for the Commander-in-Chief of the American forces.[9]

Retaliation for the Indian raids and massacres came swiftly and with merciless thoroughness. Following the harrowing experiences of settlers in the southern part of Rutherford County and in adjacent sections of South Carolina, Captain Thomas Howard set out with a small force of volunteers from the block house just south of the South Carolina line, below the present Tryon. Guided by a friendly Indian named Schuyucha, Howard crossed the mountains and went west along an Indian trail to Round or Warrior Mountain. There he surprised the encamped Cherokees and in a skirmish defeated them, capturing all those not killed in the battle. This campaign brought a cessation of Indian trouble to that section.[10]

But much more widespread action was imperative, and Virginia, South Carolina, Georgia, and North Carolina all sent troops—mostly volunteers—into the Cherokee country. On the orders of the Council of Safety of North Carolina, General Griffith Rutherford of the Salisbury District was put in command of the North Carolina campaign to be directed against the Middle and Valley towns. South Carolina and Georgia troops under Major (later Colonel) Andrew Williamson were to attack the Lower towns and then join General Rutherford. Colonel

Williams Christian was to lead the Virginia forces against the Over Hill towns. These attacks, coming from different directions, were to take place simultaneously if possible.[11]

On September 1, General Rutherford with a force of two thousand fighting white men, several hundred Catawbas, and needed pack men (making a total of 2,400) left Fort Davidson and crossed the Blue Ridge into the Cherokee country by way of Swannanoa Gap. Crossing the French Broad River, he followed Hominy Creek across the present Enka Corporation plant and then continued over the ridge to cross the Pigeon River, marching on to Richland Creek near the present Waynesville. From there he pushed on to the Middle towns, crossing the Tuckaseigee River east of Whittier and going south over the Cowee Range.[12]

Before the oncoming troops, the Cherokees fled into the fastnesses of the mountains while Rutherford's men systematically destroyed every dwelling and all crops and stored grain. When nothing was left in what is now Macon County, the troops crossed the Nantahala Mountains to the towns of the Hiwassee and Valley Rivers and those on the upper Little Tennessee. Here, too, destruction was wholesale. Except for the cattle, which the army took with them, nothing was spared. Towns, most of them newly built after Grant's raid in the region, became only blackened heaps of ashes and charred wood. The fields and orchards were merely abject specters of what had been. Here was devastation in its ugliest form.[13]

Throughout the area Rutherford and his men met with little opposition. There were numerous skirmishes, the fiercest of which took place at Wayah Bald Gap near the present town of Franklin and might be termed a battle. But the Americans found most of the towns deserted. As a result, casualties were light for both the white army and the Cherokees.[14] At the native American village on the site of the present Murphy, Williamson and his forces joined Rutherford. That was on September 26, and shortly afterward, feeling that their task had been completed, both leaders left Western North Carolina by retracing their routes.

Back at the fort of the Davidsons, however, General Rutherford learned that in crossing the Tuckaseigee and going south, he had missed important Indian towns on the lower Tuckaseigee and Oconaluftee Rivers. Accordingly, he dispatched Captain William Moore with a detachment of some one hundred men to the area. Following Rutherford's route, this contingent reached the ford on the Tuckaseigee River taken by the earlier army, but Moore and his men continued west until they reached the Cherokee village of Stekoa. They destroyed it, crossed the river, and following a trail to the Oconaluftee River, destroyed the villages and camps encountered along the way. This part of the campaign was a comparatively short one, for Moore and his men, finding their rations running low, turned back east. They had left the fort on October 29, and on November 7, Captain Moore reported to General Rutherford that the assignment had been completed and that the scorched earth policy had been accomplished in the Middle Towns.[15]

Williamson had been late in joining Rutherford since he had been delayed in the campaign through South Carolina and Georgia by strong Cherokee and Tory opposition, made especially ruthless by the additional lawless adventurers and marauders.[16] Yet Williamson had been successful in destroying the towns of the Lower Cherokees and in leaving the district in ruins as Montgomery had earlier done.

The campaign of Colonel Christian in the Over Hill section also resulted in utter defeat for the native Americans there, and all villages were blotted out except the sacred town of refuge, Echota, which was also the Cherokee capital. Altogether in this 1776 campaign, sixty-six Cherokee villages and towns were destroyed.[17] This Cherokee uprising had brought the Revolutionary War to Western North Carolina in one of its most dreaded forms. Now, although the Committees of Safety and the militia units earlier organized in the Watauga Settlements would have to continue combating sporadic Cherokee raids, the general uprising had been quelled (and with a minimum of white casualties). Rutherford's forces went east. The loss of life to the Cherokees during the march of the white forces through their territory was also small. But their casualties grew during the winter that followed when the homeless people existed on roots and berries found in the forests and constantly suffered from exposure and disease. An unknown number of them died during that mountain winter.

Sadly disillusioned with the English promise of restoring their lost lands and stunned and weakened by the crushing blows struck by the American forces, the Cherokees knew that they had once again lost all bargaining power with the whites. Bowing to the inevitable, the chiefs of the Lower Section signed a treaty with the new American Republic on May 20, 1777, at Dewitt's Corner,

South Carolina. Through it the Cherokee nation lost all of its remaining territory in South Carolina except for a narrow strip along its western border.[18] Two months later the chiefs of the Middle and Upper Towns went to the Long Island of the Holston and there made a treaty with Virginia, granting further concessions of their land in Kentucky.[19]

At this time they also made a treaty with North Carolina which relinquished forever all claims to hunting grounds east of the Blue Ridge and which made permanent the grants of territory made to the Watauga Settlements, including various areas which for some time had been disputed territory. In this treaty North Carolina arranged to purchase the eastern portion of the Cherokee lands with goods to be delivered at such a time as the financial condition of the new state would allow. Until that time, when a new treaty was to be concluded, white settlers were not to take up land in the area.[20] The once vast domain of the Principal People had dwindled to little more than the homelands in the Middle and Upper sections. Only a fraction of the Lower section remained, and the great hunting preserves were forever gone.

Throughout 1775 and 1776 a trickling of pioneers from west of the Blue Ridge joined friends and relatives in the eastern foothills and entered the American army. Some of these volunteers were with Howe's unit when General Charles Lee's forces successfully defended Charleston against an attempted British invasion in 1776.[21] Many, of course, were members of Rutherford's western campaign, and some of those went east with him. Others followed in the next few years. But on the whole, the settlers in Western North Carolina, even after the Cherokee punishment, remained on the frontier.

The western frontiersmen were ever alert to the possibilities of fresh Indian uprisings, and in their own forthright way they dealt with the desperadoes and Tories in their area. When feelings against the Loyalists rose to the fighting pitch, the king's men fled to the mountains where they hid in rocky shelters, living on the game they could shoot, on stolen cattle, and on the crops foraged from the nearby farms. To most of the pioneers the words "Tory" and "Loyalist" came to embody everything that was despicable.

The defeat of the Tories at Moore's Creek Bridge early in the conflict had kept the British troops out of North Carolina, while at Charleston Lee had discouraged their activity in South Carolina; after 1776, the main fighting was done farther north. But the South was not to be spared, and on February 26, 1780,

Charleston was besieged a second time. General Benjamin Lincoln's troops, in charge of the city's defense, held out until May. Then the city fell, and the American forces—officers, regulars, militiamen—became prisoners of the English. Lord Charles Cornwallis, British Commander in the South, was left in command of the city and of the section.[22] His plan was to subdue South Carolina and then to enter the piedmont area of North Carolina. For support in carrying out his plans Cornwallis relied upon the Tories and Loyalists in the regions through which he would pass. He was not then aware of the deterring power of many small bands of aroused Patriots under leaders who knew the territory throughly. But he was to learn.

Such North Carolina soldiers as Major Joseph McDowell, General Griffith Rutherford, William Davie, and General William Lee Davidson along with their Patriots became both hated and feared by Cornwallis and his British. For months their small bands carried out numerous surprise attacks on English units, upsetting British plans and hampering British movements, often preventing British regiments from getting supplies and from foraging about the countryside. These soldiers of the "back country" did much to put the fear of the Americans into the Tories in that region, and using methods learned from the Indians, they succeeded in being, if not an actual threat, at least a continuous nuisance to the advancing British forces.[23]

The frontiersmen could hinder and delay, but they could not stop the march of the Cornwallis army as it came westward and northward. Then at Camden it looked as though all the efforts of the "back country" men had been in vain, for the British commander, surprising the American army under General Horatio Gates, utterly routed the Americans, killing eight hundred and taking a thousand prisoners. This victory completed the conquest of South Carolina, and General Cornwallis and his army marched into North Carolina and entered Charlotte.[24] This little village, he discovered, instead of being the rendezvous of Loyalists that he had been led to expect, was a veritable hotbed of seething opposition.[25] Indeed, he found life in it disagreeable, at times well nigh unbearable. From Charlotte he planned to march his main army to Hillsboro, where supplies furnished by the Tories in the region were to be waiting. Considering the daily harassment by American Patriots that his men suffered, Cornwallis felt the need for extra help and ordered Colonel Patrick Ferguson to come from Ninety-Six with nine hundred men and to form a flank defense to the west during the march. Ferguson was to enlist the aid of all Loyalists in the area just east of the Blue Ridge and was to subdue that region.[26]

Ferguson and his men arrived in North Carolina and took up quarters in Gilbert Town in the newly organized Rutherford County. Joined by Loyalists and adventurers, his soldiers foraged through the surrounding territory, stealing cattle, destroying crops, and taking a few prisoners, despite the efforts of small groups of settlers to hamper the troops by a series of irritating guerrilla raids. The defense of the foothill country depended almost entirely upon the settlers themselves, for after the disasters in South Carolina the Americans who had escaped imprisonment had returned to their homes. Among the escapees was a unit of men from west of the Blue Ridge recruited by Isaac Shelby. After driving the last "Rebels" (led by Colonel Charles McDowell) over the Blue Ridge and after a skirmish at Bedford's Mill in the present McDowell County, it must have seemed to Ferguson that the task of subduing the "back country" was nearing completion.[27]

Then he learned that beyond the precipitous Blue Ridge were entire settlements of these stubborn, freedom-demanding Americans, many of whom had already taken up arms against the British forces. Ferguson promptly released a prisoner and sent him over the hills with an ultimatum. Shelby was given the message and rode in haste to John Sevier's home on the Nolichuky River where the two men, in charge of the militia of Washington County, grimly went about their task of recruiting. Busy with the gathering of late crops and prepared as usual for a chance Indian attack, the pioneers dropped their tools and reached for their rifles as they listened to the account of destruction and havoc taking place east of the mountains. Then the look of cold steel glinted in their eyes as they heard Ferguson's ultimatum to surrender or "he would march his army over the mountains, hang their leaders, and lay their country waste with fire and sword." Up and down the valleys to all the settlements went the word to meet at the Sycamore Shoals of the Watauga River in the present Tennessee. And swift horsemen took the call to arms into the Virginia settlements.[28]

On the evening of September 25 they gathered at the Shoals, 240 strong, led by John Sevier, a like number led by Isaac Shelby, and 400 from Virginia under William Campbell, together with Colonel Charles McDowell and his 160 refugees. They were

A New Flag for Western North Carolina / 117

TENNESSEE STATE MUSEUM COLLECTION, NASHVILLE, TENN.

Sycamore Shoals: Frontiersmen, aroused by Colonel Patrick Ferguson's command to surrender, gathered at the Sycamore Shoals (also called Flats) on the Watauga River on September 25, 26, 1780. From there, under the leadership of John Sevier, Isaac Shelby, and William Campbell, the Overmountain men grimly began their march against Ferguson's army. On the way they were joined by men from Burke, Rutherford, and Surry Counties.

N. C. DEPARTMENT OF ARCHIVES AND HISTORY

Isaac Shelby: Shelby, a prominent patriot, with John Sevier, in charge of the militia of the Watauga Settlements, led 240 frontiersmen in the march of the Overmountain men. At the Battle of King's Mountain he commanded one unit of the Americans. This picture is a copy of a painting.

quietly determined men who had left their homes to face a disagreeable task. They were all men of the woods and hills, trained by necessity in self-protection, in quick decisions, in precise timing. They spared not a thought on uniforms and army equipment, and they had no time to enlist in the American army (even had any of them by chance thought of such action).

To these settlers their immediate duty was clear and simple. The war had come to their mountains, to their homes. They would meet it east of the hills and either drive the "Tory Ferguson" from their land or force him to fight until he and his troops were destroyed. The next morning, outfitted in hunting shirts and deerskin trousers or in homemade linsey-woolsey clothes, the mountain militia was ready, armed with small-bore rifles and

ALBERT BARDEN COLLECTION, N. C. DEPARTMENT OF ARCHIVES AND HISTORY

Joseph McDowell: Joseph McDowell of Quaker Meadows in Burke County took part in the Battle of Ramseur's Mill and the Battle of Cowpens. His home was the meeting place for the groups of Overmountain men. After refreshing the men with his fine home brew, he joined them as they followed Ferguson's retreating army.

whatever hunting knives and tomahawks they had been able to lay hands to. They solemnly listened to prayers offered by the Reverend Samuel Doak, a Presbyterian minister, and then marched southeast. Their simple noon meal was eaten, it would seem, at a spring on the grassy bald of Roan Mountain, and that night camp was made at Bright's Spring on Bright's Trail.

At dawn they discovered that two of the men, William Crawford and Samuel Chambers, were missing. Breaking camp, the mountain men traveled down Roaring Creek to the Toe River, passed over the site of the present Spruce Pine, and crossing the Toe River, camped for the night at Grassy Creek. By September 29, they were at Gillespie Gap. Here, aware that Ferguson would by this time learn of their route from the two deserters, the group divided, descending the mountain range by different paths, neither of which was the route originally planned. One section under Campbell continued along the crest of the Blue Ridge and then descended to Turkey Cove to camp for the night. The following day these men went on down to the Catawba River, crossed the site of the present Lake James, and reached Quaker Meadows, the home of Colonel Joseph McDowell.

They were joined by the other section, which had spent the night at North Creek Cove and, after passing a couple of miles farther up North Creek, had crossed the southern end of Linville Mountain, descending the Blue Ridge by means of the old Yellow Mountain road. At Quaker Meadows they were joined by 350 men from Wilkes and Surry Counties, under Colonel Benjamin Cleveland and Joseph Winston. They were also joined by a small force from Lincoln County under command of Frederick Hambright, by volunteers from South Carolina commanded by James Williams and William Lacey, and by a few men from Georgia.[29]

In spite of his bold threat to the mountain men, Ferguson, upon learning of the gathering of the Americans, felt it expedient to appeal for help to Cornwallis (still at Charlotte) and to send to Ninety-Six for reinforcements. He then retreated.

Now that a battle was imminent, the Patriots paused long enough to select a leader. At Shelby's generous suggestion, Colonel William Campbell was chosen, and on October 4 Charles McDowell set out to report to General Gates and to procure confirmation for the commanding officer. By this time the army had reached Cane Creek near Gilbert Town. Finding their progress too slow, the leaders selected the best men and the ablest horses and, taking no footsoldiers, pushed after the retreating Ferguson. They chose again, at Cowpens, a select group of riflemen—master marksmen—and pursued the enemy, who had gone northwest. At King's Mountain, only a mile and a half south of the North Carolina line, Ferguson ended his retreat and established camp on a stony ridge of the hill, which was protected by a steep descent covered with woods and underbrush. He no doubt felt secure in his mountain retreat.[30]

During the steady rain of that dark October night, the frontiersmen, accustomed to endure all kinds of weather and familiar with mountain terrain, continued their pursuit from Cowpens. Learning from captured spies the position Ferguson had taken and the uniform he was wearing, the nine hundred men

A New Flag for Western North Carolina / 121

FROM A DRAWING IN DRAPER'S KING'S MOUNTAINS AND ITS HEROES, PACK MEMORIAL LIBRARY, ASHEVILLE

The Battle of King's Mountain: This diagram of the Battle of King's Mountain shows the line of march of the Overmountain men and the placement of troops that surrounded Ferguson's army. Both the English and the American forces numbered about 900 men each.

122 / *Chapter Seven*

FROM A DRAWING IN DRAPER'S *KING'S MOUNTAIN AND ITS HEROES*, PACK MEMORIAL LIBRARY, ASHEVILLE

Ferguson's Death Charge: Ferguson, leading his troops, fell from his horse, the victim of bullets fired by men he had called "Bandits."

were divided into four sections in order to ascend King's Mountain from every direction on the next forenoon. The units were instructed to advance in Indian fashion, from tree to tree, and the men were told that after the order was given to advance, each marksman was to be his own officer. Thus on the afternoon of October 7, Colonel Ferguson, like a doomed Macbeth gazing upon the approaching Birnam woods, saw the men scaling the sides of his mountain position. They were the very men of the back woods whom he had so lately defied. The opposing forces were equally matched in number, for Ferguson had 906 men, equipped with English guns and ammunition and bayonets. There was not a bayonet among the Americans, but these men had tracked wild animals in the forests and had more than once fought the Cherokees. Every shot from their rifles reached its mark.

For an hour the fighting raged, the Patriots rallying after every repulse and reattacking so that their gain was fairly steady until they reached the top of the ridge. Ferguson, blowing his silver whistle to rally his disorganized troops, fell, mortally wounded by the bullets of the men he had called "Bandits." With their leader gone, the English army surrendered. The British counted 120 dead, including their slain commander, and 123 wounded. The remainder of their troops became American prisoners. The victors lost 28 men and found 62 of their men wounded, several of whom died on the way home.[31]

With their disagreeable task successfully completed, the men of Western North Carolina, riding or trudging, weary and footsore, began the trek back to their mountain homes. They could not know that what they had done that day was unique in the annals of war. An untrained, hastily-gathered militia of frontiersmen, members of neither their state's nor their country's forces, had utterly defeated a body of soldiers of equal size on a battlefield of the enemy's choosing. Except for a group of Loyalist volunteers, Ferguson's well-equipped soldiers had been trained in the army of a strong world power. The Patriots could not know that they had freed not only the "back country," but also their entire state from the British armies' control. They could not foresee that in this battle they had made practically inevitable General Cornwallis's surrender at Yorktown.

Surprised and dismayed at the defeat of his protecting army to the west and realizing that English loyalty could no longer be counted in the piedmont section of North Carolina, Cornwallis withdrew from Charlotte and returned to South Carolina. That winter, lured by the magnificently executed retreat of Greene's American forces, he led his army back across North Carolina where he won the costly battle of Guilford Court House in March. With forces weakened by losses incurred during the long winter march through unfamiliar territory and damaged by the too dearly won battle, Cornwallis led his troops east to Wilmington and then into Virginia where he reached Yorktown. There on October 19, 1781, he surrendered the British army to the American forces.[32]

The English flag that had flown over the colonies since the days of the English explorers—the flag that had been taken by Englishmen from the Atlantic Ocean to the farthest mountain settlement beyond the Blue Ridge—was seen no more in all the land. In its place over the cities in the east and over the mountain forts in the western hills there now waved a flag of red and white stripes and thirteen stars on a field of blue.

CHAPTER EIGHT

East-West Tug-Of-War

The return of the heroes of King's Mountain was neither as rapid nor as orderly as their advance had been. The British dead and wounded they had left on the field of combat to be cared for by the neighboring settlers. With them they took their prisoners and their booty, seventeen baggage wagons and some twelve hundred stands of arms. Their own wounded they carried on horse litters. The only surgeon in the two armies—an Englishman and now a prisoner—did the pitifully little that he could to relieve the suffering men during the slow trek. At least one of them—Captain Robert Sevier, a brother of John and possibly others—died on the way and was buried in what is now Avery County.[1]

Still keyed up to battle pitch, the men now became difficult to control, and small bands occasionally deserted the ranks to pilfer and burn property of known Loyalists. The Loyalist prisoners, too, came in for harsh treatment, and nine of them were hanged before the officers could enforce restraint. The remaining prisoners and baggage wagons were left with local militias east of the mountains as the men crossed to their homes to tell of their experiences and to break the news of death to the victims' families.[2]

It is doubtful that a single man among them thought of pay in connection with what he had accomplished, and most of them were perhaps surprised when the grateful states of Virginia, Georgia, and North and South Carolina publicly thanked them for

N. C. DEPARTMENT OF ARCHIVES AND HISTORY

John Sevier: Sevier was the leader in the Watauga Settlements. In his own time he was a legend as an Indian fighter, as a local politician, and as a statesman. He commanded one unit of the Patriots at the Battle of King's Mountain. He served briefly as governor of the short-lived "State of Franklin."

their heroic service and presented them swords.³ The impoverished state of North Carolina issued them certificates in the form of pay, but since these were worth only two cents on the dollar, they amounted to no more than a gesture of appreciation. Yet the freely given thanks of their states must have been a deep satisfaction to the western settlers and might have been pleasant to recall in the stormy, confused years that followed. These years would be filled with struggles and frustration, with repeated campaigns against the resentful Cherokees, with bitter factions in their own ranks, and conflict that bordered on revolt against the General Assembly of their own state. But of all this they were fortunately unaware as they trudged over the familiar hills on an October day, hoping, perhaps, for a bit of time for "lazin' 'round" and hunting.

Such hopes were not quick to materialize, and the feverish activity of the coming years began when the men learned that what they had most feared had come to pass. Knowing that the forts of the white people were practically undefended and ignoring the pleas of their tribal leaders, bands of Cherokees from the Middle Towns had attacked the settlements. That meant just one thing—a campaign of retaliation. Under John Sevier and Arthur Campbell, seven hundred men met and soundly defeated the Indians in 1780 at a site near the present Sevierville, Tennessee. In March of the following year the intrepid Sevier with 150 picked men crossed the towering Smoky Mountains, and in a surprise attack utterly destroyed one of the chief towns on the Tuckaseigee River at the site of the present Whittier. On this compaign several smaller villages were also destroyed as were quantities of stored grain. That summer Sevier and his men felt it necessary to attack a camp made by the Cherokees near the present Newport, Tennessee, in order to prevent its use as a base for raiding parties. There, thirteen native Americans were killed. The Cherokees had had enough and sued for peace, which was granted.[4]

But this peace was merely a lull in the chaotic relations between the settlers and the Cherokees. In 1782 Old Tassel of Echota begged Colonel Joseph Martin, Indian Commissioner and Brigadier-General in charge of North Carolina's militia in the west, to appeal to the governors of both Virginia and North Carolina to restrain their people from settling in the Indian territory along the Nolichucky and other rivers. It was, the Cherokee said, impossible to prevent raids on such settlements. Nothing seems to have been done about the plea, and white settlers continued to take up and clear land in the disputed area. This meant that Indian raids, followed by retaliatory campaigns, also continued.[5]

In 1783 the North Carolina General Assembly, eager to reward its Revolutionary soldiers with land grants, passed a law that repealed the 1777 Treaty of the Long Island of the Holston and opened to white settlers land beyond the Blue Ridge as far west as the Pigeon River, extending to the French Broad and thence to the Holston and Tennessee Rivers. The land was to be paid for in goods to the Cherokees (as the state could manage it), and no grants were to be issued west of the designated line.[6]

Two years later, in 1785, the federal government concluded its first treaty with the Native Americans at Hopewell, South Carolina. For ten days the bargaining went on between the commissioners for the United States and the one thousand Cherokees gathered for the event. When the document was at last ready, thirty-seven chiefs signed it with their marks. In it the Cherokees acknowledged the sovereignty of the United States, and a boundary line was established that passed through the present Hendersonville, Biltmore, Marshall, and in a straight line, on to the Nolichucky River. A considerable strip of land formerly opened for white settlement by the North Carolina law of 1783 was now restored to the Cherokees.

This first federal treaty also repudiated the Dumplin Creek Treaty that Sevier had that very spring forced upon the unwilling Cherokees. This treaty granted the settlers land lying to the south side of the Holston and French Broad Rivers as far south as the ridge that divides the water of Little River from the water of the Tennessee.[7] Under the terms of the new Hopewell Treaty, white settlers in territory allotted to the Cherokees were given six months to evacuate their claims.[8]

Only the Cherokees were satisfied with this treaty. Four counties had by this time been organized in the western territory, and they had recently been formed by the General Assembly of North Carolina into Washington District, with David Campbell presiding over its newly organized Superior Court and John Sevier named as Brigadier-General of its militia.[9] By the new treaty the district now found itself reduced in size. To the chagrin of its leaders, it was discovered that Greeneville, the town selected as a possible capital when or if the territory was made into the hoped-for state of Franklin, was now well within Cherokee lands. The District of Washington bluntly refused to recognize the Hopewell Treaty, and the so-called trespassers in the territory given back to the Indians made no move to leave.

The Cherokees, as might be expected, made attempts from time to time to force the settlers out by attacking the farms and small villages. This, in turn, led to continued avenging campaigns by Sevier and his militia. North Carolina proper was likewise disgruntled by the new federal treaty with the Cherokees, holding that the new boundaries would fail to protect the grants already made to soldiers and civilians, (although the treaty did make provisions for maintaining the rights of those who had received such grants). The treaty that was intended to be a "peace settlement" settled nothing and brought no peace.

The Indian uprising spread west to the little settlement of Nashville, organized in 1779-80, when James Robertson led a colony of pioneers from the Watauga Settlements to the site known as the French Lick. This aroused not only the western Cherokees, but also the more westerly Chickasaws, and the trouble soon involved small settlements along the Cumberland River. The assistance given by North Carolina (through its Brigadier-General, Joseph Martin, and through its militia) was always meager and often late in arriving on the scene. In fact, a few times Martin received no order from the state for his militia to join in the campaign; therefore, to insure the safety of the settlers, Sevier and his militia continued to carry out their campaigns against the Indians, who were now determined to force the settlers from their territory.[10]

On one of these campaigns in 1788 an unfortunate event led to severe criticism of the Watauga forces and their leaders. A young volunteer named John Kirk took it upon himself to avenge the brutal murder of his family by the Cherokees. While Old Tassel of Echota, his sons, and a companion chief were waiting in a shed for a conference with Sevier under a white flag of truce, the young man attacked the group and killed all of them. The violent deed of horror was deplored throughout the settlements, and the act was condemned by Congress and by several state assemblies. Needless to say, the infuriated Cherokees sought revenge, further intensifying the warfare between the two races contending for the possession of Western North Carolina.[11]

Not all of the problems that the western settlers confronted involved disputes with the native Americans. Becoming the first pioneers to isolate themselves from the more settled coastal areas, these mountain people had early developed a spirit of independence and had learned an attitude of self-reliance in decision-making. It is possible that, without the looming dangers of the oncoming Revolutionary War, the Watauga Settlements might soon have struggled for independence from North Carolina. Be that as it may, they had petitioned the General Assembly of the state for recognition and by legislative act had become Washington County. Their representatives to the General Assembly all voted for North Carolina's first constitution in 1776.

Both the representatives to the General Assembly from Washington County and the settlers themselves soon became aware that their interests and needs differed sharply from those of the eastern part of the state. They also became aware that the government of the new state would be dominated by eastern leaders and that the laws passed would serve the planters and business men of the settled coastal region. This realization created a feeling of resentment which in time grew into general dissatisfaction. There were many factors causing this east-west tug-of-war. The basic factor was geographic—a great distance lay between the settlements beyond the mountains and the seat of government and the seaports in the east. It had taken weeks for the pioneers to learn of events taking place in eastern North Carolina and in other colonies during the crucial days of the Revolutionary War.

Roads, even in the eastern section of the new state, were in wretched condition as weary travelers repeatedly testified in the early years of the Republic. The colony and later the state made no provision for road construction except to authorize counties to lay out public roads and to establish ferries and designate bridge sites. Detailed road laws, conferring considerable power and responsibility upon the counties, had never been enforced. During the war all roads—poor at best—had been utterly neglected. Consequently even the main north-south artery through the state had become well-nigh impassable. Scant attention had been paid to possible highways to the west, especially since construction would entail bridging or ferrying the many streams flowing in northwest-southeast direction. The obstacles to be faced were numerous, including clearing tangled forests, avoiding or crossing streams, and opening swamps while keeping up with maintenance on the trade routes already in existence.

However, in 1755 a law had been passed by the colony authorizing the building of a road from Hillsboro and one from Mecklenburg County to the Cape Fear River. It had been urged by merchants hoping to profit by western trade. But until some time after the Revolutionary War, these roads, where an attempt had been made to lay them out, were scarcely more than trails and often poor trails at that. The old Pennsylvania Road to Virginia and Philadelphia, unsatisfactory as it was, continued to be the northern outlet of the piedmont and mountain settlers. The roads following ancient Indian trails along the Yadkin and Catawba Rivers still served settlers going to the southern port of Charleston. From east of the Blue Ridge the mountain men entered their own area on foot or on horseback over the trails used by earlier hunters and trappers and native Americans.[12]

This physical road handicap, deplored by the profit-conscious, eastern North Carolina merchants, meant that the settlers of both the piedmont and the mountains maintained a connection with Virginia and South Carolina rather than with their own state. It meant, too, that the cattle and hides, meal, wheat, butter, hemp, and herbs of the piedmont farmers and the furs and deerskins of the mountain men reached Virginia cities and Charleston. There they were exchanged for the manufactured articles, salt, and sugar needed by the western settlers. But it meant even more, for where their trade went, there to a marked degree, went also the loyalties of an ever-increasing portion of North Carolinians.[13]

Another factor driving a wedge between east and west was the difference in national background and interests of the two sections. Eastern North Carolina, by the time of the Revolutionary War, was a fairly settled region. Its people were largely English (with several generations of established Colonial ancestors) and Scottish Highlanders, together with a small number of French Huguenots who had arrived in the early eighteenth century. Many easterners owned large estates, and there was a substantial merchant class in the port cities. Through trade, the easterners had kept in contact with England; their sons were educated abroad, their clothes imported, and their homes supplied with furniture, hangings, linens, pottery, and silver from the leading manufacturers of England and France. Imported foods and wines supplemented the products of their own fine gardens. They held slaves as house servants and as workers on their plantations, some of which were extensive.

In fact, the eastern section of the state had emerged from the pioneer stage and had attained a considerable degree of culture, with several fine private libraries, homes of architectural interest, and talk of an institution of higher learning. The cultured and wealthy class made up a decided minority of the state's eastern population, but at the same time, its members made up the ruling class. They dominated the General Assembly, which was held in the east, and succeeded in getting laws passed that benefited planters and merchants.[14]

All of this was in complete contrast with the mountain section. The men and women living there were nearly all newcomers. They were predominately Scotch-Irish, arriving over the mountains from Philadelphia, Charleston, or from older piedmont settlements. In addition, there were Germans from Pennsylvania, Welsh, Irish, and more than a sprinkling of English. Many of these were first generation, European immigrants, and on the frontier, both east and west of the Blue Ridge, they were going through the "melting pot" process of assimilation into an American society. For them the difficulty and cost of transportation prohibited all the luxuries and most of the necessities of life. Their actual wants were reduced to a minimum, for they were pioneers carving out a way of life in wilderness valleys isolated from each other by towering ridges and hills. In the struggle against the mountains and forests there was no place for fineries, and even while fighting the Indians to keep the plots they had cleared, they sensibly adopted many of the native American modes of living.

The mountain frontiersmen depended upon themselves for most of their manufactured articles, and were satisfied with the tools turned out at their forges and with the simple household effects that they put together. They were people of the forest, and the plantations of the east were outside their world and interests. They keenly felt that the danger from Indian attacks which hovered over them every hour of every day and night, an ever-present threat to life and to property, did not interest the eastern people or the state's eastern law makers. To them their own local government and their own militia were their assurance of life.[15]

Nor were these pioneers interested in slaves and the problems that slave holding involved. The economy of the mountains generated no need or desire for slaves. Small fields were cleared, a few at a time, and cared for by members of the families—always generous in number. Work, the hard work of a new country, was taken for granted and was to most of the settlers a challenge. When the crops were "laid by," there was hunting to be done by the men and spinning and weaving by the women. The neighboring settlers were always there to give a hand when work exceeded the strength of the family, while all rallied at the fort in times of danger to ward off Indian attacks. There was no class consciousness since all worked and all were poor in worldly goods but rich in energy and visions for the future. Each man was rated according to what he could do.

Still another factor in the grievances harbored by the

mountain settlers against the easterners was the matter of taxes. North Carolina in 1775 had been utterly unprepared for war and had emerged from the five-year conflict impoverished. In order to raise even a portion of its allotted soldiers for the Continental army, the new state had issued paper currency. Then with the cessation of all trade with England, the loss of bounties for naval stores, the lack of manufactures and with the general disruption of farm life and normal interstate trade, money became exceedingly scarce. The bills of credit issued by the state were made legal tender. But the state's paper money, like the currency issued by the Continental Congress, depreciated at an alarming rate, and prices soared to unheard of heights.

Since the early days North Carolinians had been opposed to taxation, but the harassed, newly-formed state found it necessary to levy taxes, increasing them from time to time as the war continued and again during the hard-pressed years of recovery. Poll taxes were the ones first levied, followed by a general assessment on all property—land, buildings, animals, slaves, and investments. These taxes proved difficult to collect, however, partly because of the people's resentment and partly because of the scarcity of specie. The returns to the state treasury were disappointingly small; therefore, in 1780 the General Assembly in desperation passed a law setting the ratio for taxes to be paid in produce.[16]

With the exception of state representatives and a few other leaders, the mountain pioneers did not understand the economic basis for the drastic tax measures taken by the state. They saw no returns from taxation in their own areas and felt that money was far too hard to come by to be sent out of the mountains as taxes that would be used to benefit the east. The tax rates, too, they considered unjust, since cheap land of the west was taxed at the same rate as the more valuable property of the east. Western settlers depended upon their few exports to obtain necessities. They, likewise, resented paying taxes in salable products.

Some of the westerners' complaints arose from the inefficiency and dishonesty of the local officers appointed by the government, but most of the grievances against their state grew out of geographic and economic conditions. These were problems identical to those faced by the piedmont pioneers following 1760. The Regulators, who had fled west of the mountains to escape taking the British oath of allegiance required after the Battle of Alamance, found themselves seething with the old

Regulator anger. Eventually, the westerners adopted much the same course of action taken earlier in the century by the protesters against English rule. With the success of the movement for American independence from England in mind, leaders west of the Blue Ridge began planning for independence from North Carolina.

Such a step was not as radical as it might at first glance seem, for during the formation of a federal government to be set up under the Articles of Confederation, representatives of the thirteen states to the Continental Congress wrangled over the question of western lands. Those commonwealths without claims to frontier territory feared the future power of sister states when their wilderness lands should be developed, and they insisted that all such territory belonged, in reality, to the new nation. Naturally those states with western claims held other views.

The heated discussions on this subject led to practical results of a compromise nature. The federal government recognized the rights of the individual states to their western lands but invited—urged would be a more apt term—those states to cede all such territory to the Republic. Several northern states responded to the appeal and in 1787 ceded western lands which the federal government accepted in 1789 as the Northwest Territory. During the agitation North Carolina had been urged to cede its territory west of the Blue Ridge, and the federal government continued to bring pressure to bear on the state.[17]

In the Constitution of 1776, North Carolina renewed its claims to all land granted to it as a colony under the Charter of 1663 and its additions in 1665. In so doing the state claimed the Pacific Ocean as its western boundary. But England in its treaty with France in 1763 had taken a more realistic view of those old claims "as farre as the Land extends itselfe" [sic] and had designated the Mississippi River as the western boundary of English territory. North Carolina made no attempt to enforce its claims to land beyond the "Father of Waters," and when in April 1784, the General Assembly agreed to cede its western lands to the United States, that river was its boundary.[18]

There was bitter opposition to the Cession Act, which offered the state's western land to the Republic. The law as passed, however, safeguarded the state from having the inhabitants and lands of the ceded territory increase its share of the national debt incurred during the Revolutionary War. It also provided that grants already made by North Carolina to its soldiers should be respected and that one or more states should be made from the area. A further precautionary clause was added. If the area were not accepted by the federal government within twelve months, it was to revert to the state of North Carolina, and in the meantime the state was to continue its control of the region. The Act reached Congress too late in that session to be acted upon, and its opponents gained enough strength in the interval to have it repealed when the General Assembly of North Carolina met in October.[19] It was at this session, in a gesture of appeasement, that the state's western counties were organized into the Washington District, made up of four counties.

As early as 1782 Colonel Arthur Campbell, a leader in the Watauga Settlements, proposed a meeting to determine the settlers' sentiment on the question of forming a new state. Nothing came of the proposal. But in August, 1784, after news of the Cession Act had crossed the mountains, a convention met at Jonesborough with John Sevier as presiding officer. Davidson County was not represented. A second convention met in December at which a constitution modeled after the 1776 North Carolina document was drawn up for six months' consideration and at which the proposed state received the name of Franklin. During this session news arrived of the repeal of the Cession Act. The disappointed delegates promptly sent a memorial or formal request to Congress asking that the territory be made into a state.

The convention and the memorial angered the easterners, and Governor Alexander Martin roundly censured Arthur Campbell as the instigator of the movement.[20] Campbell then withdrew from active leadership, but in March, 1785, a third convention at Jonesborough set up a government under the temporary constitution. John Sevier was elected governor. Correspondence between Governor Martin and "Governor" Sevier became equally bitter and threatening on both sides. But the unauthorized state continued to function locally, and Sevier concluded the Dumplin Creek Treaty between the new state of Franklin and the Cherokees of the Middle Towns. In May it sent still another request to Congress, and in August the Franklin Assembly met to adopt a permanent constitution.[21]

By this time the western settlers had split into two camps. Those led by Sevier claimed gross neglect on the part of North Carolina and demanded immediate secession from North Carolina, hoping for early recognition by the United States. Those under the leadership of Colonel John Tipton were equally eager for a new state but felt that its formation should come through the regular channels set up as national policy. Accordingly, this latter group advocated urging North Carolina to cede the territory to the Republic as Virginia had recently ceded its land of Kentucky. They favored the organization of a government that could function as soon as a new state should be authorized by Congress.

Confusion now entered the ranks of the pioneers as each faction drew up and adopted its own constitution. The document sponsored by the Sevier adherents and modeled after the North Carolina Constitution of 1776 was adopted in November, 1785, by the "State of Franklin." But for the next few years a virtual state of civil war existed in Western North Carolina, with some counties having two opposing sets of officers.[22]

Inevitably the difference between Sevier and Tipton and their respective followers increased in bitterness until it reached open conflict and the shedding of blood. In 1788 Sevier was arrested by Tipton enroute to Jonesborough and taken under guard to Morganton for trial as a traitor to North Carolina. But there Sevier was among friends of King's Mountain days. The irons were removed from his hands and two of the McDowell family put up bail. Dr. James Cozby arranged an escape, and when Sevier rode openly out of the village, Judge Waightstill Avery made no move to pursue him.

With Sevier's return to his home on the Nolichucky River, the period of civil strife continued while he and his militia carried on their campaigns against the Cherokees. To add to the general confusion, the Spanish, who controlled the mouth of the Mississippi River, threatened to close the river to American trade, an act that would vitally affect the new settlement at Nashville and those on the Cumberland River. Rumors circulated meanwhile of a possible new country to the west.[23]

The harassed State of North Carolina, bombarded by both Congress and the westerners with demands for ceding the area, answered by censuring the pioneer leaders and appealing to their followers. In 1788, as a gesture of conciliation, the General Assembly passed an "Act of Oblivion" covering the unhappy events of the past few years in the western settlements. But it charged that John Sevier could hold no more offices. Strangely enough, during the stormy existence of the "State of Franklin," except for a few months in late 1784, every western county in the new "state" was also represented in the General Assembly of

North Carolina. Among the representatives at times were both "Governor" John Sevier and John Tipton. Following the act debarring him from office holding, the undaunted Sevier appeared as usual at the next session of the North Carolina Assembly and was seated and became a delegate to the convention called to reconsider the state's ratification of the United States Constitution. He voted for ratification.[24]

By 1789 the opposition in the General Assembly to the cession of its westernmost lands was weakened, and the state offered the territory included in the old Washington County to the federal government without reservations. It was accepted and organized as the Territory South of the Ohio. In 1794 the Territory of Tennessee was formed, and William Blount was appointed by President Washington as the territorial governor. In the following year the territory became the state of Tennessee, the first new state to be admitted to the Union from ceded western lands. John Sevier was elected its first governor.[25]

Western North Carolina, which had at one time extended to the Pacific Ocean, had shrunk in 1763 to the Mississippi River and again in 1789 to its present western boundary. The state had lost most of the estimated 25,000 settlers living west of the Blue Ridge except for those along the Watauga River in the present Watauga County and those who had crossed the mountains after the Revolutionary War to take up land opened to soldiers and other settlers east of the ceded land.

The men over the mountains had been a continuous thorn in the flesh of the General Assembly of North Carolina. In addition, the state had been in a turmoil over the questions of whether to ratify the Constitution drawn up and adopted at the Philadelphia Convention in 1787. There was bitter opposition to it on the grounds that the central government for which it provided would restrict the rights of the state governments. It was also feared that under it agriculture would be sacrificed to business and industry, and that its methods of electing the president and senators would eliminate government by the direct vote of the people. Moreover, the new constitution had no bill of rights and failed to insure democratic principles vital to the young Republic.

It was not until July 21, 1788, that a convention to consider it met at Hillsboro. There the delegates drew up a bill of rights and passed a resolution stating the necessity for such a bill. They declared that after such a bill had been presented to Congress, there should be another federal convention called to consider needed changes. Not until that had taken place, the resolution stated, could North Carolina ratify the document.[26] But before the meeting at Hillsboro had opened, ten states had already ratified the constitution, one more than the required three-fourths majority. The new Constitution had already become the law of the land, and North Carolina, like Rhode Island, was a commonwealth unto itself, out of the union of states.

For a brief period, therefore, Western North Carolina was a part of an independent state. That was far from a desirable status, however, and on November 21, 1789, a second convention at Fayetteville voted by an overwhelming majority to ratify the Constitution. By this vote the present mountain counties became a part of the twelfth state in the Union.

CHAPTER NINE

In Search of Beauty—An Interlude

It is pleasant to contemplate that during the frenzied, war-torn years and the dreary time of recovery between 1760 and 1800, a few people entered Western North Carolina on missions other than those of profit or destruction. It is also encouraging to know that some white travelers had neither sinister intentions of exploiting the natives nor of planting unwanted settlers within the confines of the Indian nation. Some whites had no idea of persuading reluctant chiefs to sign their marks on papers, depriving the Principal People of century-old rights. These unusual "tourists" to the mountains were in search of beauty.

Early explorers, understandably enough, wrote rather copiously of the extreme hardships of travel across the towering ridges and through the mountain section. A few of them went no further in their description of the country; yet some of them interspersed their accounts of struggles against the mountainous terrain with expressions of appreciation for the majesty of the green-clad hills, the arched beauty of the domed balds, the lush greenness of the valleys, and the music of the rushing streams and rivers. Such descriptions reflect the sense of marvel the travelers experienced at the sight of the prodigal abundance and variety of vegetation with which nature had endowed Western North Carolina—vegetation which, during the long centuries of Indian occupancy, had not been mutilated or destroyed.

traders in the region. Surely, it must have been comparatively easy for colonial traders to transport and deliver goods to the Indian tribes south and east of the Blue Ridge, even to the Cherokees of the Lower Towns. But men like Ludovick Grant, James Beamer, Robert Bunning, and James Adair, as well as scores of others, after once entering the mountains of Western North Carolina were held there largely by the spell of the country. They endured the slow and tortuous travel along narrow, steep, mountain trading paths for the compensating satisfaction derived from the countryside itself. They became North Carolina's first white mountaineers.

The possibility of metal resources in the area had attracted the Spaniards to the mountains in the sixteenth century, undoubtedly the first white men to enter them. Later English and colonial explorers and travelers were ever on the alert for evidences of gold, silver, and other useful metals. Sir Alexander Cuming on his trip gathered rock specimens to have assayed in England, and John William Gerard deBrahm foresaw the extensive mining that could develop in Western North Carolina. He saw, too, the possibilities of the rich, varied vegetation, once the land came into the hands of the Europeans. Soldiers who were brought into the region by the campaigns against the natives, like Henry Timberlake, wrote of the wealth of products already produced by the Cherokees and spoke of the beautiful gems reputedly held by the Indians for their ceremonial rites.

From these travelers and from accounts given by traders during their occasional trips to port cities, citizens of Charleston and Virginia cities learned of the riches locked in the hills. They also learned of the beauty of the towering ranges and the lush valleys. Merchants and officials traveling to England spread the news of the treasures to be found in Western North Carolina.

So it was that Josiah Wedgwood, English manufacturer of fine, semi-vitrified pottery and of the nation's most prized chinaware, learned of a superior grade of clay that the Cherokee Indians of Western North Carolina owned and possibly mined. After testing a sample obtained from the area, he realized that the American product was vastly superior to the clays he was using. He resolved upon an expensive course of action to get a sufficient quantity of it to make more beautiful and lovely and delicate the products of his factory that were finding their way into the palaces of royalty and the homes of the discriminating and wealthy. Accordingly, in 1767 he hired Thomas Griffiths of

Charleston to make what arrangements were necessary with the Cherokees to procure a supply of the Indian clay.

With Grant's destructive raid still fresh in their memories and protected by King George's line of demarcation at the Blue Ridge, the Cherokees were unwilling to have white men other than traders enter their territory. But Griffiths undertook the mission and left Charleston in October for the mountains. He had been told that the clay would be found in the Joree mountains—now called Cowee—near an Indian village named Ayoree. Within a month he had located the mine and had made an agreement with the Indians to buy a quantity of the clay. Gaining that agreement had not been easy, for in addition to their reluctance to bargain with any white man, the Cherokees were suspicious of any one coming for clay since, as they told Griffiths, white men had been there before for this purpose and had taken off much fine clay with only promises as payment. But this Englishman proved to be a man of tact and diplomacy. He conveyed to the chiefs that he had come from the English King, who a few years before had been happy to entertain their Great Warrior, Ostenaco. With good will thus restored, Griffiths was allowed to proceed with his mission.[1]

For three days he and his men worked strenuously to remove the debris in the pit. He estimated that before reaching the object of their search they took out ten or twelve tons of rubbish and dirt, evidence that the Indians had not used any of this clay for some years. It was also evident that earlier people, perhaps whites, had removed a considerable amount at some time. When Griffiths was ready to excavate what he planned to mine, a period of autumn rains set in, which he and his men endured with impatience. When conditions again allowed digging, he found it necessary to discard what he had and replenish his supply. Then he loaded the precious earth—five tons of it—on the backs of stout little pack horses, some 150 to 200 pounds to the horse. He paid the Cherokees for their fine product, and set out in a long caravan for Fort Prince George where the loads were taken by wagon to Charleston. By the time slowly drawn wagons reached the port city, it was February, and Griffiths gave himself a month's holiday in the active little city before taking the clay to England.

In England much interest attached to the import from Western North Carolina; even the King made inquiries about its use. The reply sent to his Majesty by the artist-manufacturer was that the American clay was used in every piece of his jaspers, his finest products. He rightly foresaw that these would need only time and scarcity to command any price one might ask for them. Today a marker designates the site in Western North Carolina, near Burningtown, where Josiah Wedgwood got the supply of fine clay which under his master hand, became the prized possessions of kings and noblemen.[2]

Seven years later, the first of several botanists to visit Western North Carolina came to revel in its spring splendor and to gather and classify many of its rare plants. He was William Bartram, a Quaker, of Philadelphia, and his trip was sponsored by Dr. John Fothergill, a well known Quaker physician of London. Eighteenth century Europeans were garden-conscious, and in the second half of the century a craze for formal gardens with sweeping vistas and with unusual hedges arranged in intriguing mazes spread over England and the continent. Even earlier there had been an awakening to the decorative possibilities of both the garden and the flower arrangements it afforded for the home. This had given rise to the profession of nurserymen. In 1730, for example, Robert Furber of Kensington published a catalogue, not only listing the plants and shrubs he handled, but also containing prints of flower arrangements suitable for home decorations each month of the year.

Housewives of all classes were soon getting flowers from their cutting gardens and grouping them in a variety of containers—Wedgwood jaspers, brass, porcelain, glass, delft bricks, fingered posey holders—to add to the interest of their rooms. Owners of fine gardens became intrigued with the idea of new and startling effects and sought strange and exotic plants and shrubs from distant countries with which to add charm and distinction to their grounds. This interest in landscaping spread to the colonies, and many are the accounts in old ledgers of orders made by colonial planters and farmers for European fruit trees, ornamental shrubs, and rare plant seeds. Both George Washington and Thomas Jefferson, farmers of Virginia, recorded the pleasure with which they received such orders and the care which they bestowed upon their imported plants.[3]

But the transfer of flowers, shrubs, fruit trees, and ornamental plants was far from one-sided. English and European garden owners were held spellbound by stories of nature's lavishness in plant forms in the southern colonies. Now and then one was willing to incur the expense of sending a botanist-collector to the region for specimens with which to "embellish" his estate. Interest in botany was rather widespread, and the work of

Linnaeus in 1753 greatly aided botanists in making accurate records of their findings. He established a binomial system of nomenclature, giving each plant and animal two names, one for the genus or family and one for the species or individual.[4]

In America the best known botanists and nurserymen were the Bartrams of Kingsessing, Pennsylvania, whose fine gardens were visited by Europeans and colonists alike. John, the father, and his son, William, were scholars and were continuously gathering and classifying the rich plant offerings of America. They were in constant correspondence with English horticulturists and gardeners and had a large group of English patrons like Peter Collinson, Quaker wool merchant of London. Collinson not only bought from them American plants, shrubs, and seeds, but also introduced these imports to other garden lovers.

Prospering in their business, the Bartrams opened a second garden in Charleston. In 1773 the firm was commissioned by Dr. Fothergill to search in Florida, the western Carolinas, and Georgia for rare and useful flora, which the London physician wished to use in his garden at Upton, near Stratford. That garden was the physician's prize possession, for in variety of specimens and beauty it rivaled the Kew Gardens. It may be that Fothergill also hoped to find some new medicinal herbs among the collections sent by the Bartrams. For several years, then, either John or William Bartram, occasionally both, made excursions into the designated areas with rich flora rewards.[5]

It fell to the lot of William, in 1775, to make the western trip that would take him into Western North Carolina. On April 22, he set out from Charleston. He was at this time thirty-six years old, a man of learning and charm and with the deep respect for people that his Quaker beliefs inspired. He was supplied with letters of introduction to the Agent of Indian Affairs and was well provided by temperament with a love for adventure and a keen appreciation of the beauties of nature. Moreover, he had a flair for transferring his enthusiasm and delight to the pages of his notebooks and from them to the record he later wrote. This account must have given sheer pleasure to the eighteenth century reader as it does to the modern historian.[6]

From Charleston, Bartram followed the old trading route along the Savannah River, veering off at times to make observations and to gather specimens. By this route he came to Keowee, the new Keowee that had risen after the destruction of the old capital in 1760. After some time spent in this area, Bartram

APPALACHIAN NATIONAL PARKS ASSOCIATION COLLECTION, N. C.
DEPARTMENT OF ARCHIVES AND HISTORY

A Carpet of Ferns: Open glades in the forest provide room for the waving plumes of ferns. William Bartram on his journey through the mountains of Western North Carolina doubtless saw and delighted in such displays.

did not wait for the return of the hunter who was to conduct him over the mountains, but went on alone. He must have felt uneasy as he entered a wild, lonely country whose inhabitants, he knew, were becoming increasingly unfriendly to the whites and who certainly would be suspicious of a stranger who peered around rocks and gathered plants and roots.

Bartram realized how terrible had been the animosity between the races fifteen years before as he passed the desolate ruins of towns and orchards in the Lower Cherokee lands where the forces of Colonel Middleton had struck telling blows. His record remarks that Fort Prince George, across from Keowee, now bore little resemblance to a fort and was used only as a trading post. Bartram also wrote that the old Keowee, which had once strung along six or eight miles of the river, was now only the tattered remains typifying the fall of a once mighty race. He knew, however, that there was still strength enough in the Cherokees to flare up into real war. But it was the month of May, and the mountainsides were aflame with azalea blooms, and the meadows were a rich carpet of ripe strawberries. He put aside his misgivings and turned his attention to the beauties of nature and the pleasantness of his task.

Later in the wilds of Western North Carolina Bartram found hospitality awaiting him. He spent the first night in the area—May 21—within the shelter of a hunter's cabin a mile or so north of the Georgia line. The next afternoon, quite by chance, he met a white trader who took the botanist to his home for the night. The following morning, fortified with a hearty and delicious breakfast, he went on to Estatoe and then on the three miles to Nikwasi. A few miles farther he reached Whatoga, where the chief of the village, a gracious host, smoked a four-foot peace pipe with him and then accompanied him for some miles on his way to Cowee, at the present West's Mill.

Cowee, he found, was a town of about one hundred houses built along the Little Tennessee River and was at this time the capital of the Middle Cherokees. There, through the letters he carried, he met and was most cordially entertained by a greatly respected and trusted Irish trader named Galahan, who had long lived in the mountains. After an agreeable visit in Galahan's home and after his rambles about the area (during which he made observations and classified flora), Bartram set out alone on the path along the Little Tennessee and across the Nantahala Mountains toward the Over Hill Towns.

Twice during his progress along the trading route the botanist had occasion to feel alarm. He records that, once, while resting, he was surprised by the unannounced appearance of a young Indian, rifle in hand and accompanied by his dogs. But his fears proved groundless, for the hunter, after asking some questions, accepted tobacco that Bartram proffered him, shook hands with the white man, and proceeded "chearfully" on his way.

The second occasion also came suddenly. According to his account, he saw to his dismay a company of mounted Cherokees approaching along the narrow path. As they neared him, he saw that the central figure was Attakullakulla, or "Little Carpenter." With the courtesy that was a part of his nature, Bartram turned off the path to let the party pass. The "Grand Old Man" of the Cherokees was touched by this gesture of respect and drew up his horse. Clapping his hand to his own heart, he then offered it to Bartram in the Cherokee symbol of friendship and introduced himself. The botanist responded, saying that he was from

APPALACHIAN NATIONAL PARKS ASSOCIATION COLLECTION, N. C.
DEPARTMENT OF ARCHIVES AND HISTORY

Carolina Clouds: Witnessing scenes like this, early botanists and other scientists coming into the mountains must have felt they were indeed above the clouds. After a violent thunderstorm, William Bartram noted in his Journal that the mists "Smoaked (sic) through the valley and over the resounding hills."

Pennsylvania where the name of Attakullakulla was revered and where the Cherokees were considered brothers of the white men. The chief then inquired of John Stuart, Superintendent of Indian Affairs, saying that he was even then on his way to Charleston to see Stuart. Bartram in turn explained that he carried letters of friendship to the Indians from Stuart. After these pleasant remarks, the old chief welcomed Bartram to his country, and the party continued on its way while the scientist resumed his journey to the Over Hill Towns.

He again became uneasy, and as he rode along the feeling of disquiet increased. He knew that Attakullakulla was on a mission to Charleston, hoping to gain a peaceful settlement of the strained relations existing between his people and the whites; he knew, too, that the fine old Peacemaker would fail to obtain his desires. Already Bartram had much information about this region and had a goodly supply of specimen—plants, roots, some seeds—to dry for the Bartram herbarium of American flora. He had classified dozens of plants and trees. It seemed pointless to go into the Over Hill section, where the feelings against the Americans were especially strong. Obeying his better judgment, Bartram turned back, retracing his route to Keowee and from there to Charleston. In the present Swain County on the highway that follows the ancient Cherokee trading route a simple marker calls attention to the spot at which two great men met on that day in late May. It reads: "William Bartram, Philadelphia naturalist, author, exploring this area, met the Cherokee chief Attakullakulla, May, 1776, near here." The year 1776 is doubtless an error made by Bartram in writing his account from notes taken on the trip. Those notes give the year as 1775. In June, 1776, the Cherokee warriors went on the warpath against white settlements. No white person would have been safe that May in Cherokee territory.

During his mountain journey nothing escaped the alert eyes of the scientist, and with the keen joy of discovery he filled his notebooks with delightful details that, transferred to his account of the journey, enable the reader today to meet a vivid personality pulsating with life. His first view of Western North Carolina he got from the mountain he called Magnolia. From its top he looked in awe across the "Vale of Tenase" (Tennessee River valley), and he watched the clear water splash down Estatoe Falls. Later he paused to revel in the beauty of the "Vale of Cowee." Into his notebooks went not only the records of his findings and the classification of plants, but also remarks, it would seem, concerning all the objects he saw—and he saw everything.

Bartram wrote of the delight he felt in seeing herds of deer, flocks of wild turkeys, the flashing wings of soaring birds, and of hearing the rich melody of their songs. His account describes the Cassine yapon, which the Cherokees considered a sacred tree, the rose rhododendron, and brings to life the astonishing variations in the shades and hues of the blooming wild azaleas and the delicacy of tiny mountain flowers. He transferred to paper the amazement he experienced in seeing such a variety of trees and the sublimity of the magnificent forests through which he passed. In crossing the mountains he had for the first time the unforgetable experience of seeing May disappear before his eyes until, upon reaching the top of the range, he was in late winter. Even a sudden and violent thunderstorm which drenched him could not dampen his spirits,

CLINE STUDIOS

Azaleas: The botanist, William Bartram, in the western mountains in May, 1775, reveled in the beauty of the spring flowers. He wrote that the flame azaleas, splashing the mountainsides with their vivid colors, gave the mountains "the appearance of being on fire."

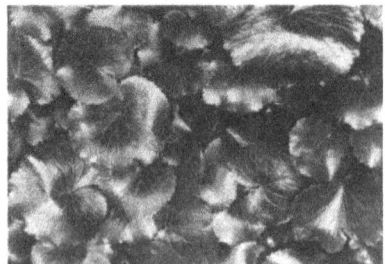

HUGH MORTON PHOTOS

Indian Pipes: The nodding Indian Pipes find their homes in nonacid humus. As plants of the woods, they refuse to be cultivated; *Rhododendron:* In the spring the white blooms of the Rhododendron Maximum reward travelers trudging rocky mountain byways; *Galax:* The shining leaves of the galax delight those coming to the mountains in search of beauty as William Bartram came in 1775. Today "galackers" find a ready market for these leaves.

and he notes that it "Smoaked through the valley and over the resounding hills."[7] He mentions the glitter of mica and the sylvan charm of a group of native American maidens gathering wild strawberries and then splashing in the waters of a nearby stream.

Bartram was alive, too, to the cultivation in the area, apparently surprised that he found so many fields. He reported that the soil was rich and fertile and noted the fields of beans and corn. He spent some time admiring the fine horses in a trader's "horse stamp." These animals, he was told, would be taken to Charleston for sale. His curiosity about Indian life led him to investigate and record his impressions of the villages he entered. He was very interested in the large, domed council house he saw in the village of Whatoga and noted that it was on an artificial mound. He passed and made note of the clay pit from which, he said, clay had been taken to England. The fine foods served him by the Cherokee wives of his trader hosts came in for comment, and his *Journal* shows that he especially enjoyed the wild strawberries covered with rich cream that they gave him.

Yet in the midst of all this natural prodigality in which his very soul rejoiced, Bartram was saddened by the evidences he saw of what man had done to man in this majestic region. Soberly he viewed the rock-covered graves and the resting places of both whites and Indians who had given their lives in the two battles of Echoee during the "Cherokee War". He was appalled by the desolate ruins of the towns and orchards and of homes never rebuilt after Grant's march through the hills. Fortunately he could not foresee that further destruction would come to the hills in the autumn of 1776 when General Rutherford's punitive forces would arrive in retaliation for the summer attacks by Cherokee warriors on homes and villages of white settlers.

In England in 1791 the account of his plant discoveries and his plant classifications in Western North Carolina, written from his notebooks, appeared in his *Travels Through North and South Carolina, Georgia, East and West of the Muscogules or Creek Confederacy, and the Country of the Choctaws*. In this volume also appeared the most complete and accurate list of American birds made up to that time. Through his account the entire region and age spring back into life, and it is surely permissible to assume that as he left this mountain country, he paused again on the summit of his Magnolia Mountain for a final view of the azaleas, splashing the sides of the mountain ranges with a kaleidoscope of flame and red and orange. As he remarked, they gave the region the appearance of being on fire.

After the Revolutionary War the French botanist, Andre Michaux, came to America on a mission sponsored by the French government to study and collect American plants. This was in 1785, and with the wealth of material to be found in the new republic, Michaux established a nursery at Bergen, New Jersey. To it he brought a vast variety of plants, shrubs, and trees, and from it he shipped choice specimens to his native country to be used in the garden of Rambouillet and Versailles. Two years later, he opened a second nursery at Charleston. That same year he followed the route taken by Bartram and entered Western North Carolina from Georgia, studying the flora along the Tennessee River.

In the autumn of 1788 Michaux returned to Western North Carolina, this time veering north from the route and going to Camden, South Carolina, and then along the Catawba River. He made observations and classified plants around Morganton and Turkey Cove. He then crossed the Blue Ridge, exploring Yellow Mountain and later that year returned to the area by way of Charlotte, exploring the Blue Ridge and along the Toe River. Again in 1793 the French botanist was on a western trip, this time going as far as Nashville, Tennessee. Two years later, he visited Western North Carolina for the last time, covering the territory around Linville, Roan, and Yellow Mountains.[8]

Francois Andre Michaux accompanied his father on some of the later trips and after his father's death in 1802 was sent back to America to study the forest of the country. Commissioned by the French Minister of the Interior, he explored fairly extensively in Western North Carolina, covering the area east of the French Broad River, Roan, Grandfather, the Black, Yellow, and Indian Mountains, and Table Rock. From that section the younger Michaux headed east over the Blue Ridge to Charlotte and then back to Charleston. Both of the French botanists wrote of their American discoveries and explorations. Andre published a volume entitled *The History of North American Oaks,* which was used later by his son in writing his book, *Sylva Americana.*[9]

Still another naturalist was John Fraser, who explored the southern states during the years when one or both of the Michaux were carrying on their Western North Carolina observations. He was a Scottish botanist with a nursery at Chelsea, England. In the last years of the eighteenth century he had gone to Russia, where he had interested the aged Catherine in new and foreign plants. After her death Fraser was appointed by Paul, her successor, as his botanical collector and in that capacity traveled in search of specimens with which to fill Russian gardens.

Upon Paul's death, however, Fraser was not reappointed to that position, and in 1802 he came to America. He had been in America earlier, engaging in botanical research in South Carolina in 1785 and again in 1789, going west until he entered the mountains of Western North Carolina. In 1799 he was making observations around Roan and Grandfather Mountains, and he recorded that from the top of Roan he had been elated at gazing into five states—Virginia, Kentucky, Tennessee, North, and South Carolina.[10]

These early botanists would, of course, be followed by others, but they laid the firm foundation for any study of plant life in Western North Carolina that might be undertaken. It was the Bartrams who found and classified the Lost Camellia or Franklin Tree, and it was Andre Michaux who in 1788 discovered the rare Shortia, a discovery that was of great interest to scientists for a hundred years. Michaux found the plant only in its fruit stage, however, and botanists needed to see it in bloom in order to complete a life cycle description of it. It was not until 1877 that the delicate plant was found in North Carolina in full bloom. In addition, Fraser discovered on one of his explorations into this section of North Carolina the glorious rhododendron that he named the Catawbensis. The work of these men, together with the specimens they sent to various countries of Europe familiarized hundreds of people with the beauty of the mountains and attracted their attention to Western North Carolina.

CHAPTER TEN

With Their Goods and Chattels

The position of the Cherokees in Western North Carolina has from colonial times been a confused one. Their struggle against the encroaching white race was basically a desperate attempt to maintain their rights and status as a nation with a recognized national territory. Neither the English government nor the French respected this right of domain, and both included the area in their claims to American lands. The issue became more confused when England split the Cherokee nation into two units in separating the two Carolinas. Under a decidedly complicated and contradictory policy, both the Carolina colonies and the English government had the power of treaty making, thus tacitly acknowledging that the Indians were a responsible government unit, if not an independent nation.

The Crown reserved the right of designating a boundary line between the races beyond which the colonists were forbidden to settle. But this responsibility was complicated by the Granville Grant that extended across the northern portion of North Carolina. Over this area North Carolina had no jurisdiction. Nor was the line of demarcation between Cherokees and whites strictly enforced, for the Watauga settlers crossed the Blue Ridge after that line was drawn and were allowed to retain the land that they cleared there. Moreover, this group of settlers made treaties with the Cherokees by which they purchased settlement rights and fixed boundaries without benefit of colonial or English sponsorship. The new state of North Carolina further divided the

the boundary line between the new state and the western territory passed through the Cherokee domain.

Under both the Articles of Confederation and the Constitution, each state was given control over the native American lands within its borders, but the federal government reserved to itself the power of treaty making with the tribes and nations. Under this arrangement, North Carolina was free to dispose of lands declared by the United States Government as cleared of Indian occupancy. The state tried to restrain its westward-bound settlers from infringing beyond the boundary limits, even though, as in 1785, the federal treaty narrowed the zone earlier declared open by the state.

During the Revolutionary War, North Carolina had confiscated the Granville Grant, declaring the land not already allotted to settlers to be the domain of the state. That tract and its western lands available to white settlers offered to the hard-pressed state government a possible means of recuperating its depleted treasury. These areas also offered a means of paying its veterans of the recent war. It was largely for these reasons that the ceding of North Carolina's western lands to the Republic had been vigorously opposed, especially by the easterners. In 1780 the state took the first step in making use of the Cherokee country for the whites; the General Assembly passed the Bonus Act, which set aside an area to be reserved for veterans' grants, both those of the state's militia and those in the state's quota in the Continental army. In 1782 a supplementary act set the scale for the land allotments. Grants allowed to individuals ranged from 640 acres for privates to 12,000 acres for brigadier-generals.[1]

Following the passage of these laws, a commission was appointed to survey soldier claims. Many veterans took advantage of the Bonus Law, taking up land in Western North Carolina, some of which later became a part of Tennessee. Other lands cleared of Indians were soon opened to white civilians. This westward migration of both soldiers and civilians was given impetus by two treaties made between the federal government and the Cherokees. Under the terms of the Holston Treaty drawn up in 1791 at White's Ford, at the present Knoxville, Tennessee, the Indians gave up their claims to lands along the French Broad and lower Holston Rivers. This area included the sites of the present Knoxville and Greeneville, Tennessee, and Asheville, North Carolina.

The second treaty, concluded in 1798, pushed the Cherokee

boundary westward to approximately the western boundaries of the present Haywood and Transylvania Counties.[2] Thus, a decade before the beginning of the new century, the double barrier of towering mountains and the presence of hostile Indians, who for a century and a half had halted the white man's compelling urge to go west, had been conquered. Into the fertile valleys of the mountain country streamed men with their guns and axes, their little bundles of household effects, their wives and children. They were coming to these ancient hills to stay.

North Carolina had earlier taken cognizance of the rapid settlement of the territory just east of the Blue Ridge. Land there had been opened to settlers since Tryon's line of demarcation of 1767; however, a sprinkling of westward-bound men and women had selected homesites and built their cabins at the very foothills of the mountains before that date.

Just when the earliest of these pioneers arrived is not known. But during the third decade of the century a few hardy frontiersmen were in the Yadkin valley, and a small number had settled on land west of the Catawba River. By 1740 the Brittain community in the present Rutherford County was the nucleus around which newcomers took holdings, and in 1742 at least one settler, Heinrich Weidner, and possibly others had taken up land in the present Burke County.[3] During the next score of years these early settlers were joined by hundreds of immigrants who streamed into the "back country" from Philadelphia and Charleston until the valleys of the streams flowing east from the Blue Ridge were dotted with the log cabins of those crowding westward. These small pioneer communities weathered the attacks and massacres of the Cherokees during the French and Indian War. They were protected, although inadequately, by forts erected by the government or by the settlers themselves, such as Fort McGaughey near Brittain Church, Fort McFadden near the present Rutherfordton, or Fort Davidson, for some years the most westerly of English forts.

As early as 1769 settlers along the upper Yadkin River petitioned the colonial government to be organized as a county. Yet it was not until January 26, 1771, that the authorization bill was passed creating Surry County from the northern section of Rowan County. That bill designated that the county court should be held at the home of Gideon Wright on the east bank of the Yadkin River. The bill also appointed Griffith Rutherford as one of the commissioners charged with surveying the boundary line between Surry and Rowan Counties.

The new county was named for the Earl of Surrey. It extended westward to the Indian nation and took in a territory along the Watauga, the Holston, the Nolichucky, and the Clinch Rivers. Later, portions of Surry territory would be formed into new counties, while another section would become a part of the state of Tennessee. Over a period of years the seat of county government shifted from one small village to another. Then Dobson was selected as the permanent county seat and a courthouse was there built.

Settlers in the new county were caught up in the Regulator movement and in May, 1771, a group of men went to join men from other counties who were gathering at Alamance Creek to confront Governor Tryon's militia. The Surry men, however, arrived too late to take part in the two-hour conflict known as the Battle of Alamance. But they were not too late to be forced to subscribe to an oath of allegiance to the colonial government.

During the Cherokee uprising in 1776, several hundred men from Surry County, under Colonel Joseph Williams, joined the militia led by Colonel William Christian against the Cherokee Over Hill towns. There they brought widespread destruction to that section of the Cherokee nation. Other Surry men were in General Griffith Rutherford's punitive expedition against the Cherokee Middle towns.

Throughout the Revolutionary War the county was the scene of conflicting loyalties. Many of the Scottish Highlanders who had earlier settled in the area remained loyal to the king and to the oath of allegiance that some of them had been forced to take following the Battle of Culloden Field. Governor Josiah Martin in 1775 stated that Surry was one of four counties that had made written pledges of allegiance to the colonial government and the English King. Gideon Wright became one of the county's most active Loyalists, while Tory sentiment was strengthened through the influence of David Fanning and the activities of his Loyalist militia.

On October 8, 1780, Tories and Patriots clashed in an encounter at Shallow Ford (now in Yadkin County). Later that month some 160 Patriots led by Major Joseph Cloyd, defeated a gathering of Tories. Yet English sympathizers continued to keep conditions in the county unstable and in both the Battle of King's Mountain and the later Battle of Guilford Court House men from Surry fought on both sides. This division of loyalty existed

FROM STATE MAGAZINE, MARCH 17, 1951
N. C. DEPARTMENT OF ARCHIVES AND HISTORY

King's Mountain: This view of King's Mountain is from the valley below. The flag on the summit of the mountain marks the site of the battlefield.

throughout the western settlements, creating conditions that would be long in the healing.

At King's Mountain, however, Surry Patriots outnumbered the Surry Loyalists in Ferguson's forces. In response to Ferguson's demand for surrender, men from Surry under Major Joseph Winston, together with men from Wilkes County under Colonel Benjamin Cleveland, totaling about 350, joined the Overmountain men on their way to meet Ferguson's army. They took part in the Battle of King's Mountain. Both Major Winston and Colonel Cleveland, for the gallantry they and their men displayed in that battle, were later awarded swords by the new state of North Carolina.

By the outbreak of the Revolutionary War, the ever-increasing number of settlers now at the very foothills of the Blue Ridge clamored for the formation of new counties. Their arguments for establishing new governmental units were in all instances the same—their distance from the county seats. With the lack of roads, distance was a telling argument, and the law creating Rutherford County recognized its validity by stating in its first clause:"...the large extent of the County of Tryon renders the attendance of the inhabitants on the extreme parts of said county to do publick [sic] duties extremely difficult and expensive."[4] The newly organized state of North Carolina answered the pleas of the frontiersmen by forming three counties. In 1777 Burke County was created from the sprawling Rowan County, with Morganton as its county seat. The following year Wilkes County was formed from Yadkin with Wilkesboro as its county seat, both county and village honoring John Wilkes.

Wiping out the name of Tryon, which to many Patriots was synonymous with tyranny and oppression, the General Assembly in 1778 separated Tryon County into two divisions, designating that portion lying west of the Catawba River and south of the old Granville line as Rutherford County. The name honored Griffith Rutherford, hero of the Revolutionary campaign against the Cherokees. The county seat was for some years Gilbert Town; however, when the new court house was constructed in 1785, the present Rutherfordton came into being, known first as Rutherford Town.[5] As soon as possible after the acts creating them, the new counties set up their county courts with the voters meeting in convenient homes. It was not until sometime after the Revolutionary War that permanent court houses were constructed.

All three counties extended across the Blue Ridge and included the Cherokee country not yet opened to white settlement.[6] These new counties were caught in the lawlessness attending the last years of the Revolutionary War, a lawlessness that increased as Ferguson's army moved in. Neither the county governments nor the county militia units could check the sporadic acts of depredation committed as Patroits and Loyalists, often neighbors, sought vengeance upon each other. Several citizens, through their personal influence, were the preservers of law during these troubled months. The success of the forces of the hillmen at King's Mountain had a quieting effect upon Tory activities. Some Loyalists, fearing the wrath of the Patriots, fled into the mountains or crossed the Blue Ridge into the western sections of their counties.

After the war, many veterans and their families crossed the mountains into the present Watauga County and on to the Toe River valley. Coming from settlements in the Yadkin valley and from eastern North Carolina, Virginia, and Pennsylvania by way of the Pennsylvania Road, they found that a few settlers had preceded them. Who these were is not known, but some had entered the region before the battle of King's Mountain and had joined the Watauga men on their way to fight Ferguson. Others had come shortly after that battle. James Holtzclaw in 1780 and

Thomas Hodges in 1781 built cabins in the Valle Crucis area. William Miller, Nathan Horton, Ebeneazer Fairchild, and a Captain Jackson soon followed, and by 1790 there was a goodly sprinkling of newcomers in what is now Watauga County.[7]

The federal census of that year listed eighty families in the Toe River valley, making an estimated population of three hundred. This fertile region had early attracted hunters and herders, and it is probable that a few tiny cabins had been erected even before 1778. In that year, having confiscated the Granville Tract, the General Assembly made an effort to protect settlers in the Cherokee country by opening to white settlement all lands north of the divide between the Swannanoa and Toe Rivers and westward to include all known white settlements. By the end of that year four large grants of land in the Toe River valley had been made to John McKnitt Alexander and William Sharpe, who took them out as speculation land and did not take personal possession of them.

In March of the following year Samuel Bright, a Loyalist, settled on land granted him near McKinney Gap. In addition to his hunting and bit of farming, he acted as a guide to men passing through the valley to the Watauga Settlements or to the land of Kentucky. The road he followed, no more than a trail but later to be known as a wagon road, was called Bright's Trail. Other settlers followed Bright into the region, the earliest being a group of Williams—William Wiseman, William Davenport, William Davis, and William Pendley. Together with those who later scaled the precipitous eastern slopes of the Blue Ridge and entered the valleys by way of McKinney and Gillespie Gaps, they took up the task of making life in this mountain-rimmed valley a self-sufficient one. Life for them was made up of hunting and trapping and clearing the land for the raising of needed crops. To a far greater degree than was true with most sections of Western North Carolina, the Toe River valley was a unit unto itself and was destined to remain so for many years to come.[8]

During the war years settlers along the Catawba and Broad Rivers must have looked with covetous eyes toward the mountain barriers, and almost certainly a few had now and then crossed the Blue Ridge to hunt in the mountain sections of their counties. News of the state's law opening up land to settlers in those areas was received with enthusiasm by some of these daring individuals, and they lost no time in taking advantage of it. The first of those known to have taken his family from Rutherford County due west across the Blue Ridge was Samuel Davidson, a member of the Davidson family that had earlier settled along the Catawba River. It was a family who had played a significant role in the history of that region. Its members, Patriots all, had taken part in the Revolutionary War.

In 1784 Davidson crossed the Blue Ridge by way of Swannanoa Gap and built his cabin at the foot of Jonas Mountain. To this new home he brought his wife, baby, and a Negro house servant, and he cleared land for his fields. This area was "cleared of Indians," although the ruins of a former village could be seen where the Swannanoa River empties into the French Broad River. The region had once been a part of the Cherokees' vast hunting domain, and this fact soon spelled tragedy for the young veteran. A band of Indian hunters saw smoke coming from the chimney of a white man's cabin, and removing the bell from his horse, the Cherokees lured Davidson up the side of Jonas Mountain where from ambush they shot him.

Hearing the rifle shot, the wife and servant hid during the day and then they made their way over the mountains to the fort. Some members of the Davidson family and some friends returned to find the body. After burying it, they searched for and found the Cherokees, some of whom they killed. So it was that the first attempt at a settlement southwest of the Blue Ridge was baptized with the blood of both races.

In less than a year Major William Davidson, the twin brother of the slain Samuel, and Rachel Alexander, his sister, along with their families and several of their friends crossed the Blue Ridge from the Catawba settlements to take up grants of land where Bee Tree Creek enters the Swannanoa River. In 1787 William and James Davidson were granted 640 acres of land on both sides of the Swannanoa. To this valley came other families—the William Gudgers from the Watauga Settlements, the William Forsters from Virginia, the John Pattons, the Robert Pattons, and James Patton. The Bee Tree and Swannanoa settlements soon became the nucleus of a new county.

Additional newcomers went into other areas, taking up land in the fertile valleys. Colonel David Vance, coming from Burke County, got a grant in Reems Creek valley. There he found that a few settlers had preceded him. Among these was John Weaver, probably the first white man to build his cabin in that area. Settlers continued to arrive in that valley, while still others took out claims in the Beaverdam valley. Among these were George

BOB LINDSEY PHOTO, ASHEVILLE CHAMBER OF COMMERCE

Mt. Pisgah: General Griffith Rutherford and his force of some 2,400 men passed this towering mountain on their punitive expedition against the Cherokees in 1776. To the veterans crossing the Blue Ridge after 1783 this 5,745 foot peak became a landmark. It was later given the name Pisgah, the biblical mountain from which Moses viewed the Holy Land. An enthusiastic guest at one of the later hotels declared that a view of Pisgah was "more effective than a dozen sermons."

DEPARTMENT OF ARCHIVES AND HISTORY

Pioneers from the Rutherfordton area, in crossing the Blue Ridge, followed this lovely Broad River and passed through Hickory Nut Gorge.

Swain, David Killian, and in 1793, Bedent Baird. These two settlements were in Burke County, while the Bee Tree and Swannanoa settlements were in Rutherford County.[9]

Other men chose their tracts of land around the present Asheville. Zebulon Baird, brother of Bedent, built his home near the French Broad River, while John Burton got several tracts, one of which was on the site of the present Asheville.[10] To the south other communities were developing. William Mills (his Loyalist father had been a victim of the Patriots' wrath following the battle of King's Mountain) took out land along the river that today bears his name. Samuel Edney also made his home in what is now Henderson County and became the first resident Methodist minister southwest of the Blue Ridge.[11] Others took out grants near the present Saluda. One of those was John Morris, probably the brother of Robert Morris, who had spent his energies and his fortune in the cause of American freedom. The extensive grants given him by the grateful new Government were both east and west of the Blue Ridge.

The call westward was a strong one, and some of the men crossing the mountains went beyond the little communities already formed to get claims farther west. One of these was William Moore. In 1787 he was granted land in the Hominy Creek section, where he and his men had camped on their mission against the Cherokees along the Tuckaseigee River in 1776. On this 450 acre tract he built his home and near it raised a small fort for protection against possible Indian raids. Today this is the site of the Enka Corporation. Moore was later granted land farther to the west. Settlers continued to enter the mountains, and in the same year that Moore was building his cabin, Jonathan McPeters was farming land on the site of the present Canton. When David Nelson, his bound servant, completed his indentureship, he in turn settled on Jonathan Creek. Here to the Pigeon River valley also came John Davidson, James Chambers, Robert Martin, and John Gooch. Other settlers followed.[12]

Still farther west were the extensive grants given to Colonel Robert Love and his brother, General Thomas Love. They made their homes on Richland Creek. The settlement that developed in that area became the nucleus of a community that would in time demand a new county, and Haywood County would eventually be formed with Waynesville as its county seat. By 1790 the region west of the Blue Ridge that had been declared "cleared of Indians" had a surprisingly large population.

As mentioned earlier, one of the hardships of the pioneers was the difficulty of getting to their county seats. This was burdensome to all but especially so to the most westerly of the tiny settlements. Going either to Rutherfordton or Morganton meant a trip across the Blue Ridge over what were mere trails. Of the communities that had so far developed, the Bee Tree-Swannanoa and the Reems Creek-Beaverdam settlements were the largest. From these two groups petitions for a new county west of the Blue Ridge were sent to the General Assembly. In compliance with those petitions, a new county was created in January, 1792, and

FLORETTA BRUMLEY PHOTO

Logs: A settler's first concern was his home. The trees he felled in clearing the acres for his crops became logs for his house, usually a cabin about 12 by 24 feet. Notched into place, these logs with their chinking insured a sturdy and warm home for his family. Some of these early cabins still stand, monuments to their builders' fine workmanship.

was given the name Buncombe County, honoring Colonel Edward Buncombe. It included all of Rutherford County west of the mountains and most of the western part of Burke County. Buncombe extended westward to the Territory of Tennessee and southward from the present Mitchell County to the South Carolina and Georgia lines; for obvious reasons it was facetiously called "The State of Buncombe."[13]

As a compromise measure, the needed court house was built on a plateau between the two most populous communities and offered road access from all directions. As was the case in the newly created counties east of the Blue Ridge, this courthouse was a small, log structure. Adjacent to it were the prison and its exercise grounds and the public stocks. The new structure faced east approximately where today Patton Avenue enters Pack Square in Asheville. John Burton, called "The Father of Asheville," from his holdings laid out a north-south street in front of it to be known as North Main and South Main. Those streets are today Broadway and Biltmore Avenue. Burton then sectioned off forty-two town lots.[14] On January 25, 1795, John Brown reached Buncombe Courthouse on a trip through Western North Carolina to select and buy up speculation land. In his *Journal* he recorded, "there is a few cabins."[15]

These cabins described by Brown were places of business, and more would be erected. Zebulon and Bedent Baird arrived in 1793 after accomplishing the almost miraculous feat of hauling a wagon loaded with supplies over Saluda Mountain. They opened a store. In addition, George Swain built a little hatter's shop, and in his home James Patton served meals and offered lodging to travelers. Silas McDowell had a tailor shop, while Phillip Smith made wagons as well as tooling "shoes for men and horses, saddles and hats." Robert Henry, coming into the Swannanoa community, opened the first school west of the Blue Ridge. Also near this little group of business houses John Burton erected a grist mill, and Thomas Forster built a bridge over the Swannanoa River. Buncombe Courthouse had become a town.

On a return trip to Buncombe Courthouse, land speculator John Brown was apparently unimpressed with the village and made the following comments in his *Journal*: "...this town stands a mile distance from the French Broad and a mile Below where the Swanno River empties into the Franch Broad the settlement is very thin and they live but very indifferently. We had very poor entertainment this town is but two days walk from the Cherokee nation [sic]." Brown was right in saying that the town was "thin." That was also true of the new county seats east of the Blue Ridge. Whatever skills and trades the pioneers brought to the shifting frontier, it was land that had motivated their coming. A merchant or a hatter typically rode into the village from his farm to ply his trade and at sunset closed his shop and rode home. Only later did homes appear on the streets of these little towns.[16]

Buncombe Courthouse had been named Morristown, but the name was not popular. When the town was incorporated, it was renamed Asheville, honoring Governor Samuel Ashe. In a few years there was noticeable growth in the village and as the only town west of the Blue Ridge, it acquired a post office in 1801, with

Jeremiah Cleveland as postmaster. In 1806 Asheville was made the distribution point for mail going to all parts of Western North Carolina, eastern Tennessee, to the western sections of South Carolina, and to northern Georgia. George Swain then became postmaster.

The formation of Buncombe County promoted the growth of the entire region, and a steady stream of settlers entered the area through every gap in the mountains. Many of them had already taken out grants or secured them upon their arrival. Other newcomers merely picked out desirable sites for homes, felled a few trees, built their cabins, and began life in the mountains. Most of the grants were comparatively modest in size, but many enterprising North Carolinians and out-of-state settlers secured huge tracts of virgin land. Part of this was usually kept for themselves and their families, and a part of it they sold to new settlers. Since they had paid only fifty shillings per hundred acres for their lands, they were able, by selling in small tracts, to make a considerable profit. In order to sell their lands to advantage, they sometimes advertised in the eastern cities. This helped to increase the number of settlers entering North Carolina from other states.

In 1795 John Brown of Lewistown, Pennsylvania, traveled through Western North Carolina. His mission was to select and purchase tracts of land for William Cathcart and George and James Latimer, eastern investors. In addition to purchases made for Cathcart and the Latimers, he succeeded in getting land for himself and for several local men whom he met during his travels. Brown meticulously kept a journal, which today is an invaluable source of information about the process of securing land grants. He wrote in detail, too, about the poor roads, the rivers he forded and reforded, the people he met, the villages through which he passed, and the "thinness" of the country. His record furnishes vivid word pictures of conditions in Western North Carolina during its pioneer days.

At the same time men within the state and settlers in the counties through which Brown passed were also taking out speculation land. Among them were several members of the Davidson family, Robert Henry, Waightstill Avery, Lambert Clayton, and Ephraim George. These tracts varied in size. Perhaps the most extensive of the speculation lands was held by Tench Coxe of Philadelphia. His acres covered huge areas, both east and west of the Blue Ridge. There were others who held grants covering thousands of acres.

With demands for land coming into the county seats almost daily, the county officials had difficulty in surveying, staking out, recording the transaction, and sending the necessary information to state officials. The fact that land was being sold both by the state government and by individuals and the incidence of numerous squatters caused some mistakes. Some lands were not surveyed, and some plots were never cleared with the state; therefore, vexing questions concerning land titles were in the making to plague citizens and lawyers of a later era.[17]

So astonishingly rapid was the influx of settlers into the opened Cherokee lands that early in the new century Colonel Robert Love and his brother, General Thomas Love, led a movement for the formation of a new county. These men had extensive holdings, one tract of which was in the area of Richland Creek, and they had built homes on the ridge above that stream. Others had settled near them. The Pigeon River community and the settlements along Crabtree, Fines, and Jonathan Creeks had likewise flourished. In their requests for a new county, these pioneers gave the same reason advanced for the establishment of Buncombe County in 1792. They declared that the distance from the courthouse in Asheville was too great for convenience at any time, and they argued that the roads were frequently, especially in the winter months, impassable. Thus an unnecessary burden was imposed upon those having to make trips to the county seat.

A petition presented to the General Assembly by Thomas Love resulted in the passing of a law in December, 1808, authorizing the formation of a new mountain county from a portion of Buncombe County's western lands. The new county extended westward to the Tennessee line but was not open to white settlers beyond the Meigs-Freeman survey line of 1803. Robert Love donated the site for the courthouse and a lot for a church, and he suggested that the new town be named Waynesville, in honor of General Anthony Wayne, under whom Love had served in the Revolutionary War. The county was named Haywood in honor of John Haywood, treasurer of North Carolina. By 1810 the settled part of the country west of the Blue Ridge had already reached the Cherokee boundary.[18]

Western North Carolina gained still another mountain county to the north when in 1799 Ashe was created by an act of the General Assembly. It was named for Samuel Ashe and the county seat, Jefferson, was a reminder to its citizens of the author of the Declaration of Independence.

CHAPTER ELEVEN

Weaving a Homespun Pattern of Living

Like the settlers east of the Blue Ridge, those crossing the mountains represented many European stocks. There were those of English descent like the Mills family, and many German names coming from Pennsylvania or directly from Europe appearing among the mountain settlers, including Shook, Gooch, or Weaver. In addition, the settlers of Dutch Cove from the Yadkin Valley were largely of German descent. There were Irish, like the Pattons, and Welsh families with names like Williams and Welsh. A few of the mountain people were of French extraction, and there were many Scotch-Irish, giving the region its dozens of names beginning with Mac. Entering the mountain area from the earlier settlements in Burke, Rutherford, and Wilkes Counties, from Virginia and Pennsylvania, from South Carolina, and from the Watauga Settlements, these pioneers were, on the whole, young men, single or with their wives and small children.

Some of these new arrivals had been trained in the ways of pioneer life since childhood, and all of them came with an optimism based upon a faith in the future of the new country. Many of them had the ability, the personality, and the qualities of leadership that would enable them to mold the trends of events and thus to justify the faith of all. As they set about developing a way of life compatible with their mountain surroundings, the days must have been adventurous, often exciting, and sometimes dangerous, but always hard. Behind them these men and women had left whatever conveniences and cultural advantages they had enjoyed, and individually as pioneers and collectively as communities, they were faced with building a social structure where none existed.

Each man's immediate concern upon arriving at his tract of land was the building of his home. In most cases that meant first the task of clearing a suitable spot near a stream. The forest was boundless, and with so much clearing of fields awaiting his axe, a man could not dawdle over the construction of a house to shelter his family. If a dwelling could be made warm and safe, it would do until the head of the household had the time to enlarge it or to build a bigger one. As a result, the first houses were almost unbelievably small. Often only twelve or fourteen by sixteen or eighteen feet, they were one or two-roomed buildings made from the logs of trees felled on the spot and notched into position for the walls. The top log was split and smoothed, and on it rested the roof of split logs, notched and held into place by poles or stones.

The floors were of rough puncheon or even, in some cases, merely the ground that soon packed into firmness. The walls and roofs of some of the cabins were high enough to allow for a loft, which was reached by means of cleats notched to the wall or by pegs below the "scuttle hole." This loft became a storage place, sleeping quarters, usually for the older children, and on occasion served as a vantage post from which to shoot at prowling Cherokees. Some lofts, like that in the home of Zebulon Baird on the east side of the French Broad River, were equipped with gun holes.[1] The one or two windows of the cabin were without glass, but puncheon shutters, hung by wooden pegs or hinges, provided protection against the elements and enemies. One end of each cabin was well taken up with the fireplace, used for both heating and cooking. It was constructed of stones mortared into place with clay. Clay or any available mud from the creek banks, mixed with pebbles and stones and even with twigs, also provided the chinking between the logs of the walls. The result of the pioneer's carpentry was rarely artistic, but it was sturdy and warm.[2]

The furniture for his cabin was also the work of the pioneer's own hands. Often in those early years the beds were bunks against the wall, sometimes attached to it with pegs. Over them the housewife could put her feather beds if she were fortunate enough

BOB LINDSEY PHOTO, ASHEVILLE CHAMBER OF COMMERCE

The Vance Home (restored):   This house, large for that time, was built by Colonel David Vance about 1795. It has a sitting room and three bedrooms in two stories and a one-story kitchen. Here David's grandson, Zebulon Baird Vance, was born on May 13, 1830. This house has been the home of five outstanding members of the Vance family.

to be allowed to bring them from the east. If not, after the first crop, she could have straw or husk mattresses, and until that time she made out with grass or reed mattresses. Buffalo and deerskin made the bed clothing, and the bunks served as seats during the daytime. The children in the loft slept on husk-filled pallets or on animal skins on the floor. Tables and chairs, which were only backless stools fashioned according to the husband's skill, completed the simple household effects.

A mantel and some storage space on the fireplace wall sometimes added to the housewife's convenience. Over the door, suspended on two forked sticks pegged to the wall, was the ever ready rifle. It was handily placed and out of reach of the children. As soon as possible a crib or cradle was made for the baby. The pioneer's farming and household tools were likewise meager. He brought into the wilderness his flint-lock, long-barreled rifle, his hunting knife, his axe, possibly an adz or a froe, and a few plough shares, together with some pot hooks and the seeds for his first crop.

The lady of the house usually had a scanty supply of "store" cloth, an iron kettle and a pot or two, an inadequate supply of pewter dishes and knives, a few spoons and forks, and sometimes a spinning wheel. Frequently she guarded a small "library," which typically included a copy of the Bible and an almanac. Perhaps in a small chest she cherished a little assortment of family heirlooms. The frontier couple brought or purchased from earlier settlers a horse or two, a cow, and a few hogs.[3]

After his home and possibly a nearby barn had been completed, the pioneer turned his attention to clearing the land. With the tools he had, he grubbed out tangled shrubs and underbrush and girdled the trees so that they would die in a couple of years. In the first year or so he planted his corn among the girdled trees, now leafless, fertilizing the crop by the Indian method of putting a fish in each corn hill. When the trees were dead, he felled them with the help of one or more of the neighboring settlers, saving some of the logs for fuel and for building. The surplus—oak, hickory, ash, walnut—was dragged to a convenient spot to be burned.

A garden plot also demanded attention and was early cleared near the cabin. It fell to the wife's lot to tend the beans, potatoes, onions, and other vegetables grown there for the family's food supply. Besides corn, as the land was cleared, the pioneer raised crops of wheat, rye, oats, and some tobacco. As he built up his herd of cattle, he used the nearby hillsides for his grazing grounds and let his hogs roam at will to fatten on the wild nuts. Bells were attached to the cows and hogs were marked with an ownership symbol. The settler usually planned to raise a sufficient number of horses to supply him with the needed farm animals and with a means of transportation to markets. Some of the settlers used oxen, and in time oxen became the beasts of burden on all farms. These pioneers, no matter what else they were, were farmers, and for the first few years of their lives in the mountains, they were all subsistence farmers.[4]

Still, the mountain settlers enjoyed a self-sufficient economy. Food was plentiful, and the pioneer's rifle, used with superb marksmanship, kept the family larder supplied with meat and fowl. The stream rippling past the house offered refrigeration and was a never-failing source of choice fish. The meadow furnished an abundance of "greens" in the early spring and a carpet of strawberries in their season. Bee trees yielded honey, and the woods offered a variety of nuts. Many kinds of wild herbs and

APPALACHIAN NATIONAL PARKS ASSOCIATION COLLECTION, N. C.
DEPARTMENT OF ARCHIVES AND HISTORY

When building a new house, a settler often kept his earlier house as a storage place or a barn. Back of this farmstead the lofty Craggies rise.

roots were gathered yearly for the home remedies so vital to a doctorless country. During those first years, the corn was ground at home by means of a stone or wooden mortar and pestle, and the many products of the garden were dried for winter use. The cows gave their milk, and the spring or creek insured a constant supply of drinking water.

For some years wild game from the surrounding forests supplied the settlers of Western North Carolina with much of their clothing. Deerskins became buckskin leggings, trousers, and shirts for the men and sometimes provided skirts for the women. Animal hides became shoes and moccasins for the entire family. As time went on, many of the settlers built up a flock of sheep and raised a field or two of flax. Then the men made hand looms, and the women spent the winter afternoons spinning and weaving linsey-woolsey cloth for the family's wardrobes and for the fine coverlets for their beds. If the women worked in the evenings, they did so by the light of the fire or of pine torches, or by the flickering light of home made beef tallow candles. Occasionally some pioneer woman would possess a lamp of iron molded in a cup shape in which floated a wick saturated in hog lard. In all the phases of their living, mountain pioneers were repeating the experiences of earlier settlers in the piedmont areas. They were continuing and extending the life style of their friends and kin folk in the newly created counties of Burke and Rutherford and Wilkes just east of the Blue Ridge.[5]

At rare intervals the pioneer went to market on horseback. East of the Blue Ridge and in the northern mountain section that meant a trip to Morganton or to Rutherfordton. West of the Blue Ridge it might mean a journey to Waynesville and often to Asheville. There the Bairds took the furs and hides from the pioneer's hunting and trapping and possibly a few hog or deer hams in exchange for salt, sugar, a few tools, or bars of iron. A bit of coffee and a few yards of "store" cloth for his wife and daughters also made the return trip. The furs and hides and hams the merchants would in turn take to Augusta or to Charleston on their next trip, exchanging them for the supplies needed by the early settlers.

Almost nothing except taxes was paid for in money, for specie was scarce throughout the state, especially in the frontier areas. When money was mentioned, however, it was in terms of English coins. It was not until 1809 that the General Assembly authorized the counties to keep their records in terms of American currency. Some of the coins appearing in Western North Carolina up to that date were English, but there was a sprinkling of French coins and even more Spanish doubloons and pieces of eight. In his *Journal*, for example, John Brown recorded the constant difficulty of exchanging the currency he had brought from Pennsylvania into pieces of eight. Entry takers often refused to make the exchange.[6]

As had been the case with the earlier settlers in the Catawba and Broad River sections, protection was every mountain settler's concern, and those pioneers living in isolated coves or along small streams had to be prepared for sudden attacks from bands of Cherokees. Each member of the family was taught to use a rifle and learned where to seek a hiding place in case of need. When forewarned, those living in the neighborhood of a block house or fort fled to a previously

THE STEPHENS PRESS, INC.

After a community or farm forge was set up, the settler had improved farm implements, and the kitchen fireplace—always a busy spot—was well equipped. The one shown above is in the restored Vance home.

designated one for safety. After 1783 there was no Cherokee "war" against the white settlements, but some native Americans, on the pretense of hunting, remained a constant menace. For instance, John Burton's miller, having crossed the French Broad River searching for his cow, was killed by a lurking Cherokee.[7] Several times the William Mills family narrowly escaped death by reaching the fort at Point Lookout before the pursuing Indians.[8] There were far too many instances in which several family members became victims of a surprise attack by prowling Indians.[9]

To protect the clusters of settlements, to prevent massacres in remote districts, and to instill in the Cherokees the fear of organized retaliation, the settlers worked out a system of patrols. Each appointed armed watchman covered a six-mile territory. Block houses or tiny log forts were erected at intervals along the French Broad River and at other strategic spots, such as Point Lookout, to which besieged families could go. Some individuals built forts at their homes, like the one constructed shortly after 1787 by Captain William Moore, probably the first white settler west of the French Broad River. His fort, which served as protection for his own family and for the families that came into the Hominy Creek region, stood on or near the present Sand Hill Road just east of the Enka Corporation plant. John Brown, in Asheville, noted that the settlers kept "near Sixty men out about seven miles distant from the Town in small garrisons to Prevent the Indians from comeing in on them [sic]."[10]

In case of need, the patrols, covering their districts on horseback, could have the assistance of the local militia. North Carolina's militia, during the Revolutionary War, had been a signal factor in quelling the English-sympathizing Cherokees. It had also been instrumental in driving the British armies from the state. Now, in 1793, it was divided into four divisions. These in turn were marked into districts, each to organize a brigade made up of freemen and apprentices eighteen years of age and over. On both sides of the Blue Ridge, Western North Carolina men, most of whom were veterans of the late war, gladly accepted the call. They furnished their own muskets, powder horns, and shot-pouches, and without the benefit of uniforms they attended called drills known as Exercises. Calls for active duty were responded to, and once a year at places designated by law or by the commanding officers, this self-made militia attended a review or inspection and recruiting ceremony known as Muster Day. This military organization, made up of seasoned soldiers, did much to maintain a state of peace between the settlers and the native American.[11]

One of the things that separates civilized man from his less

An Early Ferry: Transportation for men and their farm products was long a problem in the mountain communities. Until bridges were built over streams, ferries, like this one on the French Broad River near Asheville, served settlers both east and west of the Blue Ridge.

developed ancestors and contemporaries is a system of transportation in which roads play an essential part. Simple trails had first served the buffalo, the deer, and later the Cherokee on his hunting and raiding expeditions. These footpaths had been firmly packed into trading paths by the hooves of thousands of pack horses. They brought early settlers into the "back country," then to the foothills of the Blue Ridge, and at last across the mountains. During the peak years of this westward migration into the mountain valleys and coves, hundreds of pioneers trudged over the old paths carrying their possessions in bundles. Thousands of others rode over them on horseback with their personal effects in their saddle bags or on a pack horse or two or, in a few cases, on a crude sled or "stone boat" pulled by a patient horse or ox.

But ambitious pioneers had visions of roads over which they might use wagons in procuring needed supplies and in transporting their products to Virginia or to South Carolina markets. These visions became realities amazingly early. True, "waggon road" was more often than not a polite term for a steep, twisting, narrow, boulder-filled trail over the mountains and along the streams, yet over such trails, by near-miraculous combinations of good weather, back-breaking efforts, perseverance, and luck or destiny, determined teamsters sometimes succeeded in keeping their wagons reasonably intact and mobile.

As early as 1753 the Moravian "Brethern," arriving to build Bethabara, had actually negotiated a wagon, considered the first, over the Pennsylvania Road, a feat that had made burdensome every foot of the five hundred miles. On some of the steep inclines, it had been necessary to take the wagon apart and carry it piecemeal up the mountain, while on the equally steep descents it had been necessary to lock two wheels and to hang a log on behind to act as a brake.[12] For many years, mountain pioneers were to repeat these experiences. The first established route across the Blue Ridge was undoubtedly the one used by Boone. From his home on the Yadkin he made early trips west by crossing the range at Cook's Gap and going across the site of Boone to Hodge's Gap, then skirting the base of Rich Mountain to the present Silverstone. Then, by following a buffalo trail, he passed between the present Zionville, North Carolina, and Trade, Tennessee. This Boone trail has been marked by six markers.[13]

A later road scaled the Blue Ridge at McKinney or Gillespie Gap and, following the North Toe River, crossed Yellow Mountain or went over a gap between Yellow and Roan Mountains and on to the Watauga Settlements. New and trail-like as this route must have been in 1771, it was used by James Robertson and the sixteen Wake County families that he escorted to the western settlements. It is thought that this group took their belongings in wagons, and it is certain that the later Bright's Trail, making use of this older road which crossed over the gap between Yellow and Roan Mountains, was known as a wagon road. In 1774 Daniel Boone and eight companions, in preparation for Henderson's Transylvania colony in Kentucky, hacked out the Wilderness Road. When the settlers went over it a few months later, they took supplies by wagon train as far as the Cumberland Mountains.[14]

To the southwest the enterprising Baird Brothers—Zebulon and Bedent—in 1793 succeeded in getting a wagon and supplies over the forbidding Saluda Mountain and on to Buncombe Courthouse where they set up their merchandizing business. Two years later, presumably the worse for their mountain wear, two wagons rumbled into White's Ford, now Knoxville, having achieved the feat of scaling Saluda Mountain and the almost equally difficult feat of passing down the French Broad River gorge.[15]

As communities developed in the western mountain sections of Burke and Rutherford Counties, settlers laid out roads of a sort connecting the two counties and linking the homes of prominent citizens. Some of these were somewhat figuratively called wagon roads, and Reem's Creek boasted a "waggon

ASHEVILLE CHAMBER OF COMMERCE

Early settlers lightened their dawn-to-dark labor with home-made appliances. Here the farmer uses a sled—called a sledge—to transport his heavy implements and other burdens about the farm.

ford." When Buncombe County was created, roads were the chief, immediate concern of the new government. On the second day of the first court ever held in North Carolina west of the Blue Ridge, the problem of roads was taken up, and soon provisions were made for roads to a forge, to outlying sections of the county, and across gaps to markets. State subsidizing of roads was still far in the future, and the mountain counties both east and west of the Blue Ridge worked out a system of road construction and maintenance.

The highway was marked off into sections with one man assigned to oversee the construction and upkeep of each section. His crew consisted of "warned in" citizens, ordered by the county court to work a certain number of days. During the early settlement period when roads were desperately needed and when the lack of them might mean failure to his mountain venture, each settler responded wholeheartedly to the county's call for road duty. The system later broke down. But for the area west of the Blue Ridge a tremendous step forward had been accomplished when a usable wagon road over Saluda Gap allowed incoming settlers to bring their belongings by wagon to their new homes.[16]

Until the first quarter of the new century was ending, however, roads continued to be the stumbling block to all progress in Western North Carolina. All travelers to the area who left records take up much letter, diary, or journal space in lamenting the hardships endured on the roads over which they had entered the region. The road linking Asheville with the Hominy Creek settlement and with the Richland Creek and Pigeon River groups farther west was scarcely worthy to be so called. Its wretched condition, especially during much of the winter, was an eloquent argument for the formation of another western county.

Most of the roads followed the streams. As was true in many places along the French Broad River northwest of Asheville, a gorge frequently closed in to the river bank. This necessitated fording and refording the stream or traveling some distance by means of side fords, that is, with the wheels of one or of both sides of the wagon in the stream bed. The rocks and boulders made both types of stream travel hazardous. Bishop Francis Asbury, for instance, on his way from Tennessee to Asheville on Thursday, November 3, 1800, tried riding in a chaise. Before he reached Paint Rock, just south of the Tennessee line, he was so exhausted from bouncing over the rocks that he abandoned the carriage for his horse. It was lucky that he did, for shortly thereafter the "roan horse reeled" and fell, taking the light carriage with him. It landed bottomside up and became wedged against a sapling. As Bishop Asbury and the driver struggled to right the chaise, they saw a woman spreading the water-soaked garments and bedding of her family about on the rocks to dry. Her husband was laboring in the river to retrieve his upset wagon.

The following Sunday, the Bishop again attempted riding a chaise, this time from the Daniel Killian home north of Asheville to William Forster's house in the present Biltmore, a distance of some five miles. Again he gave up the carriage for his more reliable horse, and that night he recorded in his *Journal:* "This mode of conveyance by no means suits the roads of this wilderness; we were obliged to keep one behind the carriage with a strap to hold by and prevent accidents almost continually."[17]

Yet wagons were being used, and Asbury mentions that Phillip Smith of Asheville made wagons, as well as shoes for men and horses, saddles, and hats.[18] Between 1800 and 1814 Bishop Asbury made almost yearly trips up the French Broad Road, through the various communities surrounding the Buncombe County courthouse, and down Saluda Mountain into South Carolina. After the ordeal of getting from one preaching point to another and after the agony of descending the mountain barrier, the Bishop said farewell to Western North Carolina with relief. In 1802 he wrote that in getting down Saluda Mountain he "used time, patience, labor, and two sticks." In the next year Asbury recorded: "Once more I have escaped from filth, fleas, rattlesnakes, hills, mountains, rocks, and rivers; farewell western world for a while!"[19] Except for the hardships imposed by the more mountainous terrain, transportation conditions were scarcely better in the older counties of Burke and Rutherford and Wilkes. The ancient Indian trail from near the present Pickens, South Carolina, passed through Rutherfordton and near Morganton and on to the headwaters of Linville River and thence west to the present Boone and into Tennessee. This trail continued to be a main artery of travel.[20] Roads going east were practically nonexistent, and the products of this rich valley region went largely to South Carolina markets.

From time to time the counties laid out new roads or repaired older ones, but they were always poorly kept and frequently next to impassable. River transportation in this area just east of the Blue Ridge was necessarily stressed, and settlers living along the prongs of the Broad River were required to keep the streams navigable for small, flat-bottomed boats. Downstream the freight was reloaded onto larger boats bound for Columbia and other South Carolina river ports. In fact, so economically essential were the river highways that several "artificial towns" along streams were authorized by the General Assembly. Attempts were made by companies to build planned villages such as Burr on the Broad River and Jefferson on "Main Broad River". But all these attempts failed, for the settlers were basically farmers.[21]

Until well into the new century, the county seats were mere clusters of cabins, housing a few hundred citizens who were also farmers. Their salable products, after transportation costs were deducted, brought scarcely enough to pay for the needed but high-priced supplies. The area was forced to raise or make what was needed or go without.

Uncomfortable as traveling was, Francis Asbury made his difficult yearly pilgrimages to this frontier because, as he said, "My soul felt for these neglected people."[22] Many years later another missionary characterized the mountain dwellers as "an interesting population in great spiritual destitution."[23] It is estimated that in 1790 not more than one person in thirty in North Carolina was a member of any church; there were only fourteen to fifteen thousand church members in the entire state. Of the Protestant denominations, the Baptists, with ninety-four churches, had by far the largest membership.

Followers of John Wesley's Methodism had suffered during the Revolution because of the faith's English origin. Yet in 1784 Francis Asbury and Thomas Coke were ordained as bishops in the newly formed Methodist Church of America. After holding their first Conference near Louisburg, they began their missionary journeys that extended from Maine to Georgia.

Flocking into the back country, the Scotch-Irish brought with them the Presbyterianism of John Knox, and in 1788 there were twenty-eight Presbyterian ministers preaching in the state.[24] The Scotch-Irish Presbyterians in both Burke and Rutherford Counties early organized churches, the first in the area being the Westminster or Brittain Church in Rutherford County. Its congregation of twenty members was organized in 1768, probably by the Reverend Daniel Thatcher. That same year a church building was erected, the first house of worship west of the Catawba River; it became the first of three successive Brittain

Churches, two of them on that site. This little church wielded a wide influence and became the "Mother Church" of Presbyterian congregations both east and west of the Blue Ridge. Established later than the Brittain Church but before 1784, the Quaker Meadows Presbyterian Church was organized in Burke County.[25] However, adherents to this denomination had for some time held meetings in the homes of settlers.

In 1794 the Reverend James Hall and the Reverend Joseph D. Kilpatrick held a series of meetings in the Bee Tree settlement. As a result a Presbyterian congregation was formed there along with another in the Swannanoa community, and a third in the Reems Creek settlement. At Bee Tree the first church building southwest of the Blue Ridge was erected. It was a log structure known as the Robert Patton Meeting House. After 1797 Reverend George Newton, the first resident Presbyterian minister in the area, preached to all three congregations and to one organized near Cane Creek. In additon to his preaching duties he taught at Union Hill School, later to become Union Academy and still later, Newton Academy. The Swannanoa congregation eventually became the Asheville Presbyterian Church.[26]

Benjamin Miller, a Baptist minister, was holding meetings in homes along the upper Yadkin River in 1755 and learned that itinerant preachers of his denomination had preceded him. By 1760 a little log church building was serving a newly organized Baptist group in that area, and in 1777 a Baptist Church was organized farther west. It was called Mullberry Fields Church and was erected at the site of the present Wilkesboro. In 1779 Beaver Creek Baptist Church was organized in Wilkes County, and King Creek Church was built in what was to become Caldwell County.[27] By then itinerant ministers of this faith were entering various sections of the counties just east of the mountains, and in 1785 the Bills Creek Baptist Church was built in Rutherford County, followed two years later by the Mountain Creek Church. All of these small churches led to the formation of new congregations; and when in 1800 the Broad River Baptist Association was formed, it included not only these congregations, but also the Green's Creek Church in what is now Polk County and three Baptist churches in Burke County.[28]

Leaving the Yadkin churches, Baptist ministers crossed the mountains on horseback by means of the old Boone Trail as soon as settlers took up land in the river valleys along the Watauga and Toe Rivers. In the valley viewed almost forty years earlier by

Spangenberg and considered by him as a favorable site for an Indian mission, a little log meeting house was built in 1790 and quite appropriately was named the Three Forks Church. Nine years later the second church in the present Watauga County was built and was known as the Cove Creek Church. These, together with the few Baptist churches in Ashe and Wilkes Counties, were members of the Yadkin Baptist Association. Over the years a succession of preachers, the first of them lay-preachers, served these widely scattered congregations.[29]

As the settlements moved westward, the Baptist Convention attempted to keep pace with the pioneers, and early in the new century Humphrey Posey assumed the duties of State Mission Agent for the Convention, serving without pay. In addition to teaching short terms of school in Rutherford County, Mr. Posey made missionary journeys across the mountains. With James Whittaker as his assistant, he held meetings in the Hominy Creek and Pigeon River areas, organizing a congregation that constructed a church at the site of the present Canton. It was called the Locust Old Field Baptist Church and was the source of spiritual influence throughout the new county of Haywood. In 1817 Posey took up missionary work with the Cherokees and from stations established farther west, preached to the Indians in the western region of the state.[30]

During the Revolutionary War, a Methodist Circuit was formed, covering the Yadkin valley and extending west across the mountains and south to take in the Catawba area. The Reverend Andrew Yeargin traveled at least portions of this vast territory and may have been one of the first Methodist preachers to cross the Blue Ridge. About 1790 the Lincoln Methodist Circuit was formed, embracing a wide area that included Rutherford and Burke Counties. As ministers, Daniel Asbury and Jesse Richardson visited as often as possible the small churches established in the circuit. Methodism as a force in Western North Carolina developed largely, however, through the tireless efforts of Bishop Frances Asbury.

By 1790 Asbury was traveling from the Yadkin valley to the Catawba and west to the mountains. Wherever there were a few scattered houses he went, holding meetings in homes or in yards. In the small county seats the court houses served as meeting places. Settlers, eager to hear religious messages and glad for the news of the outside world, welcomed Asbury into their homes. In Rutherford County his headquarters were at the home of William

MARGARET MORLEY COLLECTION, N. C. DEPT. OF ARCHIVES AND HISTORY
As soon as water-powered mills were built along streams, the settlers laid aside their mortars and pestles and took their grain to the nearest mill to be ground into flour and meal.

Mills.[31] Riding over the long, muddy miles of Rutherford, Burke, and Wilkes Counties from preaching place to preaching place, he wearily recorded in his *Journal*, "This is a day of small things here."[32] But out of his sometimes tedious labors grew many churches, among them the Gilboa Methodist Church, the second religious congregation organized in Burke County.[33]

In 1793 after his journey through the counties to the east, Asbury crossed the Blue Ridge and preached to the settlers living along the Watauga River—"a neglected place," he called it. From there he followed the old road into Tennessee. In 1800 the French Broad River valley was added to his journeys, and for fourteen years he made almost yearly trips from Knoxville, Tennessee, to Asheville. From there he went to the frontier settlements farther west and through the present Henderson County, passing on into South Carolina.

In 1800 the Bishop was fifty-five years old and was already suffering from the tuberculosis that in 1816 claimed his life. Yet on horseback he came, frequently dismounting to lead his horse over the steep, slippery, rock-strewn hills. He slept wherever night caught him, grateful if it might be a hunter's cabin where he could stretch out on the hard, dirt floor. Without protection he endured the beating rains of summer and the sleet and snow of winter, for he came at all seasons of the year.[34]

The people of Asheville crowded into the court room to hear him preach, and friends and neighbors filled the David Killian home in the Beaverdam section as well as the Forster house in the present Biltmore whenever word came that there would be a meeting. Jacob Shook, in the fine log house he erected near the Pigeon River, made a "preaching" room in the attic so that Bishop Asbury could bring the Gospel message to all who hungered for spiritual food. The home of Samuel Edney in the present Henderson County was another of the Bishop's stopping places, and on one of his trips Asbury ordained Edney "for preaching." Then during the Bishop's absence from the mountains, Edney carried on the work. As congregations were gradually formed, small Methodist churches appeared in various places west of the mountains.[35]

During the years of Asbury's missionary work in the area, the camp meeting movement reached Western North Carolina. This movement was a product of pioneer and frontier life. With their previous religious background, American pioneers were interested in "preachings" and gained from them not only a needed religious inspiration, but also the social satisfaction of mingling with their neighbors. Regardless of creedal concepts and convictions, whole families managed by one means or another to attend the services held irregularly by ministers passing from one frontier settlement to another. Eventually no pioneer house could accommodate the crowds (not even Jacob Shook's with its chapel), and overflow crowds filled the yards.

The sensible thing, then, was to hold the meeting out-of-doors where all might see and hear. Nor was one meeting satisfactory to either minister or pioneers. These itinerant preachers, covering their vast circuits, arrived at meeting places badly in need of rest. Their return to the area was always uncertain, and for their own sake and that of the congregation they preferred to hold services in a community for a week, possibly two. The pioneers, on their part, felt the need of the preacher's message and, almost as strongly, the need of social life. Yet getting to and from the daily

184 / *Chapter Eleven*

WORLD METHODIST ARCHIVES, JUNALUSKA

Bishop Francis Asbury: Francis Asbury, the Bishop on Horseback, brought Methodism to the little settlements east of the Blue Ridge and to the Watauga Settlements. After 1800 he also visited the communities west of the Blue Ridge. On his trips he endured, as he said, "filth, fleas, rattlesnakes, hills, mountains, rocks, and rivers." In this painting, as he travels the wilderness, he holds the open Bible.

meetings held by the preacher presented a very real problem. It was solved with logic and good sense, and the camp meeting came into being.

With bedding and a supply of food on a pack horse or in a wagon if he owned one, each settler took his family to the meeting or camp grounds. There, roads permitting, he joined his neighbors, and all camped out for the duration of the preacher's visit. Some member of each family rode home as often as deemed necessary to see about the chores. Between the daily services, prayer meetings and singing sessions were held, but there was still time for much visiting of neighbor with neighbor and kinsfolk and for shy courting among the young people.

This type of conclave required space far greater than any yard afforded, and interested parties set aside land for campgrounds. Temporary, bough-covered shelters could be erected for the meetings, and both settlers and their wagons and horses could be accommodated. In time some of these grounds had permanent shelters.[36] Bishop Asbury, passing the "encamping places" of Methodists and Presbyterians in 1803, felt partially repaid for his strenuous missionary journeys along the French Broad River, for they made the land "look like the Holy Land."[37]

The modern American is filled with respectful awe when he realizes how much his ancestors sacrificed to settle in and tame a wilderness. One of the sacrifices involved was education. Textbooks could not be taken by settlers into the "back country" of North Carolina and certainly could not be included on the already over-laden pack horses heading westward across the mountain barrier. There was the unending task of clearing farms in a vast, forest-covered region and of making on the place practically all of the farm tools used and all of the clothing needed by a growing family. There were the additional tasks of raising and then marketing crops and of supplementing the family food supply and the exchange income with hunting and trapping. Every child in the large families was an economic asset, taking his place at an early age as a laborer in the home or in the field and woods.

If a boy had an unconquerable thirst for knowledge and if there were some member of the family capable of teaching him, the lad could learn his letters at night by the light of a pine torch or a tallow candle, with the Bible and an almanac as text books. If the compelling urge was lacking or if the boy was too work-weary for evening study, he grew to manhood wise only in the ways of frontier life. He became familiar with the mountains and their wealth of vegetation and animal life. He became alert to all forms of lurking danger; he was self-reliant, and well acquainted with hard work. But frontier youth generally went without the benefits of formal education.

The settlers coming to the mountains had had varying degrees of education in their youthful days, and as soon as the tiny settlements grew into communities, their leaders took steps to provide education for the children. The first schools in the Catawba and Broad River settlements were known as Old Field schools. These were subscription primary and elementary schools held in homes or in log houses. A teacher—usually a man, but occasionally a woman—taught community children, both boys and girls for a small fee per child. Terms were short and held between crop times. The tiny school buildings were crudely furnished with split log benches, an occasional fireplace, and a homemade desk and chair or stool for the teacher. A wooden water bucket and a gourd dipper completed the physical equipment.

Equally meager was the teaching equipment. Whatever books the teachers or parents could procure served as texts. The beginners frequently used a modified form of the old English hornbook, a shorthandled, paddle-like board with a smooth surface on which the great and small letters were written and from which the child learned his A, B, C's. A leather thong passed through a hole bored in the handle could be slipped over the head so that the child could wear his "book." In these Old Field schools the second generation, and in some cases the third, got their first contact with formal education. Among these children was young Zebulon Vance, who attended four such schools, one of which was taught by Miss Jane Hughey.[38]

The churches, always advocates of education, established elementary schools as soon as practicable, their ministers serving as teachers. Then came the academies, sponsored by church groups. The first of these in Burke County was the Morgan Academy, erected in Morganton in 1783, in which the classes were taught by the Presbyterian minister and his wife.[39] Rutherfordton Academy in Rutherford County followed, receiving its charter in 1800.[40] But the settlers in the rural sections of these counties, as in Wilkes County, continued to depend upon a bit of teaching now and then by individuals setting up private or subscription schools.

Across the Blue Ridge, the Swannanoa and Beaverdam settlements were fortunate in counting Robert Henry, a veteran of the Revolutionary War and a man of varied interests and manifold abilities, among their settlers. He opened the first school west of the Blue Ridge, attended by the pioneers' children, both boys and girls. His school became known as Union Hill School. Although necessarily handicapped by the lack of text books, Henry paved the way for the formal establishment of Union Hill Academy that provided a solid educational foundation for children of the communities. In 1797 George Newton replaced Henry, who then took up one or more of his many occupations in the pioneer town of Asheville.

In July, 1803, William Forster III deeded an eight acre tract of land to the trustees of Union Hill Academy, together with the old school building, a newly constructed one, and an additional frame dwelling. The same donor later added land on which was a brick building in the process of construction. Forster's gifts called for the dedication of the land and buildings to the maintenance and furthering of the Gospel and to the teaching of a Latin and English school. The academy was reorganized by the General Assembly in 1805, and soon after that date its name was changed to Newton Academy. At one time or another practically every prominent citizen of early Asheville and the surrounding territory served as a trustee of the institution.

The ambitious little academy was hard-pressed financially during those early years, and in 1810 it received permission from the General Assembly to conduct a public lottery as a means of raising funds with which to build new buildings and to establish a "Female Academy" in Asheville. The odds in the lottery were enticing, for the winner was to receive a prize of seven thousand dollars for his four dollar ticket. But the plan failed, and the outstanding tickets had to be recalled because, as the advertisement stated, there was extreme scarcity of cash, a prevalent condition both in the mountain section and in the state as a whole.[41] Newton Academy somehow weathered the financial crisis and for many years gave a firm educational background to boys who were to become the second generation leaders in Western North Carolina. Some of these young men were to take their places in the political affairs of the state.

Under its 1776 Constitution, North Carolina was pledged to encourage education. As a result, it established a state University, although it made no appropriations for the operation and development of the institution. Encouragement was given to elementary education by legislative permission granted to private schools and to church schools to raise money by means of lotteries or other methods considered at the time as legal. However, the day of state responsibility for carrying elementary education to the far reaches of its territory had not yet dawned. As men and women pushed beyond the villages into isolated sections, scattered communities and individuals handled the problem as best they could.

Those settlers living in more or less compact communities had Old Field schools. Those in smaller settlements or in remote coves could hope for nothing beyond a bit of teaching in the homes. It was a long time before schools reached these places, and when they did, the little log buildings were poorly equipped, books were few, and the terms were pitifully short. Through the fault of no one, the second generation of remote mountain people—those whose childhoods were spent in Western North Carolina—gave an upward swing to the state's already high rate of illiteracy.[42] In a few years the differences in available opportunity to mountain settlers became apparent, differences largely due to location, ironically enough, often a matter of only a few miles. That difference was destined to increase and to encompass every phase of life during the first third of the nineteenth century as distinct social groups evolved and as a degree of progress and prosperity came to the more accessible communities.

CHAPTER TWELVE

Boundaries and Western Leadership

Even in colonial times boundary lines were bones of contention between North Carolina and Virginia to the north and between North Carolina and South Carolina to the south. The dissensions arising from real and fancied infringements on one colony's territory by another often became prolonged and bitter. Both of the neighboring colonies laid claim to a narrow east-west strip of land along the unsurveyed boundary, and both granted settlement rights within it to westward moving pioneers. Some of these settlers, unsure of their allegiance, voted in both colonies, and dodged the tax levied by each. Overlapping land grants gave rise to inflamed feelings, and local friction and feuds wasted the energies of the newly arrived settlers and led to a state of continual confusion which at times flared into violence. Under such conditions economic progress in the border areas was impossible.

As Western North Carolina was opened to white settlers, these boundary problems were extended into the mountain area. Here they were complicated by the shifting Cherokee boundaries and by the conflicting claims of North Carolina and Georgia over their common line—claims that, at the turn of the century, led to what was locally called the "Walton War."

Virginia and North Carolina took the first practical step in solving their differences when in 1728 a commission made up of representatives from each colony surveyed the area from "north of Currituck river or inlet" westward. When the men had gone fifty miles west of any white settlements, the North Carolina commissioners, feeling it a needless expense to continue through an uninhabited wilderness and having neither an interest in the hardships arising from the surveying task ahead nor in the companionship of the Virginians, returned home. But William Byrd II, the leading spirit in the Virginia group, foresaw the coming of settlers in perhaps ten years. He and his surveyors pushed on westward until from a hill they caught sight of wave after wave of distant blue mountains. At that point they set up their marker and went home, 233 miles from the coast.[1] In 1749, with the arrival of the settlers envisioned by Byrd, a joint commission representing the two colonies extended the survey. Still another joint commission in 1779, this time representing both states, surveyed the common boundary to about the site of the present city of Bristol.

While they did much to establish settled, normal conditions along North Carolina's northern boundary, these surveys could not entirely banish the trouble, for the surveys themselves could not always be accurate. Moreover, the incoming settlers could not always locate the boundary markers, especially those on trees, and the survey could not keep pace with the westward migration.[2] It was for these reasons that one of the Watauga pioneers, running his own line, discovered that he and many of his neighbors with land grants from Virginia had actually settled and cleared land in North Carolina. It was also revealed that they were beyond the line of demarcation established between white and native American country by the order of King George. Since to the settlers vacating the region now was unthinkable and since they must have protection, the Watauga Association, as related in an earlier chapter, made a land treaty with the Cherokees and petitioned the General Assembly of North Carolina to be recognized as a county of that state.

When in 1789 North Carolina ceded its western lands to the Republic, the boundary line was designated to start on the crest of Stone Mountain where it is intersected by the boundary line of Virginia, and the line was to follow that mountain to the place where the Watauga River flows through it. From there it was to go to the top of Yellow Mountain, along its crest to Iron

Mountain, and then along its crest to the Nolichuky River; from there it was to go to the crest of the Great Iron or Smoky Mountains, thence to the crest of the Unicoi range, and thus to the southern border of the state.

After the formation of the state of Tennessee from the ceded land, each commonwealth appointed a commission to work jointly in surveying the common boundary. That group included Colonel David Vance, General Joseph McDowell, and Major Mussendine Matthews as commissioners for North Carolina and Robert Henry and John Strother as surveyors. They ran the line in 1799 from the point where Virginia, North Carolina, and Tennessee met along the designated ranges to Paint Rock. Later the survey would be completed.[3]

The last clause in the boundary line description as designated in the Cession Act gave rise to a dispute between North Carolina and its western neighbor. Tennessee held that there was no crest or main ridge of the Unicoi range west of the Hiwassee River and that a range east of that river was therefore the true boundary. This claim, contrary to the intent of those formulating the Act, would mean that North Carolina would lose a valuable strip of western territory. In his *Memoir on Internal Affairs* in 1819 Archibald Murphey urged a speedy settlement of that dispute. After the Cherokee treaty of 1819, by which the native Americans relinquished land south and west of the point at which the survey had halted, another joint commission of the two states began where the stone marker had been set up on the Cataloochee trail in 1799 and ran the survey to the Georgia line. James Mebane, Montford Stokes, and Robert Love were North Carolina's representatives on this commission, and the work was completed in 1821. The boundary line thus established was accepted by both states; yet a small area known as the "Rainbow" country at the head of Tellico Creek later caused litigation between the two states and was not settled until well into the twentieth century.[4]

The long period of dissension between the two Carolinas over their common boundary led to charges and countercharges by each state against the other and against certain governors. By 1772, however, an extension of the survey earlier made in the eastern section was carried on by a joint commission representing the two colonies, although the results were most unsatisfactory to North Carolina. A part of the trouble stemmed from the extremely irregular boundary line that jogged to the north in order to include the Catawba Indian lands in South Carolina.

According to this survey, however, the line through the western Cherokee country was to be the thirty-fifth degree of parallel. But that strip, surveyed later, also caused dissension.[5]

At the close of the Revolutionary War, South Carolina ceded its western lands, a narrow strip just below the North Carolina border, to the new Republic. Settlers from Georgia entered the area as soon as it was cleared of Indians, but they were without any state protection and petitioned South Carolina to be included in that state. No action was taken. In ceding its western lands to the federal government, Georgia asked for this territory, lying between its border and that of North Carolina. Congress complied, and Georgia created the county of Walton out of it. According to the Georgia surveyors, the northern boundary of this strip of land was north of the mouth of the Mills River, and the county extended some twelve miles into what are now Transylvania and Jackson Counties in North Carolina. By 1803 it was estimated that this area had eight hundred inhabitants, some of them from Georgia, some from South Carolina, and some from North Carolina, which likewise claimed the region and had granted land to settlers entering it.

Trouble arose between the "Walton Men" and the North Carolinians, considered squatters by the Georgians. But the Carolina pioneers were not to be driven from their claims, and for a few years there was enough bloodshed in the newly created county to warrant the term "Walton War." In 1808 Georgia sent a memorial to Congress saying that North Carolina was infringing on its territory. Since Congress took no action, the two states appointed commissioners to locate the thirty-fifth parallel through the area. This survey revealed that the entire strip of disputed land was north of that parallel and had never actually belonged either to South Carolina or to the federal government. Nor did it now belong to Georgia. In spite of a protest from Georgia and a second memorial to Congress asking that another survey be made, the work of this joint committee stood.

Georgia continued to keep the county organization it had set up, however, and North Carolina sent a militia into the region to oust the Georgia officers. The tacit state of war that had existed now broke into open conflict, and two skirmishes took place, one two miles southeast of the present Brevard and the other on land now occupied by the Ecusta Plant. At both of these clashes lives were lost and some prisoners taken by the North Carolina militia. These were taken to Morganton, but their ultimate fate is not known. Georgia, perforce, abolished the county of Walton, and North Carolina set about restoring order in the region that had for some years been an "orphan strip." As such, the area had been infested with refugees from justice and outlaws who had been a constant menace to the property and even to the lives of the settlers in the region.[6]

It was necessary to survey the boundary designated in the treaty of 1798 between the territory opened to white settlers and the Cherokee lands. Although surveys for this purpose were made earlier, the federal government did not pronounce the line as established until 1803. In that year the third survey (made the previous year by J. Meigs, commissioner, and Thomas Freeman, surveyor) was approved. From a designated point already surveyed in the Smokies, the line was drawn to run southeast. It passed about a mile and a half east of the present Sylva, thence to the headwaters of Little River in the present Transylvania County, and then to the state line.

This survey accomplished what the other two had failed to do—to work little hardship to either whites or Cherokees. By it no white family was left in Cherokee country, and the fewest possible Cherokees were left in white territory. This Meigs-Freeman line of demarcation was destined to play an important part in the counties through which it ran; since surveys were frequently inaccurate, land grants and deeds described the location of plots in relation to this government established line. The new boundary also gave rise to innumerable law suits, for after 1819, when the Cherokees moved farther west, the markings on the survey route were not kept visible. In some areas questions arose involving its actual location. These questions were not idle ones, for the authenticity of many a farm boundary was at stake. It has been estimated that at one time a third of all the deeds of Transylvania County lands depended upon the Meigs-Freeman line.[7]

Dividing lines between states and national lines of demarcation did not comprise all of the boundary troubles that plagued Western North Carolina. Counties, formed in rapid succession in the mountain region from 1808 to 1861, were created from older counties. Some were made up of sections from two or more counties. Each act creating a county designated its boundary, but the boundary, or certain sections of it, frequently proved unacceptable to the new county or to the old county or to both. Appeals to the General Assembly resulted in acts making boundary adjustments. These acts were numerous, often several for each county. In fact, Ashe County, in attaining its present boundary, required twenty-three such acts.[8]

By 1812 the attention of the settlers in Western North Carolina was sharply, although somewhat unwillingly, called to national affairs. There were disturbing episodes of impressment of American sailors into the English navy, incidents of seizure of American ships, and interference in American trade by both England and France. General dissatisfaction was also aroused by the passage of the Embargo Act of 1807 and by the later Alien and Sedition Laws. All of these factors led to a struggle in Congress for war against one or the other—the extremists said both—of the offending European nations. Led by the young members known as "War Hawks," the congressional fight culminated in June, 1812, with the declaration of war against England.

Far from the coastal areas, with no exports involved in the hazards run by the American merchant marine and busy with more immediate problems, the Western North Carolina settlers showed little interest in this war. Although men from every county enlisted for service, there were no mass enlistments from the area. Indeed, the counties just east of the Blue Ridge had as yet not recovered from the ravages of the Revolutionary War, which there had assumed the nature of a civil war. The depredations made by the troops of both Cornwallis and Ferguson in that war had brought destrucion of much property and intense suffering to hundreds of pioneers. These people had little zest for another war. North Carolina was at once assigned a quota of some seven thousand men, however, to be organized into eight companies. These were recruited largely from volunteers from the various counties. But in 1814 a call came for an additional seven thousand men. This quota was made up almost entirely by draft.[9]

The Western North Carolina counties furnished their quota of these men although most of them saw little if any action. They had been called primarily to aid in quelling the Creek Indians, urged by British agents to take the warpath against the Americans. General Andrew Jackson was in charge of the Creek campaign, and the North Carolina contingent was sent to join his forces. But it reached him after his decisive victory of Horse Shoe Bend, in which a company of Cherokee volunteers had been of service in bringing him victory and in which the Cherokee leader Junaluska had saved the American general's life. The North Carolina soldiers were then called back to their state. But the volunteers from the state in Jackson's forces went with him to New Orleans.[10]

The period of national prosperity that followed the close of the Second War with England was short lived everywhere in North Carolina and was utterly non-existent in the western counties. The financial panic of 1819 was later to affect the entire state. For the two decades after the Euro-American peace treaty was signed, however, other states began turning their attention to their own internal improvements and their economic progress. North Carolina, in contrast, was strangely apathetic. In fact, so few signs of progress were visible along any line that the state received the derogatory nickname of the "Rip Van Winkle State."

Several factors contributed to this static condition in the progress being made by the nation as a whole. Lack of harbors made North Carolina export trade a mere trickle, while lack of an east-west highway continued to divert the products of the piedmont region and the mountain area to adjoining states. Adjoining states thus reaped the profits to be gained and in exchange sent their own products into North Carolina. High transportation rates made these imports costly and discouraged farmers from raising more than they could consume. At this time, moreover, agriculture was practically the only occupation of the people.[11]

In Western North Carolina some farms along the rivers east of the Blue Ridge were large enough to warrant slave labor. But the census of 1790 showed that even in that area slaves made up a small percentage of the population. For example, in Rutherford County in 1790 only 164 of the county's 1,136 families owned slaves, and even in 1830 out of a population of practically 14,000, the county had only 3,500 Negroes.[12] In the newer and more westerly counties a few owners of extensive lands worked their fields with slave labor.

Robert Love of Haywood County owned at least a hundred slaves, and James McConnel Smith of Buncombe County worked seventy-five slaves on each of two of his farms.[13] Other men living in the fertile mountain valleys found it profitable to own slaves, but they were the exceptions. Most of the settlers neither owned nor could afford to own slaves, although some, especially those living in the towns and villages, might have an occasional house servant. The Negro population in the mountains was, therefore, almost negligible.[14]

During the first two decades of the nineteenth century there were no factories in the state with the exception of one small cotton mill erected in 1816 in Lincoln County, some scattered iron works, and three paper mills. In practically all parts of the state the people continued raising the food they ate and making the tools they used and the clothes they wore, fortunate if there was a sufficient surplus of products to exchange for the bare necessities not available in their immediate communities.

Every Tar Heel, east or west, objected to taxes in any form, and during this period the state had an annual income so small that its yearly expenditures could not exceed $132,000. Most of this amount was required to pay governmental expenses, and when it came to needed improvements, the treasury was chronically in the dire condition of Mother Hubbard's cupboard. In other words, North Carolina trailed other states in social projects while it topped them all in illiteracy.[15]

Adding to the depressing governmental impasse was the constantly intensifying struggle between East and West. As settlers pushed westward and mountain counties were formed, their representatives to the General Assembly sponsored legislation favorable to their section. North Carolina, after 1815, was a one-party state, with the Republicans (that is, the Jeffersonian Democrats) in control. But the gulf between eastern and western members of the legislature did not represent a struggle between parties; it was even more fundamental. The clash was based on the geographic and climatic differences of the two regions, on the difference in the racial and cultural backgrounds of the people of the regions, and on their widely separated interests.

It was, after all, the old Regulator struggle in a state guise. And the western representatives were treated much as the colonial representatives had been. Eastern members still dominated the General Assembly and kept this domination by forming new eastern counties as fast as western counties were authorized. From the eastern representatives the governor and the state officials were yearly elected. There seemed little hope for the men from the mountains, and the struggle, bitter and personal at times, absorbed much of the energies of the lawmakers and far too much of their time. Moreover, the struggle created deep-seated hatreds and prejudices between the two sections of the state, some of which were long in the healing.[16]

During these years vast new territories to the west were being carved into American states. Thousands of North Carolinians, thoroughly discouraged over the future of their state, joined the streams of westward trekking men and women. They planned to make homes in the Ohio River country, on lands bordering the Mississippi River, or on the beckoning plains of far-off Texas. In Western North Carolina a constant procession of people trailed along the tortuous road following the French Broad River and over the winding Wilderness Trail into Tennessee and Kentucky and the territories beyond. Still others went into adjoining states. All went in the hope of brighter prospects for themselves and their children. By 1840, thirty-two of the state's counties had a smaller population than they had had in 1830. This meant for North Carolina not only the loss of its citizens, but the loss of many actual and potential leaders.[17]

Crying for reform, the first voice in the wilderness was heard in the piedmont section. In 1812 a young lawyer of Hillsboro took his seat in the General Assembly as senator from Orange County. Born in nearby Caswell County and educated at David Caldwell's Academy at Guilford and at the University, Archibald DeBow Murphey sought expression for the strongly democratic ideas developing through rugged pioneer living in the piedmont and the mountain sections. He was ready to voice the belief of the westerners that government had a duty to perform for its people—all of its people. Thoroughly informed on the economic conditions throughout the state, Murphey offered, in 1815, the first of a series of reform measures. During the next few years he was tireless in his efforts to bring both the people and the General Assembly to a realization of the benefits that his program would bring to North Carolina.

In 1819 Murphey presented a *Memoir on the Internal Improvements Contemplated by the Legislature of North Carolina.* It was a masterly survey of geographic and economic conditions within the commonwealth, and it summed up his recommendations for a transportation system that would make use of the state's navigable streams, and that would promote the use of its coastal inner waterways. The program would also provide an east-west turnpike, together with subsidiary roads leading into it, which would funnel products from the piedmont and mountain regions into the state's eastern markets.[18]

Western North Carolina received considerable attention in these recommendations. Murphey's first suggestion concerning the area was authorization for making a new state map. The Price-Strother map, privately financed a few years earlier and

N. C. DEPARTMENT OF ARCHIVES AND HISTORY

Archibald DeBow Murphey: Murphey led a crusade for an east-west highway, a state public school system, and the revision of the state's constitution. After his death, western leaders continued the crusade that in time led to reforms. Murphy, the county seat of Cherokee County, was named in his honor.

based upon the information available at that time, was hopelessly inaccurate in its depiction of the region between the Blue Ridge and the Smoky Mountains. With the rich valleys of the Tuckaseigee and Oconaluftee Rivers open to white settlement under the Cherokee treaty of 1819, it was imperative, he pointed out, to make information available to settlers. These lands, Murphey hoped, might attract some of the North Carolinians who would otherwise leave the state for western territories. To make the lands accessible he advocated the construction of a road west from Waynesville to the southwestern border of the state where it could connect with the old Cherokee trail to South Carolina and Georgia. He felt that the Cherokee land, when sold, should bring a million dollars into the coffers of the state.

Murphey also urged that the two main highways in Buncombe County be improved and kept in good condition. The one going south from Buncombe Courthouse to Rutherford County by way of Hickory Nut Gorge was in deplorable condition, and the other, from the courthouse to South Carolina by way of Saluda Gap, was likewise in need of immediate repairs. This highway, he considered "perhaps the most public road in the state." He reflected his own recent visit to the mountain village when he added, "The Traveller is astonished on reaching Buncombe Courthouse (called Morristown on the map but now called Asheville) to find people from six states in the Union in the same Hotel."[19]

Murphey maintained that the road, which traversed the mountain section from the South Carolina border to Tennessee by way of the French Broad River would continue to be a main trade artery and must be maintained as such. East of the Blue Ridge he advocated making use of the Yadkin, the Catawba, and the Broad Rivers as transportation arteries. He stressed the need of converting the poorly constructed and illy kept roads leading westward into all-weather highways over which products could be brought from Tennessee and from the mountain section to river towns for shipment south.[20]

To carry out his state-wide transportation project, basic to any financial progress of the commonwealth, Murphey urged the General Assembly to create a board of control and to make appropriations for converting some feasible plan into a reality. Inherent in his over-all plan were future possibilities for the growth of manufacturing as well as distinct advantages for such eastern cities as Wilmington and Beaufort; therefore, he hoped that the plan would appeal to the eastern delegates to the General Assembly. He knew that without their support any proposed bill was doomed to fail. But Murphey was disappointed. The easterners were, with a few exceptions, solidly opposed to the transportation project, and in session after session the western members of the General Assembly saw their economic hopes fade into legislative limbo.

Murphey's vision for the progress of his state was not, however, limited to his dream of a state system of water and inland highways. He foresaw a partial solution to North Carolina's problem of inertia through a public school system. He was the first of the state's legislators to propose that the General Assembly set up a fund, to be administered by a state board and to be used in establishing a wholly or partially state supported system of schools. He advocated the establishment of primary schools and above them academies or high schools with the state university crowning the system. Murphey pointed out that, except for establishing the University, the provision in the 1776 Constitution enjoining the education of the people had been grossly neglected. He then cited the state's disgracefully high rate of illiteracy.

Murphey also suggested the formation of two or more primary schools in each county, supported jointly by state and county, at which enrollment would be free for children unable to pay the tuition set for other pupils. In addition, ten regional academies would be operated partly by the state and partly by local funds which would be raised in part by tuition from those able to pay. The University, which had never received a penny from the state for its running expenses, would be greatly aided by state appropriations enabling it to expand its program. Schools for the state's deaf and dumb children were, under his plan, to be entirely state supported.[21]

Again the eastern planters who, year after year, represented their respective counties were not interested. They had no desire for public education for their own sons and saw no reason for taxing themselves to educate the poorer children in their part of the state or the children of settlers in the remote areas of the commonwealth. Some of them went so far as to claim no advantage in education for the masses. Every education bill was promptly killed by the adverse votes of the eastern delegates. The leaders from the West could see no hope for enlightening the people living on small piedmont farms or in isolated mountain coves.

It gradually became clear to Murphey and to the growing group of western delegates rallying to his cause that there was, after all, only one solution for the problems facing the state. There must be either a new state constitution or a drastic revision of the one in force. The West had long felt the injustices which had grown up under the governmental regulations laid down by those designing the state's first constitution. Under it, each county, regardless of population, elected one senator to the upper house and two representatives to the lower house of the General Assembly. In addition, a few eastern cities—some of which were mere villages—elected a member each to the lower house. This borough system gave the east additional representation and power.

As the number of counties increased, the legislative body became too large, cumbersome in its work, and expensive in its operation. Since 1776 the sharp increase in population had taken place in the piedmont and mountain sections of the state, where one after another new counties had been formed until the population of those sections considerably outnumbered that of the eastern counties. But the East, with a just predominance of members in the legislature in 1776, had kept that superiority by the borough system. This was greatly resented by the mountain settlers, and so was the creation of a new eastern county for each authorized in the West.[22]

The democratic westerners, too, objected to other features of the constitution. Under it, the only popular vote enjoyed by the people was for their representatives to the General Assembly. That body annually elected from its members the state's governor and other officials. Acting upon recommendation of the county's delegates to the General Assembly, the governor appointed the county justices of the peace, the most influential county officers since they made up the quarterly or county court. Their terms were for life, and they were answerable not to the people they served, but to the governor. Under this system, the governor was naturally subservient to the Assembly that elected him.

Then, too, the privilege of voting was dependent upon a citizen's property possessions. Owning property entitled a man to vote for the county's representatives in the lower house of the Assembly, but he was required to own at least fifty acres of land before he could cast a vote for a senator. State office holders were likewise required to be land owners, one hundred acres being the minimum for a man seeking a seat in the lower house, and three hundred acres for one aspiring to a seat in the senate. Property valued at a thousand pounds sterling or more was required for one being considered by the Assembly for the governorship.[23]

All attempts made by Murphey to secure legislative authorization for a constitutional reform convention met with the same dismal fate as did his other reform measures. It must have seemed to this far-seeing statesman that the energies he had expended in behalf of North Carolina had been wasted. But such was far from the case, for his labors had set the slow mills of the gods to grinding. The progress-strangling control of the easterners was doomed. The forward-looking measures he advocated crystalized western opinions, and Murphey's dedication to the betterment of his state drew a following of younger men from the West ready to take up his work. He did not live to see any of his plans accepted, but before he passed from the scene

Chapter Twelve

N. C. DEPARTMENT OF ARCHIVES AND HISTORY

David Lowry Swain: Swain was born in Beaverdam valley near Asheville in 1801. He became the first native-born lawyer southwest of the Blue Ridge. He served as a member of the General Assembly, as Governor, and for 32 years as President of the State University at Chapel Hill, where he was affectionately known as "Old Warping Bars."

in 1832, there were small but significant victories foreshadowing the accomplishments eventually to come.

For instance, the General Assembly in 1819 created a Board of Internal Improvement and employed a state engineer. It authorized subscriptions for several eastern navigation companies, and it created a small state fund for internal improvements, to be garnered from proceeds of Cherokee land sales and from certain state stock dividends. Under this board, steps were taken for a few long over-due roads in the mountain section, shades again of Murphey's plan. Accordingly, appropriations were made for a highway from Old Fort to Asheville and for a turnpike along the French Broad River that would connect Greenville, South Carolina, with Greeneville, Tennessee, passing through Asheville and Warm Springs.

This road, known as the Buncombe Turnpike, was begun in 1824 and completed three years later.[24] It was to be a major factor in the life and progress of Western North Carolina for many years and was, for some time, the finest road in North Carolina. In 1820 an appropriation was made for improving the navigation of that section of the Broad River stretching from the South Carolina border to Twitty's Ford, and twelve years later funds were allocated for making the existing Hickory Nut Gap road an improved artery across the Blue Ridge.[25]

In 1822 the General Assembly set aside a fund known as the Agricultural Fund to aid in the program sponsored by the State Agricultural Society, which had been incorporated three years earlier. The Society had grown out of several county organizations formed with the aim of improving agriculture in the state. This measure proved a somewhat premature step, and the fund was later diverted to other projects.[26] Still, it was a promise of later developments. Another step forward was taken with the publication of state geological surveys made by Denison Olmsted and Elisha Mitchell, both members of the University faculty.[27]

In 1825 the General Assembly yielded to the increasing pressure for state-sponsored education put forth by the delegates from the West, by ministers of various faiths, and by men connected with the State University. The legislature created a Literary Fund to be built up and eventually used for public education. This fund was collected from dividends received from state-owned bank stock not otherwise allocated, from dividends of certain other state-owned stock, from taxes, from public land sales other than Cherokee land, and from appropriations. The Literary Fund was placed under a Board presided over by the governor as president and by the state treasurer. By 1836 it had received only $243,000, a part of which had been diverted to other purposes. But it kept the idea of a future public school system before the people, although the amount in the treasury of the Board was always too small to carry out its purpose. It was to be 1840 before log school houses would appear in the mountain coves.[28]

Yet the end of the do-nothing policy of the eastern Republicans was fast approaching, and the "Rip Van Winkle State" was arousing from its slumbers. Several factors were converging to bring about a change. For one thing, the demands of the now articulate West reflected the new and growing democratic movement sweeping across the entire nation and expressed in the 1824 campaign of Andrew Jackson for president. Seeing a hope for their progressive program under a "People's" president, the westerners broke politically with the easterners, and North Carolina ceased to be a one-party state.[29]

After 1832, when these same westerners had become bitterly disappointed in Jackson as president, they joined the ranks of the newly formed Whig party to oppose the easterners who had, somewhat to their own surprise, found Jackson's policies to their liking. A second factor in the forward movement was that now the voice of one man had become the voice of many; in the General Assembly a group of able and determined western leaders was headed by David Lowry Swain of Buncombe County.

Swain was born in the Beaverdam settlement in 1801 and received the thorough training given at Newton Academy to boys in families of the first settlers in the mountains. When he appeared at the State University as a student, he was placed in the junior class. After a short stay at that institution, young Swain took up the study of law at Raleigh under the tutorship of John Louis Taylor, Chief Justice of North Carolina. In 1822 he returned to his native county to hang out his shingle in Asheville, becoming the town and Buncombe County's first native lawyer. With his ability to make friends and his deep interest in the problems of Western North Carolina, it was inevitable that he should turn to a political career. By 1832, at the age of thirty-one, Swain had served five terms in the General Assembly, had been Solicitor for one year, and had been elected as judge of the Superior Court.

In the General Assembly he rallied the forces around Murphey and in advocating reforms, became an authority on taxation and on statistics showing the condition of the state. Those who worked with him came to respect his utter honesty and sincerity and forgot the ungainliness of his appearance, which was later to win him the affectionate nickname of "Old Warping Bars." His good will, tact, and diplomacy drew many friends from the eastern bloc, and his personal charm and clear-cut arguments won supporters to the cause of reform. He threw the weight of his growing popularity and the force of his sound judgment based on facts into the struggle for two of Murphey's reform measures—highway improvement and constitutional reform.

It was largely due to Swain's efforts that such desperately needed roads as the Buncombe Turnpike were authorized. As Murphey, through a series of unfortunate circumstances, withdrew from political prominence, Swain became the acknowledged leader of the Whig party in North Carolina and in 1832 was elected governor, winning the necessary support from eastern delegates in the General Assembly. Thus Western North Carolina was represented in the highest office of the state.[30]

As governor, Swain pointed out that not a major project along any line of internal improvement was in progress in the state. He set about an unrelenting campaign for the authorization of a constitutional convention. He was extremely popular in the state, and during his three terms as chief executive he led the General Assembly, to which he refused to be subservient, into the most receptive reform mood it had yet attained. By 1832 Governor Swain's constitutional reform measure had, almost by accident, found favor with two groups among the eastern delegates. One was the Roman Catholic group, whose brilliant member, William Gaston, could be removed from his position as Justice of the Supreme Court if the General Assembly desired to carry out the 1776 Constitutional provision debarring Catholics from office. The other group centered around Fayetteville, which, after the destructive fire of the capitol, put forth an effort to have the capitol moved from Raleigh to Fayetteville. Such a move would require a constitutional change.

Some degree of support was now also forthcoming from the area around Albemarle Sound because of the suggested waterway improvements for that region. Thus by the untiring efforts of Governor Swain and a group of able westerners, aided by leaders from the interested eastern groups, a law was passed in the Assembly in 1834 to submit the question of a constitutional convention to a popular vote. In the referendum that resulted a majority of almost seven thousand votes was cast favoring the calling of such a convention. For the most part, each section voted solidly according to the old line-up. At a second election delegates to the convention were chosen, and these assembled in Raleigh in June 1835.[31]

With the East and the West still opposed to each other's program, it took the tact and diplomatic skill of all the leaders, headed by the Governor, to work out acceptable compromises. But by July 11 the Convention had a list of revisions to submit to the people and adjourned. At the referendum the voters expressed practically the same majority acceptance of the amendments as they had for the calling of the convention. Again the votes were sectional in their distribution.[32] The amendments were made the law of the land, and the first major step had been taken in making possible industrial and economic progress in North Carolina. At last the "Rip Van Winkle State" was awake.

Under the revised constitution, the governor was to be elected for a two-year term by a direct vote of the people. While he might succeed himself, he could hold office not more than four out of any six years. Equal representation in the General Assembly was abolished. Instead, the upper chamber or Senate was to be made up of fifty members representing districts into which the state was divided. The lower house or House of Commons was to have 120 members elected by counties according to population; each county was to have at least one representative. The General Assembly was to meet biennially, and all voters, it stipulated, must be white males, twenty-one years of age or over. Property qualifications for voting for governor and for members of the House of Commons were abolished. But each voter casting a ballot for a senator was still required to show proof of possessing at least fifty acres of land. There were many other changes. Among them was the substitution of the word *Christian* for the word *Protestant* in the religious tests for office, the abolishment of the old borough representation, and the presentation of two methods of constitutional revision.[33]

Although much would have to be done later in the amended constitution, democracy had come to the people, and it had come through the efforts and the ideals of the West, led first by a piedmont leader and then by a man from the mountains.

CHAPTER THIRTEEN

Gold in the Hills and on the Highways

Much of the story of the European conquest of the two Americas had been the story of the white man's insatiable appetite for gold. The precious yellow metal was the will-o-the-wisp that lured DeSoto and his Spanish army into the mountains of Western North Carolina in the sixteenth century. Gold also led hopeful Spanish prospectors, during the next 125 years, to slip into the region and carry on limited mining operations that they tried to keep secret. The Indians—both the Cherokees and the Catawbas—knew of these attempts and told English traders and explorers, who, in turn, took rumors of Spanish gold discoveries back to the coastal settlements. Accordingly, those areas sent men out to "explore beyond the mountaine." Men who later pushed westward to settle were ever on the alert for gold and silver.

Small amounts of both these metals had been found, and gold in limited quantities had been panned from streams or mined from surface mines during the colonial period of western settlement.[1] But it was not until after the Revolutionary War that the cry of "Gold!" brought a wave of hopeful prospectors into Western North Carolina. The gold rush began around 1799 after twelve year old Conrad Reed found an interesting looking seventeen-pound "rock" on his father's farm in newly created Cabarrus

208 / *Chapter Thirteen*

N. C. DEPARTMENT OF ARCHIVES AND HISTORY

A Bechtler Coin: These pictures show the obverse and reverse of a gold dollar coined by Christopher Bechtler at his private mint near Rutherfordton. In his later dies he corrected the N in ONE. He also coined two-fifty and five dollar gold pieces. Between January, 1831, and February, 1840, the Bechtler mint coined $2,241,850 in gold coins.

County. The "rock" proved to be ore rich with its lode of gold. In the Reed mine that was there developed unbelievably large gold nuggets were later discovered, a few weighing from twenty to twenty-eight pounds.[2]

New discoveries continued, and mines were opened in thirteen counties, those in Burke and Rutherford being so rich that by 1825 these counties were the scene of the nation's most extensive gold mining operations.[3] These operations were carried on by any available method of mining. Gold dust floating in the waters of the streams was collected by the slow process of panning—by letting the water run through sieve-bottomed pans. A somewhat more elaborate method for the amateur was to run the gold-laden water from sluice boxes into a trough made by hollowing out a log. This log was kept in motion as the water flowed through it to keep the silt and sand afloat and moving with the water. The heavier gold sank and was caught by cleats nailed across the floor of the trough. To improve the system quicksilver or mercury might be mixed with the sand.[4]

The gold particles and dust thus obtained could be put into a cloth or leather bag to be weighed out for purchases or, if taken to the mint in Philadelphia, made into coins. Where the metal was found in the rocks, men hacked out the nuggets with pick axes and shovels. It was all slow, hard work, but it was rewarding. For example, according to Rutherfordton's newspaper, *The North*

Carolina Spectator and Western Advertiser, a man in 1830 could pan two dollars worth of dust a day from gold-carrying streams and get a similar amount from a surface mine. In 1830 in Western North Carolina the sum of two dollars, with its high purchasing power, was indeed hard to come by.[5] It has been estimated that in Burke County alone, over a period of years, a thousand men were devoting their time to this individual method of mining.[6]

As might be expected, the publicity given to the discovery of new mines spread far afield and into the gold area came thousands of eager people who had just one interest in common—the finding of gold. Indeed, these newcomers, crowding along the narrow, muddy roads of the back country and on to the foothills of the Blue Ridge, made up a motley group, representing perhaps all of the nationalities and the races that Europe was sending to the "Melting Pot" that was America. Their ideals and morals were as varied as their backgrounds. Towns and mining communities mushroomed into being, and many were the tales later told of the lusty, boisterous life of these camps.[7]

Men with money to invest, especially if it might quickly be doubled or tripled, arrived from northern states and European countries to form mining companies that were readily incorporated by the General Assembly. These men bought up mines already in operation or leased lands that gave promise of rich deposits. There they sank shafts, set up machinery to pulverize the rock and get the gold, and hired hundreds of the incoming men as "hands." The newspaper accounts, bristling with the excitement of gold fever, told of mines selling for $4,500 and $6,000. Two men declined to accept $5,000 for their joint interest in a mine, while one owner even refused the fabulous offer of $35,000 for his land.[8]

Some, although far from all, of the mines opened in the state gave satisfactory returns to the investors, who brought into the state an estimated capital investment of $100,000,000.[9] By 1814 some of the yield of the mines was reaching the government mint in Philadelphia, which that year recorded receiving $11,000 in North Carolina gold. Much more was forthcoming, and prior to 1829 the state was furnishing all of the gold minted at Philadelphia where the records show that during the period of extensive mining it received more than $9,000,000 of gold from the state, the largest amount in any single year being $475,000 in 1833. North Carolina was justly crowned the "Golden State."[10]

But that record is only a small, perhaps a very small, part of the picture of North Carolina mining. How much gold was

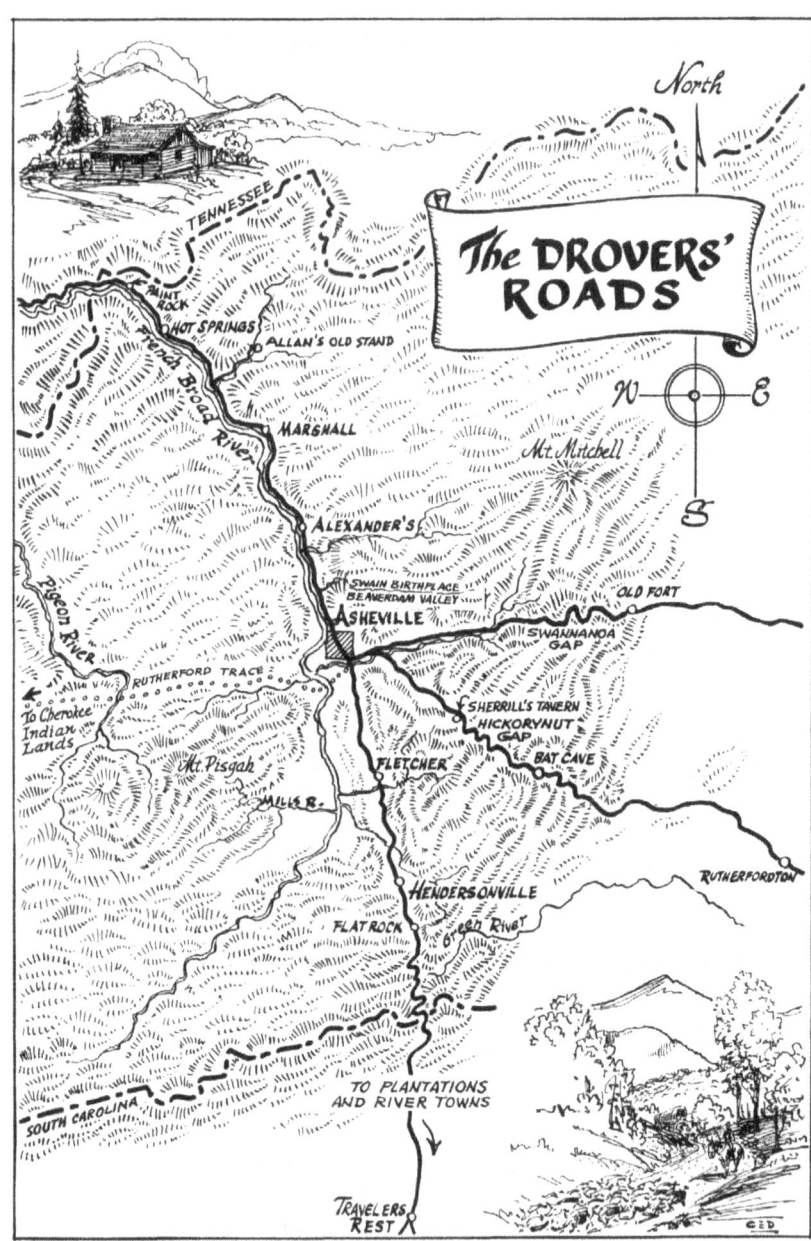

THE STEPHENS PRESS, INC.

A Drovers' Road: Horses, hogs, geese, and turkeys from states to the north joined droves that each autumn thundered and squawked along the Buncombe Turnpike. Other droves made use of roads farther west and still others passed over roads east of the Blue Ridge. All the animals were destined for markets in southern states.

extracted from the streams and mines from 1799 to 1860 will never be known. For an estimate one can only hazard a guess, for the records of most of the companies have been lost or destroyed, while the amounts panned by thousands of individuals were not kept. An untold amount went into jewelry for home demands and some was used to fill orders from other states and European markets. An estimated $600,000 worth was used for that purpose in 1832 alone. Then, too, some of the companies sent their gold to European countries. Much gold was undoubtedly lost in transactions, for both gold dust and gold nuggets or ore passed as a medium of exchange. It may well be that only a small portion of the estimated $50,000,000 to $65,000,000 worth of gold actually mined ever reached a mint.[11]

The gold boom came at a period when money was exceedingly scarce throughout the piedmont and mountain sections; in fact, many a home saw pitifully few coins of any kind—American, English, or Spanish—during a year's time. The widespread method of all purchasing was barter. Thus gold in any form meant an advantageous purchasing power to the man fortunate enough to pan a bit of the precious metal. Although coins were far more convenient than dust or ingots in making business transactions, few men had the time or the inclination to carry their gold in saddlebags that could not be protected over the long, difficult road to far-away Philadelphia. Nor were they willing to transport it by stage coach, a method slow, costly, and dangerous. So the ancient method employed by Abraham in buying a plot for Sarah's tomb was resorted to in nineteenth century Western North Carolina, and gold dust was measured or weighed out for the purchase of land or goods.

It is no wonder, then, that when in 1831 the Bechtlers set up a mint in Rutherfordton, they were able to do a thriving business. Among those arriving in Rutherfordton in 1830 were the Bechtlers—Christopher, his sons, Augustus and Charles, and his nephew, Christopher, Jr. There the elder Christopher bought land and built his home a few miles from the village. They had arrived by way of the Pennsylvania Road and on their way from New York harbor had stopped in Philadelphia long enough for Christopher and Augustus to set in motion the process of naturalization. In the Grand Duchy of Baden, their native country, they had been trained as metal workers. Now in their Rutherfordton home they again set up a shop and made and sold necklaces and brooches, cuff links and shirt studs, rings and watch chains, "executed to order, in the neatest and most skillful manner."[12] In addition to jewelry, the inventive Bechtlers also designed and manufactured rifles that would fire shots at a greater rate per minute. Since every settler was also a hunter, there was a ready market for these guns.

Christopher, who with his son Augustus, was proud of his newly acquired American citizenship, found himself deeply interested in conditions in his new country. In 1831, he took the first step in helping to solve one of its pressing problems—the lack of currency. After he and his family had designed dies and had laboriously made the necessary machinery, he advertised the opening of a mint at which, for a modest fee, he would assay gold and for a coining charge of two and a half per cent would coin a customer's gold into pieces valued at $2.50 and $5.00. The next year he added gold dollars, and for those having coins made he assayed the gold without charge. Always he gave back to the owner a sufficient amount of the gold for another assay, together with his record, so that, should the customer choose to do so, he could confirm Bechtler's record.[13]

In a shed built over a cellar the goldsmiths worked. There they assayed, refined, and coined the gold brought to their mint. Using the United States coins as their standards, the Bechtlers made each of theirs equal in value to the corresponding federal coin. But since the gold brought to them often varied in fineness, coins in each denomination varied in size and weight. Each contained the exact amount of gold used by the government, however, and each was stamped with the fineness of the gold and the weight of the coin. The name Bechtler with the initial C or A also appeared as did the name Rutherford.

In addition to North Carolina gold, the Rutherford mint also received small amounts from South Carolina and some from Georgia. Since the metal varied in color according to its source—that from the mountains being somewhat duller in color than that mined farther east and south—the coins varied in brightness. Each was stamped with the metal source. Dies had to be designed and made not only for each denomination, but also for each variety in a denomination. Until 1834 the coins bore no date, but in that year the government set up a new standard for its coins. The Bechtlers, in order to conform, had to discard their complete set of dies and make new ones. Thereafter, each coin carried the date 1834 to indicate that it belonged to the new series and thus conformed to the national standard.[14]

The federal government had established a mint in Philadelphia in 1792, but the coining of gold and silver had not yet been designated as a function of the national government alone. The Bechtler mint was the first private mint in the nation, but later contracts were entered into by the government with other goldsmiths. The government felt responsible for the integrity of the country's currency and in 1834 sent investigators to Rutherfordton to inspect the Bechtler mint. Their report was most favorable, showing that the coins made there had a slightly higher gold content than did the corresponding federal coins. No attempt was made then or later to halt or to hinder the coinage at the Rutherfordton mint. Instead, the federal government recognized the service being rendered by this mint in furnishing the region with badly needed currency, thus helping to raise the economic level of the area it served. In order to further that progress, a federal mint at Charlotte was established by an act of Congress in 1835. The new mint was open for coining in 1837.[15]

Although records are not available, from an 1840 report of the superintendent of the Charlotte mint, it would seem that the Bechtlers, during the first nine years of their mint, coined $2,241,855 worth of coins and assayed a far greater sum. No Bechtler coin carried a national symbol; yet all coins turned out by the mint were accepted at face value throughout the region and the state, in fact, throughout the nation. Many a contract called for payment in Bechtler coins, and many a westward-bound North Carolinian took with him enough Bechtler money to buy a farm when he reached his destination in some new territory. So it was that Rutherford coins sometimes came to light far from the mint that coined them.[16]

After the death of the elder Christopher, his son moved the jewelry and rifle shop into Rutherfordton. Soon afterward the work was divided, with Christopher, the nephew, taking over the mint. It continued operation until some time during the 1850's with, it seems sure, a decreasing amount of business, for after 1837 much of the gold mined was taken to the Charlotte mint for coining. In fact, many owners of Bechtler coins in time took them to the new mint for recoining into money stamped with the national symbols. That fact combined with the small size of the coins, making them easily lost, accounts for the comparatively few Bechtler coins in existence today. Still, it is impossible to overestimate the part played by these skilled artisans and their coins in the economic progress of Western North Carolina. It is a

THE STEPHENS PRESS, INC.

Early settlers drove their surplus hogs to local markets. Later these small droves were taken to the turnpikes to join animals trudging to market. The short-legged hogs could cover only eight to ten miles a day. An estimated 140,000 to 160,000 hogs squealed and grunted their way through Asheville in a single season.

shining tribute to the Bechtlers that in the years when they handled gold valued in the millions of dollars no question of their honesty ever arose. Their business transactions conformed to the same high standard of integrity that they required of their coins.[17]

While east of the Blue Ridge the economic pressure was being eased by the gold from the hills and the coins from the Bechtler's mint, the settlers west of that range were discovering a different kind of gold. The General Assembly, which in 1819 had reluctantly created a state fund for internal improvements, was induced in 1823 by delegates from the West to appropriate money for subsidizing a highway that would connect the mountain area with eastern markets. The next year the Buncombe Turnpike Company was incorporated with an authorized capital of $50,000 to be raised by the sale of shares at $50 a share. Contractors began work on the road, which connected at Saluda Gap with South Carolina's road from Charleston. It passed through the present Henderson County to Asheville, then stretched along the French Broad River to Warm Springs, and at Paint Rock joined a Tennessee road. The Turnpike thus connected Greenville, South Carolina, with Greeneville, Tennessee.[18]

In spite of the narrowness of the French Broad Gorge, necessitating numerous fords and side fords, a road had long followed the stream. The first one could have been no more than a path or trail, and it is amazing that a vehicle of any type could negotiate its ledges and rocks, its mud and its fords. Yet in 1795 at least two wagons coming from South Carolina accomplished that incredible feat. The citizens of Knoxville must indeed have had difficulty believing their eyes as the wagons rumbled into the village. Just two months earlier, Governor William Blount of Tennessee had advocated a French Broad road from his state to the Buncombe County Courthouse to be constructed by the two states.[19]

By the turn of the century such a project seems to have been undertaken, not by the states but by the prevailing method of requiring local residents along its route to do road work in their own sections. The best that could be said for the results of their rather haphazard labors was that a rider on horseback could get over it, and a wagoner with perseverance and luck might succeed in saving his stout wagon during its upsets over rocks and across fords. All travelers testified that a trip on the road required not only patience, but fortitude and endurance. As time went on, the repeated workings improved conditions somewhat, so that in 1812 Bishop Francis Asbury, making his annual journey to Asheville, commented on the "fine new road."[20] Despite improvements it was never a highway conducive to commercial travel. The mountain section had no hope of economic progress until a road suitable for trade could be constructed. With the completion of the Turnpike in 1827, therefore, a new day dawned in Western North Carolina.

With the finest highway in North Carolina to travel, settlers with their wagons piled with household goods and farm equipment now came into the region to make their homes. Strings of covered wagons wound along the Turnpike from east of the mountains, taking their owners to the hoped-for greener pastures of unseen western territories. High stepping horses hitched to light carriages—now brought into the hills for the first time or made by resident wagon makers—dashed along the road. They made unbelievably rapid time in getting their masters from Asheville or Greenville to Warm Springs, which had mushroomed into a health and recreation center.[21]

Stores in Asheville were soon showing a large and varied assortment of merchandise brought over the new highway, and on the streets of the village were hitched more horses from the surrounding areas than ever before. Wagon yards were opened to accommodate the stream of travelers. Inns and taverns sprang up along the route and carried on a thriving business, and land offices helped the incoming settlers to locate suitable real estate.

It was as a means of getting the products of the farms and woods to markets that the Buncombe Turnpike played its most important role, however, and proved to be a veritable gold mine to those living along or near it. No longer did a man have to think in terms of transporting his surplus by horseback. Wagon makers in their enlarged or newly established shops tried to make wagons fast enough to keep up with the demands. But the wagons could not be used for the meat the farmers took to market on the hoof. Up and down the French Broad River, beyond in the valleys of Tennessee and Kentucky, and north of the Ohio in Illinois the problem was—in fact, had been since the earliest settlers arrived—the task of getting products to market. The Southern Appalachians everywhere presented a barrier to towns to the east.

The enterprising pioneers partially solved the difficulty by feeding the grain they raised in the broad, fertile, river valleys to live stock and fowls and then herding the animals to South Carolina towns. There planters with broad acres of cotton tended by battalions of Negro slaves were always in the market for food for men and animals. Even before the Turnpike was constructed, the old French Broad River road had echoed with the squeals of hogs being driven along it to the Charleston highway. The new Turnpike increased the number of these drives of four-footed animals to astounding figures.[22]

When the crops had been harvested, the cool, dry days of October arrived to spread their flaunting colors over the mountain sides, and a thin blue haze veiled the peaks and sifted through the valleys. The men now rounded up their horses and mules from lush meadows or from the high, grassy balds of the uplands. They brought in their hogs from the woods, each one marked with its registered, mutilated ear or its branded flank and each one now fattened and sleek from a rich diet of nuts and acorns. Or perhaps the farmers collected the turkeys from their roosting trees and gathered the quacking ducks from the farmyard. They then began the long, slow trek to the Turnpike that crossed the mountains and followed the river that wound over Saluda Gap to connect with the road leading to distant Augusta or Charleston. For the next two months the Turnpike was alive with noisy, dust-raising animals, unwilling travelers to the slaughter.

Usually each owner preceded his drove, leading the way on horseback. Appropriately enough, he was known as the drover. Sometimes, however, a speculator would take the combined herds of neighbors and become the drover, hoping to make a profit for himself as well as for the owners when he disposed of his charges. The drover had several helpers, often young men or half-grown boys, who walked behind as drivers or at the sides of the herds to keep the animals in line and moving. These men—husky, outdoor men—cracked their long, snapping whips in the air above the backs of laggards or strays, while their strong voices rang out in calls and commands that the animals understood and sometimes obeyed.

The drovers of horses and mules had the least transportation difficulties and made comparatively rapid time from their homes to their destinations. But from eight to ten miles a day was as far as fowls would travel or as far as the short legs of hogs could take their owners.[23] The demand for hams, lard, and fatback was practically limitless, and more hogs made their deliberate way along the Turnpike than did any other live stock. Drovers of hogs entered the broad highway at any and all toll gates along its length. The animals came protestingly into it from subsidiary roads, poor and narrow, from the valleys to the east, and from the regions to the west. Roads, like the Cataloochee road, were widened from the ancient Indian trail that connected the Pigeon River area with the territory around Cosby and Newport, Tennessee.

Sometimes nightfall caught a drove of hogs some distance from a tavern, although such a mishap was more apt to occur when the travelers were turkeys. These fowl were unpredictable in their movements and at the coming of early dusk were apt to take to the first trees they saw for a well-earned night's rest.

THE STEPHENS PRESS, INC.

The Alexander Hotel: At Alexander's Inn and stand on the French Broad River north of Asheville men and animals could spend the night. Drovers were lodged in rooms with other drovers. Drivers slept rolled up in blankets on the floor of the "great room."

When that happened, the drivers stretched out on the softest spot of ground available and spent the night with the flock. But customarily, drovers and their drivers tried to manage the animals and flocks so that they would reach a stand by nightfall.

All of the live stock had to be fed enroute, and the men themselves needed food and lodging. These demands were ably met by enterprising citizens along the highway. Privately erected and operated inns and their accompanying stands were built at six to eight mile intervals along the entire route, where both men and beasts could find rest and food. The first concern of the men upon reaching the stand was for the stock. The animals were driven into wide pens enclosed with rail fences and given the day's one feeding, eight bushels of corn for each hundred hogs. With their appetites satisfied, and supplied with water, the hogs, after a few happy grunts, slept the sleep of the travel-worn. The turkeys gobbled up their portion of grain and took to the trees, and the horses contentedly swished their tails as they munched their quota of oats.

Their chores completed, the men then removed the outer layer of the day's dust from face and hands and went into the inn, a rambling one or two story building, where they did full justice to the hearty meal that awaited them. Cooked as the mountain men liked them were vegetables from the inn keeper's garden, meats from his own hogs and from the surrounding woods, hot biscuits made in his kitchen and dripping with newly churned butter, all washed down with milk, strong coffee or, if one preferred, with more potent drinks. The drovers might be lodged in rooms with several fellow travelers, but the drivers were more than content to roll up in blankets on the floor of the great hall, unmindful of the hardness of the boards beneath their thin pallets. No charge was made for those sleeping on the floor, but meals cost the drovers twenty-five cents per man. For corn for his hogs and fowl the drovers paid the inn keeper seventy-five cents per bushel.

Long before sun-up the entire establishment was astir, for the men were eager to be finished with their breakfast and to get their droves and flocks onto the Turnpike, each hoping to be the first in the onward moving van and thus to avoid the great volumes of dust left hanging in the air by previous travelers. Moreover, they wanted to make all possible mileage before the heat of the day that slowed the pace of the animals. So, one after another, the drivers got their animals from the pens and their fowl from the trees. Giving their calls and snapping whips, they got the animals and flocks once more tramping stolidly down the highway, soon screened from view by a curtain of dust.

Upon leaving the tavern, the drover might pay the innkeeper in cash, but he frequently gave a due bill, which he redeemed in a few weeks on his return from the markets. Frequently, too, he paid a part or all of the bill with hogs. The habitual laggards, the limping, and the sore-footed, together with the cantankerous, were left along the way as payment for lodging and food. These animals would later be killed and as hams, sausage, and roasts, appear on the inn keeper's table or be taken to southern markets on his next purchasing trip into South Carolina. The innkeeper was, perforce, a man of many trades. To supply the drovers with corn, he bought vast stores, filling his immense cribs. To avoid confusion, he sent word throughout the countryside that at a certain date, well in advance of the autumn drives, he would purchase corn. On that day the farmers came, their wagons bursting with corn for which they received fifty cents per bushel. They might receive payment in money. But more often each man took what was coming to him in trade, for the stand keeper was the neighborhood merchant.

Once or twice a year the stand owner put the surplus products he had received from the drovers and those he had bought from the farmers into one or more stout wagons and traveled the Turnpike to Augusta or even to Charleston. There he exchanged his load for the merchandise needed in his community. It often took six horses to pull his heavily laden wagons over the steep, curving roads. Farmers fortunate enough not to need all their payment in goods might leave the remainder due them with the stand keeper, who thus also became the community's banker. Often, to be sure, the debt went the other way, and a farmer received supplies during the year to be paid for when his corn crop was ready to deliver to the stand.[24]

For longer than most men's life-times these drives continued, and it was not until the railroads crossed the mountains and traversed the area to the west that they ceased. During those years untold numbers of men and animals traveled south over the Turnpike and through the villages of Western North Carolina. Records indicate that between 150,000 and 160,000 hogs grunted and squealed their way through the village of Asheville in a single season. David Vance, stand keeper at Marshall, said he had fed as many as ninety thousand hogs in a single month. Often fifty to a hundred men were fed and lodged, and several thousand hogs were kept in a stand during a night.[25]

Although the Buncombe Turnpike was the scene of the largest and most continuous drives, other Western North Carolina highways also served as links between farms to the north and markets to the south and east. Along the old Wilderness Road, Tennessee and Kentucky men drove their horses and hogs to Jordan Council's stand at the present Boone to sell them to Council, inn keeper and merchant. He in turn hired drivers to get the animals down the eastern slopes of the Blue Ridge, then east to Virginia markets, or once off the mountains, they might turn south on the highway leading through Morganton and Rutherfordton to Spartanburg or go by way of King's Mountain to Charleston. Farther west in the mountains, on the old Indian trails widened into roads, the droves sometimes went into Georgia and then continued east into South Carolina.[26] In the mid 1850's new east-west roads were built by incorporated companies, connecting the extreme border counties of the state at both the Tennessee and the Georgia lines with Asheville and thereby with the section east of the Blue Ridge. Horses, mules, hogs, and turkeys trudged and thundered along these roads every autumn.[27]

This autumn traffic was destructive to roads, necessitating frequent and expensive repairs. But the great, moving river of livestock brought the first wave of prosperity that the region west of the Blue Ridge had experienced. The livestock trade did even more, for it set the entire economic pattern of the mountain section. Although they were being aided economically by the gold mining that was the spectacular feature of the period, the counties east of the Blue Ridge also felt the impact of the great droves tramping southward along their highways. Farmers there profited economically, perhaps, more from the cattle and from the sale of their corn at the many stands along the trade routes than they did from the precious yellow metal being taken from their hills.[28]

CHAPTER FOURTEEN

Light and Shade in the Mountains

From the first the Buncombe Turnpike set the pattern of living along its route. To a lesser degree that was true with every road along which the drivers passed. The farmers could now market comparatively easily all the grain they could raise. Instead of feeding their corn to hogs that had to be taken to distant markets, they took it to the nearest stand. Because the demand was insatiable, they cleared more land and planted more corn, abandoning the worn out fields for new ones with no apparent concern for the future of the soil. But they prospered, those farmers whose acres lay in the fertile river valleys and so did the entire area.[1]

The pleasant new economic status of each prospering farmer was soon evident in his new house, for the original log cabin of a few years before became the "summer kitchen," a storehouse, or a shop. A roomy, comfortable home took its place as the residence of the family. The new dwelling might also be of logs or of broad, axe-hewn timbers; however, with the coming of the saw mills, some of which were water driven, it might be constructed of dressed lumber if its owner were willing to wait months or a year to cut, dress, and cure the lumber. In the villages some of the newly built homes were of brick. In any case, the new house was far more pretentious than the one it replaced. In most instances it belonged to the architectural design that became known as the "dog-trot" house or to the style called a "saddle-bag" house.

In both of these styles the builders surmounted the difficulty of preparing and handling lengthy logs or timbers by erecting two small, two-roomed buildings of equal size with a floored space between and enclosing all under one roof. In the "dog-trot" house the wide, intervening space, usually about ten feet, was open at the ends, affording the family a delightfully cool breezeway for summer days and allowing room entrances sheltered from inclement weather. This middle section served as a sheltered spot for storing gear and provisions, for curing pelts, and as an ideal retreat for the hounds. Sometimes a stairway on the breezeway led to the full height second story that practically duplicated the design of the first floor and replaced the old low-ceilinged loft. Chimneys were constructed at the outer sides of the units, and windows were placed in the ends. Except for the inconvenience of shivering across the "dog-trot" in winter to go from the kitchen-dining room section to the opposite bedroom unit, these houses were extremely comfortable and the style persisted. Many are still standing, and a few still serve as homes.

The "saddle-bag" design differed in that the space between the two units was narrow and closed at the ends. In this space the chimney was built and the stairway placed. It also provided rather ample storage space. The Sherrill Inn at Hickory Nut Gap, which for many years afforded rest and abundant refreshment to travelers weary with a day's mountain trip, proved the practical value of the "saddle-bag" style of architecture.[2]

Around his house—the old and the new—the prosperous farmer constructed a cluster of buildings, many of them still made of logs, at least until the coming of the steam-powered saw mills. Long after the Turnpike could bring finished products into the mountains, homemakers continued to need a shop and forge where tools could be made and repaired. The farmer needed barns and built large, cantilever type structures to house his horses and to store his hay. He needed shelter for the cattle, storage buildings for his grain, cribs for corn, and sheds for his gear. Essential to his food problem were the smoke house for curing and storing a supply of meat, a vegetable cellar, a spring house, and, if he had an orchard, an apple shed. Most of the farmers, too, had a structure and equipment for making brandy and a still for manufacturing a part of their grain into liquors.[3]

These stills had appeared as soon as settlers entered the region and could be found in all sections of the "back country" and the mountains. The stills enabled the farmer to get his bulky crop of

THE STEPHENS PRESS, INC.

Over the Buncombe Turnpike, called the "finest road in the state," came settlers with their belongings and wagons. Many found homes in the mountains. Others sought greener pastures farther west or north.

corn to market in the form of potent liquids sealed in jugs and strung together with long leather thongs so that they could be balanced over the back of a horse. In this way one horse could, without protest, carry the equivalent of eight bushels of corn to market.[4] The first Western North Carolina farmers had been unaffected by the early government attempt to collect an excise tax on whiskey and by the subsequent quelling of the Pennsylvania farmers who, in defiance of the tax, had instigated the so-called "Whiskey Rebellion."

The federal government later repealed the tax,[5] and the mountain settler, probably unaware that it had ever been in force, continued to take his jugs of homemade whiskey to the county seat on court days and to all the muster days of the local militia. If he were fortunate, a permit was obtained from the judge to sell his wares in the village. Failing in that, he could always find a means of disposing of the contents of his jugs. As the Turnpike led to better subsidiary roads, the farmers prospering from them and from the Turnpike itself discontinued this method of selling their corn. Instead they sold all they had to the stands. But most of them continued to distill their own year's supply of spirituous drinks.[6]

As the years rolled by, the wagons continued to rumble into Western North Carolina with their loads of supplies and luxuries. The droves of hogs continued to thunder along all the roads each autumn, and the demand for corn continued to increase. It looked as though good times had come to stay. Both east and west of the Blue Ridge every passing decade brought larger and more pretentious homes, more cleared land and larger fields, more conveniences for home and farm, and better machinery and tools. In time there developed more schools and churches, broader social contacts and more connection with the outside world.

The new roads and the improved older ones opened the way for comparatively rapid and dependable connections between communities by means of the stage coach, making regular mail service possible for the first time in Western North Carolina. Rutherfordton had acquired a post office in 1798 and Asheville in 1801.[7] Five years later Asheville was designated as the mail distribution center for a wide surrounding area that included parts of Tennessee, North and South Carolina, and Georgia.

In 1831 two-horse stagecoaches were taking both passengers and mail once a week from Lincolnton to Asheville by way of Rutherfordton and Edneyville. Departing at four o'clock on Saturday morning, passengers could be in Asheville by eight o'clock Sunday evening, having covered a distance of 110 miles.[8] A stage and mail route from Salem to Greenville, South Carolina, passing through Morganton and Rutherfordton, allowed for four-horse coaches making two trips per week. In fact, in 1831 Rutherfordton could boast of being on six stagecoach routes and of having a three-times-a-week mail service.[9]

Passengers preferred traveling on the mail coaches since their operators, under contract with the federal government, could require all road overseers along the route to keep the highways cleared of animals and fallen trees and to fill all mud holes. But all of the passengers were grateful for the rapid transportation offered by all the stagecoaches. Coaches appeared on the Buncombe Turnpike soon after its completion and in time furnished daily service. People jolted uncomplainingly along it in the springless coaches, making hitherto unheard of time from one Greenville to the other. On good roads the four-horse coaches, stopping at stands at short intervals to get fresh horses, could cover the incredible distance of sixty miles in a day.[10]

A coach could carry eight passengers inside, while several others could find traveling space on top with the driver. The baggage was carried at the rear of the conveyance and was protected from rain and dust by leather coverings. The coaches were highly decorated, and their entrance into a village, announced by the driver's horn, was the most exciting event of the day or week. As it came to a dramatic stop before the inn, men and boys gathered to witness the loading and unloading, to receive an

226 / *Chapter Fourteen*

DORIS ULMANN COLLECTION, N. C. DEPARTMENT OF ARCHIVES AND HISTORY
Dye Pots: Until after the Civil War, mountain women made their dyes from vegetables, roots, and bark. With these dyes they colored the linen thread and the woolen yarns which they wove into the linsey-woolsey cloth for their families' clothing. This picture, taken at the John C. Campbell Folk School, shows the process of dyeing as it was done in pioneer days.

occasional family letter, and to watch the driver's dextrous use of his long whip and his skillful maneuvering in getting the coach again on its way. Every young boy had hopes that some day he might hold the reins of such a fleet vehicle and guide the destiny of a glittering coach. Life in Western North Carolina had become an exciting and pleasant experience with comfortable prospects for the future.[11]

But that was not the complete story. The changes wrought by the trade arteries did not reach back into the mountain coves and small isolated mountain valleys. The groups of men and women living in these remote areas were made up of settlers arriving after the best lands had been taken, together with those who, through misfortune or their own dislike of or failure at farming, lost their rich acres and retreated to less productive land. They were joined in these more remote areas by those who were frontiersmen at heart and whose primary interest was in hunting and trapping and who had, like Daniel Boone before them, no desire to be restricted by the demands of farming on a large scale. These men and their

MARGARET MORLEY COLLECTION, N. C. DEPT. OF ARCHIVES AND HISTORY
Cabins like this one long continued to shelter families living in remote coves and away from the main highways.

families built their little log cabins in the secluded coves and in the sharp, narrow valleys on the sloping sides of the mountains. They cleared a bit of ground and with the help of their wives and children raised a few patches of corn, later one of tobacco, a field or two of other grains, and a vegetable garden. They set out a few apple and cherry trees and erected stills.

The family stock usually included a horse or two, perhaps an ox for the plowing, a cow, the hogs needed to furnish the year's supply of hams and lard and fatback, and a "passel" of hunting hounds. Most of the livestock could forage for themselves in the woods and mountain glades. The family larder received meats from the hunts, and the men took furs, a few hams, and jugs of whiskey to trade in the nearest village. They brought back the sugar, salt, and the few tools needed, along with a few yards of calico. The housewife's loom supplied much of the cloth for the family clothes, and a traveling cobbler made the family shoes. These men and women continued to live as had all the mountain settlers during their first years in the hills.[12]

Nothing worthy the name of a road entered these isolated

MARGARET MORLEY COLLECTION, N. C. DEPT. OF ARCHIVES AND HISTORY

For several generations, farm women very sensibly did their laundry out of doors near a stream. They boiled the clothes in a wash pot and beat the dirt out of them with a battling stick.

areas, and usually only the men made the necessary trips out of the community. With almost no opportunity for outside contacts, these mountain people were by-passed by the progress that came to other areas. Groups of neighbors and relatives made up the little world of cove and mountain families, walled in by the majesty of the towering hills. For this reason the types of tools they brought with them, the style of clothes worn when they first crossed into the mountains, the kind of cabins first built, the games they knew and the songs they sang, even the language spoken when they arrived as first settlers persisted while neighboring areas progressed. Daily life for these highlanders of Western North Carolina was hard. Their farming tools were crude and few, and the soil was, on the whole, unfriendly to cultivation. Conveniences were unknown. Children were born, grew up, suffered mishaps and illnesses, became old and died without the attention of doctors.[13]

Traveling ministers on horseback brought occasional messages of religion, married the young people, and sometimes succeeded in organizing a congregation and building a "churchhouse." There services could be held more or less regularly; summer camp meetings could be conducted; and in the

MARGARET MORLEY COLLECTION, N. C. DEPT. OF ARCHIVES AND HISTORY

This school house in the cove had no need for a chimney. The six or eight weeks' sessions were held when the weather was mild. Text books were few, and the teacher received about $16 a month.

surrounding grounds those who died could be laid to rest. Schools did not appear in these areas until after 1840, and long after that date the school facilities remained small and inadequately equipped. The sessions were brief, and the teachers on the whole unprepared for their work.[14]

Yet life was not all hardships. When land was being cleared, neighbors gathered for the "log rollings"—getting the felled trees into huge piles for burning. They gathered, too, for "house raisings" whenever a cabin was being erected for a newly married couple. There were quilting bees and shucking bees that brought neighbors together, while everyone went on horseback or afoot to the church services, the camp meetings, and the cemetery cleanings. On all of these occasions the rough, hand-made tables, frequently set up in the shady yard of a church or home, were laden with a cornucopia of home-grown foods. In addition, there were the "play parties," where, if the restraining influence of the local church was not too strong, young and old went through the

HUGH MORTON PHOTO

Many old cabins and farm buildings, like these in the shadow of Mt. Dunvegan, continued to be in use until well into the twentieth century.

rollicking, intricate figures of square dances, guided by the directions chanted by the neighborhood caller and inspired by the neighborhood fiddler.

Sometimes the community's recognized singer "histed" a tune, and all joined in on one of the many familiar ballads, ancient English and Scottish folk songs brought to America a generation or more before and eventually taken into the mountain fastnesses. There, in time, they were modified or lengthened by a succession of singers. Weddings and funerals also meant neighborhood gatherings. These became as the years went by not only family affairs, but also community events, for there was much intermarrying among early settlers. There came a time when all families of an entire community might be related in intricate ties of kinship.

From the mountain settlements on the border line of accessibility the men went into the villages for the gala muster days of the militia and, after 1840, for political rallies, taking with them their easily salable home-brewed whiskey, thus combining

Light and Shade in the Mountains / 231

THE BARDEN COLLECTION, N. C. DEPARTMENT OF ARCHIVES AND HISTORY
A study in contrast (circa 1880's)—the lowly beast of burden on mountain farms plods along in the shadow of the state's new capitol.

business and pleasure. Also for the men and boys there was hunting, and a trusty rifle or shotgun was each man's most prized possession. Undoubtedly the happiest hours of the mountain men were those spent tramping over great stretches of mountain forests, following the tracks or signs of animals and now and then stopping to "set a spell" on some hilltop boulder. There the mountain man could spend the time whittling and letting his gaze travel across the green ridges to the soft blue, peaceful haze of distant ranges. Around the evening firesides tales were told and repeated of the life and death struggles between men and beasts, and honor accrued to the outstanding hunters. Each community had its renowned bear hunter, a man to be respected by his neighbors and to be envied by every growing boy.[15]

APPALACHIAN NATIONAL PARKS ASSOCIATION COLLECTION, N. C. DEPARTMENT OF ARCHIVES AND HISTORY

As circumstances permitted, many settlers enlarged their homes by adding a new section to the early cabin. Here the addition is larger than the original house and a porch has been added.

The turnpikes that brought their economic prosperity and broadening influences to those living along them or accessible to them played a definite part in widening the gulf between those settlers and the highlanders, who came to be known as mountaineers. On their trips to town, the hill men looked with distrust at the changing conditions they saw and came to feel that those in the towns and open valleys were getting soft with their new luxuries and "uppity" attitudes. The townspeople and valley farmers, on the other hand, came to consider the dress, speech, and habits of the hill people as old-fashioned, even quaint.

As the years passed, the isolation of the mountain communities bred evils. Illiteracy developed, increased, continued, and finally became a virtue, so that in some areas schools were not welcome. When they came, sometimes over protests, attendance at them was poor and spasmodic. Not infrequently teachers were run off by half grown boys whose only standard of superiority was physical prowess. With life following a routine that tended to become monotonous and with a still on every farm, drinking became customary as it was in all the nation's frontier regions.

ASHEVILLE CHAMBER OF COMMERCE

The Oconaluftee Farmstead: In the river valleys farmers prospered and their cultivated acres became farmsteads, with a cluster of needed outbuildings near the house. At the Oconaluftee Farmstead, shown here, original buildings have been assembled from the area.

After the strong corn "likker" had gone the rounds or when potent concoctions like "cherry bounce" had burned its way down the pioneers' throats, there was always the probability of some social event exploding into a scene of violence. Rifles, necessary in the social order of the mountains and ever present and always sure of aim, even when fired by men whose brains were reeling with too much of their own brew, were apt to crack sharply with fatal results.

To those living a different type of life, it has been a thing of marvel that the Southern Appalachian mountain men should shoot their friends and relatives. But often there was no one else to shoot since with entire communities made up of relatives of varying degrees of kinship, a man, no matter in what direction he pointed his gun, aimed at a kinsman or neighbor. And tempers were easily aroused when the affairs of every family—even every individual—were the common knowledge of all. No one could so rile a man as his friend or brother or cousin.

In the early settlement days protection had of necessity been a personal or intra-community affair, and to a large extent it continued to be so in the remote mountain areas. Thus there grew up a feeling that what happened in an isolated cove was the concern of the settlers alone. To the close relatives of a slain man belonged the revenge for his death, a code which inevitably

N. C. DEPARTMENT OF ARCHIVES AND HISTORY

Quaker Meadows: Quaker Meadows in Burke County, the home of Major Joseph McDowell, gave evidence of the growing prosperity of farmers east of the Blue Ridge. It was here that the Overmountain men met on their way to meet Ferguson's forces.

developed feuds, some of which might rage for years (even into the second or third generation) and might result in a series of deaths. Inevitably, too, the code gave rise to resentment toward outside law. Entering these regions in attempts to carry out their duties, sheriffs were regarded as intruders and fair marks for the rifles of local hunters. Later, the federal revenue officers were "varmints" sneaking into the private affairs of mountain men to deprive them of their rights. Many such an officer, entering a cove, made a one way trip.[16]

Yet the isolation of the mountain also developed much that was admirable. Thrown upon their resources, the mountain families built up a self-sufficient way of life. Many of the women became expert in collecting and preparing the healing herbs that abounded in the woods and were skilled in caring for the sick and wounded. For example, the entire family gathered ginseng. It is said that it was Andre Michaux on his visit to the Blue Ridge Mountains in 1794 who taught the people living near Grandfather Mountain how to gather and prepare the plentiful ginseng for the Chinese markets. The information spread throughout Western North Carolina, and many a mountain family, both adults and children, gathered "sang," which could be taken to markets in the towns. There it was made ready for shipment. For some areas, "sang" became the principal cash crop, but the slow growth of ginseng discouraged its cultivation. Gathering the wild roots continued to be fairly widespread throughout the mountains until recent years.[17]

Another of the attributes of self-sufficiency was that hundreds of mountain men became adept at making their simple tools. A few achieved the construction of rifles that met their own rigid standards. Others, with no tools except knives, carved out fiddles that gave forth tones of sweetness and grace, while some unknown artist designed and made the first mountain dulcimer, an instrument that has been copied hundreds of times. This instrument has a body somewhat like a guitar except that it is much narrower and is strung with a varying number of strings, often three. It is held across the player's knees, and the strings are plucked to give the surprisingly tuneful notes that make a perfect background for the ancient ballads of English and Scottish origin.

Perhaps the greatest gift of isolation has been the spirit it engendered in the hearts and lives of the mountain men and women. Cut off from the world at large, they cherished the spirit of independence and the love for freedom that had first lured them into the untamed Appalachians to carve out with their own minds and hands a satisfying way of life. This spirit intensified as the years passed and took on the character of the mountains themselves. The deep, silent language of the hills spoke to the men who tramped over them and built their cabins by the streams that splashed down from the heights.

The hills of home imparted to the people something of their

own strength and uprightness, something of their mystic revelation of infinite greatness and goodness and peace. The mountains also instilled something of their own towering poise and quietness, something of their own lofty, wind-swept heights of calm. The dwellers in the uplands, both east and west of the Blue Ridge, sometimes misused the outward strength and inner power gained from their mountains. But when they turned these traits to their proper uses, the mountain people made contributions to their state and nation that were distinct and worthy of their land of majestic peaks and beauty.

It was, however, largely from the prosperous valley farming areas, benefiting from the turnpikes and roads both east and west of the Blue Ridge, that the early leaders came. And it was largely from the towns and from these areas that the demands for public schools and for general improvment in economic and living conditions came. It was this area that gave David Lowry Swain to Western North Carolina and to the state.

Completing three terms as governor, Swain went to the University as president in 1835, following Joseph Caldwell, who had recently died. During his term as a delegate from Buncombe County in the General Assembly, the young Swain had favored Murphey's program for public education and as governor had recognized the dire need of enlightening the people of the state. His energies were necessarily concentrated, however, on the task of getting a constitutional revision. He felt, too, that because of the poverty of the masses and the remoteness of many sections, a state-wide public school system would not at that time be feasible. Now with the constitutional reform an accomplished fact, he found himself, as president of the state's only authorized educational institution, in charge of a faculty and of a student body made up of ninety boys. That number, he realized, was a pitifully small enrollment for a state having a population of almost 750,000.

With characteristic energy and tact, he set about the task of improving educational opportunities for the youth of North Carolina.[18] Since the state admitted that a third of its adult population was illiterate, that task had to include a consideration of the general educational conditions throughout its length and breadth. At the beginning of 1836, the outlook for establishing public schools was dismal indeed. The Literary Fund established in 1825 by an act of the General Assembly had scarcely increased since that date and was far too small to allow for financing a state system of elementary schools. Additional funds were nowhere in sight.

But in that year a happy incident opened the way for taking the first step in Murphey's plans for education of the masses. The federal government had by that time paid its debts and found itself with a large surplus in the treasury as a result of the rapid sale of its western lands. In 1836, therefore, Congress passed the Distribution of the Surplus Act, by which the funds in the federal coffers in excess of $5,000,000 were to be distributed to the states on the basis of each state's representation in Congress. It was hoped that the states would use the money for needed internal improvements and education. North Carolina received as its share $1,433,757.39, and in the state legislature the eastern bloc of Democrats, satisfied as always with the status quo, urged that the sum be applied to the state's debt. Once more they were defeated by the Whigs, including those from Western North Carolina, and except for the sum of $100,000 allocated to meet governmental expenses, the entire amount went into the Literary Fund. To state it more accurately, perhaps, the federal allotment went into investments, the proceeds of which under the 1825 law went into the Literary Fund.[19]

When the Public School Law was passed in 1839, it set up a system based upon Murphey's plan, although greatly modified in details. Whereas Murphey had advocated tuition for those able to pay and had suggested that only boys continue past the lower grade levels, this bill provided for free schools for all white children, both boys and girls. Under it, each county was to lay off school districts and appoint a school committee for each. Every district was to raise the sum of $20 by taxation, which would be supplemented with $40 from the Literary Fund, the resulting $60 to cover the expenses involved in operating a two or three months' term of school a year. The decision to establish this system was not to be thrust upon the counties, for in a general election voters could cast their ballots for or against the establishment of schools in their county.[20] In the remote areas of Western North Carolina, where illiteracy was prevalent and where schools were desperately needed, many of the people were either indifferent to the issue or were opposed to the necessary taxation or to education in general. Yet only one western county, Yancey, which had been created only a few years earlier and had an extremely mountainous terrain, voted "No Schools." At a later date that vote too was reversed.[21]

N. C. DEPARTMENT OF ARCHIVES AND HISTORY

Pleasant Gardens: This home in McDowell County was built before the Revolutionary War. The logs of the original house have been covered with clapboards and a porch has been added. The interior of the house and its furnishings have kept the character of the early home.

In 1840 the state's first public schools opened, and during the next ten years there were 2,657 such schools established. A portion of these were little, one-roomed log buildings in the mountains where for two or three months a year (in some sections, six weeks) the children who attended could learn their letters and whatever else the teacher could crowd into that time and had the knowledge to teach. In the villages and in many of the prosperous farming communities the privately operated and the church-owned schools and academies continued the fine and thorough work that they had performed for decades. And in these regions the public schools attracted only those pupils whose parents could not afford the tuition charged by the older and better equipped schools. In these areas, naturally, the public schools acquired no prestige. Even in sections where there were no other schools, many district schools were given little respect or support. Advocates of the public schools system were openly disappointed in the results obtained and began a careful study with revision in mind.[22]

The lack of popularity and the slow acceptance of the public schools, they found, were due to several defects in the system. Perhaps the chief cause of the slow progress made by the system was the lack of a general directing head. Allied to this shortcoming was the poor teaching carried on by untrained teachers, poorly paid men with no supervision. Joseph Caldwell had recognized teacher training as a basic need in a state system and had urged, unsuccessfully, the establishment of a school for that purpose.[23] Swain, trying to increase the enrollment at the University, was also deeply interested in the teaching problems involved in the system. But there were other weaknesses. The school law had been revised in 1841 so that counties were authorized but not required to raise in taxes half the sum allotted from the Literary Fund, and some counties took advantage of that escape clause, thus reducing their school money.

Still another fault in the system was the allocation of the Literary Fund, which was based not upon the white population, which it actually served, but upon the total population of a county. The counties lying just east of the Blue Ridge had a small Negro population, but except for Buncombe, those west of that range had practically no Negro population. Thus the schools in Western North Carolina received less money than was their just due, often too small a sum to accomplish anything like satisfactory results. Perhaps the best that can be said for those first mountain schools is that they helped to get people used to the idea of schools and that in them a few children learned their A.B.C.'s.[24]

One of the most vigorous advocates of the public school system was Calvin Henderson Wiley, a University graduate and a young lawyer. He went to the General Assembly with a determination to further education in North Carolina. To do so, Wiley became an authority on conditions throughout the state and succeeded in getting a bill through the General Assembly for the appointment of a state superintendent of public instruction. Under the law, this official was to plan a course of study, set up teaching requirements, assist and advise the local school committees, select proper texts, and keep the public informed on the schools' progress and their needs. Wiley was appointed to that position and became North Carolina's first Superintendent of Public Instruction in 1852.[25]

He faced a task of staggering proportions, but strong in his knowledge of conditions and armed with the courage of his dreams for the state, he went to work. He set up a system of licensing teachers through examinations and established Teachers' Associations and Library Associations to inform, encourage, and make professional those teaching in the public schools. The new Superintendent selected, even wrote, suitable text books, and gradually brought unity and order out of the chaos. In time the Educational Association of North Carolina was organized and began its official publication, the *North Carolina Common School Journal,* later to become the *North Carolina Journal of Education.* As he worked, Calvin Wiley gained friends for the public schools.[26] As the years passed, his labors brought visible results. In the towns and villages of Western North Carolina and in the prosperous rural sections, the public schools steadily grew in prestige. Better buildings were erected and more able teachers hired. At last these schools rivaled and then surpassed the private schools in enrollment and took their respected places in the life of the communities.[27]

But in the remote areas the schools' progress was not that rapid. In time the mountain people came to realize that the schools had come to stay, and opposition to them died down. But the buildings remained small and inadequately equipped, and the pittance paid to the teachers— in some counties as little as $16 a month—attracted men who perhaps had failed at other undertakings and had managed by hook or crook to pass the required examination and to obtain a license.[28] It was to be another decade followed by a war with its devastating aftermath before the dream of education envisioned by Murphey, Wiley, Caldwell, and Swain would become a reality in Western North Carolina. Yet a light had been kindled, a light that would one day dispel the darkness of illiteracy and give added beauty to life in the land of mountains.

CHAPTER FIFTEEN

The Crack of Doom in the Mountains

In a weirdly Satanic mood, Fate took a lump of gold picked up in 1815 by a little Cherokee boy in northern Georgia and in the boiling caldron of the white man's hatred and greed, spun it into lightning that cracked over the child's nation with the unmistakable warning of swift doom. With DeSoto's flamboyant appearance in the mountains in 1540, a cloud of destruction arose on the horizon of the Indian nation. But the Cherokees became a strong people, and the cloud was no bigger than a man's hand. It was all but forgotten as a century and a half passed into the days that are gone.

Then came the English and the French, and there were times when the cloud grew and darkened. But the Cherokees always retreated and ceded land, treaty by treaty, until their vast hunting grounds were no more and their homelands had shrunk into the westernmost section of North Carolina beyond the Meigs-Freeman line, spilling over into the mountains of Tennessee and Georgia.[1] In 1815 there was nothing more to give up except the fields of grain and the orchards and the gardens, except the yards and the cabins. Now the white man demanded even these.

In the fifty years following the coming of white settlers into the region west of the Blue Ridge, the Cherokee nation developed with phenomenal strides. The raids on the first isolated settlements were soon over, partly because of the effective system of sentries and the strength of the local militia units, but partly because of the restraining influence of Cherokee leaders. When the second war with England seemed inevitable, the great Shawnee chief, Tecumseh, one day appeared in the council of the Cherokees. To the gravely listening chiefs and braves he spoke of his plan for a concerted Indian uprising against the Americans, soon to be weakened through their war with the English. All of the tribes and nations east of the Mississippi River were being asked to join in a widespread federation to make a last struggle against the constant encroachment of the Americans, an encroachment that would eventually mean destruction for all native Americans.

The Cherokees heard him through, and restive young braves nodded approval of his plea. But the leaders spoke through the answer that Chief Junaluska gave. That answer was "No." War against the whites had been tried by their fathers, and it had always brought loss of life and of land. It would again. The Cherokees must be content with the twelve thousand square miles left them. They were now unused to war. They must live in peace with their American neighbors. They must stay out of the white man's wars.[2]

The Creeks gave another answer, and in 1813 they went on the warpath, massacring some five hundred men, women, and children at Fort Mims. Then it was that a group of Cherokee volunteers led by Junaluska joined the forces of General Andrew Jackson against their century-old enemies. It was the Cherokee warriors at Horse Shoe Bend on March 27, 1814, who turned a probable defeat into victory for the Americans. On a punitive campaign against the Creeks in January, Jackson had been forced to retreat when his camp was attacked by warring Indians led by the brilliant Billy Weatherford. He had withdrawn to Fort Strother. By March his inadequate forces had been strengthened by the addition of troops from Tennessee and by six hundred Indians, some of them Cherokees from the Lower Towns, some of them Junaluska's volunteers from Western North Carolina, and a small number of them friendly Creeks.

Learning that Weatherford's army was assembled at the bend in the Tallapoosa River, Jackson returned with a force of two thousand men to find the Creeks intrenched behind breastworks on an island in the river with their women and children on the nearby fortified peninsula. Jackson divided his forces. Sending General John Coffee with seven hundred Tennessee men and the Indians, under the command of Colonel Gideon Morgan, three miles down the stream with instructions to cross the ford there, the General gave orders to take a position opposite the rear of the fortifications. They were to prevent the Creeks from escaping while he led his main force in a frontal attack.

With the Creeks doubly protected by the stockade and the river, the Americans gained no headway in the day's fighting. During this impasse Junaluska and another Cherokee, braving possible fire from the guns of their own side, swam across the river and, tying together the canoes that the Creeks had in waiting for escape in case of need, brought them back. Swarming into the light boats, the soldiers, both Indians and Americans, crossed the stream and reached the stronghold for hand-to-hand fighting, while Jackson's army stormed the opposite side. The result was the annihilation of the Creeks. Two weeks later, Billy Weatherford surrendered, and the Creek War was over.

The battle of Horse Shoe Bend has been considered the greatest of all Indian battles in the long history of the westward moving American frontier. It prevented further Indian uprisings against the Americans in the southeast and forced the removal of several Indian nations to western territory. This battle also paved the way for the formation of two new states—Alabama and Mississippi.[3] It was before this battle that Junaluska saved General Jackson from the poised weapon of an attacking Creek. So in 1815 the Cherokees were living peaceably with their American neighbors.

The native Americans were learning something of the white man's government and in 1820 reorganized their nation, following a pattern similar to the government of the United States. They divided their country into eight districts and drew up a constitution modeled after that of the white man's nation. New Echota in Georgia, named in memory of their ancient sacred town, was their capital and there the legislative body met. The Cherokee assembly was made up of two houses, to which four representatives from each district were elected by popular vote. At the head of the nation was the president of the council, who was also elected. John Ross was first chosen for this high office.[4]

The Cherokee people had a group of able leaders. A few of these were revered chiefs, conscientiously guiding their people with the paternal love and solicitude felt by their ancient predecessors. They had the wisdom handed down by generations of wise men and possessed the knowledge gained by their own long years of living. Perhaps most honored in this group was Yonaguska, who lamented that his people had adopted so many of the white man's evils. One of these evils he had been able to combat. During an illness, when his people grieved that he must soon leave them, he spoke to them of the sin of drinking. He said that he must come back from the very grave to save them from the curse placed upon them by the white man's whiskey. Slowly he recovered, and more than a thousand of his people took a solemn oath of temperance. Those who broke their pledges—and they were few—were whip-lashed as a public disgrace.

Yonaguska, also known as Drowning Bear, governed his people like a father. Through his wisdom and understanding and with his gift of oratory, he exerted a telling influence upon the nation and won the deep respect of the Americans. In the unhappy days during which exile faced his people, he was known as a "peace chief." Yet when removal came, he refused to go west. Going to a new land was useless, he maintained, for it would be merely a matter of time until the white man's greed would demand these western lands, too. Along with many others, he fled into the Smokies.

After the withdrawal of federal troops, he led the remnants of the Cherokee nation back to the acres that were no longer theirs. Now more than three score and ten years of age and enfeebled by the privations and exposure endured as a fugitive, he was not equal to the task of leading the destitute Cherokees. At his suggestion, William Holland Thomas was asked to assume that responsibility. With the leadership of his people thus provided for, Yonaguska was ready to depart. In 1839, at the age of seventy-five, this man, one of the great Cherokee chiefs, closed his eyes in his last sleep.[5]

Younger than Yonaguska was Junaluska, whose parents had called him Gul-nu-la-hun-ski, "One who tried but failed." The name was bestowed when he admitted failing to fulfill his earlier boast to destroy all Creeks. This title the white man corrupted into Junaluska. He was a brilliant strategist and in 1811 was strong in the strength of mid-manhood and clear in his thinking. He was not content to remember the past glories of the Cherokee nation. Sanely and sensibly he looked at the present and did what he could to build the future security of his people. He counseled against the alliance with Tecumseh and the English, and for this gesture of friendship with the Americans the Cherokees won a promise of aid in case of Creek attack against their nation.

The attack came, instead, against the Americans, and true to the pact he had made, Junaluska led a band of perhaps a hundred men from the mountains to join General Jackson's forces. After Horse Shoe Bend, Jackson extended to Junaluska and his volunteers the gratitude of the American people. Personal gratitude was given to Junaluska for the Cherokee's quick action in averting a death blow meant for the American General. Junaluska returned to his home, carrying in his heart a deep friendship for Andrew Jackson and sure that, if wisely led, his people in the future could live in peace and harmony with the Americans. He did not realize what a lump of gold could do.[6]

Of their able leaders, John Ross was chosen to head the reorganized government of the Cherokees. He was well fitted for the position. The son of a Scottish father and a Cherokee mother, he was one of the few men of his nation to receive a formal education. His selection for their highest office proved the confidence his people placed in him and the respect they awarded him. So did the name they gave him—Guwisguwi—the name they had bestowed upon a rare bird reputedly seen only once in their land. Both their confidence and respect were well placed. In the crushing and chaotic days ahead he was to exert all of his energies and all of his personal fortune in the struggle to avert the oncoming catastrophe. Perhaps no other Cherokee was so well equipped to present the cause of the Indian nation to Congressional leaders in Washington. There, however, by a narrow margin, he failed. In spite of the fact that he was able to win the support of a few outstanding men, he could not stem the avalanche of destruction already crashing down on a helpless people.[7]

The greatest of all Cherokee leaders never attained the title of chief. He was a shy, retiring man, given to thinking. He had no ambition to sway his people in the council and no desire for power; yet deep within him was a driving urge that would not let him rest. It was an urge not understood by neighbors and family, an urge that set him apart. Possibily he himself did not understand this strange thing that was in him.

On an unknown date shortly before the time that the Cherokees became involved in the American Revolutionary War, this man had been born in the Over Hills country not far from the ruins of old Fort Loudon. His mother was a Cherokee named Wut-tah, a sister of the influential chief Old Tassel of the Over Hill Towns. His father was Nathaniel Gist, a white man who was in Western North Carolina only temporarily and whose name was his only gift to the Cherokee boy whom he never saw but whom, years later from his home in Tennessee, he acknowledged as his son. The mother called her baby Sequoyah, a name with no descriptive meaning.

As the boy grew to manhood, he became adept at handwork and without training began drawing and then fashioning metals into tools and jewelry. After watching white men at their forges, he made his own forge and set up a blacksmith shop where he worked iron into the tools his neighbors needed. He also loved to make silver into a variety of trinkets. But he longed for something he did not have, something his people did not have. He learned that, by making symbols on a piece of bark or paper, white men could know each other's thoughts. In curiosity, he asked his friend, Charles Hicks, who had attended one of the mission schools, to write the name *Gist*. Hicks, probably following Sequoyah's pronunciation, wrote the name *Guess*. Sequoyah made a die of the queer marks and with it stamped each piece of his silver. He knew then the meaning of the urge that was within him, and he set about devising a set of symbols that would give the Cherokees this power of silent speaking when absent, the power that the white man possessed.

For years Sequoyah worked, moving into a small house alone and ignoring the ridicule and scorn of his neighbors. In time he was swamped with the characters he had designed, and he knew that unless he could reduce their number, he would fail. He put aside what he had done and started his self-appointed task anew, using a different approach. Now instead of trying to make a symbol for each word, he reduced the Cherokee language to its elemental sound units—syllables, the white man would call them. He found there were eighty-six such units. He then set about devising a symbol for each one of them.

In this endeavor he was aided when, quite by chance, he came by a piece of American printing. The Roman type letters, he saw, were far simpler to form than many of his own and, without knowing the sound that each English letter represented, he borrowed what he needed. The result was a queer looking but easily learned set of syllable symbols covering every Cherokee sound out of which words were made. By 1821 he had completed this supreme task of his life. He had in his hands the means by which his people could become literate. At the time, no one was interested—not his family, not his neighbors, not the missionaries, not even the Superintendent of Indian Affairs. Sequoyah turned to any who would listen, teaching little groups of children and young people. Quickly they learned and proved to the skeptics the marvel of this thing that the inventor, untutored and unaided, had brought to pass.[8]

In less than a year Cherokees were a literate people. The Council voted to establish a newspaper and through the recommendations of the Reverend S.A. Worchester, President of the Brainard Mission School, his Mission Board in Boston had the type of the new symbols cast in that city. The type, together with a press, was shipped by water to Augusta, Georgia, and from there by wagon to New Echota. Two white printers worked with a Cherokee apprentice to put out the first issue of the *Cherokee Phoenix,* which appeared on February 21, 1828. The editor was Elias Boudinot, an educated Cherokee. During the struggle over the removal to a western reservation, the paper was forced to suspend operations, but was later continued at Tahlequah, Oklahoma, under the name of the *Cherokee Advocate.* For some years it was printed in both Cherokee and in English and was distributed free to all Cherokees who could not read English.[9]

Four years before the arrival of the press at New Echota, John Arch had translated a portion of the Gospel of St. John and had circulated the handwritten copies. It was the first Bible translation ever made in a written native American language. David Brown, a half-Cherokee preacher, later translated the New Testament into Cherokee. In the first four and a half years of its operation, the press printed some 14,600 copies of the Testament, hymns, and religious tracts. Practically every Cherokee could read them.[10]

In grateful recognition of his gift to them the Cherokees, through their Council, presented Sequoyah with a silver medal, and the Nation gave him a life pension. News of what he had done reached Washington where the Bureau of Indian Affairs and the Government of the United States presented him with a gift of

FROM McKENNEY AND HALL'S COPY OF THE ORIGINAL PAINTING OF 1828, THE STEPHENS PRESS, INC.

Sequoyah: Unlettered and untutored, Sequoyah spent long, lonely years perfecting a system by which his people might "speak when absent." With his syllabary the Cherokees became a literate nation within a year.

money. In 1917 the state of Oklahoma presented a statue of him to be placed in the Hall of Statuary in the nation's capitol. But the most fitting tribute to this man, who, in the short span of twelve years, bridged the gap of thousands of years and lifted himself and his nation into the sphere of literate peoples, came when his name was given in honor to the giant trees of California. They too, lift their heads above the lowland up into the clear, pure realm of light and sunshine.

Sequoyah went with the Cherokees on the long trek to their new home. From there, when he was an old man, he set out in search of the "lost Cherokee tribe," said to have gone into Mexico. He was not equal to the arduous journey, and he sickened and died. There by the Rio Grande, the boundary of the land he sought, he was buried, this greatest of all Cherokees and one of the most remarkable of all men.[11]

The Cherokee nation during the decade of the 1820's developed a stable government. The people were reasonably prosperous on their little farms, raising their grain crops, fruits, and vegetables, and tending to their cattle. The clack of the loom sounded from every cabin. Many of them were accepting, or at least listening to, the white man's religious teaching. Early in the century the Moravians had established missions in their territory, followed by the Baptists, who, in 1820, had four missions in Western North Carolina. The most influential mission school, however, was the Brainard School in Tennessee. It was established by the American Foreign Mission Board in Boston, with the Reverend S. A. Worchester as its president. The federal government aided this school in its industrial education program; it was perhaps the first school in the nation to carry on such work. During this decade, too, the Cherokee nation became a reading and writing nation, reaching a rate of literacy that shamed the white section of Western North Carolina. The Cherokees were also far more temperate and law-abiding than their neighbors.[12]

But unfortunately, gold had been discovered on their land. That fact the white men could not tolerate. The idea spread that the Cherokees must leave. There was Indian land beyond the Mississippi River. Let them go there. In 1817, cajoled by the whites, a few chiefs signed a treaty ceding their territory and agreeing to a removal to the west. This settlement was at once repudiated by the Council, and sixty-seven chiefs signed a memorial of protest, pointing out that the signers of the treaty had no authority to represent their government. This document was sent to Washington, and John Ross began a series of trips to the national capital to present the case of his people. Such Congressional leaders as Daniel Webster, Edward Everett, and Henry Clay championed the rights of the native Americans. The unauthorized treaty hung fire; yet the Cherokees felt that it would not come up again.[13]

Agitation for removal continued in Georgia, and in 1819, hoping to appease the whites, the Cherokees by treaty sold their land along the Tuckaseigee River, thus ceding all land north and east of the Little Tennessee River and east of the Nantahala Mountains. It was a big price to pay, and for the Indians it availed little.[14] Georgia became vociferous in its demands for removal, and the ensuing ten-year period was a time of growing confusion and bitter feelings. The possibility of expulsion from their homeland hung over the Cherokees like a Damocles sword. Georgia then began a series of petty indignities that developed into persecution. The Indian leaders kept their people in check only with the hope that the government at Washington would protect their national rights. John Ross continued making trips to confer with congressmen and justices.

This explosive state of affairs flamed into warlike activities when in 1828 new gold discoveries were made on the Georgia holdings of the Cherokees. That state, snatching at any angle that would present a legal facet, grimly and determinedly set about getting possession of the Indian land. No quarter was to be extended to the Cherokees. Seizing upon the convenient political theory that no nation could exist within the confines of the American government, the General Assembly of Georgia declared that the Cherokee nation did not exist. Hence the Cherokee laws were also non-existent. By another act, it declared that the Cherokees living within its boundaries were incapable of owning land. Thus the state acquired the power of removing unwanted Cherokee occupants, who were given until June 1, 1830, to leave the state.[15]

Remembering the service rendered to General Jackson at Horseshoe Bend and recalling his declaration of friendship of the Cherokees, their leaders still had high hopes of saving their nation. Junaluska tried to quiet the fears of his people with the conviction that Jackson, now entering the White House as President of the United States, would champion their righteous cause.

The confusion that existed before now swelled into a state of pandemonium. Georgia sent state surveyors into the Cherokee territory to mark off the land into "land lots" of 160 acres each and "gold lots" of 40 acres each. These were offered by lottery to the white residents of the state and to the inrushing hordes of gold-hungry speculators. At the same time the Cherokees were forbidden to hold meetings of the Council, in fact, to hold any meetings. Friend and industrial advisor of the Cherokees, the Reverend Worchester, was imprisoned; and at one time John Ross and his guest, John Howard Payne, were held prisoners in the home of Joseph Vann, a well-to-do Cherokee. The *Cherokee Phoenix* was forced to suspend operation.[16] °

Protests against Georgia's treatment of the Cherokees as criminals were sent to the federal government, and in 1831 the Indian nation appealed to the Supreme Court of the United States for an injunction against the state of Georgia. They also appealed to that court concerning the seizure of a Cherokee charged with murdering a fellow tribe member, a case, the Cherokees felt, that was within the jurisdiction of their own courts. John Marshall's decision that the Cherokees had the right to their land until an authorized and voluntary treaty with the federal government compelled them to relinquish it brought some hope to the Indian nation. But Georgia openly defied the decision, and President Jackson, besieged by appeals from that state, uttered the crisp rejoinder that rang through the Cherokee nation like a death knell. "John Marshall has made his decision," said Jackson, "now let him enforce it."[17] The faith in General Jackson, to which Junaluska had clung, crumbled, and a hopeless spirit of fatality gripped the aging warrior.

Two factions now divided the Cherokees. One, led by the brilliant young John Ridge, who had been educated in the white man's schools and who had a white wife, argued that compromise with the Americans was no longer possible. His followers felt that the only practical course open to the Indians was to conclude a treaty with the federal government on as favorable terms as could be arranged and to move to the western lands. On March 14, 1835, this faction agreed to a treaty drawn up by the Reverend J.F. Schermerhorn, commissioner for the government. Under its terms the Cherokees were to receive $3,250,000—a sum later raised to $4,500,000—for their eastern lands, and they were to move west. This treaty was not to be in effect, however, until it was approved by the Indian nation meeting in full council.

In October the Council met and overwhelmingly rejected the treaty. In desperation the federal government called for a meeting of all Cherokees at New Echota for the purpose of drawing up a new treaty. John Ross, who opposed any removal plan, was held prisoner in Georgia until after this meeting. Other leaders were also absent. Out of the total Cherokee population, only some three hundred men, women, and children gathered at New Echota. Although this small group was in no way respresentative of the nation, a committee was appointed and another treaty worked out by which the Cherokees agreed to cede all their eastern domain in return for government land in Indian Territory and which offered a sum amounting to about fifty cents an acre for their homeland. This forced treaty was ratified in the Senate on May 23, 1836, and a Removal Bill arranged for evacuation by May 26, 1838.[18]

The frantic appeals of John Ross were fruitless. Near the end of the allotted time, however, only some four thousand Cherokees

WOOLAROC MUSEUM, BARTLESVILLE, OKLA.

The Great Migration: Because gold had been discovered on their land, the Cherokees, now a literate people living under a written constitutional government, went from the land of their fathers in what has been called "The Great Migration." On their way to Indian Territory many died from exposure and exhaustion.

had gone west, leaving approximately seventeen thousand still on the eastern domain. The government, impatient with this lack of response to orders, sent General John E. Wool with an army into the area to implement the removal. Upon learning that the Cherokees were being removed against their will and after seeing conditions at the fort "at the mouth of the Valley River," General Wool asked to be relieved of the assignment. He was replaced by General Winfield Scott, who was given an army of seven thousand regulars whose orders were to complete the evacuation as rapidly as possible, although Martin Van Buren, now President, agreed to extend the time beyond the designated date.[19] What followed is stark tragedy, a total eclipse of all the principles of freedom for which the new Republic had been formed. Stockades were erected in various parts of the Cherokee country (North Carolina, Tennessee, Georgia, Alabama), and into them the soldiers herded the men, women, and children taken without warning from their fields and homes. In June, 5,000 of the people, traveling in bands of 800 to 1,000, said a tearful goodbye to the land of their ancestors and started west, going by water as much of the way as possible. They were removed on government-provided steamers down the Tennessee River to the Ohio River

THE TRAIL OF TEARS

FROM THE 19TH *ANNUAL REPORT OF THE BUREAU OF AMERICAN ETHNOLOGY*

The Trail of Tears: The second group to leave the Cherokee land numbered more than 12,000 and traveled in groups of 1,000. They began their journey in October, 1838, and reached their new home in March, 1839. An estimated 4,000 died on the way.

and then to the Mississippi, eventually crossing Arkansas into designated Indian Territory. It was a hot, dry summer and the wanderers suffered greatly. In the intense heat of a western August they reached their destination. Word sifted back to the mountains that many had died enroute. It was reported that in one group of 875, some 350 had died and had been buried along the way.

John Ross then requested that the remaining twelve thousand of his people be allowed to go in the autumn and asked that they have charge of their own removal. His request was granted. In October the heartsick people, in groups of a thousand each, set out by an overland route for the remote land they had never seen. Government-furnished wagons held household goods and tools and carried the children, the aged, and the sick. The few who owned horses, rode, but most of the men and women, each with a bundle on back or in hands, trudged every step of the thousand miles on foot. Starting from the north bank of the Hiwassee River, their course led through Nashville, Tennessee, where they got government supplies, and then headed northwestward through a forested area of abundant game to the Ohio River. They crossed it by ferry near the mouth of the Cumberland.

The exiled people then crossed southern Illinois, fording the Mississippi River at Cape Girardeau, and passed across southern Missouri into Indian Territory. The journey which had begun on October 4 ended in March. Six months of daily plodding through the rains, sleets, and snows of an exceptionally dreary and cold winter had proved disastrous to a third of their number. About four thousand died along the "Trail of Tears."[20] So powerful was a lump of gold!

The best known tragic episode in this macabre drama took place, however, back in the mountains. A Cherokee farmer with no understanding of the causes behind this historic event or of its future significance was its hero. He was a little-known man in his sixties named Tsali and called by the whites "Old Charley." Through his death, a thousand Cherokees hiding in the fastnesses of the Smoky Mountains received government permission to remain in the hills and thus eventually to build for themselves a new nation—the Eastern Band of the Cherokees.

During the gathering of the people at the departure forts, scattered individuals, families, and groups of neighbors escaped into the mountains, seeking whatever shelter the towering Smokies afforded and existing on the scanty food supplied by the autumn forests. Among these refugees was Tsali, and with him were his wife, his grown son Ridges, a second son (still a child), and his brother-in-law Lowney. Over the years, as the story of his death was told and retold around the nation's camp fires, the man Tsali was clothed with heroism. His death was regarded as a sacrifice, the voluntary assumption of the role of scapegoat for the salvation of a thousand of his people.

According to the traditional story, two soldiers came to Tsali's cabin home to take him and his family to the fort. Along a steep stretch of the path one of the Americans prodded the lagging Indian woman. Tsali, controlling his wrath at this indignity to his wife, spoke in Cherokee to his son and Lowney. At the first turn in the path, he said, he would fall, pretending injury to his ankle. Then the soldiers would halt momentarily, giving the Indian men an opportunity to leap at them and sieze their guns. The Cherokees would then flee into the nearby hills. The plan almost worked, but one soldier rushed to the fallen Tsali while the other was being overpowered by Ridges and Lowney. From the ground, Tsali tripped the man bending over him, and in his fall the soldier's gun went off, killing him instantly. Sadly picking up the dead man's gun, Tsali led his family up into the mountains.[21]

The sequel came after the autumn departure of the Cherokees. General Scott's troops attempted to round up all fugitives hiding in the mountains. They were unsuccessful, for these hills had been the hunting grounds for generations of Cherokees. The refugees were familiar with hiding places that no strange white men could locate. Nor was it possible to starve them out of their hidden recesses, for the Indians knew how to exist on the nuts and roots and plants they found in the forests. It began to look as though this final phase of the removal would drag on indefinitely. With his men eager to be finished with this unpleasant task, General Scott sought some way to bring it to an "honorable" close.

He found it. If he could capture Tsali and publicly avenge the death of an American soldier, he would forget the others. According to tradition it was William Holland Thomas who took Scott's message to Tsali and brought back to the American officer Tsali's reply, "I will come in." True to his promise, the Cherokee farmer, unaware of the heroism of his sacrifice, stood unblindfolded with Ridges and Lowney, while at his request his own people fired the shots that made them martyrs. His younger son, because of his youth, was allowed to live.[22] This is the traditional story of Tsali, familiar to every Cherokee and to thousands of white Americans who have seen it come to life in the Mountainside Theater at Cherokee Village.

The reports of the officers rounding up the Cherokees, however, present a somewhat different version of the episode. In an attempt to gather in the fugitives, General Scott assigned Colonel William S. Foster and his Fourth Infantry to the upper Oconaluftee River valley and the Smoky Mountains. In October Colonel Foster, detaching units of his men to various sections of his territory, sent Second Lieutenant A. J. Smith and three soldiers through the upper Oconaluftee valley district. These men, finding no Cherokees, started for Fort Scott. On their way they surprised a camp of fugitives near the Little Tennessee River. Tsali and his family were reportedly among the dozen men, women, and children taken into custody by the soldiers.

In a report to his superior officer, Lieutenant Smith told of the ensuing tragedy. He was aware, he said, of the spirit of resentment seething through the captive group and, fearing trouble, ordered his men to seize a long knife that one of the Indians had. The officer later gave a similar order when he discovered that one of the refugees had an axe. This second order came too late, for, apparently at a signal, the men in the group attacked the soldiers, killing two and wounding the third. Lieutenant Smith owed his own escape to the dexterity of his horse. This act, the only instance of bloodshed during the removal of the Cherokees from Western North Carolina, called for drastic and immediate retaliation. The members of the Indian band were identified by

William H. Thomas, James Welch, a settler, and Lieutenant Smith. General Scott sent Captain C. H. Larned after Tsali, considered the leader of the outlaw group.[23]

It was at this juncture that General Scott, evidently wishing to avoid a search of undetermined length and hoping to enlist the aid of other refugees, issued an order of immunity to all hiding in the hills, provided that Tsali and his men were captured and turned over to the army. After a two weeks search the men were brought in by two of their own people, Wecheecha and Euchella, and were taken to Fort Lindsey, which had been erected at the junction of the Nantahala with the Little Tennessee River. According to Lieutenant Smith's report, Wacheecha and Euchella had asked permission to capture Tsali and to mete out his punishment in order to expiate the disgrace that the murdering of two white men had brought to their nation. In carrying out Tsali's execution the deaths of the two American soldiers had been avenged. And what was of supreme importance to the hundreds of Cherokees still hiding in mountain caves, the terms of the conditions upon which their immunity from punishment depended had been met. General Scott and his army, considering their removal assignment completed, withdrew from the mountains of Western North Carolina.[24]

Then from their hiding places came the pitiful remnant of a once proud and populous nation. They now owned not an inch of ground in the land that had once been theirs. They had neither money nor personal possessions. Their great chief Yonaguska was old and now ill from the months of privations in the mountains. They were bewildered and without confidence in their own power or in the justice of the federal government. In their extremity they turned to the one man they could trust. They turned to a trader named William Holland Thomas.[25]

They could not have done better. Born in 1805 near what was to be Waynesville, William Thomas grew up on the frontier and in the Cherokee country. Since his father had died before the boy's birth, young Thomas assumed a man's work at an early age. Already at age twelve he had gained the confidence of business men and was manager of an Indian trading post at Qualla. He was hired by Felix Walker, a farmer, trader, land speculator, and representative to Congress, who in 1808 had come from Rutherford County to the newly organized Haywood County. In his work Thomas came to know and to admire the Cherokees, and

THE BARDEN COLLECTION, N. C. DEPARTMENT OF ARCHIVES AND HISTORY
William Holland Thomas: Thomas, who was reared in the mountains, became the white chief of the little band of destitute people left in the hills. Through his efforts these native Americans became the Eastern Band of Cherokees.

they grew to love and trust him. They approved when Yonaguska adopted the white boy as his own son, and they accepted him as a member of their nation. Before he was fourteen, young Thomas found himself, through the gift of the now financially hard-pressed Walker, the owner of a trading post with its meager stock and of a set of law books. He was now not only the manager of the post, but also its owner.

William Thomas was educated in Cherokee through Sequoyah's syllabary, and he had studied the law books until he was familiar with American law. Politics already interested him. He had prospered in business and had been justified in the establishment of five trading posts. At maturity he lived on a farm on the Tuckaseigee River near the ancient Indian town of Stekoa, destroyed in 1776 by Moore. What was more important, as events proved, was that he could feel, think, and speak like a Cherokee. It was logical, then, that when the aged Yonaguska died, Thomas should be chosen chief of these eastern Cherokees.

It is hard to visualize the fate of these men, women, and children—a thousand of them—had William H. Thomas refused the responsibility of becoming a later-day Moses for a persecuted people. The first step taken before he became chief was to go to Washington in behalf of his people, pleading for aid for them and asking for their share of the $5,000,000 that the federal government had agreed under treaty to pay the Cherokees for their eastern land. It was a slow, strenuous task, this wresting from an unwilling government even a token of justice for a forlorn group of defenseless people. It was only after years of effort and after the expenditure of much of his own financial resources that Thomas succeeded in his aims. He was eventually appointed the Federal Agent for these eastern Cherokees and as such could hold in trust the money turned over to him for the Indians under the Removal Treaty of 1836.

Consistent with the theory adopted as a basis for their expulsion, the Cherokees were not granted the right of citizenship by either North Carolina or by the United States, and they could hold no land. Both as the government's representative to the Cherokees and as the Cherokee spokesman to the government, Thomas purchased with the Indians' money paid to him a tract of some 57,000 acres around the present village of Cherokee in addition to a smaller tract known as the Snowbird Reservation near the present Robbinsville. This land he held in trust for his people until they could become citizens and have the right to own it individually. Once more there was land in the mountains of Western North Carolina that the Cherokees could call home.

Under Thomas' guidance, the Cherokees divided the area into five communities called Bird Town, Paint Town, Wolf Town, Yellow Hill and Big Cove. Thomas helped them devise a form of government, and this eastern segment of the Cherokees began the slow process of rebuilding a nation.[26] In time, a few of those who had gone west came back and were allowed to remain. Among them was Junaluska, old and homesick. Somewhat tardily, North Carolina manifested its gratitude to him by conferring citizenship upon him and by giving him land on which to live out his life. On November 20, 1859, in his little cabin near the present Robbinsville, he died.[27] He had lived, some have thought, more

THE BARDEN COLLECTION, N. C. DEPARTMENT OF ARCHIVES AND HISTORY
Junaluska: Tired, footsore, and disillusioned, Junaluska, the great Cherokee warrior and leader, returned from Indian Territory to the mountains he loved.

THE STEPHENS PRESS, INC.

The Grave of Junaluska and His Wife Nicie: In recognition of his having saved the life of Andrew Jackson at the Battle of Horse Shoe Bend, Junaluska received citizenship and was allowed to return from Indian Territory. He was given a farm on the Snowbird Boundary reserves of the Cherokees. There he died on November 20, 1859.

than a hundred years. He had seen his people rise to their brief period of greatness and then fall before the greed of the white man. He had been a great warrior and a revered counselor of his nation. He had been a wanderer and a refugee. But he had come back to the land of his birth and the hills he loved, and he died as he wished, in the mountains of his ancestors.

CHAPTER SIXTEEN

More Government for Western North Carolina

After the formation of Haywood County from the "State of Buncombe" in 1808, the two counties furnished local government for an extensive area west of the Blue Ridge for twenty years. Rutherford, Burke, Wilkes, and Ashe Counties continued to serve both their more settled sections east of the Blue Ridge and their mountain lands west of that range. For the mountain regions especially, it was a period of settling and of evolving a mountain way of life. It was a time for developing the river valleys into comparatively large farms and a time of organizing self-sufficient communities in many rich but mountain-rimmed geographic pockets. In time, however, several factors combined to raise the familiar clamor for the creation of new counties out of portions of these far-flung older ones.

Perhaps the basic factor was what might be considered the normal influx of settlers. The general restlessness giving rise to a westward trend of migration that characterized the national life style also affected Western North Carolina, bringing people seeking new homes in western areas. Some of these westward moving people passed along the mountain highways into Tennessee or on to more distant territories. But many of them stayed to take up land in Western North Carolina. After the

APPALACHIAN NATIONAL PARKS ASSOCIATION COLLECTION, N. C.
DEPARTMENT OF ARCHIVES AND HISTORY

Settlers going into the remote sections of newly formed counties often encountered rushing mountain streams and virgin forests.

completion of the Buncombe Turnpike in 1827, a second factor entered the picture. The prosperity that the road brought to the mountain region increased the number of incoming, mountain-minded travelers. Because of this new, easy access to the hill-country, men could now bring their families and household goods in wagons over the finest road in the state of North Carolina.

For some thirty years the Turnpike rumbled with heavily laden wagons, some of which used the road as a passageway out of the state, but a far greater number of which came to rest in mountain coves and along mountain streams. Thus, during the 1830's half of the counties of the state declined in population, but the population of Western North Carolina increased.[1] Still another factor in the demand for new counties was the opening of Cherokee lands. The Meigs-Freeman line of demarcation between the races was no longer in effect after 1819. The reduction of the size of the Cherokee nation allowed North Carolina to open such "cleared" acres for settlement.[2]

In 1819 the Cherokees, in a desperate attempt at appeasement, sold the federal government all their homeland north and east of the Little Tennessee River together with the rich Tuckaseigee and Oconaluftee River area, as well as a more southerly strip extending to the Nantahala Mountains. The area was then opened for white settlement. White settlers rushed hastily into every part of the opened territory, taking out grants and building homes. Their successors settled near them or bought lands still left in the older sections. In once remote parts of Haywood County the population became sufficient to justify the machinery of a new government. Buncombe County also had areas in both its northern and its southern districts that were fully ready for their own local government.

The reasons advanced in the petitions for the formation of new counties were the familiar ones of distance from the county seats together with poor road conditions. Farmers in the valley of the South Toe River had to travel a distance of about forty miles to reach their county seat of Asheville. At certain seasons of the year, the roads, scarcely more than trails, were impassable. Even at best they were wretchedly poor, the "pooriest, rockiest roads in the country," according to one traveler.[3] It took a man on horseback two days to make the trip and the farmers living in the valley of the North Toe River had a similar distance to go to reach Morganton, their county seat. They had to descend and, on the return trip climb, the forbidding Blue Ridge Mountains. Not only did this waste precious work time, but also the slowness of travel could well impede the process of justice.

The first western petition acted upon favorably by the General Assembly after the formation of Haywood County came from the citizens recently flocking into the lands opened for settlement in the western portion of that county. Many settlers had purchased land tracts in the area in September, 1820, when a general auction sale of Cherokee lands had been held in Waynesville, the county seat. The number of residents increased steadily. In fact, so populous did the region become that after 1824 it was necessary for Haywood County to keep a deputy sheriff in the area as the county's officer of law enforcement.[4]

The new county was named Macon, in honor of Nathaniel Macon, leader of the North Carolina Republicans and at one time Speaker of the United States House of Representatives. There for many years he was his state's outstanding political figure. It was somewhat ironic, however, that this western county should receive Macon's name in view of the fact that Western North

ASHEVILLE CHAMBER OF COMMERCE

Dry Falls: These falls are so called because one can pass behind them without getting splashed by their spray. They are in Macon County.

Carolina opposed practically all of his economy measures and eventually helped to bring about the end of Republican control of the state. The county seat was named for Jesse Franklin, governor of the state for a term prior to the bill authorizing the formation of the county.[5] The town of Franklin was built on the site of Nikwasi, the ancient sacred city and capital of the Middle Cherokees.

The mound near the new town was made by a people of the

forgotten past and had been used by the later Cherokees as an elevation for their council house. There they may have entertained DeSoto and his Spaniards in 1540, and there in 1730 they drank to the health of King George with the persuasive Cuming. Today the mound broods over a modern mountain town, a sub-capital known as a county seat. That its brooding may be undisturbed by thoughtless persons seeking relics of a past civilization, the citizens and school children of Macon County purchased the mound in 1946 and presented it to the city of Franklin to be held as a public trust. A marker designating the site of old Nikwasi has been placed at the mound.[6] As soon as the new county was formed, the county court set about its road building. Citizens working in shifts under an appointed overseer opened a road from Franklin along the Little Tennessee River to the mouth of the Tuckaseigee River. This connected with a highway being constructed to the Tennessee line.[7]

In the third decade of the century three more petitions from mountain sections received favorable action in the General Assembly. Yancey County was authorized in 1833, Henderson County late in 1838, and Cherokee County in 1839. The new Yancey County comprised all the Toe River valley. It was an old country, bearing evidences of ancient battles between the Cherokees and the Catawbas, who had spasmodically contended for coveted hunting rights in the fertile region. Here, too, was evidence of Spanish invaders, coming after 1540, not to settle, but to sink mine shafts in search of gold and silver and possibly other metals.[8]

Across this area in 1771 James Robertson had led sixteen families from Wake County to the new Watauga Settlements to the west. And through it in September, 1780, had tramped the aroused frontiersmen on their way over the hills to stop once and for all Ferguson's raids east of the Blue Ridge. Scattered settlers along the North and South Toe Rivers had joined these marching men and had taken part in the battle of King's Mountain. Here, too, a few years later speculators like Waightstill Avery, John Gray Blount, and William Cathcart had received vast grants of land with an eye to the rich wealth of minerals known to be locked in the hills.[9]

From 1777 to the formation of Buncombe County in 1792, both the North and the South Toe valleys had been a part of Burke County, and the northern section remained so until 1833 when both areas were again united in the county of Yancey. Contrary to

ASHEVILLE CHAMBER OF COMMERCE

Linville Gorge: The Linville River makes its way between Linville Mountain and Jonas Ridge. This wildly beautiful gorge in Burke county was viewed by the French botanist Andre Michaux in 1802. Today it is designated as a Wilderness Area.

the experience in many new Western North Carolina counties, the selection of a site for the county seat submitted by commissioners pleased all sections of the county. The selected town was named Burnsville in honor of Captain Otway Burns, an officer in the navy during the second war with England. The county name honored Bartlett Yancey, twice a member of the United States Congress from North Carolina.

Much of the legislative energies of the new county was consumed during the succeeding years in forming plans for making the county seat accessible to all its sections by the construction of badly needed roads. Ambitious plans were also drawn up for an east-west highway across the county, giving access over the Blue Ridge to Morganton and connecting in the west with Buncombe Turnpike along the French Broad River. Access routes to both Tennessee and South Carolina markets would thus be established. An alternate plan for the western section, should the original one prove impractical, called for a highway going directly south to Asheville.[10]

PHOTO BY BARBARA GREENBERG FOR THE APPALACHIAN CONSORTIUM

The Valley Crucis Mission School: Originally purchased for "a shotgun, a pair of leggins, and a hound dog," acreage in this beautiful valley was later purchased by Bishop Levi Silliman Ives in 1842 and became the site of a training school for the Episcopal ministry. In later years the Mission School has served as a classical and agricultural school for boys, a preparatory school for girls, and a parish training center for theological students. The original structure, shown here, today serves as part of a year around conference center for the Episcopal Diocese of Western North Carolina.

Some progress was made in these projects by improving the narrow, inadequate existing roads and by constructing a few new local ones, all by the system generally employed of impressing citizens for road construction and maintenance. But the new county was pathetically poor and not enough help was forthcoming from the state to convert the dream of an east-west artery of trade into a reality. As time went on, however, sections of it were built and maintained after a fashion. Because of its lack of anything like an adequate system of roads and the resultant difficulty of getting its products to suitable markets, mountain-encompassed Yancey County was thwarted in its economic and social progress until well into the present century.

Henderson County, created by an act of the General Assembly in December, 1838, comprised the southern section of Buncombe

MARGARET MORLEY COLLECTION, N. C. DEPT. OF ARCHIVES AND HISTORY
Ploughing small patches of ground with an ox or a horse or with a mule as this boy is doing was long a familiar sight in many Western North Carolina counties.

County and was a well-developed and populous area with several well-defined rural settlements. The first road ordered built by the new Buncombe court in 1792 extended into this area, and in it some of Buncombe County's first industries had been established. Around the turn of the century Phillip Sitton had built ironworks, getting his ore from what is now known as Forge Mountain. His output of needed iron justified the bounty he received from Buncombe County. Matthew Gillespie set up a forge nearby where he and his sons, Harvey, Phillip, and Wilson, made long rifles for the pioneer hunters. Both of these enterprises had been invaluable to the early settlers west of the Blue Ridge.[11]

The southern boundary of the new county was also the dividing line between North and South Carolina, and throughout the county's length had passed the first roads built as links between the mountain area and the distant South Carolina markets. There were several of these, most of them following original native trails that had been glorified into pony paths during the days of the

N. C. DEPARTMENT OF ARCHIVES AND HISTORY

Back in the hills getting to the "church house" on Sundays often meant crossing a stream on a foot log.

Indian trade. One of these roads crossed the mountains into South Carolina by way of Caesar's Head. Another took the mountain traveler—one presumes on horseback—southeast by way of Hickory Nut Gorge into Rutherford County, while a third led over Saluda Gap, connecting with a road to Greenville, South Carolina. Still another link was the widened Indian and traders' path leading to the Spartanburg area of South Carolina.[12]

It was the Saluda Gap road over which the dauntless Bairds had brought their wagon and goods to set up merchandizing in the newly created Buncombe County in 1793. It was this same mountain road that, nine years later, Bishop Asbury had found negotiable only on foot and with the aid of two sticks. In 1806 Asbury had tried the road into Rutherford County, finding it equally bad and recording that for nearly a mile its descents were like the roof of a house.[13] These roads, poor as they were, had been the means of developing the region west of the Blue Ridge.

The area that became Henderson County had been especially favored by these highways over which settlers first entered the mountains. The geography of the country had also been an asset to this territory, for in it was the broadest, most open valley to be found in all Western North Carolina. Its fertility was early recognized. By 1838 the county had well established settlements in

270 / Chapter Sixteen

THE STEPHENS PRESS, INC.

In remote coves and on hillsides in both old and new counties families continued to live much as the first settlers had. Their cabins were small; they tilled a few acres; they raised their food; and they hunted for game. Away from the changes brought by the improved highways, they kept the habits, the dress, and the speech of their ancestors.

the Mills River and French Broad region as well as along the Green River and along Mud Creek and its tributaries. These farming areas profited greatly after 1826–27 by the Buncombe Turnpike that ran through the length of the county. The Turnpike furnished the farmers with a ready market for their corn at the many stands along it and also provided a means of getting their hogs and horses and turkeys to South Carolina.

The westernmost parts of North Carolina continued to grow. Hotels and inns catered to the travelers entering by every gap. At Fruitlands, the home of the Edneys, apple raising was proving practicable. Each community had its established private school, like the Mills River Academy, as well as churches of various denominations. And there were already several camp grounds for the annual summer religious meetings.[14]

PRINT FROM THE ORIGINAL GLASS PLATE NEGATIVE, BARBER PHOTO
Henderson County's First Court House: Although the formation of Henderson County was authorized in 1838, a dispute over the site of the county seat was not settled until 1841. In 1842 the new court house in Hendersonville was ready for use. This picture was taken at a much later date.

Both the new county and its county seat were named in honor of Judge Leonard Henderson, one of the associate justices of the state's Supreme Court. A county government was duly set up in 1839 at a court held in the home of Hugh Johnson in the French Broad area, but disagreement arose among the eleven commissioners appointed to select the site for the county seat. On the location of the town the citizens were also divided into two bitterly opposing camps, one contending for a site on Shaw's Creek (on land offered by Hugh Johnson) and the other for a site on Mud Creek that would take advantage of the Buncombe Turnpike. For two years the court held its sessions in the Mills River Academy; meanwhile, the Grand Jury asked permission to heat and use one of the permanent shelters on the camp ground that adjoined the campus of the Academy.

During this time litigations concerning the county seat location dragged through the courts. At last the General Assembly ordered the matter settled by a direct vote of the county's citizens. At the elections held in January, 1841, the Buncombe Turnpike site received a majority of 109 votes. In spite of the fact that fraud was at once charged in connection with the voting in the Flat Rock

DORIS ULLMANN, *HANGING PHOTOGRAPHS*, N. C. DEPT. OF ARCHIVES AND HISTORY

The inner strength and the spirit of accepting daily toil as a way of life have been bequeathed by mountain women to their daughters and their granddaughters.

area, the courts upheld the election returns. The town of Hendersonville was then laid out on land given by Mitchell King, John Johnson, and James Brittain, and in 1842 the courthouse was ready for use. Although no deeds to lots were recorded until 1846, a village had grown up around the courthouse by that time. In 1850 the General Assembly altered the boundary line between Henderson and Buncombe Counties, and by another act in 1844 it ceded a small portion of Rutherford County to the newly formed county. This strip of land was to become a few years later a part of Polk County.[15]

DORIS ULLMANN, *HANGING PHOTOGRAPHS*, N. C. DEPT. OF ARCHIVES AND HISTORY

Aunt Curtis: For several generations the life of a woman in the mountain sections of the newly formed counties was hard. Yet there were chores in which a woman's heart delighted—gathering the fruit, weaving at the loom, and planting the garden. Good times came in joining neighbors at church and at "play parties."

In 1839 a portion of Macon County was formed into the state's most westerly county, Cherokee County. Along its rivers in an age long past, primitive people had come to build their homes and to live their simple community lives. But the region was destined to be a land of changing nations, and these first citizens of the mountains had been forced to give way to successive tribes of mound builders, who, in turn, succumbed to the Cherokees. Now

274 / Chapter Sixteen

N. C. DEPARTMENT OF ARCHIVES AND HISTORY

A Cherokee Home: By the time the most westerly counties were formed, the Cherokees had long been accustomed to the white man's dress. They no longer lived in lodges but in cabins like those of the white settlers.

the Cherokees had been deported by the white man, who had built his little government village on what had been the site for a succession of native American towns. Above the site on a knoll along the Hiwassee River was Fort Butler, erected at the time of the Cherokee removal. To it the reluctant Indians had been brought, and from it they had started on their weary westward journey.

On this old village site, where a hundred years earlier English traders had distributed their wares to the Cherokees, was a trading post built before 1835 by Colonel Archibald Russell Spence Hunter. The county seat was for some years known as Huntersville. In 1873, however, it was officially named Murphy in honor of Archibald D. Murphey. Through an error, the "e" in his name was omitted in naming the town. The county's name of Cherokee perpetuates that nation's long association with the land of mountains and streams. By 1839 there was a sufficient number of settlers in the area to justify a county government, for people had followed Hiram Lovingood, who had come from Burke

County back in 1830, building a log cabin in the upper Andrews section and taking out land.

The newly organized Cherokee county already had a forge or two in operation, and each community had its church, the oldest being the Whitiker Church where George Washington Lovingood, brother of Hiram, preached on Sundays and labored at his land clearing during the week. The first court was held at Fort Butler on March 19, 1839. Two years later a courthouse was ready for use and served the county until it was destroyed by a fire set by raiding Federal troops in the Civil War.[16]

East of the Blue Ridge two additional counties were authorized shortly afterward, Caldwell in 1841 and McDowell in 1842. Named for Dr. Joseph Caldwell, first president of the state University and one of the state's early advocates of educational reforms and internal improvements, Caldwell County was formed from portions of Wilkes and Burke Counties. From Wilkes it received Fort Defiance, the Happy Valley plantation home of William Lenoir. He was an outstanding officer at King's Mountain and an early community leader. Lenoir's private fort had offered protection to settlers during the Indian raids preceding and during the War for Independence. Since 1805 there had been a post office at Fort Defiance with mail brought by carrier on horseback from Wilkesboro. Caldwell received from Burke County another early fort, Ford Crider. Also privately built around 1765, it was the gathering place for nearby settlers in times of danger. Near this fort, in 1841, James Harper operated a store and for nine years a post office as well, getting mail once a week from Salisbury.

In a log house in 1843 Judge Frederick Nash presided over the county's first court that set up the machinery of government. The county seat was happily named and located, honoring William Lenoir and being placed at Tucker's Barn. This structure, large for a pioneer building, had been built by the Tucker family near Fort Crider. As the most commodious structure available, and with the added advantage of being close to the fort, the barn early served as a gathering place and social center for the settlers. There meetings were held, speeches given, celebrations conducted, and barbecues enjoyed. For more than a generation much of the life of the surrounding settlers had centered around Tucker's Barn, now Lenoir. As was the case with other counties, Caldwell at once concerned itself with road building and in time had a highway

JUNE GLENN, JR. PHOTO, *ASHEVILLE CITIZEN-TIMES* COMPANY
Transylvania County's Looking Glass Falls are in the present Pisgah National Forest near modern Highway 276.

connecting over the Blue Ridge with Boone and one going south to Morganton.[17]

The following year, 1842, by an act of the General Assembly, Burke County's southern portion and Rutherford County's northern portion were combined to form McDowell County. It was named for a local hero, Major Joseph McDowell of Pleasant Gardens, whose patriotism had been an embarrassment to

Ferguson's forces. McDowell had been one of the leaders in the Battle of King's Mountain. With the Blue Ridge on its western border, the more gentle South Mountains to the east and southeast, and with the broad, fertile Catawba River valley traversing it, the area had early been settled. In it Fort Davidson, now Old Fort, had protected the settlers from the Cherokees and had provisioned pioneers crossing the Blue Ridge to make the first communities in the country beyond. Many of the settlers coming into the area after the Revolutionary War had been veterans of that conflict, and some had become large land owners.

Among those holding large grants was Robert Morris. He had been financial director of the Revolution and had been given some 200,000 acres in this region by an impoverished new national government unable to repay the patriot for the use of his time and fortune in the cause of liberty. Robert Morris's will was recorded in the McDowell courthouse. The county seat was named Marion in honor of Francis Marion, leader of the guerrilla band dogging Cornwallis's army on its march through South and then through North Carolina. Both Caldwell and McDowell Counties had been scenes of pillage and struggle during the War for Independence and had suffered at the hands of Tories and Loyalists.[18]

In 1849, still another county was formed west of the Blue Ridge. It was made up of the southern portion of Ashe County, the western part of Wilkes County, the northeastern portion of Yancey County, and a small section of the new Caldwell County. The name *Watauga* selected for it was an old one and an appropriate one, for the settlers in its western borders had at one time been a part of the old Watauga Settlements. It had been the country of hardy hunters and herders, the country of Howard and of Daniel Boone. It was fitting, that its seat of government should receive the name Boone, although it was 1850 before that name was given to the village.[19] The site selected for the seat of government was located near Howard's cabin for herders where it is thought that Boone was in the habit of seeking shelter when on hunting expeditions in the region. This was also the valley viewed earlier by Bishop Spangenberg and his party and considered by them as a site for an Indian mission.

In 1849 the community was known as Council's Store. On the highway running through it from Tennessee and Kentucky and connecting with roads leading into Virginia and South Carolina, Jordan Council, Jr., had his store and stand and, after 1823, a post office. Council was active in urging the formation of the county

THE STEPHENS PRESS, INC.

The sheer cliffs of Whiteside Mountain have long been landmarks for travelers through Jackson County. High on one of the cliffs Spanish writing has been found, a message perhaps left by some gold-seeking Spaniard.

and donated the land for the town's first school house. Although the Watauga County government was set up in 1849, it was allowed no representation of its own in the House until 1851 and was allowed none in the Senate of the General Assembly until 1864. During the intervening years it was represented by legislative members from Surry and Wilkes Counties.[20]

The formation of western counties had been long over due because of opposition on the part of the eastern bloc in the General Assembly. Frequently petitions were not considered until eastern counties were ready to be formed. Their rapid authorization after 1836 is a considerable indication of the growth of population and of its distribution in Western North Carolina, for opposition in the east decreased after that date. In fact, while nine counties were formed in the mountain region, between 1835 and 1860 only two were authorized for the east.[21] Four of these western counties came into being during the decade of the 1850's. They represented four sections of the total area: Madison, bordering Tennessee; Alleghany, bordering Virginia; Polk, bordering South Carolina between Henderson and Rutherford Counties; and Jackson, farther west and bordering South Carolina between Henderson and Macon Counties.

The authorization bill for the formation of a county to be carved from Buncombe and Yancey Counties and to extend to the mountain border of Tennessee was passed in 1851, and the new county was given the name of Madison, honoring the fourth President of the United States. The first court was held on the last Monday in February at the tavern operated by Adolphus E. Baird. Attempting to profit by the dissensions over the selection of county seats that arose in Henderson and Polk Counties, the General Assembly arranged for a popular vote in the event that two or more sites were suggested. Jewel Hill, now Walnut, was selected and several terms of court were held there, although no courthouse was erected.

The dissensions foreseen by the General Assembly developed, and in its 1852-53 session that legislative body appointed a new committee to make the choice. The committee selected the site on the French Broad River where Baird had his tavern on land belonging to T. B. Vance. In 1855 this site was chosen by the voters by a one vote majority, and plans were made for building a courthouse. Court continued to be held in Jewel Hill until 1859 when apparently, the new building was ready for occupancy. The village along the French Broad River was named Marshall in honor of John Marshall, first Judge of the United States Supreme Court.[22]

That same year, 1851, Jackson County was formed from sections of Haywood and Macon Counties and named for Andrew Jackson. It embraced a rugged mountain area that for an uncharted time had been a part of the Cherokee homeland where the native Americans had left one of the few hieroglyphic inscriptions to be found in Western North Carolina. This writing appears on an outcropping of slanting rock, called by the Indians the Judaculla Rock. Its weird markings were uncipherable to both the later Cherokees and to the coming white men and gave rise to a whole cycle of Cherokee myths and sagas dealing with the exploits of its mythical maker, the giant Judaculla. Whether its inscriptions were made by the Cherokee or by an earlier people is not known at the present, but some students of history think that it is a Cherokee description or diagram of a battle.[23]

Jackson County had been more than once the scene of bloodshed during the struggle between the Cherokees and the whites. In 1776 Rutherford's forces had traversed it to leave its villages in ruin. Through it had passed the Meigs-Freeman line, running north and south about a mile and a half east of the present Sylva. On the white man's side of this line that divided the two races, the Foster Trading Station had early been established for trade with the Cherokees. Somewhat later Colonel Robert Love had built a trading post between what is now Sylva and Webster.

These posts had prospered, and settlers had come into the area, crowding to the line. Some, without doubt, slipped across into the forbidden territory. Among the early settlers in the county was a group of French Huguenots, coming from South Carolina and going into the Tuckaseigee valley where they established at the mouth of Caney Fork Creek, a settlement they named East LaPorte. Today that name is one of the few reminders of the presence of the French in Western North Carolina. The first court was held by Judge John W. Ellis, later to be governor of the state, at the home of Daniel Bryson, Sr., and the second session was held at "Allen Fisher's new store." The county seat was established at Webster on a broad elevation above the Tuckaseigee River. It was not until the railroad made the village of Sylva more desirable as a center of county government that the citizens voted in 1913 to move the county seat to that town.[24]

When war or opposition struck Western North Carolina from without its borders, its citizens, strong in their sense of independence and jealous of their democracy, fought it as a unit. Whether the disturbance came from the Cherokees to the west, from the forces of Ferguson to the east, or from the dominating eastern members of the General Assembly, these mountain settlers were quick to respond. But, like a family, they could and often did fight each other fiercely over issues arising within their own borders. As happened in Henderson County, factions now and then developed that split the county and that, in the case of Polk County, led the General Assembly to repeal its Authorization Bill.

Early in its 1847-48 session, the General Assembly authorized the formation of Polk County from a western section of Rutherford county and an eastern portion of Henderson County. This county, named in honor of Colonel William Polk, straddled the Blue Ridge Mountains. Its eastern section had been settled before the Revolutionary War, and the pioneers there had been divided in their sympathies during that conflict. As a result, it had suffered from the violence that had flared up. It had suffered, too, from Cherokee raids.

Under the Enabling Act, the new county was to set up its local government but was to have no representation in the General Assembly for some years, its citizens being represented as in the past by members from Henderson and Rutherford Counties. The county seat was to be named Schuywicker in memory of Captain Howard's Cherokee guide and was to be not more than five miles from the residence of Marvil Mills at whose home the first court met.[25] But dissension over the site immediately broke out and became bitter, resulting in an injunction to stop the appointed commissioners from selecting the site and ordering the laying off of lots. Although meetings of the county officers were held from time to time during the next year and a half, little was done as the quarrel went through the courts.

At last, on January 16, 1849, the General Assembly repealed the act authorizing Polk County, and the legislature's right to do so was upheld by the state's Supreme Court. It was not until January, 1855, that a new bill was passed, identical to the first one except for the clause concerning the county seat. This bill provided that the town should be situated in the center of the county. It was named Columbus for Dr. Columbus Mills, who had been instrumental in getting the county formed a second time. Before March of the next year, a temporary courthouse was erected, and the machinery of government was set up. Polk had finally become a permanent county.[26]

The most northeasterly corner of Western North Carolina became the county of Alleghany in 1858. It was formed from Ashe County but later received small strips of land from other counties, necessitating numerous boundary adjustments. It was given the name of one of the Appalachian mountain chains, which was also the name of an Indian tribe early met by the Spaniards. Alleghany County's first court met at Shiloh Church and continued to meet there until a courthouse was built at the county seat, Sparta. It was ordered by the General Assembly to be established in the center of the county. The new county bordered Tennessee and the trade of the settlers there had long been with that state and continued to be. The government of this mountainous area was incomplete when war broke out, and the county was caught in the turmoil of internal dissension.[27]

Just at the outbreak of the Civil War, Western North Carolina gained three additional counties—Transylvania and Clay along its southern boundary, and Mitchell on its western border. Across the territory organized into Transylvania County was the ancient Indian trail leading from the present Henderson County to the Davidson River. From there it ran over the mountains to the French Broad and on to Estatoe, the most easterly of all the Cherokee towns and now the site of Rosman, and then down into South Carolina. This trail was early made into a road, and along it had passed the volunteers on their way to the Mexican War.

This region had been settled earlier when a grant of 640 acres had been made to Colonel Charles McDowell of Quaker Meadows in 1787. After 1790 a little colony was established along the Davidson River, and other settlers went to the forks of the French Broad. A private fort erected by John Carson was reassuring to these first settlers who were living so close to the Cherokee country. When Henderson County was formed, the settlers in its western area voted solidly for the French Broad or "River" site for a county seat. They were never reconciled to the returns of the election that placed the seat of government on Mud Creek, or the "Road" site, and they began an agitation soon afterwards for the formation of a county out of the western portion of Henderson.

After years of impatient waiting, the petition for such a county was presented in the General Assembly and granted in 1861. An organizing group met at James Neill's Hattery Shop on the old Boylston road near the site of the present Ecusta plant. Contrary to the custom of naming counties for prominent North Carolinians, this district received the name Transylvania, a name possibly suggested by residents who had in mind the Transylvania colony in Kentucky. Brevard, the county seat, was ordered established within five miles of the home of W. P. Poor. It was named for Ephraim Brevard, secretary of the Mecklenburg Convention. The new county was to have no direct representation in the General Assembly until later and was in the meantime to be represented by the members from Henderson and Jackson Counties.[28]

In the same year that Transylvania was formed, Clay County was formed from Cherokee County and named for Henry Clay. Its county seat was established at Hayesville, honoring George W. Hayes. Like the other counties formed just prior to the outbreak of war, its government was incomplete when the conflict came, and the county suffered greatly from the unsettled conditions.[29]

The third county to be formed that year was Mitchell County, named for Dr. Elisha Mitchell, explorer of the peak that now bears his name. It was formed from portions of Yancey, Watauga, Caldwell, Burke, and McDowell Counties. The county seat was to be named Calhoun. Like the history of many counties, however, there was again disagreement over the placing of the county seat, and the justices refused to levy taxes for the courthouse at the village of Calhoun. They pointed out that it was inconvenient for at least three-fourths of the residents of the county. The deadlock that resulted was referred to the General Assembly and that body in 1863 ordered a site to be selected in the geographic center of the county. Under that stipulation, Davis was chosen, but the name of the village proved unsatisfactory to the citizens, who were, for the most part, Union sympathizers. In 1868, therefore, the name was changed to Bakersville. Over a period of time, by act of the General Assembly, the boundary lines of this county were adjusted and readjusted.[30]

By the beginning of the Civil War, Western North Carolina had twenty-one counties, although several of them had as yet not been permitted to have representation in the General Assembly. A few had not yet erected courthouses, and most of them would require boundary adjustments. Moreover, the local governments in those established last were still incomplete and not strong enough to cope with the unsettled conditions arising in connection with the turmoil of war.

CHAPTER SEVENTEEN

The Lure of the Mountains

After 1838 the first stage of frontier life rapidly disappeared in Western North Carolina as settlers took up land in the old Cherokee nation and transplanted their ways of living to the newly opened areas that extended to the borders of the state. That is not to say that the pattern of living throughout the region became one of prosperity and progress. On the contrary, until the Civil War every county had mountain sections in which people lived much as the earliest settlers had, but they were no longer experimenting with a type of living suitable for their mountains. The pattern had already been formed, and they were following it as a settled way of life. Indeed, they were to follow it, with a few gradual changes, for years to come.

Occasionally the people coming to these isolated areas left records of the conditions they found. The Reverend W. W. Skiles, for example, taught from 1842 to 1862 in the Episcopal school at Valle Crucis and had a tiny, log church nearby in which he preached on Sundays. He saw in the people "an interesting population in great spiritual destitution." The community, he declared, was "of the rudest kind," while in his congregation he observed "more feet than shoes."[1]

Natives of Western North Carolina also recorded illuminating word pictures of conditions in areas more or less remote and hence cut off from the benefits of rich river valleys and from the turnpikes. Riding the circuit in 1853-54 to county courts in

Buncombe, Henderson, Yancey, Madison, Haywood, Jackson, and Cherokee, Judge Augustus S. Merrimon of Asheville complained of the wretched state of the roads he had to travel. He complained of the filth he found in the little villages and of the lack of anything like comfortable or clean accommodations to be had in the little log houses that served as inns. He recorded the residents' utter lack of outlook or interest in anything beyond their own problems of hog marking, "boars, mountain boomers, and the like," and he lamented the low moral standards everywhere in evidence. Merrimon was shocked at the prevalence of ill will and vengefulness, which it seemed to him, rankled "in the bosom of every one." County officers, appointed by the governor upon the recommendations of the General Assembly, were, he found, often "ignorant as heathen, and corrupt as demons." He deplored, too, the prevalence of drinking that characterized all court days.[2]

Temperance societies had appeared in the state before 1830, and the North Carolina Temperance Societies had held a meeting in Rutherford County that year, while a local society was formed at Brittain Church the following year.[3] After that, temperance agitation soon crossed the Blue Ridge to the regions beyond. But in a country where every farm had its still, where no form of license or supervision was required for the manufacture of spirituous drinks, and where it was held that a man had the right to do what he chose with the grain he grew, the temperance cause got little support from either the people, their leaders, or the church congregations.

Yet even in these sections of Western North Carolina in the years before the outbreak of war there were signs of better times to come. The establishment of schools, both church sponsored and public, the gradual improvement of roads, and the broadening outlook gained from general political meetings, together with the building of churches were all factors which could bring about the improvements desired by Judge Merrimon.

In the areas opened to trade, however, the picture was a brighter one. In the quarter of a century before the war, easing the transportation situation brought not only a degree of prosperity to people living in these favored regions, but also an economic stability. Luxuries were slow to cross the Blue Ridge and did not appear in mountain homes until well into the 1850's. Yet the homes were comfortable, with the growing cluster of outbuildings and twisting rail fences enclosing the fields as testaments to

N. C. DEPARTMENT OF ARCHIVES AND HISTORY

St. John-in-the Wilderness: This church, built before the Civil War, is one of the three Episcopal churches constructed by South Carolinians and Georgians who had summer homes in and near Flat Rock. It is still in use.

the high standard of well-being enjoyed by the farmers. They told, too, of the efficiency of operation and the diversification practiced on their farms.

Speaking at a meeting in Asheville just before the Civil War, Nicholas W. Woodfin deplored the fact that looms had disappeared from the homes, and homespun was no longer seen on the village streets.[4] More forges and mills and tanyards made work easier, and when the plank road came into the region, so did a steam engine for the saw mill that cut the lumber into planks. Schools, both private and public, and churches in this area increased in numbers; overall, a greater social life was enjoyed. In fact, with all of the hard work and continuous grind still involved in a self-sufficient economy, there was enough leisure time to turn every election day, every political rally, and every muster day with its fifes and drums, its parades and drills, into festive occasions. The protracted church meetings continued their social character. The highways, the stagecoaches, the newspapers, more imports, and incoming travelers widened the interest and horizons of Western North Carolina citizens. They developed a sense of being a part of the greater state unit. An increased interest in state politics brought with it plans and demands for their section's share of good roads and railroads, the ante bellum version of a "Finer Carolina."[5]

In the quarter of a century preceding the war, the complexity of life that was gradually coming into the mountains was apparent in the many events taking place simultaneously in the same or widely separated parts of Western North Carolina. They were events varying in character, but all looked both to the present and to the future. While Rutherford—including Polk—and Burke Counties were caught in the fever of the gold mining earlier described and were reaping the benefits of coins coming from Bechtler's mint, people in the western counties were watching with eager interest the struggle between the federal government and the Cherokees. Many were ready to rush into the opened lands as soon as the last Cherokee had been rounded into the stockades.

As the long queue of dejected, displaced native Americans disappeared into the west, the voters in all sections were rejoicing over their victory in gaining, through the revised state constitution, a fuller degree of democracy for Western North Carolina. While county after county eventually gained self-government, William H. Thomas was welding his remnant of the Cherokees into a nation. So well did Thomas succeed in this task that Charles Lanman, visiting the reservation in 1848, considered the Cherokee community self-sufficient, including churches and native preachers, its own courts, well-kept farms, and locally made farm tools. And the Cherokees now had a population at least three-fourths of whom were literate. He considered the Cherokees the happiest community encountered in his southern tour.[6]

While local dissensions in some counties were dividing the people into factions, roads and highways were being chartered and built to unite all Western North Carolina into a single district.

BARBER PHOTO

The Farmer Inn: Members of the Flat Rock community built this inn before the Civil War. Henry Farmer was its manager and later its owner. It was the earliest of the resort hotels west of the Blue Ridge. Today it is operated under the name of Woodfield Inn.

Every county established its county seat, and a few additional towns came into being during this period. But the pattern of life that was set and maintained remained a rural one, and the towns grew slowly. Asheville and Rutherfordton were the only incorporated villages in the area. In 1850 Asheville had a population of 800, and Rutherfordton claimed 484. It was 1860 before Asheville could boast of having passed the thousand mark with a population of 1,100. For an ever-broadening area, Western North Carolina came to mean to its citizens no longer merely a place to wrest a living from the hills, but a place of settled life and prosperity and future hopes.

To travelers coming in over the fine Buncombe Turnpike or plank roads it meant still other things. For some years before the Turnpike was built, a sizable colony of men of wealth and influence from Charleston and the surrounding coastal area had brought their families to northwestern South Carolina for the summers. A little summer community on the Reedy River was

N. C. DEPARTMENT OF ARCHIVES AND HISTORY

Warm Springs Station: After the railroad was built along the French Broad River, summer guests could arrive at Warm Springs by the "cars." They could find accommodations at the nearby Warm Springs Hotel.

formed and given the name Pleasantburg. A resort hotel was opened in Greenville for the accommodation of these summer guests. From time to time groups of these low-country people made excursions into the foothills of the Blue Ridge, and some of the more adventure-loving braved the poor, rocky roads to cross the range. After the opening of the Turnpike, it was possible for them to travel in comfort across the mountains into that section of Buncombe County later to become Henderson County. These excursions made the South Carolinians recognize Western North Carolina as an ideal place to escape the enervating heat of the flatland summers as well as a place which furnished a complete change from their customary environment. They became the region's first "summer people."7

Their idea of a summer home in the mountains, however, was not the modern one of a rustic retreat in an undisturbed natural setting. Nor did their idea of life in the hills imply reverting to a simple, unencumbered mode of living combined with the study of nature that their contemporary, Henry Thoreau, was advocating. To them a summer in the mountains meant transplanting the life they knew and enjoyed to the new environment. Between 1826

N. C. DEPARTMENT OF ARCHIVES AND HISTORY

Warm Springs Hotel: At the warm springs, considered medicinal, an inn was opened in 1831. It was later enlarged as a resort hotel. It could accommodate 250 guests and their servants and could provide for their horses. It attracted summer visitors and turnpike travelers. Drovers stayed at the stand that it operated.

and 1830 perhaps a half dozen South Carolinians, soon followed by friends and relatives, bought mountain land, acquiring hundreds and sometimes more than a thousand acres each.

The early comers chose an area surrounding an outcropping of flat rock pitted with holes. These man-made depressions and the fact that several Indian trails converged at this rock gave rise to the belief that the rock had at one time been of special significance to the Cherokees, possibly as a station for fire signals.[8] It was known as the Flat Rock. Unlike the people living in Western North Carolina, these purchasers were not interested in raising corn for the tramping hogs and horses. In fact, most of them were not interested in any phase of mountain farming, and as the years went by, only now and then did one clear land for crops. Instead, they made of their acreages great estates with winding, tree-lined avenues over which elegant carriages arrived at the elegant homes that sat, mansion-like, in expansive park settings. The extensive grounds allowed for hunting in the English and low-country manner and for tracks for horse racing. Several estates could boast of having deer parks.[9]

Following the custom of the coastal area, these estates

received charming names, and the houses were built in the styles their owners would have chosen for low-country homes. Most of them were of English or modified English architecture, taking on the appearance of English manors, complete with porter's gate and lodge, rambling stables, servant quarters, and kennels. A few were modifications of French architecture, while others were created according to the unrestrained ideas of their owners or of employed architects. All were large, with spacious parlors and drawing rooms allowing for lavish entertainment and for balls and for the presentation of the popular private theatricals. These were directed by Mrs. Charles Baring, for years the acknowledged social leader of the colony.

Some of the furnishings for these homes came from the coastal cities, but much of it was made on the grounds by cabinet makers brought from Charleston or by those in Asheville or those in the little factory set up by Henry T. Farmer in Flat Rock. The hangings, china, and silver were brought with the family. The Barings, who were Episcopalians, as were most of the group, were accompanied by their rector. Besides furnishing him with a home, they built a little church known as St. John-in-the-Wilderness, which was attended by many of the summer residents.[10] The colony grew, and as it expanded so that distances became too great to travel easily, a second Episcopal church was established by those living in the area known as Fletcher. A building there was constructed of hand-made bricks on land donated by Alexander Blake. It was dedicated on August 21, 1859.[11] Still another Episcopal church was formed through the efforts of Robert Hume of Charleston, and a building was constructed farther west in the present Transylvania County. It was called St. Paul's-in-the-Valley and served the summer residents of that area.[12]

After 1836 the number of South Carolinians making Western North Carolina their summer home increased rapidly until "Charleston in the Mountains" extended from Flat Rock to Fletcher and west to the Davidson River and the upper French Broad River valley. In the group were many men of prominence. Judge Mitchell King, owner of some seven thousand acres, was one of the promoters of the plan for a Charleston to Tennessee railroad to pass through the mountain area. He later gave a part of the land needed for Henderson's county seat. Charles Baring, who with his wife was a leader in the social life of the colony, had come to Charleston from England as a representative of the English banking firm of Baring Brothers.

292 / *Chapter Seventeen*

APPALACHIAN NATIONAL PARKS ASSOCIATION COLLECTION, N. C.
DEPARTMENT OF ARCHIVES AND HISTORY

The Paint Rock: With its mysterious colors, this rock was a favorite for sightseers. Guests at the Warm Springs Hotel were taken to it on picnic jaunts. Those daring enough climbed it.

Another prominent summer resident was C. G. Memminger, a Charleston lawyer. He was an advocate of public schools in his state, and as an able political leader, he helped to draft the Constitution of the Confederacy. For a short time he served as treasurer of that republic. Marie Joseph Gabriel St. Xavier, Count de Choiseul, at one time a political refugee from France, was now French Consul at Charleston, and the members of his family found their mountain estate, The Castle, so satisfactory that they became year-round residents of Western North Carolina. Christopher Hampton, brother of Wade Hampton, who was later to be governor of South Carolina, built his home near the present Cashiers. Other "summer people" included the Reverend John Grimke Drayton and Dr. Mitchell C. King, son of Judge King. Scores of others before 1860 enjoyed their mountain homes, either for the summer months or for the entire year.[13]

Each spring the families of these "summer people" arrived by stagecoaches or more often by carriages, traveling over the good turnpike that South Carolina had constructed on the route of the old trading path. It had been used a hundred years before by the state's traders as they took their wares by long pony trains into the Cherokee country. The carriages, for the most part, crossed the Blue Ridge by way of the Buncombe Turnpike to reach the summer destinations by the end of the second week of traveling if all went well. Wagons bringing baggage, necessities, and servants trailed them or, more often, preceded them. To accommodate these discriminating travelers and those arriving later for visits at the estates, hotels were built and suitably furnished along the route. Flat Rock itself early had a hotel.[14]

The mountain "Charleston" was, of course, practically self-sufficient, and socially there was no connection between this group and the farmers of Western North Carolina. Yet a new way of life had come to the hills, and a fairly extensive strip of accessible territory was now the home of people who, although of the same stock as the mountain dwellers, had for several generations been removed from pioneer life. As the family fortunes made on the rich, spreading plantations increased, they had acquired a broad, even cosmopolitan, culture and outlook. This segment of Western Carolina's population brought to their summer homes an ease of living, a degree of luxury, a charm, and a diversity of interests never before seen in Western North Carolina. Their presence had an effect, even though slight, on the region. For one thing, they created a small but noticeable market

N. C. DEPARTMENT OF ARCHIVES AND HISTORY
Round Knob Hotel: The coming of railroads into the mountains made possible such luxury hotels as this one at Round Knob. Here an added attraction was the fountain known as Andrews Geyser.

for grain for their horses and for meat and vegetables and fruits for their own tables; futhermore, they paid for these commodities in welcomed cash. A few mountain people worked when needed with the cabinet makers turning out furniture for the estates, and still others found employment in the hotels that catered to the "summer people."

A more noticeable result of the growing summer population in the community was the opening of resort hotels by the local owners of springs considered medicinal. In 1831 James Patton bought the hot springs located on the French Broad River. He improved the grounds around them and built a magnificent hotel on the Buncombe Turnpike. The springs had long been known. The Cherokees, believing in the curative powers of the water, had made pilgrimages to them for perhaps centuries. In 1778 Thomas Morgan and Henry Reynolds, two settlers of the Watauga Settlements, had stumbled upon them as they searched for horses stolen by the Indians.[15] Built more than fifty years later, Patton's two-story hotel, with its wide, pillared piazza facing the river, was designed to accommodate 250 persons and had an ample dining room, a bar, parlors and a ball room. Clustered near it were a half dozen brick cottages for guests, and nearby there were stables to take care of the horses that brought these guests.

These buildings, together with those necessary to such an establishment, and coupled with the nearby stand operated during the autumn drives, gave Warm Springs the appearance of a little village. The fame of Patton's hotel spread along the length of the Turnpike, and to it in fine carriages drawn by high-stepping horses came people from North Carolina, Tennessee, and South Carolina. All hoped to benefit from the water, and they were certain of enjoying the fine fare and entertainment offered. Patton and later his sons, John E. and James. W., were genial and lavish hosts. To occupy the hours pleasantly for their guests, they arranged sightseeing and picnic excursions to the Paint Rock and to other places of interest. Musicales and balls and parlor games were organized for the evenings, and for those desiring more manly forms of enjoyment, there were deer hunts in the surrounding forests and hills.[16]

West from Asheville some four miles another resort was developed at the sulphur springs discovered in 1827 by Robert Henry and his servant. There three years later Henry's son-in-law, Colonel Reuben Deaver, built a resort hotel, and by 1848 it was also village-like, with a little cluster of buildings which could accommodate two hundred guests and their accompanying servants and horses.[17] Stopping there that year on his journey through the mountains, Charles Lanman found the resort occupied, apparently to capacity, by South Carolinians from Charleston and Georgians from Augusta. He was deeply impressed by the magnificence of the resort itself and was charmed with the delightful guests and the pleasing entertainment they enjoyed. He declared that both in natural beauty and in the society gathered there, Sulphur Springs was superior to the better known Saratoga Springs in New York.[18]

Shortly after Lanman's visit, other sulphur springs were discovered near Waynesville by a slave of James R. Love, and some time afterwards a resort was also developed there called White Sulphur Springs.[19] This resort attracted its share of visitors. These spring-inspired resorts caused glowing reports of Western North Carolina to be taken far beyond the borders of the state. They foreshadowed the time when the pure water of the mountain streams, the buoyancy of the mountain air, and the calm and majesty of the hills themselves would yearly attract not hundreds, but thousands of visitors in search of renewed health.

296 / *Chapter Seventeen*

THE STEPHENS PRESS, INC.

Mount Mitchell: This view is from a drawing that appeared in Scribner's Magazine soon after Dr. Mitchell lost his life on its heights. The Half-Way House: This small cabin was a stopping place for those climbing the rugged Mount Mitchell.

Dr. Elisha Mitchell: In the summer of 1857 Dr. Elisha Mitchell returned to the Black Mountains to verify his former measurements of their highest peak. That peak, later named for him, became his final resting place.

As mentioned earlier, for succeeding generations of scientists the land of mountains continued to be a divinely equipped laboratory in which to gain further knowledge of nature's lavish gifts. In the early years of the nineteenth century, John Lyon, a Scottish botanist who had recently resigned his position as manager of a Philadelphia nursery, came to Western North Carolina. Here he roamed the hills, reveling in the wealth of mountain offerings and leisurely gathering plants to send to European gardeners. He made Asheville his headquarters, taking up lodging at the Eagle Hotel. His interest in the surrounding hills and the charm of his personality made him an admired visitor.

When the ravages of tuberculosis at last confined him to his room, he was the concern of many citizens. He was tenderly cared for by another lodger at the hotel, James Johnston, one of the town's blacksmiths. This devoted friend carried the frail Lyon to the window on September 14, 1814, to view for the last time the western range of mountains silhouetted against the flaming afterglow of the setting sun. Unlike the earlier visiting botanists, Lyon left no written record of his experiences in Western North Carolina, but this gentle, sincere lover of nature deeply impressed the mountain people, who long cherished his memory.[20]

A glossy-leafed mountain plant bearing ethereal, bell-shaped, white flowers was the will-o-the-wisp enticing Harvard University's botanist, Asa Gray, to the Southern Highlands and sending searching parties scouting over the hills and along the streams. The modest little flower had earlier intrigued Andre Michaux, who had taken a plant and its fruit back to Europe. But Michaux's trip had not been at the blooming season for the plant and he was only able to note, "blossom unknown." Yet this discovery held so much interest for him that he left a detailed description of the location in which he had found it in 1788. Asa Gray, in France in 1839, saw the preserved plant and read the French botanist's record of it. He resolved to locate this mountain dweller, and he gave it the name *Shortia galacifolia,* honoring his friend and fellow botanist, Dr. Charles W. Short.

In 1840 Gray visited Western North Carolina, searching for the plant on the mountains of Ashe, Watauga, and Yancey Counties, but all efforts of his searching parties failed to locate the elusive, little mountain plant. Another expedition three years later also ended in failure, and for years the Shortia was known to botanists as a "lost" plant.[21] The failure to find it had been due, however, to the difficulty of locating the region described by

ASHEVILLE CHAMBER OF COMMERCE

Mount Mitchell Falls: On his way to engage "Big Tom" Wilson for his guide, Dr. Mitchell followed a stream. At the head of these falls he slipped and fell to his death in the pool below.

Michaux. In 1877 George McQueen Hyams, seventeen-year-old son of a herbalist, finally discovered the plant growing east of the Blue Ridge at an altitude much lower than Gray's party had searched. Upon receiving the plant, Gray made another trip to Western North Carolina, but the Shortia was not in bloom.

It remained for another botanist, Dr. Charles S. Sargent, director of the Arnold Arboretum of Cambridge, Massachusetts, to locate the area described by Michaux and to see the carpet of

Shortia plants just where the earlier botanist had witnessed them. Michaux's account applied to a section of the Toxaway country in the present Transylvania Couny. Dr. Gray at last received a blooming Shortia, although he did not see the expanse of blooming plants in their mountain home. Thus almost a hundred years after Michaux first noted the delicate, charming little Shortia, its blooms could be added to the botanical information, for the mountains had given up their secret of the Shortia or Oconee Bell.[22]

During these years interest developed not only in the flora of the mountains, but also in the mountains themselves (an interest foreseen by Sir Alexander Cuming and John William Gerard deBrahm a century earlier). Local people and scientists became interested in the contours of the individual peaks and ranges, in their rock formations, and in their minerals. Increasing attention was likewise given to their heights. Naturally the two areas attracting the greatest attention were the Smokies, with their many jagged, towering peaks and domes, and the Blue Ridge where Roan, Grandfather and the Black Mountain groups claimed special consideration.

The question of mountain altitudes became quite controversial. Many were the conjectures by local enthusiasts and by scientists regarding the relative heights of Western North Carolina mountains and those in New England. New Hampshire's Mount Washington was at that time considered the highest peak in eastern United States. John C. Calhoun of neighboring South Carolina, familiar since young manhood with the mountains of Western North Carolina, expressed the belief that the great Alleghany chain reached its greatest height as it did its width in the Southern Appalachians.[23]

This opinion was shared by Thomas Lanier Clingman. This statesman from Buncombe County was always deeply and genuinely interested in his mountain district, and he took up the study of measuring land elevations in order to test his theory. He spent several summers trudging over the Smoky Mountains and the Black Mountains. With him he took his measuring instruments to estimate altitudes and to record his findings for publication. On these scientific excursions he sometimes worked with only a guide and the necessary helpers; at other times he was one of a party, as was the case in 1858. Of the peaks he measured, two have special significance, for he measured in the Smokies the towering dome that now bears his name. In 1855 he measured the present Mount

MARGARET MORLEY COLLECTION, N. C. DEPARTMENT OF ARCHIVES AND HISTORY

"Big Tom" Wilson: *"Big Tom" Wilson, famed bear hunter, had earlier acted as guide for Dr. Mitchell. Heading a searching party of Yancey County men, he located Dr. Mitchell's body and the long search was over.*

Mitchell, which he found to be 6,941 feet above sea level. That same year he published his findings, claiming that his measurement of the highest peak in the Black Mountains was the first ever to be made. Clingman thus refuted Dr. Elisha Mitchell's claim of a much earlier measurement and asserted that the scientist's measurement was actually that of another mountain, one in Buncombe County. Dr. Mitchell, he maintained, had never been on the peak now bearing his name.[24]

Dr. Elisha Mitchell was one of two outstanding men of science who did pioneer work in geological studies in Western North Carolina's mountains, including the measurement of several peaks. He actually measured seventeen peaks during two of his many trips to the region. Elisha Mitchell had been trained originally for the ministry, but like many of his profession in the first half of the nineteenth century, he combined preaching with teaching. After a year as tutor at Yale, his alma mater, he joined the faculty of the University of North Carolina at Chapel Hill as professor of mathematics. He was a man of abundant energy and almost limitless interests, and as President Caldwell broadened the scope of the University's offerings, Dr. Mitchell added to his teaching load classes in chemistry, minerology, and geology. He was also keenly interested in botany. Under a meager appropriation made by the General Assembly, he and Dennison Olmsted, his colleague at the University, carried out a geological survey of North Carolina, publishing their findings. These reports were the first of such summaries to be published in the nation.[25]

Dr. Mitchell was acquainted with the records of Western North Carolina trips made by the two Michauxs and by William Bartram and from the first he was eager to make excursions into this section of the state. In the summer of 1828 Mitchell was using Wilkesboro as headquarters for geological excursions into the surrounding areas. These took him into Ashe County and through Watauga County where Henry Holtzclaw acted as his guide. During this trip he climbed the rugged Grandfather Mountain, arriving footsore and weary but feeling well repaid by the view he saw. He felt sure, however, that this mountain, high as it was, was not the highest point in the Blue Ridge.[26] It must have been the fulfillment of a long desire when he took upon himself the task of exploring the majestic mass known as the Black Mountains, with their peaks reaching skyward. With barometric measuring instruments, Mitchell found the highest of these peaks he climbed to be 6,476 feet above sea level. He published his report in 1835. The Black Mountains called him again and again, and altogether he made five trips to them, carefully measuring and rechecking his earlier findings. As a result, he revised his first records to 6,708 feet and again to 6,672 feet.[27]

Dr. Mitchell was amazed at the allegations in Clingman's publication of 1855 and wrote an article refuting them and giving his account of his work. Clingman, never one to give up an opinion or to retract a statement, replied with a bitter article, and the difference between the two men took on the nature of a personal quarrel aired in the newspapers. Perhaps the only gain derived from this unfortunate turn of affairs was the widespread publicity given to the North Carolina peak. But the measurements offered by both men answered the question about the 6,288 foot Mount Washington. The New Hampshire peak was definitely not the highest in eastern America. Clearly that distinction, whoever was right, belonged to a North Carolina mountain.

Politically devoted to Clingman as the mountain voters were, they knew him as a man whose self-confidence often reached the stage of arrogance and as one unrelenting in a quarrel. It may be, therefore, that the sympathies of the local residents were with Dr. Mitchell from the start. It is certain that the wholehearted good will of the people went out to this professor painstakingly doing his work in the interest of science when the aftermath of the pamphlet warfare led to tragedy.

In June, 1857, Dr. Mitchell, with his son, Charles, a daughter, and a servant, came back to the Black Mountains for still another excursion and additional measuring. He hoped this time to prove his claims. The little party set up camp headquarters at the home of Jesse Stepp at the foot of the mountain. From there Dr. Mitchell and his son worked. On June 27, he left Charles at the Half-Way House, a lodge built as a summer home on a ledge of the mountainside by William Patton of Charleston, but now operated as an inn for mountain climbers by Colonel T. T. Patton of Asheville. The scientist planned to go to the home of Big Tom Wilson, who had been one of his guides during the 1844 explorations, and to arrange for assistance in the final phase of the work. It was already afternoon, and Tom's mountain cabin on the other side of the mountain was a goodly distance to cover. He told his son that he would return Monday afternoon, but no one saw him alive after that parting.

When he did not return to camp at the appointed time and still did not arrive Tuesday or Wednesday, Stepp and Charles began a search. At Big Tom's cabin they learned that Dr. Mitchell had not arrived there. Now, thoroughly alarmed for his safety, searching parties were organized to scour the wild mountain country. Big Tom Wilson, Yancey County's honored bear hunter, who had tramped the tangled sides of the Black Mountains with his gun in search of wild game, now headed a party made up of other Yancey men, men of the hills and the woods, bent on a solemn mission. When the news of Dr. Mitchell's disappearance reached Asheville, citizens of the town, including Zebulon Baird Vance, and men of Buncombe County formed another search party. For two days hundreds of men fanned out over the mountains and pushed through laurel and rhododendron thickets, over boulders, and up steep, uncharted inclines through the dark, wood-covered slopes of the massive peak. It began to look as though the mountain would not reveal its secret.

But in the end it yielded. The Yancey men found Mitchell's trail along the narrow Caney River. It was their Big Tom Wilson, whose keen hunter's eyes noted the broken laurel twigs, the crushed moss, then the prints of a heel on a rotten stump, some leaves turned wrong side out as though they had been grasped by some one, and finally unmistakable ground evidence of some one slipping. The men followed the stream until they discovered it flowing over a rocky ledge into a pool forty feet below. In this basin their search ended, and the chain of events became clear. Dr. Mitchell had attempted to follow the little river which he knew flowed eventually through Big Tom's small farm. But darkness had over-taken him in this wild region, and he had slipped and fallen to his death. His watch had stopped at ten minutes after eight o'clock.[28]

News of the discovery was taken to the other searchers. They began the difficult task of getting the body down the mountainside to Asheville where services were held at the Presbyterian Church, with burial in the churchyard. Perhaps no event had so stirred the men of the mountains as did the death of Dr. Mitchell. The people of Yancey, recognizing that "Greater love hath no man than this, that a man lay down his life for his friends," knew now that the highest peak in the Black Mountains belonged not only to them, but also to this man of science who had given his life to it in his search for truth. The people asked that he be buried on its crest, and in the following year, when the family consented, the men of Yancey tenderly carried the body of Elisha Mitchell up the mountain to its final resting place on the peak which was later given his name.

The next summer, 1858, a slightly-built, energetic, bespectacled man arrived in Western North Carolina to study the Southern Appalachians. He was a scientist of international reputation. Arnold Henry Guyot, like Mitchell, had been educated for the ministry in his native Switzerland. Also like the American, his intense interests had branched out into many fields—languages, botany, physics, the work of glaciers, mineralogy, geology, and geography. His studies in these fields took him to many European universities, and in 1848 he came to America to lecture in Boston. In America he stayed and in 1854 accepted a position at Princeton as professor of physics, geography, and geology. The list of Guyot's accomplishments is an amazingly long one. He wrote books in many fields of science, including geography text books. He established a museum at Princeton. He began weather observations under the Smithsonian Institution, and he undertook the exploration and measurement of all outstanding peaks in the Alleghany chain, from Maine to South Carolina.[29]

In connection with his mountain work it was inevitable that Guyot should be drawn to the Southern Appalachian region, and with the exception of 1857, he spent the summers between 1856 and 1860 in Eastern Tennessee and Western North Carolina. During these months he lived in mountain homes and employed mountain men as guides and assistants in his work. From them he learned the tales of the country, the history of the region, and the names given locally to the peaks and ridges. Guyot tramped up and down the mountains in the Smokies, determining their altitudes by barometric pressure. Not only did he measure the mountains, but he also gave them names. To some he gave significant Indian names. To others were attached the names of early settlers, and still others received names appropriate because of their contours or the appearance gained through their woods and vegetation.

Arnold Guyot's work in the Black Mountains was also extensive, and he found the highest peak there to be 6,701 feet above sea level, a figure later revised to 6,707, differing by only one foot from one of Dr. Mitchell's findings. As a summary of his work in the southern mountains, Professor Guyot made topographical maps of the Applachian region. His studies in the long chain of mountains in eastern America justified John C. Calhoun's belief that the Alleghanies reached their greatest height as well as their greatest width in the Southern Highlands.[30]

New and more accurate instruments and methods have changed the measurements of Western North Carolina mountains arrived at by Clingman, Mitchell, and Guyot. The official measurement of Mount Mitchell has been established at 6,684 feet, with Clingman's Dome in the Smokies approaching it at 6,642 feet above sea level. The third highest mountain in the Southern Appalachians, a 6,621 foot peak in the Smokies on the boundary line between Tennessee and North Carolina, has most appropriately been given the name Guyot in honor of perhaps the most eminent scientist ever to study these mountains.

To Charles Lanman, yet another visitor, Western North Carolina meant a country of wonder and majesty with waterfalls of sheer beauty and sunsets of unbelievable range and intensity of colors. It meant spectacular views from mountain tops and a riot of color up the hills. It meant hospitality in mountain cabins and in little villages. Western North Carolina also meant being christened "The Wandering Star" by the friendly Cherokees. It meant riding alone over the crest of wild mountains and then spending a few days in the company of the charming, cultured South Carolinians gathered at Sulphur Springs. To him it also meant a trip to the Black Mountains and back in a deluge of rain that completely obscured the famous peak. It meant, too, a deer hunt arranged by John Patton at Warm Springs. But above all, Western North Carolina meant to him the unforgetable experience of seeing Hickory Nut Gorge, of viewing Grandfather Mountain, and of climbing Roan Mountain.

Charles Lanman did not come to Western North Carolina to buy land and settle. He did not come to study its plants. Nor did he come to drink its medicinal waters or to pass a season at one of its resorts. And he brought nothing to sell. He came to see and to revel in the rugged expanse of mountain scenery and to catch glimpses of life in the hills. He was, perhaps, Western North Carolina's first "tourist." What he saw of the land and its people and his impressions of the trip that took him from Murphy to Roan Mountain, he expressed in accounts written in the form of *Letters*. These he published in magazines so that others might also enjoy the region.

To the modern mountain dweller these *Letters*, penned in 1848, make fascinating reading. They must have been the finest pieces of "advertising" that the region received before the Civil War. One wonders how many, if any, of their readers were lured by them into experiencing for themselves the spell and beauty of the Southern Highlands. Yet it is somewhat significant that when Lanman later collected his many travel sketches, he included *Letters From the Alleghany Mountains* and named the two-volume work *Adventures in the Wilds of the United States and British American Provinces*.

By 1860 the widely diversified future development of Western North Carolina was clearly foreshadowed. It is intriguing, even though futile, to envision the next two decades in the mountains had there been no interruption of progress, no devastation, and no crushing of hopes by man's most destructive self-made force—war.

CHAPTER EIGHTEEN

Whigs in the Mountains

People were coming to the mountains for many reasons, and while local government was being brought close to the people of all sections of Western North Carolina, state and national politics were claiming an increasing share of their interests. As noted in an earlier chapter, mountain voters in 1824 rallied to the banner of Andrew Jackson, considering him a representative of their own independent and democratic frontier politics. From him they expected to gain national action on issues that promised betterment of their counties. They were disappointed when, in the close election that gave no candidate a majority of electoral votes, John Quincy Adams was chosen by the House of Representatives as President of the United States.

Four years later, the mountain people again pinned their faith to Andrew Jackson, who had actually been born in Western North Carolina according to those living near the South Carolina border. During the years of Jackson's two terms as president, however, the mountain people learned, both to their surprise and disappointment, of his defeat of the bill to turn the federal surplus over to the states for improvement projects. They learned of his successful fight against the national bank and of his veto of the bill for granting federal aid for improvements. All of these economy measures meant for them no help in their economic struggle. At the same time President Jackson's states rights theory, as it applied to letting the commonwealths work out their own improvements, crushed the hopes of the westerners for their section since the opposition of the eastern representatives in the General Assembly was strong enough to kill all improvement and reform bills.

David Lowry Swain, then Western Carolina's representative—at first in the General Assembly and then as Governor of the state for three terms—had been opposed to Jackson as early as 1824. As the easterners gradually came to accept the President as representing their own economy policies, Swain, fighting for reforms, switched to the Whig party. It was nationally organized in 1834 in opposition to Jackson's Democratic Republicans, or Democrats, as they came to call themselves.[1] Except for the Toe River area, the voters in Western North Carolina followed Swain into the Whig Party along with voters in the piedmont and sound regions. Soon there were enough to warrant a formal organization of the Whigs in North Carolina in 1835.[2] Standing for federal and state aid for road and waterway improvements and favoring railroad building and state educational and constitutional reform, this party gave North Carolina a two-party system. The Whig party became the party of Western North Carolina, to remain so until the 1850's.

As the western voters saw their leaders achieve places of prominence and influence, they won decisive victories on such issues as constitutional reform, public education, and transportation projects. The mountain people were gaining a feeling of political importance in the state. They rightly felt so, for the Whig Party in the next fifteen years elected satisfactory majorities in the General Assembly four times and continuously kept their candidates in the office of governor as well as a goodly number of their representatives in Congress. They controlled the state's most influential newspapers and, through their closely knit organization, carried their issues directly to the people.

In the election of 1836, the first held under the new constitution, voters for the first time cast their ballots for the governor of the state and were eligible to vote for candidates seeking seats in the state House of Representatives without having to present property qualifications. But until 1857 only voters possessing at least fifty acres of land could vote for senators. Throughout Western North Carolina this election took on the nature of a victory celebration, and the new Whig party swept its candidate, Edward B. Dudley, into the governorship.[3]

Even more colorful was the election of 1840. It had been especially prepared for by the organizations of both parties, and it established a pattern for future elections. Party conventions—new in the state—were held in Raleigh to draw up the party platforms, and county organizations were set up throughout the state. Candidates for governor along with other office seekers jolted and bumped over the roads in stagecoaches or rode on horseback to county seats to "electioneer." The crowds traveled the back roads to see these aspirants for office and to hear them explain the issues before the state.

The political rallies that characterized this and succeeding elections were, in effect, glorified court days. They reached their climaxes when rival candidates—of necessity traveling together—debated the issues. Political debates in the years preceding the Civil War became exceedingly popular throughout the nation. Some, like the Lincoln-Douglas series, became historically famous. But often in Western North Carolina, as elsewhere, the debates had increasingly little to do with logic and much to do with personalities and jibes directed at the opposing speaker and his party. This enhanced their entertainment value for the mountain men, who appreciated broad wit on either side.[4]

As on court days, the men from the coves and from farms along the little streams and creek banks brought their jugs of whiskey, and it also became customary to have a general barbecue at noon. Since a political meeting meant an entire day, the men made the most of it. To these meetings and rallies the candidates distributed copies of their political newspapers, tracts, and broadsides, often bitter attacks on the opposition. These the mountain men took home to be read by or to those who missed the rally and to be discussed at firesides or along rail fences as neighbor met neighbor. As might be expected, the rallies were used by some spectators as occasions for settling personal grudges, and when political fervor rose dangerously high, angry words were exchanged and brawls resulted.

They were lively affairs, these early rallies in Western North Carolina, for the men of the hills were men of action, determined in their opinions, bitter in their disagreements, and quick to resent real or fancied insults.[5] Along with his political tracts, a man might take home from the rally a resentment against neighbor or acquaintance, even a heretofore stranger, that deepened into a lifetime animosity. The candidates themselves were quick to anger when insulted. Today in reading the broadsides, filled with personal attacks and what seems like fantastic charges against the other party, the historian wonders how the listeners or candidates knew that the "unpardonable insult" had been uttered. That they knew that the "unpardonable insult" had been uttered. That they did know when that delicate line had been crossed is evident from the duels arising out of political differences. In remote areas these duels between voters took the forthright form of shooting, without the frills and niceties of dueling etiquette. Most of these incidents are today forgotten, but a few between candidates of prominence and position are remembered.

In November 1827, for example, bad blood was engendered between Dr. Robert Brank Vance, Buncombe County's first native physician, and Samuel B. Carson over allegations and counter-allegations hurled during the campaign in which they were rivals for a seat in Congress. The resulting duel was strictly carried out according to the rules of dueling and took place just south of the dividing line between the two Carolinas. Dr. Vance, a promising young politician and uncle of Zebulon Vance, died from the wounds inflicted by Carson's gun.[6]

Another memorable incident occurred in 1845 when Thomas L. Clingman, then in Congress, was a participant in a duel with William Yancy of Alabama. It took place just outside the capital city and was brought about by political animosity aroused by debates concerning the bill for the annexation of Texas, which Clingman opposed. It was conducted in the approved fashion for "affairs of honor." Fortunately, neither of the principals was injured. Apparently for both men "satisfaction had been given," and the affair was over before officers of the law appeared.[7]

Going to a political rally on horseback or on foot over the rocks and around the fallen trees and mud holes that obstructed their roads, the mountain men could look expectantly to a day filled with pleasant social contacts with friends. They could anticipate feasting and entertainment, with the enjoyment of humor and clever sallies of the speakers, high political emotions, and probably moments of tense excitement. Yet these rallies, with their speeches and debates, served a far deeper purpose and performed a more serious service to the voters of Western North Carolina than mere entertainment.

By 1840 Raleigh newspapers, both Democratic and Whig, were entering the mountain region by means of the stagecoaches, and for ten years Rutherfordton had had its own paper, *The North Carolina Spectator and Western Advertiser,* which gave way in 1836 to *The Carolina Gazette.* In 1840 under new management, it became the weekly *Western Star of Liberty,* espousing the Whig principles.[8] In 1840, too, *The Highland Messenger* appeared in Asheville. It was

310 / Chapter Eighteen

PACK MEMORIAL LIBRARY, ASHEVILLE

Thomas Lanier Clingman: Clingman was a lawyer, a scientist, and a Congressman. In honor of his achievements in measuring the heights of Western North Carolina mountains, one of the peaks in the Great Smoky Mountains National Park bears his name. As a Congressman in the trying times preceding the Civil War, he became a spokesman for the South.

the first newspaper to be printed west of the Blue Ridge, and in 1849, *The Asheville News,* expressing Democratic party principles, printed its first issue.[9] These newspapers were small, usually four pages, with little attention paid to local news. As Rutherfordton's rapid succession of newspapers indicates, they were all financial risks to the owner-editors and many were short-lived. Others survived by becoming mouthpieces for one or the other of the political parties. Their subscription rates were high and their circulation was limited; yet they had more readers than their short subscription lists would seem to indicate. They all played a definite part in molding the political thinking of their readers.[10]

But these politically biased newspapers did not reach far beyond the main roads suitable for stagecoaches. An overwhelming majority of settlers in Western North Carolina never saw newspapers except as they might acquire one at a political rally. And a distressing proportion of the population could not read them. The people living back from the arteries of trade came to depend upon the rallies, therefore, for their political information. Knowing this, each candidate or speaker was quick to stress the advantages to the mountain section to be gained by the measures and policies he advocated. He was sure to point out how the planks in his party's platform would result in concrete benefits to the mountain district, and at the same time he demonstrated how all that the mountain men held dear would be swept away if the opposing party or candidate came into office. Largely through verbal information, thousands of small farmers came to believe that the Whig party would achieve economic improvement for their section of the state in the form of better roads, railroads, and freer money. For this reason, Western North Carolina became one of the state's Whig strongholds.

The western Whigs were not disappointed in their political faith. By controlling the state offices, the Whig party was able to inaugurate reforms and to set in motion the machinery for state-wide improvement projects. David Lowery Swain of Western North Carolina, who had been the leading force in the first realizations of these plans, which took the form of constitutional revision, left the governorship and took up work as an educator. He exerted his energies mainly in behalf of the state's school and university problems. Swain's place of political influence within the party was taken by another man from the mountains.

In 1836, Thomas Lanier Clingman, a twenty-four year old lawyer from Surry County, opened a law office in Asheville. He had graduated with honors from the University of North Carolina at Chapel Hill in 1832 and, after studying law in Hillsboro, had served a term in the General Assembly as representative from Surry County. He was both striking in appearance and forceful and convincing as a speaker. Born of pioneer stock which included a Cherokee ancestress, Clingman could readily identify himself with the mountain people who were struck with his ability, his fearlessness, and his honesty. The voters of the 49th District, made up of Buncombe, Haywood, and Macon Counties, elected him on the Whig ticket, therefore, to the state Senate in 1840. Although

FROM DOWD'S *LIFE OF VANCE*, THE STEPHENS PRESS, INC.

Vance's First Law Office: After being licensed as a lawyer in 1852, the twenty-one year old Zebulon Baird Vance opened his law office in this small building on College Street in Asheville.

he was too much of an individualist to adhere strictly to party lines, Clingman took over the leadership of the Whigs in the Senate. He threw his energies into the improvement measures they advocated, always taking the side of the West in sectional differences arising within the state party.

The Senator worked for east-west highways, championing the construction of a turnpike from Raleigh to Tennessee by way of Wilkesboro and Jefferson. He also advocated another from Fayetteville to Asheville, which would connect with the Buncombe Turnpike, thus giving access to Tennessee. Clingman asked for state aid in building these roads, and he proposed the incorporation of a Nantahala Turnpike through the western section of his mountain district. He favored improved educational conditions in the state and the establishment of more colleges. In addition, he vigorously advocated state aid for railroads.[11]

In 1842 Thomas Clingman was elected as one of the state's representatives in Congress, taking office in the January, 1843, session. He was returned to this office, serving until 1855 as a Whig, except for the 29th Congress when he was returned as a Democrat. In 1858 he was appointed by Governor Thomas Bragg to the seat in the United States Senate left vacant by the death of Asa Biggs. Clingman won the seat in his own right at the next election and was a member of the Senate until war broke out in 1861. In Congress he threw his tremendous energy into upholding the interests of his state. Although he was frequently charged with inconsistencies in his policies, he gradually helped to crystalize not only North Carolina's position on slavery but he also became a voice of the South. As such, Clingman interpreted the attitude of the South and warned against measures ignoring the economic problems and welfare of that section of the nation.[12]

Attending political rallies and early imbibing political opinions, still another Western North Carolina leader was growing to manhood in the hills in the 1840's. Zebulon Baird Vance was a grandson of David Vance, who had presented the petition for the formation of Buncombe County from the Burke County settlers living west of the Blue Ridge. He was also the grandson of Zebulon Baird, Buncombe County's resourceful first merchant. Members of the Vance family, who derived from sturdy English stock of Norman French extraction, were politically minded and alert to local needs. Those of Zebulon's grandfather's generation had done their parts in the Revolutionary War to win independence and democratic principles for their country.

From these ancestors, Zebulon Vance inherited a talent for leadership, which was intensified by his inheritance from the Baird family. Zebulon Baird, his maternal grandfather, was born in Scotland. Coming to Asheville in 1793, he had represented the new Buncombe County in the General Assembly, first in the lower house and then in the Senate. From the Bairds, Vance inherited the flashing wit, the shrewdness, and the quickness of mind that characterized his mother's family.[13]

For the part he was destined to play in the history of this state, Zeb Vance had the advantage of a boyhood in the mountains. He was born on a farm in Reems Creek valley some ten miles from Asheville. Like the other boys in the neighborhood, he attended "Old Field Schools" (short-term, subscription, elementary schools). He later attended Washington College at Jonesboro,

BARBER PHOTO

Judson College: Until after the Reconstruction Period the education of children and young people was largely the concern of the churches. In addition to private schools, churches established academies, often called colleges. Some of those in operation before 1860 were Rutherford College in Burke County, Mars Hill in Madison County, and Judson College in Henderson County.

Tennessee, which was under the management of the Reverend Samuel Doak. Still later, he was a student at the University of North Carolina where David Lowery Swain was President.[14]

As a farm boy and for a time as a helper earning his living at John Patton's stand in Madison County, Vance came to understand the economy of the area as it ebbed and flowed according to the droves of livestock thundering down the Buncombe Turnpike to southern markets. From the farmers bringing their corn and from the drovers and drivers, he became familiar with conditions on the broad, river bottom farms and in the coves with their mountain grazing lands. The young Zeb Vance was genuinely interested in people. He had a word, a jest, and a genial, infectious laugh to share with all who passed. As he went through his teens, he was learning to understand people—his mountain people, all people.

From his forebears and from his environment Vance

developed a fearlessness of opinion and action, together with an honesty that was never questioned, a singleness and loftiness of purpose that seemed to be gifts from his native hills, and a dogged determination that smacked of their granite. Perhaps more than any other individual, Zebulon Baird Vance typified the strength and sturdy virtues, as well as the independence and the intellectual capacities of the people making the mountains of Western North Carolina their home. Perhaps it was for those very qualities that he became one of his state's most beloved citizens.

Following his study of law in 1854, Vance, then twenty-four years old, was sent by his native county of Buncombe to the General Assembly and four years later was elected to Congress as a Whig. His career there was interrupted for twenty-four years by the Civil War. During that time he gave his abundant energies to the cause of the Confederacy and to the welfare of North Carolina, serving as Governor during the war and for one term afterward.

It was during this period of Whig activity that the little log school houses, discussed in a previous chapter, appeared in every western county. These schools gradually increased their service to the people as Dr. Calvin H. Wiley's educational program strengthened their curricula and increased the efficiency of the teachers. Although from today's standpoint these schools left much to be desired, they were a leaven raising the degree of literacy, and hence the outlook, in Western North Carolina. By 1860 in the prosperous areas, these mountain schools were as efficient, perhaps, as the schools in most of the new areas of the nation.

The Buncombe Turnpike and the road connecting the citizens of Watauga County with Morganton, Rutherfordton, and with South Carolina markets, together with other north-south roads, continued their beneficial services to Western North Carolina; nevertheless, roads and their upkeep remained the major problem of the mountain country. For the first time the region looked to the state with some degree of confidence for aid in constructing additional trade lanes. In Governor Morehead the section had a champion in its road demands. John Motley Morehead had been one of the young liberals supporting the reforms advocated earlier by Murphey. In his 1840 campaign he had promised to work for state aid for internal improvements. Western North Carolina received encouragement from his 1842 message to the General Assembly in which he listed as one of the state's most pressing

THE STEPHENS PRESS, INC.

The Young Congressman: In 1858, at the age of twenty-eight, Vance won a seat in the House of Representatives in the Thirty-Fifth Congress of the United States. He took the seat made vacant by the resignation of Thomas Lanier Clingman, who became a senator.

needs the construction of the east-west highway earlier envisioned by Joseph Caldwell. Extending from the coastal area westward through the mountains to Tennessee, such a highway would, he pointed out, open the mountain-locked region to eastern markets.

Morehead echoed the convictions of the mountain people when he pictured the development that such a highway would bring to Western North Carolina. "When good roads shall be established in that region," he contended, "it is believed the population will increase with rapidity, agriculture will improve, grazing will be extended, and manufactures and mechanic arts will flourish in a location combining so many advantages and inviting their growth. The improved highways will be additional inducements to the citizens of other sections of our State to abandon their usual northern tours, or visits to the Virginia watering places for a tour more interesting among our own mountains, much cheaper, and much more beautiful—a tour in which they will inspire health in every breath and drink in health in every draught."[15]

The first road that could be considered an adequate highway across the Blue Ridge, linking Buncombe County with the counties directly to the east, came when a company was chartered in 1840 to construct a road from Rutherfordton to Asheville. Six years later the Hickory Nut Turnpike was chartered, authorizing a road from Rutherfordton across the mountains to Henderson County and on to Asheville and the Buncombe Turnpike. These improved highways made possible regular stagecoach travel between the areas.[16] The citizens of Western North Carolina still impatiently awaited the coming of the east-west highway advocated by Governor Morehead. But the waiting period was far too long, for it was not until 1849 that the General Assembly authorized the chartering of a company to construct the western section of the long promised road.

With a capital stock made up of shares owned by the state and shares purchased by citizens of the counties through which the road passed, the turnpike company constructed the highway from Salisbury to the Tennessee line. It went by way of Morganton, Old Fort, Asheville, Waynesville, and continued westward to Cherokee County and Tennessee. A southern branch extended to the Georgia line. Thus the new highway was somewhat the fulfillment of Clingman's plan for a Nantahala Turnpike. By 1855 this highway was linking the western border counties with Asheville and the Asheville and Greenville Plank Road.[17] During these years, too, western counties were constructing new, subsidiary roads and were improving others. Yancey County had a fairly adequate road from Burnsville to the Buncombe line, and in other counties roads were built to connect with turnpikes. But the secondary roads in all mountain counties continued to be poor, often practically impassable during the winter months.[18]

By the time the Whigs gained control of the state government, railroads had made their appearance in North Carolina, and Western North Carolina joined in the clamor coming from all counties for state aid for railroad construction. Many leaders saw in the railroads the solution to North Carolina's vexing transportation problem, and the Whig party advocated a complete network of railroads. As early as 1833 a privately constructed, mile and a quarter stretch of railroad at Raleigh had been the means of hauling stone from the quarries on mule-drawn flat cars to the site of the capitol then being built.

Following that successful venture, private capital had succeeded in building and operating two railroads. The Wilmington and Weldon was built 161 miles in length, and in 1840 it was the longest in the world. The Raleigh and Gaston was 86 miles long. But the cost of construction and maintenance of these railroads, with their iron-covered rails, was too excessive for private enterprise, and by 1836 both faced bankruptcy. It was then that the Whigs succeeded in inaugurating the policy of state aid. By 1845, when the state had actually had to purchase the Raleigh and Gaston line, North Carolina had spent (lost, the conservatives claimed) almost a million dollars in its railroad aid program.[19]

The building of railroads was recognized, however, by many leaders in all sections of the state as being so necessary to the economy of the commonwealth as to warrant further state aid to this enterprise. The question of railroads was the popular topic of the day. Their value to the state and state aid for their construction were themes debated pro and con by speakers. Newspapers also aired the rising controversy over state aid for the roads. Politicians envisioned railroads passing through the counties of their constituents.

Many plans, both practical and visionary, were advanced for the development of intrastate lines, some running north-south and others east-west, but all with an eye to funneling the state's products to its eastern markets. Interstate railroads were also discussed, and Joseph Caldwell's plan for a Beaufort to Murphy line was revived.[20] Governor Morehead expressed the belief that such a line would bring products from as far west as Memphis through the length of the state to its eastern ports. It might even serve as a European market line for cities in California.[21]

In Western North Carolina this cross-state plan was welcomed as the solution to its transportation problem; yet the region's first hope for a railroad came from a plan for an interstate line from Charleston to the growing West. South Carolina was profiting from the trade that passed south over the Buncombe Turnpike, connecting with the fine new road that Joel Poinsett had constructed along the ancient trading path to the Cherokees. Charleston, Robert Y. Hayne pointed out to his fellow statesman, was the natural outlet for products not only from the mountains, but also from Kentucky, Illinois, and Ohio—indeed, from all territory in the Mississippi valley. Moreover, a railroad from Charleston to this area might offer a political link between the new west and South Carolina, an advantage not to be overlooked.[22]

With such leaders as Hayne, Mitchell King, Joel Poinsett, and James Bennett interested in the project, plans progressed, and investigations were made for a route through or around the mountains. The choice settled on a line from Saluda Mountain to Asheville and down the French Broad, which had an easy grade of thirteen feet per mile, to Knoxville. The road would thus extend 107 miles through Western North Carolina and could be constructed, engineers estimated, at a cost of two million dollars.[23]

Following the pattern set for crystalizing public sentiment for railroads, delegates from the states concerned attended a railroad convention in Knoxville in 1836. Reports were heard from committees earlier appointed to make investigations into all the phases of such a far-flung project. Then the Louisville, Cincinnati, and Charleston Railroad Company was formed with Robert Y. Hayne as president. The plan was that each state would incorporate a company within the larger framework to build the section passing through its territory. An atmosphere of optimism pervaded the convention, and the meeting closed with an admonition to state representatives "not to suffer the work to fail."[24]

During the next few years enthusiastic citizens of Western North Carolina subscribed for stock in the company. They attended meetings of stock holders to hear reports of the company's progress and of the surveys made by the engineers. At such a meeting in Asheville in 1839 Robert Y. Hayne was stricken with a fatal illness and died. Mitchell King was then elected president of the company. The ambitious plans for the railroad collapsed soon afterward when South Carolina refused to incorporate a company that would be a part of an out-of-state organization, and Tennessee followed her example. Western North Carolina's hopes for getting a railroad faded.[25]

That hope was later revived when in 1848, under the Whig controlled government, the state began the policy of issuing and selling interest-bearing bonds as a means of raising money for aid for improvements, including railroads. The following year the North Carolina Railroad, to run from Goldsboro to Charlotte, was incorporated with the state subscribing two million dollars and private capital sponsoring another million.[26] The state later found it necessary to subscribe an additional one million dollars. The bill authorizing this road was a bipartisan, compromise measure. It called for the construction of a railroad that would connect Goldsboro with Charlotte by way of Salisbury. John M. Morehead was elected president of the company.

Construction began from the two terminal points, and in 1856 the 223-mile line was in operation, opening the piedmont to the markets of the state. Almost at once its effects throughout that section and in the mountain counties east of the Blue Ridge were apparent. Freight rates were cut in half; prices of incoming commodities were drastically lowered. Farmers, able to get their products to market and at a cost insuring profit, raised more grain. A general air of prosperity came to the region that was once known as the lagging "back country."[27]

The construction of this railroad brought again into prominence the idea of extending lines across the Blue Ridge and on to the Tennessee border. Joseph Caldwell in 1828 in his *Numbers of Carlton* had pleaded for a line stretching from the eastern cities of Beaufort and New Bern westward to Tennessee.[28] Now that plea was revived. Accordingly, the Western North Carolina Railroad was incorporated in 1854. It was to be the western extension of the North Carolina Railroad, and construction was to start at Salisbury.[29]

This railroad, which was favored by both Democrats and Whigs, was to be constructed in sections. The bill designated that each section was to be in full operation before any work might begin on the succeeding section. That clause included the selling of stock. The maximum stock was to be $6,000,000 and the state was to own two thirds, with one third raised from private capital in the counties through which the road would pass.[30] Four possible routes were presented, but because of the absence of gaps in the precipitous Blue Ridge, only two seemed practical enough to warrant surveys.

One of these proposals would take the railroad across the Blue Ridge into Watauga County and along the Watauga River, entering Tennessee at a point thirty-three miles from the East Tennessee and Virginia Railroad. This was the shortest of the suggested routes, 121.77 miles from Salisbury. Because of the extreme construction difficulties it presented, however, Walter Gwynn, the surveying engineer, recommended the longer route going by way of the Catawba valley and crossing the Blue Ridge at Swannanoa Gap. This route would necessitate a series of tunnels. From the west portal of the last tunnel the road would go to Asheville and from there down the French Broad River to Paint Rock. This line would be 186.78 miles long.[31]

Almost at once another route from Asheville to the Tennessee border was suggested. It would go west from Asheville to Waynesville and on to connect with the Blue Ridge Railroad or on to the Tennessee line near Ducktown. Both of these routes were later surveyed, and the advantages of each became the subject of much local publicity. Citizens of Buncombe and Madison Counties favored the French Broad route. Citizens of the western counties favored the Ducktown route, pointing out that such a road would reach the thriving copper mines of eastern Tennessee and would, as Morehead had made clear, open for Memphis its shortest route to sea ports.[32]

East of the Blue Ridge counties were contending for routes stretching west from Salisbury. Caldwell County had favored the Watauga route but gave up the struggle for that, demanding that the line pass north of the Catawba River. Burke County urged that Morganton be made the terminal for the first section of the Western Railroad and, winning its point, its citizens subscribed $100,000 to the capital stock. R. C. Pearson of Burke County was elected president of the company and James C. Turner was appointed chief engineer. Rutherfordton, which was not on the route of the Western North Carolina Railroad, looked forward after 1854 to a road from Charlotte. The year before the western division had been chartered, the General Assembly had passed a bill under which the Wilmington, Charlotte, and Rutherfordton Railroad was incorporated. Work on it began almost at once. As the project progressed, the company made plans to extend the line over the Blue Ridge to the Tennessee border in Watauga County where it would connect with a road from Jonesboro, Tennessee.[33]

In the meantime, South Carolina revived its earlier plan for a Charleston to Cincinnati railroad that would cross Western North Carolina by way of the French Broad River, and it incorporated the Greenville and French Broad Company. It also chartered a company to construct a railroad from Anderson through a section of Georgia, to continue for a distance of seventy-three miles across the western counties of North Carolina into Tennessee. This line was to be called the Blue Ridge Railroad. By 1855 it looked as though Western North Carolina might have a network of railroads.[34]

It soon became evident that the clause requiring the construction of the Western North Carolina Railroad to be done in sections would greatly impede the progress of the work and therefore delay its advent into the counties west of the mountains. To the citizens of Western North Carolina this delay was both unwarranted and intolerable. For several reasons they felt that haste was imperative. In the first place, it was felt that the state would be unwilling to invest in two roads across the mountains and that contentions arising over a choice between the Western North Carolina Railroad and the Rutherfordton line would inevitably lead to a prolonged delay, resulting in the abandonment of both plans.

In the second place, the mountain citizens much preferred that the road west of the mountains be constructed by a North Carolina company; yet, unless the Western Extension reached the area within a reasonable time, the South Carolina company would doubtless have its line along the French Broad in operation. As a solution to the railroad problems facing the area, the residents of the mountain counties began agitating for the removal of the sectional clause in the Western North Carolina Railroad Bill. Feelings ran high, with railroads an issue in the 1858 campaign. A bill presented to the General Assembly for striking out the objectionable sectional feature failed to pass. The reaction of the citizens west of the Blue Ridge was immediate and bitter.

The editor of the *Asheville News* wrote a stinging economic declaration of independence from the eastern part of the state, declaring, "We have no doubt the people of the West will readily embrace this tender of a dissolution of every tie that binds us together as one people, and will henceforth regard themselves as having neither part nor lot in the internal improvement system of North Carolina." He went on to predict "that the people of the

French Broad Valley will never again ask for a connection with any North Carolina Road."³⁵

Aroused citizens gathered at a mass meeting in Asheville and heard Nicholas W. Woodfin, who had led the section's struggle for a railroad, deliver a fiery speech, advising his fellow westerners not to invest a penny in the Western North Carolina road. Instead, the people of Henderson, Buncombe, and Madison Counties were urged by Woodfin and other leaders to purchase stock in the South Carolina road. At elections held in these three counties in the summer of 1859, each county was empowered to purchase stock in the Greenville and French Broad Railroad. On July 28, 1859, the officials of that road met in Hendersonville with citizens of Henderson, Buncombe, and Madison Counties to formulate plans.³⁶

During this time, the construction of the first section of the Western Extension was progressing slowly, far more so than had been anticipated. The contractor was badly in need of additional state funds, but under the bill, these could not be forthcoming until the completion of that section. To alleviate this embarrassing situation, the General Assembly early in 1861 revised the incorporation bill, making the entire distance from Salisbury to the western end of the Swannanoa tunnel the first section.

At the same session the Assembly ratified the Ducktown route for the line from Asheville to the Tennessee border, the route earlier adopted by the stockholders upon the recommendation of the surveyor. The act allowed for a branch road, however, to be constructed from Asheville to Paint Rock, but that could begin only after the western portion had reached Waynesville.³⁷ With the prospect of a state-sponsored road reaching their area, citizens of Western North Carolina were somewhat placated. Surely one of the many plans under consideration would result in a railroad for the area. But the western citizens were again to be disappointed.

By April, 1861, the Wilmington, Charlotte, and Rutherfordton road had not yet reached Rutherford County, while the Western Extension lacked more than five miles of entering Morganton. When the Civil War broke out, the contractor of this section left for the army and was later among those killed at the First Battle of Manassas. Another contractor was employed to carry out the work. But with workmen enlisting or being drafted and with the added difficulty of getting the necessary metal for the rails, the work could go on only at a snail's pace. It stopped altogether before reaching Morganton. The Rutherfordton line ceased construction activities at Cherryville, and at the time of the Civil War only a few miles of track had actually been laid in Western North Carolina, none of them across the Blue Ridge.

The early railroads in the state furnished conclusive evidence of the prosperity that would follow with adequate systems of transporation. But the excessive cost of railroads, even when partly assumed by the state, and their expensive upkeep made them financial risks. Those risks often prevented private capital from being invested in stocks of the incorporated companies or in state bonds issued to aid them. Then, too, as Western North Carolina painfully learned, railroad construction was a slow process.

For those reasons engineers and interested citizens sought a quicker, cheaper way of supplying satisfactory highways in areas untouched by the existing railroads. As a solution to this problem some inventive person came up with the idea of the plank road, and in the 1850's the building of plank roads took second place only to railroads in the interest of transportation-conscious Carolinians. The first of these roads, later called the "Appian Way" of North Carolina, was chartered in 1849 and opened in 1854, connecting Fayetteville with Salem. It proved to have many advantages over the old type of highway.[38]

A plank road was constructed by allowing the graded bed to settle and then placing over it pine sleepers or sills placed end to end lengthwise. Across these sills pine planks, from nine to sixteen inches wide and from three to four inches thick, were laid. Wider than the turnpikes, these roads were usually about eight feet in width, with frequent turnouts to allow for the passing of vehicles. With their firm beds and their two thicknesses of planks, they were all-weather roads, enabling the farmers to market their grain at all seasons of the year. Over them a team could haul a vastly heavier load than on the old highways. Their cost, compared with railroads, was modest, for the plank roads usually followed the old roads, whose beds could easily be put into condition for the sills. The pine lumber used was cheap, costing about three dollars per thousand feet. They seemed to be the answer to the needs of several sections of the state in Western North Carolina.[39]

The Buncombe Turnpike by 1850 was badly in need of repairs from years of heavy animal traffic. The company was dissolved, and in 1851 the Asheville and Greenville Plank Road Company was incorporated, taking over sections of the older turnpike bed.[40] Over the new plank highway the great droves continued until the incoming railroads in states to the north could take the livestock to market by rail cheaper than the animals could transport themselves. By the late 1850's the number and size of the droves passing along Western North Carolina roads decreased, although they did not cease until the Civil War and were continued for a time after the end of the conflict. But the plank road era was of short duration. Even without the destruction brought by war, it would probably have passed, for the life of a plank highway was from seven to nine years. By that time even the sills had to be replaced, and long before that, expensive repairs were necessary. These were often made by using crushed rock, a more durable material.

In the decade before the war the Whigs, who had given to North Carolina its greatest period of internal improvements, lost their control over the state offices. Now fully aware of the prosperity brought about by the Whig projects, the Democrats by 1850 had shrugged off their cloak of inertia and were espousing the continuance of improvements. They had also become alert to the ominous trend in national issues involving the slave question. To safeguard the state's economic order, the Democrats stressed their old policy of the state's right, as opposed to the national government, to deal with all matters concerning its internal affairs. In so doing, the Democrats became the party of the South and of Southern interests.

By 1850 the party was revitalized and vigorous enough to place its candidate, David S. Reid, in the governor's chair, and the Democrats continued to control that office until the outbreak of the war. They also gained a majority in the General Assembly. Within the next few years, the slavery issue assumed a larger place in national politics and, therefore, necessarily in state politics. As a result, many of North Carolina's political leaders left the Whig Party, which remained silent on the slavery issue, and joined the Democrats. Among them was Thomas L. Clingman, who found the rejuvenated Democratic Party expressing his own views of the slavery question.[41] William W. Holden, later to play a partisan role in North Carolina affairs, also left the Whigs to become a spokesman for the Democrats through his newspaper, *The North Carolina Standard.*

The Democrats now made a bid for western votes by a

movement for free suffrage, long desired by the small farmers of the western counties. In 1857 the movement crystalized into action, and by a constitutional amendment property qualifications for voting for state senators were discarded.[42] This constructive and long overdue action won adherents for the party in the west. The party also gained followers as it took up its new role of sponsorship of internal improvements, including turnpikes, plank roads, and railroads for the mountain section of the state. In fact, even though originally planned by the Whigs, whatever highway improvements reached Western North Carolina in the 1850's came through Democratic sanction.

As a series of slave measures came up in Congress, the feelings of both Northerners and Southerners became ever more bitter. The Southern men in Congress now came to foresee in the near future a predominance of northern Congressmen with steadily growing anti-slavery views. They recognized that the passage of each slavery bill into law was a defeat for the South. Accordingly, North Carolina leaders continued to leave the Whig party, which still took no stand on slavery issues, to join the ranks of the Democrats. A decisive blow came to the national Whig Party with the passage of the Kansas-Nebraska Bill and the subsequent bloodshed in that unhappy area. Those events were followed by the formation of the Republican Party, pledged to slavery-free territories and to the belief that the Union was indissolvable. Many northern Whigs went into this new party, while in protest to it, many Southerners joined the Democratic Party.

During the 1850's the North Carolina Democrats actively took up the issue of slavery, favoring the extension of slavery in the new territories and incoming states and denying the expediency of federal restrictions in the territories as advocated by some Whig extremists. In all these policies the Democratic Party was, as it had earlier been, the party of the slave-owning plantation East. But the growing tension throughout the nation and in the state made these policies, especially the state's rights policy, the platform of the South against the increasing abolitionism of the North. The Democrats now took into their ranks former Whigs who had become alarmed at the turn in national affairs and who feared "Black Republicanism."

Many of the voters in Western North Carolina were still unwilling to join the Democratic Party, and a goodly number of them cast in their lots with the United American or Know-Nothing Party, which formed an organization in North Carolina in 1855. This party had no slavery policies and very little to offer in the way of a constructive platform. In its origin and character it was generally negative in its approach to the problems with which it concerned itself.

The Know-Nothing Party centered its attacks on the unrestricted European immigration to the United States, which annually brought into the nation hundreds of thousands of economically low-class families from southern European countries. Thousands of these were poverty-stricken people who entered regardless of their physical, mental, or moral ability to be absorbed into the American pattern of life. A high percentage of these undesirable immigrants was Catholic, and the Know-Nothing Party, which veiled its objectives in secrecy, was anti-Catholic. For the voters of Western North Carolina this party was a poor substitute for the Whig Party, and when in 1859 the Whig Party was briefly revived in North Carolina, the Know-Nothings disappeared from the state. The mountain members then returned to their old party. Among them was Buncombe County's Zebulon Baird Vance, who that year was elected to the Congress on the Whig ticket.[43]

CHAPTER NINETEEN

War in the Land

The presidential election of 1860 was a tense one. The Union was literally at stake. The series of hotly contested slavery issues had weakened the Whig Party four years earlier and brought into prominence the Republican Party, organized in 1854. Differences brought about by the slavery issues also caused the Democratic Party to split over its platform in 1859. The Southern delegates walked out of the Convention, organized their own wing of the party, and nominated John C. Breckenridge of Kentucky for president. The Northern or Regular Democrats nominated Stephen Arnold Douglas of Illinois. The newly organized Constitutional Party, made up largely of Whigs unwilling to join other parties, nominated John Bell of Tennessee, and the Republicans named Abraham Lincoln. Voters in North Carolina had only three presidential choices, however, for Lincoln's name was not on the ballot for the presidency.[1]

Chiefly because of the split in the Democratic ranks, the Republicans succeeded in electing Abraham Lincoln as President of the United States. South Carolina's reply to the election returns was prompt and emphatic. Considering the state sovereign and endowed with the right of self-determination, it seceded from the Union in December. Early the following year Mississippi, Alabama, Texas, Florida, Georgia, and Lousiana also seceded.[2]

In North Carolina the idea of secession had earlier entered political discussions. The Republican Party had nominated John

Charles Fremont as its presidential nominee for the 1856 election. Thomas Lanier Clingman of Western North Carolina was then a member of the United States House of Representatives. In 1855 he voiced his belief that, should Fremont be elected, the Southern States would be justified in withdrawing from the Union, and he outlined a plan of secession. His views were echoed by several other state leaders.[3]

North Carolinians knew that Lincoln had been active in opposing the extension of slavery into western territories. They also knew that he was outspoken in his belief that the Union could not be dissolved. The idea of secession was repugnant to most Whigs and ex-Whigs and to most of the members of the Democratic Party. As a result many state leaders were active in their efforts for peace. In February, 1861, delegates from North Carolina attended a Peace Conference in Montgomery, Alabama. There the delegates hoped to work out settlements of a compromise to the sectional differences. Nothing constructive came out of that meeting, however, and in that same month a Peace Conference, called by Virginia, met in Washington. Delegates from twenty-one states attended, including those from North Carolina. As compromise measures that might be acceptable to both North and South, seven proposed amendments to the Constitution were presented to Congress. All were rejected. Here and there within the state Peace Rallies were held, but they also failed in obtaining their objective.[4]

Among those opposing secession was Zebulon Baird Vance of Buncombe County. In 1858 Thomas L. Clingman was appointed to the United States Senate to fill the unexpired term of Asa Higgs, and Vance was appointed to fill Clingman's seat in the House of Representatives. He was elected the following year and served in the Thirty-Sixth Congress, the last before the outbreak of the war. Throughout the session he was a staunch supporter of the Union, and back in his native state he vigorously urged adherence to the Union.[5] On February 26, 1861, in response to the Convention Act passed by the General Assembly, citizens went to the polls to vote on calling a convention to consider secession, but the convention proposal was defeated. Vance and other Union leaders were disappointed. They felt that Unionists would dominate the convention and thereby insure a negative vote for secession.[6]

But that spring the tide of public opinion abruptly turned. On April 12, troops of the new Confederacy fired on Fort Sumter. They captured it two days later before reinforcements could

THE STEPHENS PRESS, INC.

Young Confederate Colonels: Vance opposed secession, but his views abruptly changed when North Carolina was ordered to furnish federal troops. "If war must come," he said, "I prefer to be with my own people." He entered the war as a Captain of the Rough and Ready Guards but soon achieved the rank of Colonel in the Twenty-Sixth Regiment.

reach it. Both North and South knew that this was war, and almost at once public opinion became unified. President Lincoln's call to arms included an order from the Secretary of War for two North Carolina regiments. In a speech delivered before the Andrew Post No. 15 of the Grand Army in Boston on December 8, 1886, Vance told of his own experience. News of this order reached the village of Marshall while he was "pleading for the Union" with his arm upraised in a gesture. When that arm came down, he said, it fell sadly by the side of a secessionist. If North Carolina had to fight, he pointed out, it must be against Northerners.[7]

The days following the first shot at Fort Sumter were brimming with excitement and crowded with war preparations. Governor John W. Ellis called a special meeting of the General Assembly. He ordered Forts Caswell and Johnson seized at the mouth of the Cape Fear River, as well as the Federal Arsenal at Fayetteville and the Government Mint at Charlotte. Ellis then issued a call for 30,000 volunteers, promising the Confederacy to get from 1,000 to 10,000 state troops within a few days. He made arrangements with the Confederate Government to have these volunteers enter training as state troops, and he entered into an agreement with the Confederacy whereby North Carolina was to clothe and arm its own soldiers, the only Southern state to do so.[8]

In the emergency the General Assembly dispensed with the referendum and called an election for electing delegates to a convention to be held in Raleigh on May 20. These delegates, after organizing the convention, voted to withdraw from the union existing between North Carolina and the other states of the United States. They declared North Carolina a sovereign commonwealth and ratified the Provisional Constitution of the Confederacy. Thus Western North Carolina became a part of a new Republic, and to its mountains was to come yet another war.[9]

The war began with an outburst of patriotism and enthusiasm. James Green Martin was appointed Adjutant General of the state troops and was put in charge of organizing the military program and mobilizing supplies. Under the county units that he set up, the volunteers offered their services for six months. Military companies were hurriedly formed as both the state and its people prepared for what all considered would be a short war. Western North Carolina was active in these preparations.

Even before secession, Burnt Chimney, now Forest City, organized a unit which it proudly called The Burnt Chimney

THE STEPHENS PRESS, INC.

The Battle of New Bern: Taking a prominent part in this battle was Colonel Vance with his Twenty-Sixth Regiment, which was largely made up of men from the western counties of North Carolina. This picture is from an 1863 drawing.

Volunteers. This unit left for Raleigh on June 3 to become Company D in the Sixteenth Regiment of North Carolina Infantry. The unit formed at Rutherfordton, called The Rutherfordton Riflemen, became Company G in the Sixteenth Regiment.[10] The first volunteer unit in Western North Carolina was formed in Buncombe County, however, by William Wallis McDowell of Asheville. It was organized prior to Governor Ellis' call for troops and was called The Buncombe Riflemen. On April 18 it left Asheville for Raleigh to become Company E of the First North Carolina Volunteer Regiment. On June 10 these men from the mountains, with little more than a month's intensive training, saw action at Big Bethel, the first land battle of the Civil War.[11] On May 4 Zebulon B. Vance organized another company, called The Rough and Ready Guards. It left Asheville to become Company F in the Fourteenth Regiment. Later as a part of General Robert E. Lee's army, it fought brilliantly in Virginia, Pennsylvania, and Maryland. Vance, now Colonel Vance, was later transferred to the Twenty-Sixth Regiment. He left that Regiment in 1862 after being elected Governor of his state.[12]

Haywood County organized a unit that became Company A of the Sixteenth Regiment.[13] On May 18 The Henderson County

Guards left Hendersonville, filled with zeal to fulfill the motto on their banner, "To the Henderson Guards: Follow your banner to victory or death."[14] In August Thomas L. Clingman helped to form yet another unit in Asheville, made up of men from Buncombe, Haywood, Cherokee, Henderson, Jackson, and Transylvania Counties. This unit was mustered in on September 18. Eleven days later it reached Wilmington and became a part of the Twenty-Fifth Regiment.[15] In Madison County Lawrence M. Allen formed a mounted company called Allen's Rangers, later to be known as Allen's Legion. These men became a part of the Sixty-Fourth Regiment.[16]

What was happening in these counties was repeated in every section of Western North Carolina as young men from the hills volunteered in county units or joined with men from neighboring counties to organize groups leaving for Raleigh or Wilmington where they went into training. During the next year this volunteer effort continued, and in 1862 two companies were organized at Brevard,[17] while the Sixty-Second Regiment was made up almost entirely of mountain men. Hundreds of others entered state regiments already formed, while still others joined the armies of the Confederacy. In their first outburst of enthusiasm, some of the counties, like Rutherford, backed by their county courts, levied a tax to provide money for clothing and equipment for their own soldiers. Transylvania County went so far as to borrow fifteen hundred dollars from the Cape Fear Bank at Asheville in order to give each of its volunteers the sum of fifteen dollars.[18]

As these first volunteers prepared to leave home, the communities made each occasion a public demonstration of patriotism. The villages from which they were mustered were crowded with friends and relatives of the departing men. Speeches were made by prominent citizens. Prayers were offered by ministers, and in some instances the men were presented with Bibles. Flags made by young women of the town were presented with appropriate remarks. After these colorful ceremonies, weeping families and well-wishing friends followed the marching men until darkness compelled them to return to their homes. There the awful reality of war became a part of their daily living.[19]

Volunteers responding to the first call enlisted for six months, but the General Assembly in May authorized the calling of an additional fifty thousand volunteers for a year's service in addition

THE BARDEN COLLECTION, N. C. DEPARTMENT OF ARCHIVES AND HISTORY
The Ad-Vance: Purchased for the state by Governor Vance through an agent, this sturdy blockade runner, named The Ad-Vance, made eleven cargo-filled trips into Wilmington before its capture in September, 1864.

to the organization of ten regiments of state troops for the duration of the war. Although the state hoped for a short war, it prepared for a long one. Recruiting offices were opened in villages, and training camps and drilling grounds were laid out in the mountain counties. Mountain men continued to enlist in the armies of their state and in those of the Confederacy.

Products of the forges of the mountains (and there were perhaps a score of them) were contracted for by the state, and new forges were established to furnish the iron needed for the manufacturing of rifles and for the various purposes of war. A private factory for the manufacturing of rifles was set up in Asheville. The following year it was taken over by the Confederacy, and Major Benjamin Sloan, a West Point graduate, was placed in charge. At first much scrap iron was used, but Major Sloan was able to get iron from the Cranberry mines to enable the Asheville factory to turn out, at the rate of three hundred guns a month, thousands of the best rifles made in the South. Later in the war the factory was moved to Columbia, South Carolina, but before the end of the war it was blown up to prevent its falling into the hands of the Federals.[20]

The issue of slavery affected the mountain counties very little,

NATIONAL PARK SERVICE

Cherokee Veterans of the Thomas Legion: To protect citizens in the western counties William H. Thomas in 1862 formed what became known as The Thomas Legion. Of its 17 companies, two were made up of Cherokees. This picture was taken in New Orleans at the last reunion of these Cherokee veterans. Those in the picture, as named by the son of Colonel Thomas, are: front row, 1 Young Deer; 2 unidentified; 3 Pheasant; 4 Chief David Reed; 5 Sevier Skitty; back row, 1 the Rev. Bird Saloneta; 2 Dickey Driver; 3 Lieut. Col. W. W. Stringfield of Waynesville (officer); 4 Lieutenant Suatie Owl; 5 Jim Keg; 6 Wesley Crow; 7 unidentified; 8 Lieutenant Calvin Cagle (officer).

for geographic conditons had made slave labor impractical. Only a few owners of river valley farms had found it profitable to invest in slaves. In the villages and on some of the farms a few slaves were used as house or stable servants, and the summer residents in Henderson and Transylvania Counties brought with them from the low country the slaves they needed to staff their estates. But the majority of mountain people had neither the money nor the need to own many slaves.

The counties on the eastern slopes of the Blue Ridge with their broad river farms had more slaves than did those farther west. In 1860 Rutherford County, with a total population of 11,573, had 2,391 slaves; Burke County, with a population of 9,237, had 2,371 slaves. Across the mountains Buncombe County (population 12,654) had 1,905 slaves, while Cherokee to the west had only 520 slaves out of a population of 9,166. Madison County, with a population of 5,678, had 213 slaves and 17 free Negroes. Other counties varied in their slave population, depending largely upon the area's terrain.[21]

For years the western counties had been aligned in interests against the eastern plantation section of the state and had opposed governmental concessions to the slave-owning planters; however, there had been no special movement in the area directed against slavery itself. Nor is there evidence that such publications as Hinton Rowan Helper's *The Impending Crisis* had exerted any influence upon the few readers it may have reached in the mountains. But certainly the men of Western North Carolina had no desire to give their lives for the cause of slavery. They justified their participation in the war on other grounds. Both their environment and their heritage enabled the mountain men to espouse the cause of a state's right to determine its own course of action and caused them to resent what was considered the insult of Lincoln's call for North Carolina troops.

Not all mountaineers accepted as justifiable the causes for war as explained by the state's leaders and by the newspapers. During the Revolutionary War the mountain area had been a region of divided loyalties with accompanying bitterness and destruction. That pattern was repeated from 1861-1865, and since the settlements in Western North Carolina were more numerous than in 1776, both the hatred and the devastation were more widespread. Thus while the boys and men were reporting to camps to be enrolled in the state's troops, a trickle of men quietly disappeared from their mountain homes to cast their lots with the Union.

Neighborhoods were thus divided, and men long friends went in opposite directions to enlist, some to don the uniforms of gray and others to wear the uniforms of blue. All hoped not to meet again until after the conflict had ended. The number of those joining the Union forces from mountain counties will never be definitely known. They had to enlist in other states, and their home counties were not listed in the records of their units. But during the four years of war there were many who took up arms against the Confederacy.[22]

Union sentiment was evident throughout the region but was especially strong in Henderson and Transylvania Counties and in the Toe River valley counties of Yancey, Madison, the newly created Mitchell County, as well as in Watauga, Ashe, and Alleghany Counties. In Henderson County in 1863 a Union company was organized with James Hamilton of Little River as captain. It became Company F in the Second North Carolina Federal Volunteers. It has been estimated that for every ten men in Watauga County who enlisted in the Confederate armies, one man enlisted in the Union forces. The ratio of Union soldiers was probably higher in Mitchell County, and in Gloucester and Little River Townships in Transylvania County more than half of the men were Unionists.[23]

Early in the war secret means of getting Unionists safely to Northern recruiting stations were set up and remained active throughout the conflict. They were known as "underground railroads," one of which took men coming from east of the Blue Ridge to Boone. Working in relays, scouts got them from there to the underground station at Banner Elk where they were taken on or directed to the Cranberry station or to the one at Crab Orchard in Tennessee.[24] Another of these "railroads" crossed Polk County from South Carolina and linked with one in Henderson County that passed men through the Bat Cave community and on north to Buncombe County where they were aided on their way to Tennessee.[25] Still another underground network along which escaping prisoners from Andersonville, Georgia, passed, entered Western North Carolina in Transylvania County, passed through Little River Township and through Gloucester Township into Jackson County, and continued on to the Tennessee line. Over these "railroads" went Unionists, escaping prisoners, deserters, and fleeing slaves.[26]

In addition to the men whose Union sympathies were strong enough to compel them to take up arms in its defense, many within the age limits of soldiers were too loyal to the Union to join the Southern armies but were unwilling to fight against their fellow Southerners. They were called Tories, the word used for the English sympathizers in the Revolutionary War. They avoided enlisting in either army, and when they were in danger of being conscripted, many of them hid in the hills to become known then as "outliers." During the first year of the war many families added to the worries and heartbreak of family division the growing distrust that came to characterize community relationships.

By the end of the first year, hopes for a speedy end of the conflict had almost vanished, and life in the hills grew increasingly austere. As the months passed, the weakness of a largely agricultural South pitted against a more industrial North became distressingly apparent. The South had few factories. It shipped its cotton and wool to England and to Northern industrial markets and did the same with its other raw products. Turpentine and naval stores were its chief manufactured exports. North Carolina, like the other Southern states, depended upon imports from England and the New England area for its cloth, tools, guns, railroad metals, and other manufactured articles. In 1860 North Carolina had 39 cotton mills, 49 ironworks, more than 300 saw mills, and 639 grist and flour mills. With the exception of three cotton mills employing more than a hundred workers each, however, these factories were small, often operating in connection with the owners' other little enterprises and often designed to supply only local needs.[27]

With the beginning of the war the state took over most of the cotton and woolen mills to insure uniforms for the soldiers, and even then it had to purchase additional cloth from other countries. The state could and did stress raising grain needed to feed its troops and to supply the Confederate armies. To insure the hundreds of manufactured articles needed for civilian and army use, North Carolina and the South had to depend upon two things: the establishment of factories that could begin rapid production of essential articles and the importation of supplies from other countries.

The Federal Arsenal at Fayetteville had yielded 37,000 guns, and the state bought more from private citizens. It established several gun and ammunition factories, some of which it later turned over to the Confederacy, and the state bought products made by owners of ironworks already in operation. Increased production was encouraged in all the existing mills, and stores of meal and flour were bought from the owners of grist and flour mills. The state also levied its first tax on the manufacturing of spirituous drinks in an attempt to funnel more grain into food channels. It also encouraged raising more hogs and cattle for food for armies and civilians. All of these efforts, however, could furnish only a small amount of what was needed. In the end winning the war would depend upon getting manufactured goods from other countries.

Whatever hopes Southern leaders might have had of recognition by Great Britain faded when Parliament passed the Neutrality Act in May, 1861. English ship owners and manufacturers were willing to sell their products to private buyers, however, or to states in the new Confederacy. The major import problem consisted in getting the goods and ships into Southern ports. As one of the first war measures Congress declared a blockade of all Southern ports, and thereby set the pattern for one of its war objectives—cutting off the South from all sources of manufactured goods. Until this plan became effective, Southern ships managed with comparative ease to reach their destinations. But as the months went by, Wilmington became the only Atlantic port city still held by the South. It was thus the only port of entry for the sturdy little blockade-runners that were zig-zagging through the Federal defenses and worming their way around the dangerous shoals to discharge their precious loads. By the second year of the war the shortage of goods was beginning to be felt throughout North Carolina and the South.

To supply the armies and, as much as possible, the civilian population with needed goods, civilian owners of vessels were daring the hazards of blockade-running to bring in machinery for the factories, hand cards, shoes and leather, cloth, arms, coffee, hospital supplies, food stuffs, and items of merchandise. On the advice of Adjutant General James G. Martin, Governor Vance purchased through an English agent a blockade runner for North Carolina. Captain Thomas M. Crossan christened it the Ad-Vance. The ship was captured by Union forces in September, 1864, but it had completed eleven trips. The state also purchased interests in other blockade-runners, and the civilians sold their cargoes at an enormous profit after turning over to the Confederacy the share required of all runners. This profiteering was allowed because of the great demand for the goods and because of the odds against the success of each venture. At least half of the ships participating in this dangerous business were captured or destroyed by the Union forces.[28]

Governor Vance and his officials hoped to allocate the civilian portion of these imports equitably, but transportation was greatly hampered and by 1864 was completely disrupted in some sections of the state. Western North Carolina, having to depend upon cross-state transportation for its share, received only an uncertain supply. According to needs, definite amounts were allotted to the counties and stored there to be supplemented by local agencies and used for the relief of the families of soldiers. Wagons of salt from the Virginia salt mines and those from Wilmington were also sent to the western counties for distribution, but those amounts were often meager. Some counties, like Buncombe, arranged for one of their own citizens to go east for salt at the expense of the county, and at times individual citizens took the long trip east in order to supply the neighborhood merchants. Even so, before the end of the war some farmers in desperation were digging up the earthen floors of their smokehouses to extract the salt deposited there over a long period of usage.[29]

North Carolina's military and civilian leaders were responsible for supplying men, animals, and food to the armies of the Confederacy, in addition to raising, equipping, and feeding its own state troops. Much dissatisfaction with the Confederacy thus early arose. Dissension also flared within North Carolina's state Democratic Party, which was now the state's only political party. Gradually two factions took shape, the Confederate wing and the Conservative wing. The Conservative group became strong enough to defeat the Confederacy-inspired movement to eliminate the 1862 election and thus to retain as governor Henry C. Clark, a Jefferson Davis sympathizer. As a result, on the ticket offered the voters at the election were the names of William J. Johnston as the Confederate candidate and Zebulon B. Vance as the Conservative candidate for the governorship. Neither man campaigned, but the general opposition to the Confederacy's war policies and its recent war measures was reflected in the election of Vance, who carried sixty-eight of the state's eighty counties.[30] Western North Carolina now had a leader in the highest office in the state.

When the six months' term of the first mountain volunteers was over and the year's enlistment period for those volunteering under the May call terminated, many of the men from Western North Carolina, as from other sections of the state, reenlisted. Others had had their fill of battles and, after the first brave enthusiasm, returned home. This failure to reenlist and the decreasing number of men volunteering became fairly general throughout the South; therefore, the Confederate Government felt it necessary in 1862 to pass a Conscription Law under which men between the ages of eighteen and thirty-five were subject to draft into the Confederate army.[31]

That law was especially offensive to the mountain men. They resented the stigma attached to being drafted; moreover, to insure a continuing supply of foodstuffs, the law provided that overseers of twenty or more slaves on plantations would be exempt from the draft. To the mountain men this was evidence that, regardless of the speeches they heard, the war was based upon slavery and the protection of plantation owners. This law was one of several factors in the breakdown of morale in the mountains. Governor Vance also objected to the Conscription Law, although he had considered conscription necessary when the law was first passed. Its administration, he found, resulted in forcing men into the armies of the Confederacy at the expense of the pledged quotas of state troops. Conscription also resulted in unpleasant incidents between state recruiting officers and out-of-state officials sent in to man the Confederate draft offices.

By the end of the second year of the war the mountain section was keenly feeling the lack of essential imports. Farm and household tools were now needing replacement, and no new ones were available. Nor could iron be procured for fashioning tools at the farm forges, since the forges in the area were under orders to send all their products to the state or to the Confederacy for war equipment. "Store cloth" was no longer on the shelves of the village stores, and the supply of thread and yarns had long been depleted. Whatever new clothes the members of the family got now were of the old pioneer material, linsey-woolsey, made in the homes. The state was asking for any products of home looms that could be spared, but in home after home the task of making cloth was becoming increasingly complicated as new hand cards, used in making thread and yarn, were needed to replace the ones rapidly wearing out. Coffee, although it had been carefully hoarded that first year, now disappeared altogether, as did sugar, prepared medicines, and the all important salt that preserved the meats.[32]

The women, with their vein of pioneer iron, were raising more products than their farms had ever yielded. The pattern of life in the hills was made even more grim as the men began to return too crippled or ill for further soldiering and too incapacitated to take up work on the farms. Even worse, word reached village homes and mountain cabins of sons, husbands, or brothers who had fallen on far-away battlefields or who were suffering in war hospitals. Some, too, had been captured and were enduring the horrors of war prisons. Mountain women must have now and then wondered at that first outbreak of patriotic enthusiasm. Also in many sections there was a growing animosity between the Union sypathizers and those faithful to the Confederacy, developing into a distrust of former friends and neighbors.

Because of the need of more protection for their citizens than the western counties had, William Holland Thomas in 1862 recruited what became known as the Thomas Legion. It was made up of men from Haywood, Jackson, Macon, and Cherokee Counties, with a few other counties being represented. Of its seventeen companies, two were made up of Cherokees who probably had been influenced by a visit to their region by Colonel Gideon Morgan, an Indian who had commanded the Cherokees at Horse Shoe Bend. The Legion was assigned to patrol and scout duties, which took on great significance as guerrilla warfare swept into Western North Carolina. It may be that Colonel Thomas' Legion did some mining at Alum Cave, actually a bluff overlooking a river valley. This place had long been known to the native Americans for its medicinal treasures. If the mining took place, the medicinal treasures were sent to Confederate hospitals, along with the herbs and medicinal roots collected and sent from Asheville and Wilkesboro.[33]

In addition to its assigned duties, the outstanding achievement of the Thomas Legion was the construction of the Indian Gap road. No road had ever been constructed across the main ridge of the Smokies, and to those entering the region early, a road over the forbidding heights seemed a permanent impossibility. Now a road allowing direct access between Western North Crolina and Tennessee was needed as a supply line and as a means of defense for the mountain area. The road began at Quallatown or near it and followed the Oconaluftee River. From there it wound up the steep inclines of the high range to Indian Gap and then down the Tennessee side to near Sevierville. Today sections of it can still be discerned along the Oconaluftee River at the Pioneer Farmstead Museum north of the village of Cherokee. Travelers to Clingman's Dome cross it at Indian Gap. Travel over this road was never a pleasure, and from a modern car owner's viewpoint it was impassable. Rugged and narrow and crude as it was, however, it was used during the remainder of the war. In January, 1864, Brigadier General Robert Brank Vance took his soldiers and equipment over it. In many respects this road, a product of the Thomas Legion's efforts, remains one of the engineering achievements in Western North Carolina.[34]

CHAPTER TWENTY

War Comes to the Hills

By the middle of 1863 affairs in Western North Carolina were getting desperate. In addition to the extreme scarcity of needed goods, there was no money to buy what trickled in.[1] Taxes were steadily rising, and they were many, reaching into every avenue of life. Some of the counties had earlier levied extra taxes to enable them to clothe and equip their own troops. State taxes had been drastically raised, and it had been necessary to levy new ones. Then, too, the Confederacy ever needed new sources of income in order to meet its needs; thus it levied taxes on occupations, on necessities such as flour, corn, oats, and drygoods, on salaries over one thousand dollars a year, and it placed an eight percent tax on all agricultural products on hand July 1, 1863.

The Confederate tax that most drastically affected the mountain people, however, was the tax in kind. It required that ten per cent of all farm products above a specified exemption for home use must be delivered by the producer to the nearest railroad for shipment to Confederate warehouses. This tax tended to reduce surplus raising of food, and it meant transporting the grain and the vegetables produced on farms in the hills to the railroad at Greenville, South Carolina, or to the station east of Morganton. Such journeys would be difficult at best and sometimes almost impossible as women took over practically all the work on the mountain farms.[2] That problem ceased to exist by 1864, for by that time raiding troops that lived off the land and bands of outliers from the mountain recesses were taking not only the surplus but much of the food raised for families.

From the first each county had had its militia, which was charged with local defense. In 1863 these units, which had been under county control, were disbanded, and Home Guard units were organized as a part of the state's military program. All men between the ages of eighteen and fifty years not already enlisted in the State Militia or the Confederate armies automatically became members of the Home Guards, and training centers were set up in the counties. John W. McElroy was made Brigadier General in charge of the western units and made his headquarters at Burnsville.[3]

In addition to guarding the counties against enemies, both those from the outside and those on the inside, the Guards were charged with the duty of rounding up deserters and renegades. The Home Guards were an improvement over the county militia units, but by the end of 1863 they were made up almost entirely of young boys and old men. In the counties bordering Tennessee they were unable to cope with the spreading lawlessness. Then, too, members in these Guards constantly decreased in numbers. Lieutenant Colonel William W. Stringfield, in charge of defending the most westerly counties, by 1865 had only some three hundred Home Guards for covering the area from Asheville to Murphy. This made it necessary to keep several regiments of State Militia in Western North Carolina to insure order, to protect property and citizens, and to render assistance to the Home Guards.

Except for two small skirmishes in 1865—one at Craggy near Asheville and the other near Waynesville—Western North Carolina saw no battles during the years of the war. Instead, war in the hills took the form of raids, and as bitterness and distrust among the citizens deepened, personal attacks by individuals or small bands became frequent. There was also the problem of deserters and "outliers." Deserters from both the State and Confederate forces steadily and stealthily returned to the mountains. Some of them, satiated with the scenes of war, came back to work on their farms. Others were unwilling to return to their homes or having returned, found themselves unwelcome in their communities. They became "outliers." As the war went on, bringing each month greater privations and suffering to the families of soldiers, men, with no criminal intent, sometimes left the ranks in response to appeals from members of their families.

Men from Western North Carolina served in every area of war activities and took part in most of the battles. North Carolina topped all of the Southern states in its numbers of deserters, but some eight thousand of these later returned to the armies. Since North Carolina had furnished more soldiers than any other Southern state, the ratio of desertion was about that of both the Confederacy and the Union. During the entire conflict about 23,000 soldiers and 423 officers from North Carolina deserted the army.[4]

Madison County, with its many Union sympathizers, was reported in 1862 to have some 160 deserters. Many of them lived at their homes although some became outliers, and all, in case of need, could get into the hills. The Shelton Laurel section of the county had been from the first almost solidly for the Union. In January, 1863, a group of perhaps fifty armed men from there went into Marshall where they broke into stores, taking salt and whatever else they desired. They claimed that because they were Unionists, they were denied salt and other commodities being sent into the county. After the looting, they set a few fires and ransacked the home of Lieutenant Colonel Lawrence M. Allen, whose Legion made raids against Unionists in Tennessee.

Brigadier General William G. Davis, whose headquarters were at Warm Springs, sent Lieutenant Colonel James A. Keith and his command in pursuit of the Shelton Laurel men with orders to arrest all known to be of "bad character," whether involved in the looting party or not. He was to have the aid of the Thomas Legion, which was already in the county engaged in scouting duties along the North Carolina-Tennessee border. Keith's command rounded up thirteen of the renegades in the Shelton Laurel area. Governor Vance was then notified by Brigadier General Davis that the mission had been successfully carried out. The Governor's reply was to have those captured turned over for trial. Instead, all thirteen were shot and buried in a common grave.

Upon hearing this, Governor Vance asked Augustus S. Merrimon, State Attorney for this Judicial District, to investigate the affair. Merrimon gave Vance a preliminary and then a detailed report in which the names and ages of those shot were listed. Two were mere boys—thirteen-year David Shelton and fourteen-year-old Aronnota Shelton. Another victim, James Shelton, was more than fifty years old and therefore beyond the age for conscription. The handling of this affair shocked Governor Vance as it did both Union and Confederate sympathizers throughout Western North Carolina. In a letter to James A. Seddon, Secretary of War, Vance enclosed the Merrimon reports. He closed the letter with these words, "I desire you to have proceedings instituted at once against this officer, who, if the half be true, is a disgrace to the service and to North Carolina." As a result, Lieutenant Keith was removed from command but was never tried.[5]

Another incident of looting (but without the loss of human lives) took place in Burnsville on April 10, 1864. There some seventy-five Union sympathizers broke into the ammunition magazine. The group, said to have been led by Montravail Ray, took what ammunition and guns they wanted and destroyed the remaining weapons. The previous day a group of angry women, wives of Union sympathizers, charging that the state had food for the families of Confederate families but not for their families, broke into a storehouse and carried off bushels of government wheat and other food items. Brigadier General John W. McElroy, who had moved his headquarters to Mars Hill College, wrote of the affair to Governor Vance. With only a hundred men under his command, all of whom were needed to protect against the raids of Colonel George W. Kirk and his volunteers, and with the Home Guards few in number, it was impossible, he said, for him to prevent such incidents. Besides, men who were arrested immediately applied for a writ of habeas corpus and so could not be brought to trial. He also reported that swarms of men, fearing conscription, had become Tories and that people were leaving the county.[6]

In June, 1862, with the sanction of his government, President Davis suspended the writ of habeas corpus under certain conditions. As a result, some forty persons in North Carolina were arrested and imprisoned at Salisbury without trial. On charges of disloyalty to the Confederacy, several men in Cherokee County were arrested by armed soldiers and taken to Georgia where they were forced to join the army. Of these, two were past the draft age. Perhaps no act of the Confederate Government so aroused Governor Vance as did the suspension of the writ of habeas corpus, for it involved the right of a fair trial by jury for the citizens of North Carolina.

Vance wrote letters of protest to Secretary Seddon and to President Davis. When he received only negative responses, he insisted that the North Carolina General Assembly nullify the

Confederacy's decree by passing a law making it mandatory for North Carolina judges to issue the writs. After learning of the arrests in Cherokee County, he ordered the State Militia to resist by any means necessary the arrest of any persons discharged by the courts of the State. But there continued to be instances of misuse of the state law guaranteeing the protection of citizens against unwarranted arrests. By invoking it, citizens seized in raids could, and did, escape arrest to repeat their offenses.[7]

Governor Vance also objected to the seizure of private property permitted by the Confederacy under certain conditions, and he condemned the right given the Confederate troops of impressing food and horses in the areas of their operations at set prices, which were always lower than the current market value. Another act of the Confederacy that brought sharp words from Governor Vance was the pasturing of broken-down cavalry horses in counties where the civilians were held responsible for their food and care. This, he pointed out, worked an added hardship upon the women and children in a region where food was exceedingly scarce. Also, in these western counties the unsettled conditions were rapidly approaching a state of lawlessness, a condition which would be made worse by the act. The Governor declared, therefore, in a letter to Secretary Seddon on February 25, 1863, that unless this burden was taken from citizens of these counties, he would be compelled to call out the State Militia and drive the animals from the state. When the Confederacy had done nothing about the horses a month later, Governor Vance wrote a second letter of protest in terms that could not be misunderstood.[8]

By mid-summer of that year Western North Carolina, because of existing conditions there, was organized into a separate military district. Brigadier General Robert Brank Vance was placed in command of the area. In his address to the General Assembly at its 1864-65 session, Governor Vance told the lawmakers, "The western border is, however, subject to constant raids and the situation of the inhabitants is distressing in the extreme. Bands of lawless men, many of them our own citizens, acting or pretending to act under commission from the enemy, swarm into the mountain frontier, murdering, burning and destroying. Totally regardless of the laws of civilized warfare, they have inaugurated a system of cruelty at which humanity shudders."[9]

During the last years of the war deserters from both the Union

N. C. DEPARTMENT OF ARCHIVES AND HISTORY

The Carson House: This house, built about 1810, had briefly served as McDowell County's first court house. It was a stagecoach stop, and during the Civil War a small private school for girls was conducted in it. Emma Rankin, a teacher, has left a vivid account of the destruction caused by a unit of Stoneman's raiders searching for Colonel Carson.

and the Confederate forces and draft evaders continued to come to the hills. They were joined by roving outlaws. All lived off the land, and from their mountain hideouts they swooped down on valley farms, taking horses and food and frightening the woman and children. At times several banded together for these forays, but occasionally the raids were made by individuals. There were those, too, working alone or in small groups, who seized the opportunity of settling old grudges or striking at those considered personal enemies.

Transylvania County was the victim of such groups. This county had been formed just before the outbreak of the war and had only a skeleton government. It was wholly unprepared, therefore, to cope with these bands of deserters and renegades that used its mountains and those of Henderson County for their rendezvous. Some appeared at the farms in uniforms, either blue or gray as they had been able to get them, and occasionally they posed as members of the Home Guards.[10] In addition to stealing horses and cattle and stored grains, they sometimes murdered an official or officer. Among their victims were Robert Thomas, Henderson County's first sheriff, General Baylus E. Edney, and Huett Allen. William Deaver, answering a knock on the door of the Deaver home, was shot by a band seeking his son, Captain James Deaver, conscription officer in the area.[11]

The fine mountain residences of the South Carolinians likewise became their targets. Members of the South Carolina "summer people," many of whom were living in Western North Carolina the entire year to escape the dangers threatening Charleston and the Southern ports, buried their jewels, silver, and money. Occasionally a group of raiders would force entrance at one of the estates and loot the house, destroying the furnishings and taking whatever of value they found. On one such raid Andrew Johnston of Flat Rock, owner of the Beaumont Estate, was killed. In Polk County Dr. Columbus Mills was badly beaten, and in Macon County William West, a mill owner, was attacked by a band of roving outlaws and left for dead. Fortunately, his life was saved by members of his family.[12]

Distressing as conditions were in the counties just mentioned, they were worse in the northern border counties. Madison, Yancey, Mitchell, Watauga, Ashe, and Alleghany Counties were subjected to almost constant raids, while their neighboring counties in Tennessee were subjected to frequent raids by bands of Confederate units. As early as December, 1862, some officials in Yancey County considered it unwise to call out any more men for the State Militia or for Confederate armies. They felt that all those at home now would be needed to maintain order in the county in view of the growing intensity of emotions and the rapid deterioration of the people's morale, coupled with the fact that deserters were entering the county in increasing numbers. Alleghany County was forced to ask Surry County for aid in handling its local problems.[13]

Governor Vance was well aware of the tense situation in the area he had known since boyhood and acknowledged in a letter to Secretary Seddon that, "in Yancey, Mitchell, and Watauga the tories and deserters are in strong force." Yet he clung to the hope that tolerance and understanding might be used in dealing with the rising disturbances.[14]

All counties suffered from sporadic raids, but the raids most feared were the invasions of Colonel George W. Kirk's Third North Carolina and Tennessee Federal Volunteers. One of the policies of the Union was to take the war directly to the people and thus destroy their morale and arouse among them a feeling of futility for carrying on further resistance to the Union. With headquarters in Greeneville, Tennessee, Kirk's Volunteers were assigned to guerrilla warfare in Western North Carolina. Colonel Kirk was bitterly condemned by the Confederate forces and by Confederate sympathizers in the regions he entered. By them he was looked upon as an outlaw, and his Volunteers were considered ruffians and brigands. But he was considered by his superiors in the Union forces as an able military leader carrying out a successful, guerrilla operation.[15]

The chief targets of Kirk's men were public offices and records and buildings connected with military operations and military supplies. They frequently took horses and food supplies from private citizens, however, and in the villages and surrounding countrysides they engaged in some looting. In August, 1863, about 120 of the Volunteers crossed the mountains into Cherokee County. At Murphy they set fire to the courthouse, destroying the county records. Outside the village they took horses and mules and killed a few work oxen.[16]

In early March, 1865, Haywood County, which had been comparatively free of border raids, girded itself for defense as scouts reported the approach of the Kirk Volunteers, estimated to be six hundred strong. The hastily gathered local forces, few in number, were unsuccessful in preventing the invaders from crossing the Smokies and entering Waynesville, which could offer little resistance. There Kirk's men liberated the county prisoners and burned the jail. After setting fire to the home of Colonel Robert Love, Revolutionary patriot and founder of the village, they left the town. A small force led by Lieutenant Robert Conley of Cherokee County, a member of the Thomas Legion, forced the Volunteers across the Balsam Range, but they returned the following day by way of Soco Gap. The Thomas Legion succeeded in preventing depredations in the territory of the native Americans and the Legion, augmented by three hundred Home Guards directed by Lieutenant Colonel William W. Stringfield, turned the Kirk Force back at Soco Gap as they attempted to return on March 6.[17]

In the spring of 1864 a contingent of Kirk's Volunteers went through Watauga and Alleghany Counties, taking horses and arousing the hatred of the citizens there. In July of that year, Kirk himself appeared at the head of some 120 Volunteers, a few of them Indian deserters from the Thomas Legion. Accompanying them as scout was David Ellis, a Unionist who had been active in the underground railroad in the region. After burning the home of a Confederate officer, the Volunteers crossed the Blue Ridge and went on to Camp Vance, six miles from Morganton. The hundred or more Junior Reserves stationed at the Camp were no defense against Kirk's men and surrendered. The Volunteers then destroyed a locomotive, some cars, and a few commissary buildings. They captured 1200 small arms, some ammunition, and took or destroyed about 3,000 bushels of grain. The Volunteers failed, however, in their main objective of destroying the railroad bridge across the Yadkin River. On their way back to Tennessee they took the Reserves as prisoners and took horses and mules to carry the food and goods taken from homes.

The returning Volunteers were pursued the next day by the Burke County Home Guards and a group of citizens. At the overnight campsite of the invaders a brief battle took place during which Kirk suffered the only wound of his military career. In that same skirmish North Carolina lost one of its outstanding political leaders when William Waightstill Avery, at that time a member of the Guards, was mortally wounded.[18]

While most of the guerrilla raids conducted by Confederate units took place in Tennessee, there were others directed against Union sympathizers in the mountain counties. One of the most effective of these took place in 1864 when Colonel John C. Vaughn's Confederate Cavalry entered the border counties. This unit, ignoring the North Carolina law against seizure of property, took what they wanted and destroyed more. They came, as one staunch Confederate sadly admitted, "seeking whom they might devour." In this unfortunate region where it was from the first inevitable that suspicions should deepen into hatreds, these raids by both sides in the conflict added fuel to the lightly slumbering fire, and the citizens themselves came to open battle. Those sympathizing with the Union met with those on the Southern side near the present Banner Elk in a skirmish that was later called Beech Mountain Battle, an affray in which blood was shed on both sides.[19]

In the following year Captain James Champion of Indiana and a small force entered Western North Carolina, rounding up deserters from the Union army, Northern sympathizers, and men who could act as scouts. Some local men joined the force at Banner Elk and, with James Isaacs as guide, the unit reached

352 / Chapter Twenty

FROM BRADY'S *HISTORY OF THE CIVIL WAR*, N. C. DEPARTMENT OF ARCHIVES AND HISTORY

General George Stoneman: General Stoneman, shown here seated with his staff, conducted a series of raids during the final months of the Civil War. The counties just east of the Blue Ridge suffered much during those raids.

Camp Mast, about four miles from Valle Crucis, during the night of February 5. The men were stationed in groups around the Camp. Major Harvey Bingham, who was in charge of the Camp, was absent on a mission attempting to get help needed due to the unsettled conditions existing in the county. At daybreak Captain Champion gave the men in the camp ten minutes to surrender. At the end of that time some seventy-five Home Guards appeared and were taken prisoners. These men represented about half of the local Home Guard unit since the men weekly alternated their camp service. The surrendering group was made up largely of boys and disabled Confederate soldiers.[20]

On April 3, 1865, the citizens of Asheville, so far spared the devastation of guerrilla warfare, learned that some nine hundred infantrymen of the Hundred and First Ohio Infantry under the command of Colonel Isaac M. Kirby were approaching the town from Tennessee by way of the old Buncombe Turnpike. Asheville had little protection against this number of men, and there were those who counseled surrendering. But to most that was unthinkable. Hastily assembling a group of volunteers, some of whom were home on furloughs, Colonel George W. Clayton led his volunteer troops northward. They met the Union army at Craggy, four miles from the town, at a place now on the campus of the University of North Carolina at Asheville. After a five-hour skirmish during which no Condederate was injured and only two Union men were reportedly wounded, Colonel Kirby's troops withdrew and returned to Tennessee.[21]

The best organized and most devastating Union raid in Western North Carolina took place in the last weeks of the war. Knoxville and eastern Tennessee had been taken by the Union armies late in 1863, and Knoxville had been made the headquarters of General Ambrose Everett Burnside. From those headquarters General George Stoneman, with a select cavalry unit of veterans, was sent into the North Carolina mountains for a rapid but destructive raid. His men traveled light, carrying only rations of bacon and coffee (which could not be obtained in the raiding area), extra sets of horse shoes and nails, and their fire arms and ammunition. They were to live off the land, but General Stoneman gave orders for no looting and no needless destruction of private property.[22]

The hand-picked cavalry reached Boone on March 28. There was only ineffectual opposition from the weak Home Guards, who lost several men in the exchange of shots. A few public buildings were burned, including the county courthouse and its records. Colonel George W. Kirk's Volunteers entered Boone and General Stoneman's troops went on across the Blue Ridge to Wilkesboro. The Volunteers did further damage to property. One contingent of the cavalry under Brigadier Alvan C. Gillem went from Boone to Lenoir where the men destroyed public buildings and a cotton mill. This unit then joined General Stoneman at Wilkesboro. From there the General swung northward into Virginia, returning to Salem, where little damage was committed, and then pressed on to Salisbury.

When Salisbury was taken, the prison, cotton mills, government storehouses, and supply depots were burned. Detachments were sent to tear up the tracks of the railroad, and fifteen miles of tracks were thus destroyed. Railroad shops and water tanks were burned, bridges and roads were damaged beyond repair, and some railroad equipment was destroyed. General Stoneman's Cavalry continued on to Statesville. Among other buildings destroyed there, was the office of the *Iredell Express*. By April 15, the Cavalry was in Lenoir, and two days later General Stoneman left for Blowing Rock and Boone, heading back into Tennessee. Before that he dispatched a part of the Cavalry under the command of Brigadier General William J. Palmer to go south into the Catawba country to Lincolnton. Palmer attempted to enforce General Stoneman's rule of no looting or useless destruction of private property. In fact, in Statesville he ordered some soldiers to return articles belonging to Mrs. Zebulon B. Vance, who was at that time living in the village. But it was not always possible to restrain his men, especially those sent on foraging expeditions.[23]

Another contingent of General Stoneman's Cavalry under Brigadier General Alvan C. Gillem was sent to Asheville. On April 18 his men entered Morganton, destroying whatever might be of use to the Confederates. From there this unit went to Marion, planning to go to Asheville by way of Swannanoa Gap, but Confederate forces west of the Blue Ridge had effectively blocked that road. The Cavalry then returned to Marion and took the longer route through Hickory Nut Gap, arriving in Asheville on April 25. This unit was followed by the arrival of Colonel Kirk's Volunteers. Here the old gun factory, and a few other buildings were burned. The guns of Porter's Battery atop the town's western hill, the slight fortifications on Beaucatcher Hill to the east, and the Confederate flag on its pole were all captured. But little looting took place, and order was maintained throughout the incidents.

Brigadier General James G. Martin with his command was in Asheville at this time. There under a truce made possible by the armistice agreement between General Joseph E. Johnston and General William T. Sherman, he furnished the Federal troops with a three-day ration allotment. The Cavalry left Asheville, preceded by Kirk's Volunteers. On the morning of the twenty-sixth, however, a unit of the Cavalry, made up of the Tenth and Eleventh Michigan Regiments, returned to Asheville. They took captive some Confederate officers and soldiers and looted some homes and burned others, including that of Brigadier General Martin and that of Dr. Robert H. Chapman, minister of the Presbyterian Church. Upon receipt of an order from Brigadier General Palmer, written at his headquarters in Hickory Nut Gap on April 28, the captured officers and men were released. Federal soldiers roamed the countryside during the next few days, however, taking animals and food stocks from the farms.

Early in May Lieutenant Colonel William C. Bartlett of the Federal forces stationed in Asheville broke the proclaimed truce and went through Buncombe County and Haywood County "requisitioning" horses. On May 6 he was surrounded on the grounds of the White Sulphur Springs near Waynesville by the Thomas Legion and Home Guards under the direction of Colonel James R. Love. In the skirmish that took place a Federal soldier was killed; thus the final shot of the Civil War in North Carolina took place in the hills of Western North Carolina. Upon receiving official word of the cessation of hostilities, Lieutenant Colonel Thomas disbanded his Legion, and Lieutenant Colonel William W. Stringfield took his troops into Tennessee to surrender them. There he was jailed for a month.[24]

Whatever means of communication Western North Carolina may still have had with the outside world had been utterly destroyed by General Stoneman's raid, and news of the surrender of General Lee at Appomattox did not reach the people of the mountains until the soldiers returned. It was even then hard for the people, who for four long years had been the victims of a war that filled their region with bitterness and suffering, to grasp the fact that the war had ended.

CHAPTER TWENTY ONE

The Rebirth of a State

War ceased, but long months and even years were to pass before peace would come to North Carolina and to sections of its mountains. In April, 1865, mountain men laid down their arms at Appomattox Courthouse and at other formal surrenderings. They took the oath of allegiance and began their slow walk back to the hills. Others, learning that the war had ended, left their camps and started for home without the ceremony of taking the pledge of loyalty to the Union. Men long in Federal prisons were released and with aid or through their own efforts made their way back to Western North Carolina. Over all the mountain passes they came, weary of war and eager for the sight of the hills of home. Reaching their valley farms and their cove cabins, they found their waiting families somber and gaunt, the hardships of the past years written in their faces and stooped shoulders. The eyes of their children filled with horror at the sight of their fathers' uniforms.

Sections of Western North Carolina lay prostrate. Many of the fields were untilled, and there was little if any grain for the spring planting. Tools were worn out or had been destroyed by the marauding bands that had driven off the horses and some of the cattle and hogs. In a few cases anything of value that the homes possessed had passed into the hands of raiders. Signs of the destruction of orchards and occasional charred buildings gaped like wounds on the spring landscape.[1]

On their own tables the men found the kind of food that had sustained them as soldiers during the last years of the war—bread made of coarse, handground corn, cowpeas, perhaps sweet potatoes, and with luck, a bit of sorghum or honey. To some of those living in the remote coves this was the food they had known since childhood. Now even this humble fare was limited in quantity. Had a wider variety of foodstuffs been available, there was no money with which to pay the high prices brought on by the increasing inflation. That inflation resulted from the steady depreciation of state bonds and the even more rapid depreciation of Confederate bonds and money. With the fall of the Confederacy, its bonds were repudiated, and the State war debt was repudiated in October, 1865.[2]

By early 1865 the cost of bacon had soared to $7.50 a pound, and the price of wheat flour had reached $500 a barrel. The pay of a Confederate soldier had been insufficient for even one person; thus the families of soldiers had been, from the beginning of the war, dependent upon what they could raise. At first in the mountains that amount had been enough to supply the family with food, but as the men steadily left for the war fronts and as the armies of both the North and the South sent foraging units through the countrysides, want became widespread. Money, never plentiful in the western counties, had practically disappeared by the time the soldiers returned. Barter, which in the newer or remote sections of the counties had never been completely abandoned, was again the trading system in the hills.[3]

In the few western counties in which slavery had been a part of the economic pattern of life, the owners of large farms had suffered, in addition to their other misfortunes, a loss of thousands of dollars as their slaves were freed. These men faced the problem of arranging for laborers to plant and later to harvest the year's crops, but there was far more work to be done than could be accomplished by the reduced number of men available. North Carolina furnished more soldiers than any other Southern state and suffered proportionately more casualties than any other state. A considerable number of these men had come from Western North Carolina. In addition to those slain, many men returned home hopelessly crippled or incapacitated by lingering illnesses.[4]

Also adding to the labor pinch were some Negroes who sought out their new freedom and left the fields and their old quarters.[5] To alleviate the labor shortage, Major William Wallis McDowell of Asheville wrote to his friend, Gilbert B. Tennent in London, to investigate the possibility of arranging for Scottish immigrants to Western North Carolina. The reply he received

Carolina. The reply he received was discouraging since workmen coming to America would have to come under the auspices of the Emigration Society of Scotland, which was under government patronage. They would thus command higher wages than the mountain farmers were able to pay. The task of raising food crops and farm products that might be marketable became each man's private problem. Both men and women set about solving it in light of what they had and could do. In many sections of the mountains life for the people was again at subsistence level.[6]

Sections of Western North Carolina shared in the unsettled conditions that prevailed in the state during the Reconstruction years. The bitterness that had disrupted communities and unleashed the horrors of guerrilla warfare in the border counties continued to embroil mountain men in long-drawn-out lawsuits and murder cases. These consumed the energies of those involved and retarded the restoration of their sections to normal activities. There were instances of men returning from the Confederate army to find themselves objects of persecution in their own neighborhoods. There were even more cases of men released from the Union armies who dared not return to their homes.

Men known to have been in the foraging units of either army or in raiding groups were almost certain to be the victims of mistreatment. Many were indicted on these charges. In Madison County, for example, trials of this type dragged through the courts, and many cases involved men who had been in General Stoneman's forces or in Colonel George W. Kirk's Volunteer Infantry. Some were of a more serious nature. One such concerned the murder of Ransom P. Merrill, sheriff of Madison County, on May 13, 1860, when the citizens had gathered in Marshall to vote on the secession question. Barrels of liquor had been brought into the town, and at least a part of it had been consumed by the time of the shooting. Merrill, a shouting secessionist, started a near riot during which a bullet he fired wounded Elisha J. Tweed. Tweed's father then shot the sheriff. Both the Tweeds later entered the Union army and the father was killed in a skirmish in Kentucky. When Elisha Tweed returned in 1865, he was charged with creating a riot and with murder while a group of others were charged with being accomplices. The trial was still in progress in 1867, and lawyers were getting affidavits from men involved in the broil.[7]

Madison County was not alone in these unfortunate cases.

Trials on similar charges occurred in the courts of many of the western counties. All of them kept alive the spirit of disunity and partisan emotions. Added to the unhappy atmosphere thus created was the fact that the mountains in these counties offered hiding places for men afraid to go home, for bitter and disillusioned men planning vengeance on society, for refugees from justice, and for many coming for these or other reasons from other states. These men, riding singly or in bands, rendered property and crops unsafe. As the months passed, some of them organized into gangs.

One renegade group—the Adair gang—roamed Rutherford County, stealing horses and mules and burning well-filled barns. They went fully armed and on at least one occasion were present at voting places, bent on preventing the citizens from casting their ballots. They were open in their activities and boastful of their depredations. The Adair gangsters were known to have killed a Negro and his family. They aligned themselves with whatever Reconstruction organization served their purposes, and they perpetrated crimes in the names of organizations to which they did not belong.[8]

In Wilkes County such gangs so menaced the region that in desperation citizens formed a posse and captured "Fort Hamby," the mountain hideout of the desperadoes. This counter attack cost the lives of several citizens. Those members of the gang that were taken prisoners were brought to trial, and the leaders were executed.[9] Conditions in nearby Ashe County reached such a stage of lawlessness that the citizens appealed for help to the federal military unit stationed at Salisbury.[10] Many communities throughout the mountain counties organized Home Guards for protection of life and property during the months following the end of the war.

Confusion and unrest were general throughout North Carolina. Govenor Vance was for more than a month a prisoner in Washington. Both the southern states and the Confederate government had been repudiated, resulting in a period of uncertainty. It was a new situation in American history, and it presented many problems and challenges to the national government. Mistakes in judgment and execution were almost inevitable. North Carolina leaders could understand but they clung to the repeated assertion that the federal government had undertaken the war to preserve the Union. They held to the hope, therefore, that the way would be opened with all possible speed for the readmission of their state into the Union in order that it might evolve from its shattered economy a new and stable way of life.

On April 29, 1865, General John Schofield, federal officer in charge, issued a proclamation declaring hostilities over and announcing the emancipation of all slaves within the state. He then divided the state into three districts, placing General Jacob D. Cox in charge of the western area. On May 29, 1865, President Andrew Johnson issued an Amnesty Proclamation in which he pardoned all who would swear allegiance to the United States and its Constitution. In this he was following the program earlier worked out by President Lincoln. Whereas Lincoln had excluded six classes from the pardon, this Proclamation excluded fourteen classes of Southerners. Among those excluded were men in high civil and military offices in the Confederacy, all who had resigned federal service to join the Confederacy, and persons whose assets totaled more than $20,000. These restrictions affected leaders in all southern states; yet pardons might be granted to persons requesting them through petitions. The rather liberal administration of petition granting resulted in about 13,500 Southern men receiving pardons.

On the same day that President Johnson issued the Amnesty Proclamation, he issued an order appointing William W. Holden as Provisional Governor of North Carolina. Holden was charged with calling a constitutional convention which would define the qualifications for future office holders and voters and which would abolish slavery in the state. He was also to set up the machinery for a November election for members of the General Assembly.[11]

The people of North Carolina were not pleased with the amnesty terms, and many leaders were opposed to the choice of William W. Holden as Provisional Governor. Holden's political career had been a long one, and as owner and editor of the *North Carolina Standard,* he had exerted much political influence throughout the state. Like many other leaders, he discarded the Whig Party in 1843 and joined the Democratic Party. He was an able and energetic writer, and his paper had endorsed free suffrage and state aid for internal improvements, helping to incorporate into the Democratic Party the policies once advocated by the Whigs. This endorsement won him the support of voters in Western North Carolina, who felt the need of state aid for highways and railroads in their mountain counties. [12] At the

Democratic Convention of 1858 most of the delegates from the West had voted to nominate him as their Party's candidate for governor, but the eastern bloc had stopped that movement. John W. Ellis headed the Democratic ticket in that election year and won.

As slavery became a national issue, Holden had urged the annexation of Texas and the protection of slave property by the national government. He had attacked abolition and free soil sentiments to the extent of getting a Free Soil University professor dismissed from the faculty for expressing a desire to see John C. Fremont, the Republican candidate, elected as president of the United States. Largely because of the editorial in the *North Carolina Standard,* the man was hounded out of the state.[13] In 1860 Holden voted against secession. During the first year of the war his paper crystalized the Conservative attitude developing within the Democratic Party, and he had thrown the weight of his influence and the force of his editorials into getting Colonel Zebulon Baird Vance elected as Governor in 1862.

As the war went on, Holden came to oppose the Conservative wing of the Democratic Party. After the disastrous loss of Vicksburg and the defeat at Gettysburg, he realized that the cause of the Confederacy was lost. He was then accused of sympathizing with, if not instigating, the rash of peace meetings held throughout the state.[14] His attitude precipitated a break with Governor Vance, and in the bitter election in 1864 he opposed Vance as a candidate for the governorship. In the election Holden received over 14,000 votes but carried only Johnston and Randolph Counties. Able as he was, the various political shifts he made lost Holden the confidence of various blocs of voters. For these reasons many opposed his appointment as Provisional Governor of North Carolina, a position he was to hold until December 12, 1865.

As mentioned earlier, the new Provisional Governor Holden called for an election to be held on September 21, for the purpose of electing delegates to a Convention to be held in Raleigh. At the meeting of the Convention the Act of Secession was repealed, and slavery was declared abolished in the state. Additionally, the machinery was set up for an election in November for governor and for representatives to the General Assembly. The Convention members also repudiated the state war debt, arousing opposition both in the Convention and throughout the state, for it meant the loss of most of the state's assets and of its credit, as well as the loss of thousands of dollars to private holders of state bonds. In the November election Holden was defeated in his race for the governorship, and Jonathan Worth became Governor of North Carolina. Union men were elected as the state's representatives to Congress, and the Thirteenth Amendment was ratified.[15]

When Congress met in December, 1865, the members sent to it by the Southern states were refused their seats on the grounds that not the President but Congress alone had the authority to determine a state's readmission to the Union. In March, 1867, Congress enacted the Reconstruction Act, making it a law over President Johnson's veto. Under its terms, whatever had been done under President Johnson's plan was set aside, and the entire South was put under a military government. North and South Carolina were designated as the Second Military District and were put under the command of General David E. Sickles, who was later replaced by General Edward R.S. Canby. Each state was required to draw up a new constitution to be ratified by the voters and then submitted to Congress for approval. Negroes were not to be denied the right to vote and the General Assembly to be elected under the new Constitution would have to ratify the Fourteenth Amendment before the state would be readmitted to the Union. Jonathan Worth was allowed to continue as Governor of North Carolina, but his authority was limited since the military regime in each district was given rather full powers over its territory, including authorization to remove state and local officers from their positions.[16]

It was the military commander, General Edward R. S. Canby, who issued the call for an election of delegates to a state constitutional convention. Some of the state's leaders were not yet eligible to vote, and many others, thoroughly disgusted over the Reconstruction Act, did not register or if they did, failed to vote. At the prompting of Republicans who had come into the state, more than 72,000 Negroes registered for the election.[17]

A year before the convention was called, the Republican Party had been formally organized in North Carolina through the efforts of Northern men who had entered the state in connection with the various phases of the Reconstruction program. During the year the Party had attracted newly enfranchised Negroes and thousands of white Union sympathizers, together with small farmers long opposed to the plantation system. There came into it, also, some very able men, but on the whole these were not the

Party leaders. At the Constitutional Convention meeting in Raleigh from January 14 to March 17, 1868, the Republican Party had a majority of delegates.[18]

The Constitution drawn up at this Convention was, to a large extent, modeled after those of Northern states. Most of the provisions it contained were progressive and democratic and forward-looking. Many of them have stood the test of time and are today in force. In addition to abolishing slavery within the state and repudiating the state war debt, it contained a bill of rights. It forbade the suspension of the writ of habeas corpus and upheld the freedom of the press. The new Constitution abolished property and religious qualifications for voting and for holding the office of governor; furthermore, it provided for a "general and uniform system of Public Schools" to be in operation for at least four months each year. It provided for a superintendent of public instruction. And finally, this improved model provided for the election of local officers by qualified voters, and it set the voting age at twenty-one years.[19]

A month after the close of the Convention, voters went to the polls where they ratified the new Constitution. They elected state and county officers and representatives to the lower house of Congress, and William W. Holden, now Republican candidate for governor, swept into the state's highest office. The Republican Party won most of the seats in the General Assembly, carried most of the county elections, and won all but one of the representative seats in Congress.[20] The General Assembly, at its convening, elected Republican Senators to Congress and ratified the Fourteenth Amendment. Congress received the newly elected Representatives and approved the state's Constitution. After four years of war and more than three years of Reconstruction, North Carolina was again a state in the Union.

CHAPTER TWENTY TWO

Long is the Night

The federal officers sent into Western North Carolina by General John Schofield and under command of General Jacob D. Cox administered the oath of allegiance to all county and town officers appointed by the Provisional Governor. They set up a county police force charged with arresting marauders, maintaining law, and seeing that justice was carried out. As might be expected, the mountain people resented the presence of federal troops. Their resentment increased when, in 1867, under the Reconstruction Act of Congress, a more or less permanent military government was set up.

Almost immediately trouble arose as military officials began setting aside some decisions of the civil courts. Eventually a compromise was worked out. Civil authorities were to be allowed to arrest both Negroes and whites. Civil courts were to have the authority to try the accused whites, although no civil court could inflict corporal punishment. Negroes were to be tried in military courts only, and the military officials also had the authority to make arrests. The governor had the power of pardoning those sentenced by civil courts.[1]

Many, perhaps most, of the military personnel worked to maintain law and order, but some had no understanding of or sympathy with the people among whom they were stationed. A few did not rise above the character of conquerors chastening a defeated people. There were some who saw in their assignments the opportunity for financial gain and others who caused friction between the races. It is true, however, that some complaints against the military personnel were unjust.[2]

The Civil War began as a means of saving the Union; furthermore, after the Emancipation Proclamation, it had the added objective of freeing the slaves in the Southern states. Now the Southern states were in the process of attaining the requirements for readmission into the Union, and the slaves had been freed from their bondage. One of the difficult problems facing the bankrupt South was dealing with its Negro citizens, who had been suddenly released from their old pattern of life with no preparation for a new economic and social pattern. Except for a small number of educated and free Negroes, the race had generally had no opportunities to learn to read or write, and it had no funds and no land to call its own.

Because of the increasing numbers of Negroes following the Union armies, Congress in 1862 established what became known as the Freedman's Bureau. Its purpose was to be of service to the Negro refugees in the army camps. On March 3, 1865, Congress passed a new Freedman's Bureau Bill, which provided for headquarters to be established in Washington with General Oliver O. Howard as chief. Units were then set up in all the Southern states. The Bureau's work as outlined by the law that created it, was to help the Negroes establish themselves economically through work, through an opportunity for education, and through favorable relationships with both whites and fellow Negroes. It was to aid the Negroes in securing employment, in getting land, and in establishing schools. Its work in North Carolina extended over a three and a half year period, and it accomplished much that was beneficial to the newly freed race. The Freedman's Bureau also served needy white people.

The immediate problem was food. The Bureau distributed about $1,500,000 worth of food to needy Negro and white families. It gave vast amounts of clothing and supplies of medicines. In addition, as it could, it aided Negro farmers to secure land. One of this agency's fine services was the establishment of schools. It established or supervised day schools, night schools, Sunday schools, and industrial schools; moreover, it aided colleges, among them Hampton Institute and Fisk University. During the years of its activities in North Carolina it set up and operated 431 schools, which had an enrollment of more

PACK MEMORIAL LIBRARY, ASHEVILLE

Nicholas W. Woodfin: During the Civil War Nicholas W. Woodfin served as the agent for the distribution of salt from the mines in Virginia to the mountain counties of North Carolina. In 1870 he was appointed chairman of the legislative committee charged with the investigation of the railroad dealings of George W. Swepson and Milton Littlefield.

than 20,000 Negro children. It also established hospitals which, its records show, treated some forty thousand Negro patients.[3]

The manifold activities carried on by the Freedman's Bureau necessitated a large staff of workers and administrators. This need brought into the South several thousands of Northern men and several hundreds of Northern women, who became teachers in the Negro schools. Most of these men and women were sincere in their efforts and served well. Many had a missionary zeal to bring the enlightenment of the North into the dark South. But few had any concept of what the people in their assigned areas had undergone during the war years. On the other hand, the North Carolinians felt that these men and women were interfering in a problem southern in character and wholly within the province of the state. They felt, too, that these outsiders were responsible for a growing resentment against white people by the Negroes.

Teachers in the Negro schools were especially disdained. The Freedman's Bureau was never intended as a propaganda or political medium, but its influence helped to draw the recently franchised Negroes into the Republican Party. In the counties west of the Blue Ridge there was little work for the Bureau, but in the counties on the eastern slopes of the mountains, with their larger Negro population, it was active. The Bureau was abolished in 1872.[4]

Growing out of the bitterness of war and the Reconstruction were several secret organizations. During the last desperate years of the war, men sympathizing with the Union organized in Tennessee a "society" that was made attractive and binding by its secrecy. Either before the end of the conflict or soon after that, units of it appeared in North Carolina where it gained hundreds of members in the western counties. It had been given the patriotic name of Heroes of America, but because its symbol was a red string, it became known as the Red Strings. It was complete with ritual, password, and oaths obligating the members to obedience to its orders.[5]

After the war the Heroes of America became a perfect instrument through which leaders could direct the actions of members and shepherd them into the Republican Party. Its membership was made up of mountain men who had been sympathizers with the Union (perhaps soldiers in the Union army), small farmers, laborers, and some Negroes, together with a few "blockade runners," that is, men making and selling whiskey illegally. For a time Albion W. Tourgee, one of the most influential and active of the Northern men who had come into the state, edited a paper called *The Red Strings*. It was intended to be the official organ of the Heroes of America. The organization was active in all the western counties with Rutherford County having the largest membership. There its activities were directed by George W. Logan, who had been a slave owner and in 1860 had been an ardent secessionist. He had come out of the war a Unionist, however, and had been made a judge. Using the wide powers granted him in that position, he was able to dominate the organization in his territory. At its meetings guards were stationed outside the building to preserve the secrecy of its proceedings.[6]

For the Negroes there was the Union League, founded in Philadelphia in 1862 to promote loyalty to the Union. It entered the South with the conquering armies. There it began organizing

N. C. DEPARTMENT OF ARCHIVES AND HISTORY

Augustus Summerfield Merrimon: Judge Augustus S. Merrimon of Asheville "rode circuit" to the county seats of western counties. He deplored the state of the roads and the general ignorance he found everywhere. In 1870 he served as one of the three members of the House Legal Council Committee at the impeachment of Governor William H. Holden.

the Negro branches of the League. At first the mountain membership included some white men, but as the months passed, the white members gradually withdrew. The organizer of the branch would initiate those joining into the secrets of the organization, which included a ritual, a password, a catechism, and oaths. Then followed a period of instruction in which the rights and political duties of the members were dwelt upon. Governor Holden was for a time president of the state organization and was succeeded by General Milton S. Littlefield. James H. Harris, a Negro, was vice-president of the clandestine organization.

After its introduction into the state in 1865, it spread rapidly until it was estimated that most of the male Negro population were members. Both the Union League and the Freedman's Bureau were accused of forcing their members into the Republican Party, but it is more probable that the members voluntarily became Republicans because of the interest shown them by the leaders of the groups. To the "stable" citizens there was much that was pathetic about the gatherings and motley parades of the men who had but recently been workers on their plantations. There was also a lurking fear of what might happen should these members of the Union League be supplied with arms.[7]

The general state of affairs was further complicated by the federal officers sent into the region to enforce the revenue laws. From the time of early mountain settlement, farmers had constructed stills on their farms just as they had built barns and granaries. They stocked their cellars with homemade liquors, selling whatever surplus they had. Since colonial days there had been regulations governing the conditions under which intoxicants could be sold at taverns and inns; yet after the repeal of the excise tax on whiskey in President Washington's administration, no restrictions had been placed by state or nation upon the manufacturing of spirituous drinks.[8]

But Civil War made imperative the conservation of grain for food purposes. Two laws were passed by North Carolina during the early years of the conflict, prohibiting the manufacture of all alcoholic drinks by banning the use of the farm products that went into their making. A tax was also levied upon imported liquors. In 1862 the federal government had levied a twenty-five cent tax on every gallon of spirituous drinks, and that tax had been raised from time to time until by 1864 it amounted to two dollars per gallon. When the Reconstruction was set up in North Carolina, federal officers were sent into the state to enforce this revenue law. The men coming for that purpose were roundly hated by the farmers, who looked upon the tax as a war punishment and a flagrant interference into private affairs.[9]

The result of this situation was that the mountain men placed their stills in secluded spots not too easily ferreted out and "ran the blockade" in selling their surplus products. During these stormy Reconstruction days the attitude prevailed that, however extreme, all methods were fair in outwitting the revenue officers trying to thwart those making and selling their products without

THE STEPHENS PRESS, INC.

Zebulon Baird Vance—Post-War Governor: In January, 1877, Vance became Governor of North Carolina for the third time.

benefit of licenses or taxes. Despite the tacitly declared war between officers and farmers, stills were occasionally taken and men arrested for violations of the federal law. In a four-year period from 1877 to 1881, more than 4,000 illicit stills were seized in North Carolina, and more than 7,000 arrests were made. That was accomplished at a price. In fulfilling their duties, 26 officers lost their lives, and 57 others were wounded. There were further casualties on the civilian side during these raids.[10]

By 1870 the excesses of the outlaw gangs, coupled with stories alleging the destruction of property (including the burning of two churches) had produced a condition of fear and unrest in the piedmont and mountain counties just east of the Blue Ridge.[11] This unsettled situation gave rise to another secret organization, the Ku Klux Klan. This group was organized in Tennessee probably in June of 1866, and on June 5, 1867, it held an anniversary parade in

Pulaski, Tennessee. Its original purpose was stated as being the protection of women and families and defense in case of attack. The attack, it seemed to assume, would come from the Freedman's Bureau or the Union League or the Heroes of America. Under three separate but allied "Brotherhoods" the Klan entered North Carolina in 1867.[12]

The Klan was a secret organization, and its activities were directed against members of both the Union League and the Heroes of America. Its leaders saw in it a means of maintaining white supremacy; however, many of the small farmers joining it were not concerned with far-reaching or philosophical objectives. They were led to believe that they were avenging atrocities committed by the newly freed Negroes and the white people who had joined them in the Union League or the Heroes of America. Klan members, along with their leaders, objected to the Negroes being given the political right of voting and the opportunity of getting an education. They readily accepted the stories related to them by their leaders of atrocities committed by Negroes. The Klan at its secret meeings made plans for revenge and the methods of carrying them out. Then a group of members usually masked and riding at night, "warned" the victim. If the warning was not heeded, Klansmen at a second visit administered whippings and might also destroy property. In some cases this or a third visit resulted in the murder of the victim. It is estimated that the Klan in North Carolina had a membership of 40,000 and it has also been estimated that in this state the Klan was responsible for 260 attacks that included seven murders and the whipping of 141 Negroes and 72 whites.[13]

In Western North Carolina, Rutherford and Polk Counties suffered the most from Klan activities and from raiders going about the countryside in Klan disguises. Recently returned to Rutherfordton from a newspaper venture in Asheville, Randolph Shotwell was asked to take over leadership of the Klan there. He agreed to the request although he claimed never to have been a member of the organization. It may have been too late for moderation. At any rate, Shotwell was unwilling or unable to control the lawless element now working inside the lodges and those carrying out their midnight rides. Several incidents of violence aroused widespread tension.

One such "visitation" was to the home of Aaron Biggerstaff, a former Union scout, now considered a community trouble maker. His daughter saved him from an attempted hanging, and he

N. C. DEPARTMENT OF ARCHIVES AND HISTORY

Vance at Lenoir in 1876: Wherever Vance went during his many campaign trips about the state, crowds like this one at Lenoir greeted him and eagerly listened to his speeches.

claimed to recognize some of his assailants. These men were arrested under federal warrants. Aaron Biggerstaff and his daughter, on their way to court as witnesses, were again "visited" as they stopped at Grassy Branch on May 12 to spend the night. Little known as these people were, this case created a tense situation. George W. Logan, Judge of the Superior Court of the Ninth District, reported the incidents to Washington. Officials entered the scene and arrested thirty-five of the old man's neighbors.[14]

Other incidents involved people holding more prominent positions. One of these was James M. Justice, Republican Representative from Rutherford County in the General Assembly. He had been a frequent speaker at the Union League meetings. On Sunday night, June 11, two groups of masked men rode into Rutherfordton and captured Representative Justice, demanding that he stop his propaganda and that he leave town. Justice later claimed to have recognized some of his attackers, and those he named were arrested. The riders on that Sunday night also broke into the office of the *Rutherford Star* and wrecked its equipment. They arrested Robert Logan, son of Judge Logan, and J. B. Carpenter, owners of this active Republican newspaper.[15]

All of these outrages were reported to Washington, resulting in the passage of the Ku Klux Klan Act. It banned all secret societies and increased the penalties for the violations of the Fourteenth Amendment. It also established punishments for violations of the newly ratified Fifteenth Amendment and allowed suspension of the writ of habeas corpus in areas of disorder. Additional troops were sent into the state, and a detachment of soldiers was sent to Rutherfordton. There many arrests were made, and among the men arrested was Randolph Shotwell. In September he was taken from the Rutherfordton jail to Marion and then to Raleigh where he was one of the 981 North Carolinians indicted by the Federal Grand Jury on charges of participating in Ku Klux Klan activities. He was sent to a federal prison in Albany, New York, where he spent two years before being pardoned by President Grant.[16]

As early as 1868 the Reconstruction Assembly eyed with alarm the spread of the Ku Klux Klan. In October, 1869, William W. Holden, now Governor by popular vote, issued a proclamation declaring the conditions in Lenoir, Jones, Orange, and Chatham Counties bordering on insurrection. In January, 1870, the General Assembly passed the Shoffner Act enabling the Governor to declare a state of insurrection in lawless counties and to call out the militia to squelch disorders. He was also granted the privilege of hiring detectives. In light of the numerous "visitations" by the Klan that resulted in the deaths of a Negro office holder and a white senator, who was also a detective, Alamance, Chatham, Caswell, and Orange Counties were considered dangerous counties by the administration. Two of these counties, Caswell and Chatham, were declared to be in a state of insurrection. Orange County was later added to this list as the condition in these counties steadily deteriorated.[17]

In June Governor Holden asked Colonel George W. Kirk to organize state troops and to police the area. In Marshall, Burnsville, and Asheville handbills then appeared calling upon all those who had been in Kirk's Third North Carolina and Tennessee Volunteer Infantry of the Union to rally to their old Colonel and join his regiment. Recalling the havoc Kirk's raiding units had wrought in the mountains, distressed citizens of Asheville petitioned Governor Holden not to raise troops, and above all, not

E. DOUGLAS DE PEW AND BOB LINDSEY PHOTO

A Still in the Mountains: Until the Civil War no restriction had been placed on the manufacturing of spirituous drinks. Almost every farm had its still. After that war, federal officers came into the mountains to collect the liquor taxes levied by the national government. Farmers then hid their stills and protected them with whatever means necessary. Stills continue to be hidden in unlikely places as is shown in this posed picture.

to put Colonel George W. Kirk in charge of them. The petition went unheeded, and by early July Kirk had raised a force of about 600 men, ranging in age from 16 or 17 to 60 or 70 years of age.[18] Military courts were set up, and Kirk obtained from Governor

Holden a list of men to arrest, a list that had been made up by Republicans.[19] The list included men from almost every official position, every age bracket, and every social position. Many were prominent men.

Among them was Josiah Turner, editor of *The Raleigh Sentinal* in which Governor Holden had been sharply criticized. Arrests made in these counties aroused the entire state. One of the sharpest criticisms was the refusal to honor writs of habeas corpus issued for the release of those arrested. In an attempt to restore order, George W. Brooks, Federal Judge, then issued writs of habeas corpus requiring all prisoners taken during the purge to appear before him at the next session of the court at Salisbury. To Governor Holden this constituted interference by a federal officer, and he appealed to President Ulysses S. Grant. In reply the President ordered Governor Holden to honor the writs. The only course left open to the Governor then was to order Colonel Kirk to produce the prisoners and then to disband his regiment. Following that, the Governor declared the state of insurrection at an end. Technically, the "Kirk-Holden War" was finished. Under pressure of the Enforcement Act passed by Congress on May 31, 1870, and as a result of the "Kirk-Holden War," the activities of all secret organizations gradually subsided.[20]

Another reason for the lessening of Klan activity was the 1870 election, which brought new Democratic members into the General Assembly. The Democratic Party had been steadily gaining strength during and after the Reconstruction Period; moreover, Holden, both as Provisional Governor and then as Governor, had lost the support of many politically prominent leaders. The militia campaign conducted during the elections meant his political defeat. At the December session of the General Assembly the Democrats were strong enough to present a resolution of impeachment against Governor Holden. Of the eight charges placed against him, the Governor was found guilty on six, which accused him of exceeding his authority in raising a militia and of making illegal arrests. Western North Carolina was represented at the trial, which lasted from February 2 to March 25, 1871, and was presided over by Judge Augustus S. Merrimon. Joining him as counsels for the House Committee during the proceedings were William A. Graham and Thomas Bragg.[21]

Neither at the impeachment nor later was Governor Holden charged with personal misuse of state funds or of using his high office for bettering his own financial fortunes. But certain decisions he made and certain acts of the Reconstruction government, while not corrupt in themselves, almost completely destroyed the assets of the state and also its credit. These acts affected every section of North Carolina. The repudiation of the state debts and the war debts brought widespread financial loss to citizens already suffering from the loss of slaves, property, and crops. This repudiation also closed every bank in the state and swept away most of the Literary Fund, a large portion of which had been invested in bank stock.[22]

With its state source of income gone, the state school system could no longer survive. Making the collapse complete, Governor Holden refused to recognize Calvin Henderson Wiley as Superintendent of Common Schools and declared the position vacant. The General Assembly promptly abolished the office and that of treasurer of the Literary Fund and turned what assets remained in it into the public treasury. By almost superhuman efforts, Calvin H. Wiley had kept the public schools in operation during the years of conflict and had saved the Literary Fund from being invested in Confederate and State war bonds. Now, he was forced to watch the schools close, and for two years not a public school in the state was in operation, from the first grade through the University. In Western North Carolina the little log school houses that had brought the beginnings of educational enlightenment to the hills stood silent, with sagging doors and empty benches.[23]

Even though Governor Holden could not be accused of using his office for personal gains, the government that he headed could be. Before his downfall came, every county in the state had suffered from the waste, extravagance, and in some instances, from the deliberate fraud of men in positions of political responsibility. Western North Carolina was a victim of the most devastating of all of these frauds perpetrated in the name of government.

The debilitating state of North Carolina's government during Reconstruction had far-reaching ramifications. For example, in answering Major William W. McDowell's plea for laborers from Scotland, Gilbert B. Tennant in 1865 had offered the suggestion of industry as a means of relieving the economic stress in Western North Carolina. He pointed out that the region was admirably adapted for industry, and he thought the time was ripe for forming corporations in the mountain area. But industrial development was not possible during the Reconstruction days. There was little private money to invest in business enterprises, and the lack of transportation facilities and the tense, post-war conditions discouraged outside capital.

Roads and highways, neglected and abused during the war years, were badly in need of repairs, even of rebuilding. Projected railroads into the area had been halted soon after the outbreak of the war. In 1865 stagecoaches were again in use, although they were frequently delayed by the highway conditions. Mail service, completely abandoned in 1861, was also resumed, but it was slow and uncertain.[24] At the close of the war, the railroads seized by the federal government were returned to the state practically unfit for use. Lack of equipment and materials needed for repairs—even spikes—crippled the efficiency of those lines kept in the hands of the state. Both Federal and Confederate armies had destroyed bridges, water tanks, shops, cars, and rails. The state and Confederate debts owed the railroads could never be collected, and the sinking funds were almost a total loss. Damage claims against the roads took most of the remaining assets; yet if the railroads were to function, vast amounts would have to be spent on repairs and new equipment.[25]

In spite of the bleak outlook, the people of Western North Carolina still looked forward to the extension of the railroad over the mountains. Stoneman's raiders had seriously damaged and in some places utterly destroyed the completed section of the Western North Carolina Railroad running from Salisbury to Icard Station east of Morganton. In 1865 this railroad had only three engines, one usable passenger car, and a small number of freight cars. During the summer of that year temporary repairs made it possible to provide three trips per week over the line. By 1869 there was daily service.[26]

At a meeting in Morganton in 1868 plans were revived for extending the line westward. By this time a series of encouraging legislative acts relating to the Western North Carolina Railroad had been passed. The Assembly repealed the old clause on sectional construction and authorized the state to subscribe two thirds of the capital stock after the remaining one third had been subscribed by private capital. The line was divided into two divisions, with Asheville the line of separation. The Western Division was to include both the Ducktown route and the Paint Rock route. The Buncombe Turnpike Company was empowered to grant the necessary right-of-way along the French Broad River. Each division was to be organized into a new company, possessing a capital stock of $6,000,000.[27]

In 1867 contracts were let for that section of the Eastern Division between Morganton and Old Fort and in the following year for that from Old Fort to the western end of the projected Swannanoa tunnel. George W. Swepson was made president of the company that was duly formed for constructing the western road. When the required $2,000,000 of stock had been subscribed by citizens, Swepson let the contract for the Paint Rock branch to Samuel Tate and the longer Ducktown route to General Milton S. Littlefield. All of this Swepson reported to Governor Holden, preparatory to receiving the state's bonds for its pledged $4,000,000. During the next two years, Swepson and Littlefield engineered a fraud for which Western North Carolina paid a high price.[28]

General Milton Littlefield had come into North Carolina during the Civil War and at its close had made his presence felt as a banker in Raleigh. George W. Swepson was a native of the state. He too, was a banker and through the influence of Governor Holden was granted political favors, including the presidency of the Western North Carolina Railroad.[29] These two men formed the nucleus of a small group of opportunists who used not only the Western North Carolina Railroad, but eastern lines as well as a means of funneling money from the state treasury and from private capital into their own pockets. General Littlefield's role was that of a lobbyist. He bribed members of the General Assembly to pass laws favorable to Swepson's railroad interests, and he bribed attorneys to secure decisions favorable to Swepson. It has been estimated that more than $333,000 were paid out in bribe money coming from the illegal sale of bonds intrusted to George Swepson.[30]

During the year of Swepson's presidency, little actual work was done on the roadbed of the Western Division. Because of a rising tide of complaints, Swepson, as was permitted under the original contracts, relet contracts for a 45-mile link of the Paint Rock branch and a 55-mile link on the Ducktown road. Some grading was done on both of these stretches, most of which was useless by the time the road was actually constructed. At a Director's meeting in Asheville in 1869, Swepson, using a complaint of excessive criticism as his excuse, resigned as president of the company. General Littlefield was then given that position. He promised to push the work on the road, but by that time there was little left with which to pay contractors and workmen.[31]

In March, 1870, a legislative committee was appointed to investigate Swepson's widespread railroad affairs. With Nicholas W. Woodfin of Asheville as chairman, this committee found the transactions of both Swepson and Littlefield so involved that they were never able to clarify all of them. Swepson was arrested and for a time was held in Raleigh, and Littlefield was finally located in London. Upon orders of the General Assembly, the committee tried to retrieve what it could by making arrangements with the two men individually for certain settlements. These yielded little, however, since Littlefield made no attempt to honor his agreements and the Florida railroad stock which was put up as security by Swepson could not be collected because of a previously given lien on it.

Of the millions of dollars worth of state bonds that disappeared, the committee was able to collect only $295,876.26. The General Assembly repealed the railroad appropriation bills of 1868 and required all unsold bonds returned to the State Treasurer. Later, all the bonds originally issued to Swepson were repudiated. Because of this scandal, the state debt rose from $15,000,000 to more than $28,000,000. Out of that vast fund the counties west of the Blue Ridge got two short strips of graded roadbed.[32]

Meantime, however, work on the Eastern Division had progressed steadily, and late in 1869 the section from Morganton to Old Fort was ready for use. The "Iron Horse" finally puffed its way into the town where the fort built by the pioneers once stood guard. Two years later much of the work of grading was completed on the section between Old Fort and the projected Swannanoa tunnel. Grading work was also in progress on the section westward toward Asheville. By 1871 the Eastern Division, although free from corruption, was in serious financial straits, but it refused to purchase the Western Division offered it at a foreclosure price. Four years later, on June 22, 1876, the Western North Carolina Railroad was put up for sale and was purchased for the state by Augustus S. Merrimon. Again the people of Western North Carolina dared to hope for a railroad across their mountains to the Tennessee border.

The Swepson-Littlefield scandal broke about the time of the "Kirk-Holden War" and may have been a factor in the Governor's impeachment. In 1874 the Democrats took full control of the General Assembly, and in that year many of the Federal troops were withdrawn. By 1876 the Reconstruction days were over.

CHAPTER TWENTY THREE

Dawn Breaks Over the Mountains

During the Reconstruction days, with their high taxes, their unrest, and their secret organizations, hundreds of peace-loving men and women said goodbye to their mountains and joined the thousands of fellow North Carolinians leaving for new homes in the beckoning West. Discouraged over conditions in their native state, they sought, as had their forebears in coming to the mountains, a place where they and their children might live in peace and might prosper. But many of the veterans, discontented with post-war conditions or preferring the life of woodmen, did not leave the state. Instead, they moved west into the sparsely settled sections of their own or nearby counties. They joined the small number of hardy pioneers who had preceded them and were joined by those coming from farther east. As a result, during this period Western North Carolina gained two new county governments.[1]

In 1871 Swain County was formed from the western parts of Jackson and Macon Counties. Quite appropriately it was named for David Lowery Swain, the state's first Governor from Western North Carolina. In this new county was one of North Carolina's last great uninhabited areas. Its wild and magnificently forested mountains culminated in the lofty Smokies, along whose crest runs the dividing line between North Carolina and Tennessee. It was in this region that Tsali and his band took their last stand against the encroaching white man.

The bill for the formation of the county passed the General Assembly on February 24, 1871, and the commissioners met for their first meeting at Cold Springs Church. A tiny settlement on the banks of the Tuckaseigee River, along which Indian villages had once flourished, was selected as the county seat. The following year a two-story courthouse was constructed there, which also served as a school building and a church. The village was known as Charleston, but when it was incorporated in 1887, the name was changed to Bryson City, honoring Thaddeus Dillard Bryson, through whose efforts the county had been formed.[2]

When, years later, the Smoky Mountain National Park was formed, approximately two thirds of the area of Swain County were transferred by North Carolina to the Federal Government. Its lands were also taken for the T V A project at Fontana. For a quarter of a century after its organization citizens of the county, except those in the village of Bryson City, lived the lives of mountain pioneers, repeating the farmer-woodsman type of life practiced by their forebears. It was not until the mid 1880's that a railroad would pass through the county on its way to Tennessee. This would link Swain County with the counties farther east and would foreshadow the coming of industries to be followed by a slowly changing pattern of life.

In 1872 the second of these westernmost counties was formed from the northern section of Cherokee County. It was given the name of Graham, in honor of William A. Graham, who as a young Whig member of the General Assembly had advocated Murphey's reform measures, including railroads for the western section of the state. Graham's later political career had included a seat in the United States Senate, the governorship of his state, and the post of Secretary of Navy. The village of Robbinsville, the last home of Junaluska, was selected as the county seat and a courthouse was there erected. Like Swain to the east of it, Graham is an area of mountains with only a small amount of its land suitable for farming. Its first citizens combined hunting with working their hillside farms in sheltered coves. This county, too, borders Tennessee and reaches its highest altitude in the Unicoi Range that is shared by the two states.[3]

In spite of the dissatisfaction and unrest of the people in this Reconstruction period, thousands of men and women in every county in Western North Carolina remained on their farms. Looking for a better future as they quietly repaired the damages wrought by the war, these tenacious people planted and harvested

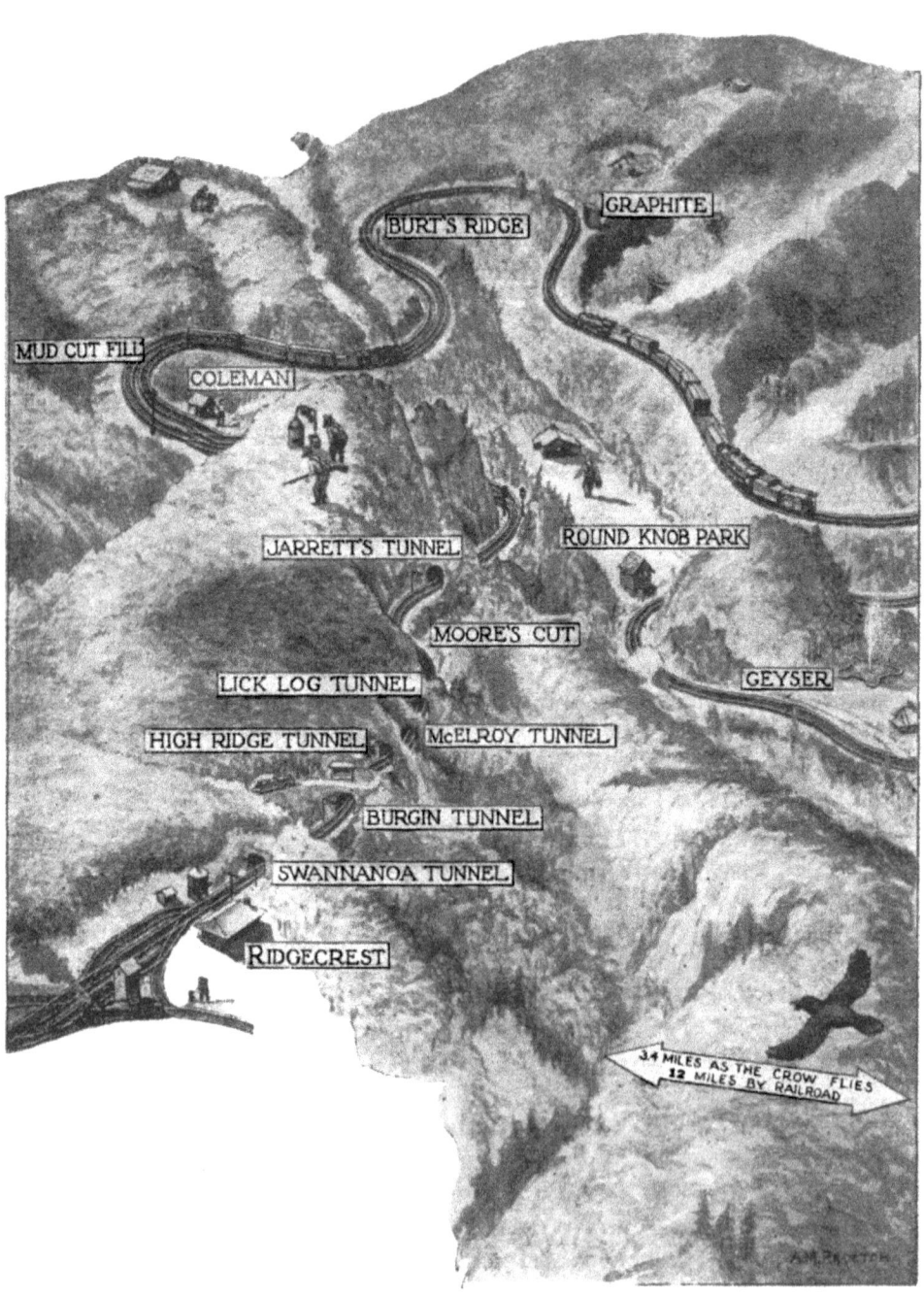

ILLUSTRATED MAP BY AURION PROCTOR IN *THE RAILROAD MAGAZINE*,
DEC., 1943

The Railroad Crosses the Blue Ridge: Spanning the Blue Ridge with bands of steel was a constant contest between determined men and resisting mountains. Between Old Fort and Ridgecrest, a distance of 3.4 miles as the crow flies, the curving tracks made 10 complete circles and covered 12 miles.

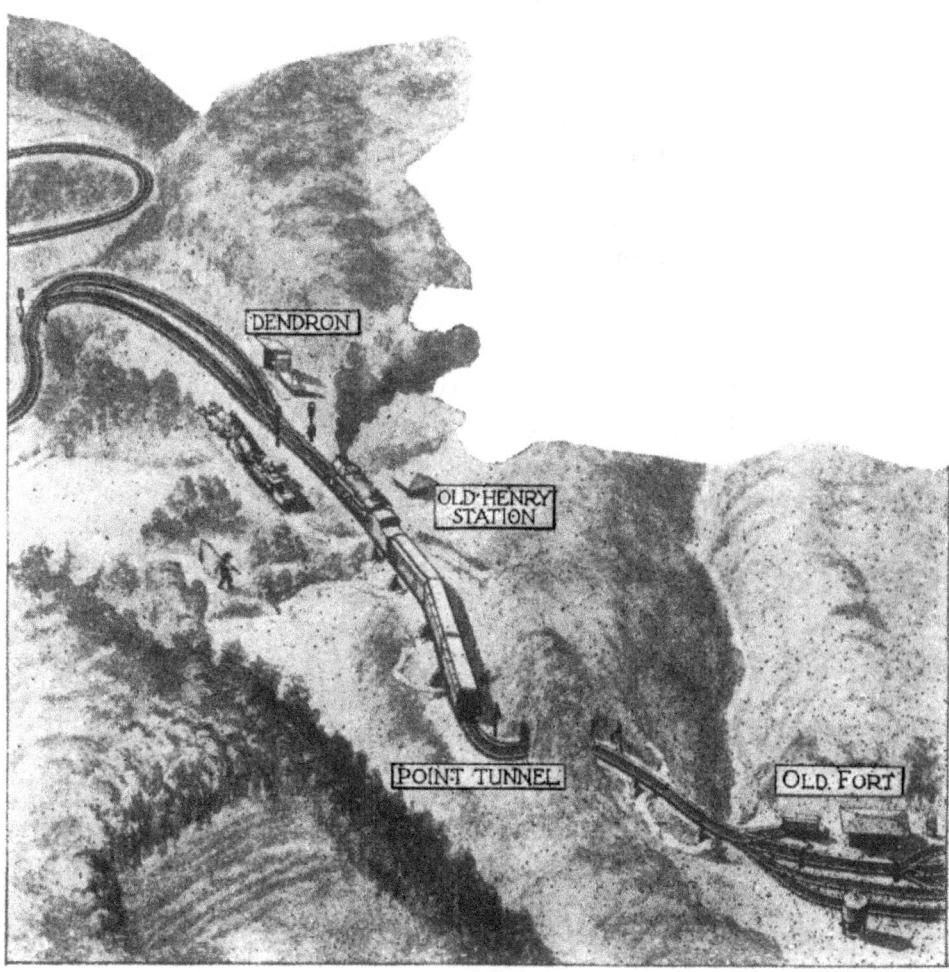

their crops and built up their herds of cattle, horses, and hogs. Under the old county system main highways were gradually made passable again. Once more in the autumn months clouds of dust billowed over them as the noisy droves of animals made their way to southern markets. Again the stand keepers bought the farmers' corn and furnished them with supplies in return. But compared with the pre-war droves, these tramping animals were few in number, for neither the South Carolinians nor the freed Negroes on the plantations could now afford to "eat high off the hog." Then, too, railroads were pushing westward resulting in fewer tramping animals from states to the north.[4]

Forges were once more turning out tools as well as iron bars that could be fashioned into needed articles at the home forges. The water-powered mills continued grinding the farmers' grain into flour and meal, and new cards were now available, making the housewife's work easier. On winter days with a rhythmic thumping of her loom she turned out the coverlets and yards of linsey-woolsey that made her family comfortable. The traveling cobbler resumed his rounds, working up the tanned leather into sturdy shoes that ranged in size from the miniature ones for the toddlers to the boots large enough and strong enough to endure a man's tramping in all kinds of weather over the fields and hills and through the woods. Returning ministers opened many of the closed "church houses," and "preachings," "singings," "cemetery workings," and family gatherings gave a sense of restored normal living to the mountain communities.

Gradually, too, a sense of security returned. With the exposure of the government excesses and scandals, resulting in a Conservative majority in the General Assembly and the impeachment of Governor Holden, many of the carpetbaggers left the state. The federal enforcement of the Ku Klux Klan Law subdued the activities of that organization as well as those of the Union League and the Red Strings, allowing for the restoration of law and order.

In 1875 Western North Carolina sent its quota of delegates to the Constitutional Convention called by the General Assembly. This Convention, made up of an equal number of Democrats and Republicans and three Independent members, revised the 1868 Constitution by the addition of some thirty amendments. Among the changes was one by which the county justices of the peace were to be appointed by the General Assembly. The number of Supreme Court Judges was reduced from five to three, and the number of Superior Court Judges from twelve to nine. Negro and white schools were to be separately but equally maintained, and secret political societies were banned.[5]

In 1876 the pre-war spirit of political fervor again sprang into life throughout the mountain area, as it did everywhere in the state. Zebulon Baird Vance, Western North Carolina's favorite son and North Carolina's honored war-time Governor, was again a candidate for the state's highest office. He represented the Conservatives, who earlier had affiliated with the national Democratic Party. His opponent was Thomas Settle of Rockingham County. Settle was a man of recognized ability and integrity and was a former Supreme Court Judge of North Carolina. The campaign was carefully planned by both party organizations, and Vance and Settle toured the state together and faced each other on open-air platforms. Their main speeches lasted an hour and a half, after which they refuted and ridiculed each other's claims in half hour rebuttals. Each man interspersed his speeches with jokes, anecdotes, and jibes at the expense of his opponent.

The people of Western North Carolina crowded into the county seats for these political rallies. Mountain-bred Zebulon Baird Vance spoke the language of the mountain people. Hundreds had heard him in earlier campaigns, and there were those who had been in his regiment in the early part of the war. They knew that nowhere was his equal in clear, forceful thinking and speaking, in hilarious story-telling, and in witty rebuttal. So it was that Rutherfordton, boasting a population of slightly more than 1,000, overflowed with a crowd of more than 4,000 when Vance and Settle appeared in the village.[6]

On August 3, 1876, the farmers of Mitchell County, many of whom had fought each other through four years of war (and had continued to do so in trials and law suits and feuds during the troubled years that had followed) jostled each other along the roads and trails leading into Bakersville. They stood shoulder to shoulder as they listened spell-bound to the verbal battle between Vance and Settle. The town had prepared for the rally and was gala with banners made by the women and strung across the street. Processions of party members formed and, led by their musicians, marched out of the village to meet their respective candidates and to escort them with proper fanfare to the rallying place.[7] Never had this border county witnessed such an assemblage, and political fervor mounted as each candidate aimed

N. C. DEPARTMENT OF ARCHIVES AND HISTORY

Hydraulic Work: In the absence of explosives such as dynamite, railroad workers poured water over heated rocks to crack away jutting ledges.

his barbs and shafts at vulnerable spots in his opponent's arguments.

Similar rallies were held in other Western North Carolina towns, and perhaps nowhere in the state were the election returns more eagerly awaited than in the western counties where a man's Republican vote might be offset by his neighbor's Democratic ballot. With the election of Vance by a comfortable if not large majority, the Democrats were once more in full control of North Carolina, and Western North Carolina again had a man in the governor's chair. The carpetbag rule was over, and in 1875 federal troops were withdrawn from the state. The mountain people, even those who had cast their votes for Settle, now hoped for economic recovery.

Both the Governor and the General Assembly were concerned with economy measures that would inspire confidence. They were also eager to fulfill campaign pledges of reduced taxes, but at the same time two projects were recognized as worthy of state aid and demanding immediate attention. One was the westward extension of railroads; the other was the acute problem of public education. The Constitution of 1868 made provision for a state system of schools that would furnish free education to children and young people between the ages of six and twenty-one. Primary schools were to be operated for at least four months each year.[8] But little had been done to carry out these provisions, and for two years all schools in the state were closed. In 1870 in North Carolina fifty per cent of all citizens over ten years of age were illiterate.[9] In his 1872 report to Alexander McIver, State Superintendent of Instruction, Haywood's county official described the school conditions in Western North Carolina when he penned this dismal statement: "Our school system is a failure."[10]

Many factors combined to counteract the efforts to reopen and to maintain the public schools. The basic one was lack of funds. The remaining assets of the old Literary Fund had been diverted to other purposes, and the appropriation made by the General Assembly in 1869 was never paid.[11] In 1870 the State Supreme Court declared unconstitutional a clause in the state law providing for local school taxes. New and more effective school laws were from time to time passed, but no effective machinery was set up for their enforcement.[12] Under a law passed in 1873, however, a township without funds for operating even one school could levy, upon the vote of the people, a special school tax.[13] Paying an extra tax was impossible for most farmers in Western North Carolina, many of whom were fortunate to have twenty to thirty dollars in cash in a year.

During the early years of Reconstruction some of the teachers sent into the area were from the North and were distrusted by the people.[14] But more important was the fact that many of the little log school houses had been destroyed during the war, and those remaining were badly in need of repairs. The state would assume only half of the cost of construction or repairs. Textbooks were also a problem.[15] The supply of school books, purchased from Northern printers, was cut off at the beginning of the war.

N. C. DEPARTMENT OF ARCHIVES AND HISTORY
Round Knob and Mill: From Round Knob three levels of tracks can be seen. In the foreground is a water-powered mill.

Following an educational meeting in July, 1861, school books were hastily written by school leaders in the state. They were printed on the poor, yellowing paper turned out by newly established mills, and once in the hands of pupils, they were short-lived. As late as 1876 there were no depositories for books in the counties, and old copies were soon lost.[16] Like those in the early pioneer days, the schools were then forced to use as texts whatever books could be gathered from the homes, regardless of subject matter or grade level. "Anything we can get" was the standard many an official reported concerning books used in his district. A majority of the pupils had no texts of their own.[17]

To make practical use of the meager and varied assortment of books at hand required skillful adaptation by experienced teachers. But their number was few. Certification of teachers had from the first been generously done, and now as schools reopened, county examiners at times issued certificates on the basis of the financial need of the applicant or to any neighbor who could be induced to apply. The pay was low, as it had always been, and the four months' term could not be reached. Often it was ten weeks in a year. No attempt was made to enforce the compulsory attendance law, requiring at least sixteen months in either public or private school between a child's sixth and his eighteenth birthday.[18]

In the western counties having a Negro population there was the added burden of maintaining separate schools for the Negro children. Some mountain counties had no Negro children of school age. Some had too few to justify the expense of a school and had to make other arrangements for the education of those children. One township in Macon County reported one little Negro girl for whom the officials were making arrangements for schooling. Mitchell County reported too few Negro children in any one district for a school, and the children were too scattered to attend a centrally located school. One district in Transylvania County reported no Negro school in operation because no teacher was available.[19]

In his opening address to the General Assembly Governor Vance urged the establishment of at least two normal schools. As a result, a summer normal school for white teachers was set up at the University at Chapel Hill, and one for Negro teachers was established at Fayetteville. Both proved popular.[20] After 1877 any township having a population of five thousand or more had the authority, upon a petition of a hundred voters, to submit to the public the question of establishing a graded, eight-month school through the levying of a special school tax. Under this law Buncombe County voted such a tax, and two years later the village of Lenoir was empowered to submit a similar referendum to the voters.[21]

In order to bring the teacher training program closer to the people, the summer school at the University was discontinued, to be replaced by short term normals held in various parts of the state. Three of these were held in Western North Carolina—at Sparta, Franklin, and Asheville.[22] From time to time new laws were made under which more taxes were appropriated for the school fund and more efficient use was made of each county's share. In 1881 a county Superintendent of Schools replaced the county examiner, and the lax third grade certificate for teaching was discarded.[23]

Later the short term normals were replaced with county institutes, which teachers were required to attend. Then Edwin A. Alderman and Charles D. McIver, two dedicated educators, were employed by the state as institute leaders. They worked with the teachers, citizens, and local organizations in bringing improvement and prestige to the public schools. They were aided

N. C. DEPARTMENT OF ARCHIVES AND HISTORY

The Swannanoa Tunnel: The Salisbury, one of two locomotives used, was taken across the mountain so that this tunnel might be worked from both directions. On March 11, 1879, "Daylight entered Buncombe County, grades and centers meeting exactly."

in this by the Farmers' Alliance, in which thousands of the state's farmers held membership. Even so, in many of the mountain communities schools continued to be taught by poorly paid and poorly prepared teachers. Equipment and books were still inadequate, and in some districts not more than fifty per cent of the community children attended school. In far too many mountain valleys and coves this condition prevailed until the dawn of a new century.[24]

Since the public schools of Western North Carolina were inefficient or lacking, church and privately owned schools that had closed during the war were reopened, and new ones were established. Many of the new ones were made possible by funds from Northern people genuinely interested in the educational problems of the mountain area. Other private institutions were established by North Carolinians who saw little prospect of the public schools meeting the pressing needs for education.

In Rutherford County both the Male and Female Academies in the county seat were reopened. Oak Hill, Round Hill, and Burnt Chimney Academies also resumed operation, with several private schools giving instruction to primary children.[25] In 1868 Robert

Abernethy began the school in Burke County that grew into Rutherford College.[26] The Academy in Sparta also reopened, and others were established in Alleghany County. In spite of the fact that its boarding house had been destroyed during the war, the Finley School for Boys at Lenoir reopened as students returned from the army.[27]

The same pattern prevailed west of the Blue Ridge. At Burnsville the Yancey Collegiate Institute, in operation for some years prior to the war, reopened its doors to continue serving until the 1890's. The college established by the Baptists at Mars Hill weathered the stormy Reconstruction days and had continued to serve the mountain area and the state as an outstanding church college. Weaverville College, incorporated in 1856, occupied the site of an old Methodist campground. It, too, reopened after the war. In Asheville the Lee School for Boys reopened while in 1887 the Northern Presbyterians established a Normal School on a tract of land which today is the site of the Memorial Mission Hospital.

A school building was started in Hendersonville by the Baptists on the eve of the war. A part of the unfinished building was used briefly as barracks by federal cavalry units during their passage through the town. The school was completed in 1873 and became the home of the Western North Carolina Female College. Among its students for a period of time were about one hundred Cherokee girls placed there by the federal government. In time it became a co-educational school and, when sold by the Baptists, was reorganized as Judson College.[28] During the last decade of the nineteenth century practically every town or village had an academy and a mission primary school. Some of those academies have today become parts of the University of North Carolina.[29]

During the last score of years of the fading century the long-cherished dream of the mountain people for a railroad became a reality. As the new century dawned, railroad engines were puffing their way along the rails, trailing strings of freight cars along the valley floors, over the mountain grades, and through the tunnels. The clouds of smoke that testified to the efforts they were forced to make could be seen from Old Fort to Murphy and from Tryon to Paint Rock. Gleaming, newly laid rails connected towns in the eastern foothills with each other and with the east and the south.

With the incompleted Western North Carolina Railroad now the property of the state, construction of the Western

N. C. DEPARTMENT OF ARCHIVES AND HISTORY

The Salisbury: Locomotive 25, the little wood-burning Salisbury, is on a trestle by the French Broad River near Asheville.

Division began on the first day of October, 1875. By the end of 1876 the records showed a disappointingly small profit. Despite the cheap convict labor furnished by the state for pushing the road westward, only three additional miles of track had been laid. The General Assembly then declared the Western Division a corporation, having a total stock of $850,000. The next year a twelve-member Board of Directors assumed control with Major James W. Wilson as president.[30] During the next three years, working under the most difficult physical conditions and under a constant financial strain, Wilson and his chief engineer, Colonel

Thaddeus Coleman, and their assistants took the road across the Blue Ridge.

Since Colonial times, the abrupt and forbidding granite walls of this range had said to the white man, "This far shalt thou go and no farther." At last the mountains were conquered by parallel ribbons of steel, making the East and the West one. The gaily bedecked stagecoach drawn by "six fine horses" that had taken passengers from the railroad terminal at Henry, just west of Old Fort, over the Blue Ridge to Asheville could now eliminate the precipitous curves of the Swannanoa Gap.[31] Early in 1880 it was picking up its westward traveling passengers at the terminal near Azalea, seven miles from Asheville. Freight wagons rumbled with their loads over the shortened route to warehouses in the mountain towns.[31]

The Blue Ridge had not tamely submitted to man's determined efforts to conquer it. Every step of the way it fought the engineers and their laborers with slides of rock and rain-soaked earth and with grades so steep that the only hope of successfully navigating them was gouging out tunnels through the solid rock walls. Indeed, the story of this engineering feat reads like a modern version of the ancient tale of the Aegean stables. Work on the short sections of grading done four years earlier was practically lost, and new surveys were necessary over the range itself. These showed that the only method to combat the sudden rise in altitude would be a looping track and a series of tunnels.

With the help of five hundred convict laborers furnished by the state, Wilson and his assistant engineer, H. Heaton Coleman, laid a curving track that doubled and redoubled on itself, enough, it was said, to make almost eight complete circles. This looping required 9 miles of rails to cover 3.4 miles, but it insured a negotiable grade over the 1,092 foot ascent. Shearing the jutting towers of rocks down to the level of the roadbed meant removing tons of mountain wall and often the forming of narrow gorges, a backbreaking task for the convicts. They had picks and shovels as their tools, and with the help of ox and mule teams, the laborers dragged away the boulders and carted off the finer debris in wheelbarrows.[32] Now and then a sudden storm or a landslide would undo the labor of days or even of weeks. These events were numerous, but the most disastrous of them all occurred at Mud Tunnel. There, when all but some 8,000 of the 77,000 cubic yards of earth and rock necessary to be removed had been cleared away, a series of landslides crashed down the mountain sides. They filled the man-made cut with 110,000 cubic yards of rock and debris, every boulder and pebble and grain of which had to be removed.[33]

The blue prints called for seven tunnels, ranging in length from 89 to 1,800 feet. Their construction presented the project's greatest problems, both to the engineers and to the workmen. Holes for the blasting of the rock had to be hand-drilled and are visible today, mute evidence of the prodigious human efforts expended in the struggle between determined men and resisting mountains. These holes were filled with a paste made on the spot by mixing nitroglycerine with sawdust and corn meal.[34] When work began on the Swannanoa Tunnel, longest of the series, Wilson and Coleman conceived the bold idea of getting a locomotive over the crest of the ridge so that work could be carried on from the western as well as the eastern portal. In defiance of the mountain's forbidding slope and height, temporary skid tracks were laid across the range. Over it the "Salisbury," one of the two locomotives in use on the eastern end of the tunnel, was hauled and pushed by the sheer, main force of straining oxen and crews of sweating men.

With the construction proceeding from both directions, the work progressed so that Major Wilson was able on March 11, 1879, to send the following well-known telegram to Governor Vance: "Daylight entered Buncombe today through Swannanoa Tunnel. Grade and centers met exactly." The seemingly impossible had been accomplished. But the Blue Ridge had taken its toll, not only in the form of physical efforts that sometimes stretched the point of human endurance, but also in accidents claiming lives. Nearly 125 convicts, toiling under the poised guns of guards, paid the supreme sacrifice in order that the counties of Western North Carolina beyond the Blue Ridge might have the benefits of a railroad.[35]

On October 3, 1880, every one of the 2,610 citizens of Asheville who were able to put one foot ahead of the other assembled to see the town's first train pull into the tiny station. The village was in a holiday mood, for each one prophesied that this long awaited event was the dawn of a new day for the Western Highlands, a day that would bring a prosperity never before known in the mountains. In addition to the freight cars bringing commodities into the area and taking out the produce of the region, the trains now crossing the Blue Ridge from Salisbury soon boasted one passenger-coach. It had a central division so that one half of it was the first-class section on the westward trip, and the other half claimed that distinction on the returning eastward journey. Once out of the mountains, these trains gained enough speed to cover the distance of 120 miles from Henry to Salisbury between daylight and dark, stopping at Hickory for the mid-day meal.[36]

Shortly before the road reached Asheville, it was sold by the state to William J. Best of New York City and his associates. They took over the $850,000 mortgage and agreed to extend the line westward to Murphy and along the French Broad River to Paint Rock. The state, which in the transaction lost all it had invested in the road prior to October 1, 1875, agreed to furnish convict laborers for the company's combined projects. For several years an economy group in the General Assembly had been advocating a retraction of the state's railroad enterprises. The income received by the state from the three lines in which it had significant investments had always been negligible, and it was argued that the roads could be leased or sold, using money thus realized to advantage in furthering education in the state.

As a result, a proposal to merge the three roads, making a great east-west trunk line extending from the coast to Murphy, failed; and in 1871 the North Carolina Railroad was leased to the Richmond, Danville System for thirty years, thus passing out of the control of North Carolina. Shortly afterward, the lessees further separated the road from other North Carolina lines by changing its guage to conform to the Virginia lines held by the company. Now the old Western Division of the Western North Carolina Railroad likewise passed out of the hands of the state. For the third time it was organized as the Western North Carolina Railroad, but it, too, shortly became the property of the Richmond, Danville System. Later, when that road was transferred to the receivers, these lines were taken over by the newly organized Southern Railway Company. In 1895 it secured a ninety-nine year lease of the Western North Carolina Railroad.[37]

In the meantime, both routes through the mountains to points on the Tennessee border were completed. The route following the French Broad River used a part of the old Turnpike bed, but in some sections a new roadway had to be blasted from the solid walls of the river gorge. The work was slow, but it progressed steadily until 1882 when the last spike was driven that connected the newly laid tracks with those in Tennessee. Because of the difference in the gauge of the lines, however, all freight had to be unloaded from one train and reloaded onto the other. The workmen from the completed section were transferred to the western route. Construction of this segment had been progressing satisfactorily, and in 1882 a train puffed its way into Waynesville, to be enthusiastically welcomed by the citizens of that village.[38]

From Waynesville westward the engineers ran into construction difficulties, for between Waynesville and Murphy the road had to cross both the Balsam Range and the Nantahalas. Earlier plans for tunnels through these barriers had to be abandoned, necessitating a rerouting of the track through wild mountain terrain and over the crests of these towering ranges. In the Balsams that meant attaining an altitude of 3,315 feet above sea level. The problems connected with the work in this difficult territory greatly delayed the completion of the road. The company asked for and received an extension of the construction time allotted in their contract with the state. But by 1891 these lofty mountains, like the Blue Ridge to the east, had been conquered, and freight trains were pulling into the switching yards at Murphy.[39] The great east-west line envisioned by Caldwell and advocated by Clingman had at last become a reality. But it was not the transportation system of their dreams. Nor did the educational fund ever receive one penny from the sale of this western road.

Chartered in 1855, the Spartanburg-Asheville section of the old French Broad Railroad began long-deferred westward construction from its Spartanburg terminal in 1873. Slowly the track crept over the Blue Ridge. The original plans called for the road to pass through Columbus and along Tryon Mountain and across Howard's Gap, passing through a series of tunnels. These plans were now abandoned and a new survey made. To avoid the tunnels the track was laid up the steep mountain to Saluda. This was a prodigious feat of mountain construction, for in one three-mile section the bed had to climb 600 feet and at some points the grade was 220 feet per mile. On the steepest part two safety tracks were laid, and the trains required an additional engine from Melrose to the village of Saluda.

As on the Old Fort-Asheville road, convict labor was used on this line after it crossed into North Carolina. Once again, the wild terrain took its toll of lives, and nineteen graves mark the resting place of convicts killed in accidents. But the Blue Ridge was forced to yield to the human endeavor, and in 1882 trains were passing over the rails into Hendersonville. There the road terminated until work was again resumed in 1883, and the line reached Asheville in 1886, connecting with the roads to Paint Rock and the branch creeping westward from Waynesville.[40]

The old pre-war plan for a line from Georgia to Knoxville, worked out by the Blue Ridge Railroad Company and intended to pass down the Hiwassee River, took form in the shorter Marietta and North Georgia Railroad with thirteen miles of track in Cherokee County on the route to Tennessee. Its tracks reached Murphy three years earlier than did those of the Western North Carolina line. In 1894 a line was constructed from Hendersonville to Rosman. Chartered as the Hendersonville-Brevard Railroad, it was reorganized as the Transylvania Railroad and later, like other roads west of the mountains, became a part of the Southern Railway System.[41]

During the last two decades of the nineteenth century the railroads extended their lines, and the General Assembly chartered new ones in the counties just east of the Blue Ridge. Some of these progressed no farther than the charters, but others sold the required amount of stock and set about building their road beds. The enormous cost of railroad construction and the heavy upkeep of road beds and equipment after the lines were in operation, together with the nation-wide depression following the 1873 panic, affected railroads throughout the country. Bankruptcy was the fate of some of the new companies, resulting in reorganizations and recharterings. There were also consolidations of roads through merger, purchase, lease, or the absorption of small lines by larger ones. With all of these frequent changes in the railroad pattern, Western North Carolina was being supplied with needed railroads.[42] By 1890 a line was in operation from Spartanburg, South Carolina, through Rutherfordton to Marion. To the towns in Western North Carolina this meant connections also with Camden, South Carolina. In 1884 a road linked Lenoir with Lincolnton and Charlotte.[43] One more railroad would come to this area in the new century, and once more the Blue Ridge would submit to parallel rows of steel linking counties to the west with their neighbors to the east.

Western North Carolina was, after long years of waiting, getting its railroads. With them came the beginning of a new day in the mountains. It would be a day when once more the people could follow the pursuits of peace, and they could say, as Henry Woodward had written two hundred years earlier, "We have discovered a country so delitious."

398 / *Chapter Twenty Three*

THE STEPHENS PRESS, INC.

The Statue of Vance in the U. S. Capitol: In 1879 Governor Vance resigned his office to enter Congress as a United States Senator.

THE STEPHENS PRESS, INC.

The Vance Monument: This monument to Buncombe County's native son is on Pack Square in Asheville.

CHAPTER NOTES

Explanation: In the Chapter Notes, references to Collections are by title only. After their first appearance, other references, where clear, are by authors only.

CHAPTER 1
The Land of Mountains

1. Jasper L. Stuckey and Warren G. Steel, *The Geology and Mineral Resources of North Carolina*, 3.
2. *Ibid.*
3. H. J. Bryson, *The Story of the Geological Making of North Carolina*, 13.
4. Stuckey and Steel, 5-6.
5. *Ibid.*, 6.
6. *Ibid.*
7. In some places in the Smokies the shales and limestones of the Ordovician period are actually below the older Ocoee rocks owing to this overthrust.
8. The oldest life forms found in the region are in Cades Cove. These fossils belong to the Ordovician period. Stuckey and Steel, 31.
9. *Ibid.*, 4.
10. The ancestor of the Pigeon River flowed east and south into an ancient French Broad River near the site of the present Asheville. It reversed its flow northward, leaving a section of its old bed dry. Other Haywood County streams show that they once flowed east, while beds of yet other ancient rivers can still be discerned, mute evidences of the work of pirate streams. See W. C. Allen's *Annals of Haywood County*, 11-12.
11. The fascinating geological history of Western North Carolina is traced through succeeding geological ages by Bryson and by Phillip B. King and Arthur Stupka in "The Great Smoky Mountains—Their Geology and Natural History," *Scientific Monthly*, LXXXI, 31-43. See also Henry S. Sharpe, "The Geologic Story" in *The Great Smoky Mountains and the Blue Ridge*, 290-319.
12. Stuckey and Steel, 9.
13. *Early Travels in the Tennessee Country*, 193. Henry Timberlake, in the Upper Cherokee towns on a good will tour in 1761, found that the

Notes / 401

13. *Early Travels in the Tennessee Country,* 193. Henry Timberlake, in the Upper Cherokee towns on a good will tour in 1761, found that the Cherokees had ornaments of gold and silver and copper and that they had gems. Some of these were so fine that they used only in the religious ceremonies. See his *Memoirs,* 57–103.
14. The gold deposits and their effects upon Western North Carolina are treated in Chapter XIII.
15. See Stuckey and Steel for a list of the mineral deposits, 26-33.
16. King and Stupka, 41; Charles A. Shull, *The Lure of Western North Carolina for the Explorer-Naturalists.*
17. Bill Lord, *Nature Notes on the Blue Ridge Parkway.*
18. Donald C. Peattie, "Men, Mountains, and Trees," in *The Great Smoky Mountains and the Blue Ridge,* 152-171; King and Stupka, 40.
19. William Bartram, climbing up the mountain ranges in May, 1775, recorded his amazement as he watched spring give way to winter. *Travels Through North and South Carolina,* 273-275. Charles Lanman, traveling on horseback from Franklin to the Qualla Reservation in May 1848, noted this same rapid shifting of the seasons. *Adventures in the Wilds of the United States and the British American Provinces,* 1, 385. See also King and Stupka, 41.
20. King and Stupka, 43.
21. The display of wild flowers is not as extensive as it was before the white man came to cultivate the land and to clear the forests. William Bartram, viewing the flame azalea on a mountainside, wrote: "We are alarmed with the apprehension of the hill being set on fire," *Travels Through North and South Carolina,* 264.
22. The parade of blooms and hence of color through the months is given by Stupka in "Through the Year in the Great Smoky Mountain National Park, Month by Month," in *The Great Smoky Mountains and the Blue Ridge,* 263-289.
23. King and Stupka, 40.
24. *Ibid.*

CHAPTER 2

Eden Is Discovered

1. Miguel Cavarrubias, *The Eagle, the Jaguar, and the Serpent,* Chap. II. John R. Swanton traces the pre-historic Indian movements in the southeast in his *The Indians of the Southeastern United States,* 21-33. Although writing in an unorthodox style for a scientific study, Harold S. Gladwin in his *Men out of Asia* has presented an interesting discussion of the movements of Asiatic migration to America, 1-183.
2. Cavarrubias, Chap. V; James B. Griffin (ed.), *Archeology of Eastern United States,* 207 ff.; Powell, "Mound Explorations in Caldwell, Burke, Wilkes, Haywood, Buncombe, and Henderson Counties," *Report of the Bureau of American Ethnology,* XII, 331-350, and Powell, "Mound Builders," in the same volume, 595-730.

3. Dickens, Roy, *The Pisgah Culture and its Place in the History of the Southern Appalachians.*
4. Extensive excavations have been made at Hiwassee Island at the junction of the Hiwassee and Tennessee Rivers. See Thomas M. N. Lewis and Madeline Kneberg, *Hiwassee Island,* and their *Tribes That Slumber.*
5. See Note 4.
6. Mooney, 14-22; Adair, 11-15.
7. See Note 6.
8. The map (Plate III) given in Mooney's *Myths of the Cherokees* shows the Cherokee boundaries at the period of the nation's greatest expansion and its subsequent losses of territory.
9. Mooney, 14-23; Adair, 237-241.
10. Adair, 16-20. See also his "General Observations," 405-480.
11. The most important, and doubtless the oldest, of these trails was the Warrior Path. It entered from the north by way of the Tennessee River, passing up the Hiwassee River, where, near a village on the site of Peachtree Mound, it forked, one branch going to Nikwasi, on the site of the present Franklin, and the other continuing along the Hiwassee to its headwaters, then crossing the mountains to villages in the present Georgia. From Nikwasi the other branch passed through a gap in the mountains into northeastern Georgia and then southeast into the present South Carolina. Along this in 1540 came De Soto and his army. Frank M. Setzler and Jesse D. Jennings, *Peachtree Mound and Village Site,* 9-10. Branches from these main trails led to the scattered Indian villages. The early trails eventually brought English traders into the mountains and became pack horse routes. They were later widened into wagon roads, and some of them are today serving as paved highways. The white man's railroads also used these ancient trails. Sections of a few of the old Indian paths are still visible.
12. See the myths given by Mooney.
13. Adair, Timberlake, Bartram, and Schneider all tell of Cherokee food and its preparation. Adair says that one method of cooking potatoes was to boil them in bear's grease. Adair, *History,* 337; Timberlake, 57, 61, 68; Schneider, "Journey to the Upper Cherokee Towns," *Early Travels in the Tennessee Country,* 257.
14. Adair, 442-446; Swanton, 386-439; Timberlake, 57-103; Schneider, 260. Until the English traders, as more or less permanent settlers in the Cherokee nation, brought the white man's way of constructing log houses, the Indians made the walls of their lodges or houses of upright poles or saplings set close together in a trench.
15. William Bartram was impressed with the village of Cowee and recorded a description of it. He pictured the council house in detail. It was, he said, in the shape of a rotunda that would seat several hundred people. In it he witnessed some of the Indian activities typical to the Cherokees. *Travels,* 297-298. See also Timberlake, 59.
16. Such a feather robe was made by Cherokee women for use in the drama, *Unto These Hills.*
17. Adair, 342-446; Swanton, 351 ff. Schneider also describes the food, crops, dress, and customs of the Cherokees, 250-265.

16. Such a feather robe was made by Cherokee women for use in the drama, *Unto These Hills.*
17. Adair, 342-446; Swanton, 351 ff. Schneider also describes the food, crops, dress, and customs of the Cherokees, 250-265.
18. Schneider found that the Cherokees made earthenware that was so efficiently treated that it looked like ironware from a foundry, 257.
19. *Ibid.*; Timberlake, 68.
20. At the Oconaluftee Indian Village at Cherokee the visitor can enter a typical, seven-sided council house. In this village, too, he can watch the processes of making boats, fashioning implements, making pottery, and weaving baskets, all according to the ancient methods employed by the ancestors of the present Cherokees. He can also see demonstrations of the amazingly efficient blow-guns. The buildings in the palisaded village are authentic types used by the Cherokees in 1750, some of them showing the influence of the white man's method of construction. Under the general sponsorship of the Cherokee Historical Association, research work for this project was done by the Anthropology Departments of the Universities of North Carolina, Tennessee, and Georgia.
21. They also used the semi-precious stones found in the mountains. Henry Timberlake was told that, according to an ancient Cherokee legend, an especially brilliant stone, considered too sacred to be used except in religious rites, was found in the head of a serpent. *Memoirs,* 73-74.
22. Schneider, 262.
23. A special game was arranged for Charles Lanman when he was the guest of William H. Thomas at Qualla in 1848. He describes it in his "Letters From the Alleghany Mountains," 414-416. See also Chapman J. Milling, *Red Carolinians,* 378-380.
24. It would seem that this name was not applied to the Cherokees alone. Lederer was told that beyond the Blue Ridge lived the Rickahockans, who would at that time have been the Cherokees, but Indians appearing earlier in coastal towns and so designated were not Cherokees. Swanton, 217.
25. *Ibid.*
26. The Smithsonian Institution, working with the Civil Works Administration, made excavations between December 21, 1933, and April 1, 1934, at Peachtree Mound, five and a half miles east of Murphy, near the confluence of Peachtree Creek and the Hiwassee River. Much interest attached to this excavation, since it was thought the mound might prove to be the site of Gau-ax-u-le (Quasili) visited by De Soto in 1540. Its location, both in relationship to the rivers and to the Indian trail, aptly fitted the description of that town left by the Spaniards. The excavation revealed only one culture, which was "probably Cherokee." Setzler and Jennings, *Peachtree Mound Site;* 9-10; *Final Report of the De Soto Commission,* 188-191.

CHAPTER 3
Two Races Meet

1. *Final Report of the De Soto Commission,* 187-188.
2. John R. Swanton and the members of the Commission suggest that the

word Chalaque in the Spanish records may not have reference to the Cherokees, since it seems to have been applied to Indians farther east, who were not Cherokees. *Final Report,* 49-51.
3. *Final Report,* 2-3, 103-105. Extracts from these four accounts are given in *Early Travels in the Tennessee Country,* 5-14.
4. *Final Report,* 187.
5. Sondley, *History of Buncombe County,* 130-137.
6. *North Carolina History Told by Contemporaries,* 3; Lefler and Newsome, 6ff.
7. Sondley, I, 329.
8. *Ibid.,* I, 330-334.
9. *Colonial Records,* I, 208. Woodward made four western trips, on one of them going as far west as the Chattahoochee River, through the lower Cherokee country.
10. This is the route given by S. C. Williams in his "Introduction" to Wood's account of the Needham trip. *Early Travels in the Tennessee Country,* 24-38.
11. The Hickory Nut Gap has been considered by many writers as the most likely taken by Needham.
12. *Early Travels in the Tennessee Country,* 24-38.
13. Heath conveyed rights to others. One of these men made claims upon the English government for his share of the Heath land. The claim was finally settled in 1769, when the Crown and Council substituted for the Carolina land some 100,000 acres in New York. Sondley 1, 265-272, 386.
14. W. S. Powell, *The North Carolina Charter of 1663.*
15. Sondley, I, 324-329; Lefler and Newsome, 34.
16. Lefler and Newsome, 32.
17. Sondley, I, 345-352.

CHAPTER 4
Along the Trading Paths

1. Mooney gives their names: Coran, the Raven; Sinnawa, the Hawk; Nellawgitechi; Gorhaleke; Owasta (all from Toxawa); Canacaught, the Great Conjuror; Gohama; and Caunasaita (these three from Keowee), 31.
2. *Ibid.*
3. *Ibid,* 31-32.
4. Logan, *History of the Upper Country of South Carolina,* 188. In 1694 the taxable population of the entire colony of Carolina was 786, making an approximate total white population of 3,000. Hugh T. Lefler and Newsome, Albert R., *North Carolina,* 50.
5. The act to make public the Indian trade passed the South Carolina Legislature on June 30, 1716. While the previous arrangement could not be called a colonial monopoly, the process leading to one had begun with the establishment of the first Board of Indian Commissioners and the beginning of supervision over traders.
6. *Journal of the Commissioners of Indian Affairs,* 126.
7. Logan, 262.

8. *Journal of the Commissioners*, 2. Burdeners were allowed whiskey at the fort, but the Board ordered, "Mix what rum is disposed of to the Indians, one third part water," 103. Logan says that this order was an attempt to halt Indian drunkenness at the fort. Workers there more often than not diluted the whiskey two thirds. Logan, 256-257.
9. A separate trading house was arranged at the fort. For a vivid description of a busy day's bartering there, see Logan, 252-253. For the attack on the burdeners in 1717, that resulted in the loss of 770 skins and in the death of several burdeners, see Logan, 263-264.
10. *Ibid.*
11. The price list is given in the June 30, 1718, entry of the *Journals of the Commissioners*. On July 19, 1718, William Hatton, Hasting's successor, asked that the list be revised to compete with prices used by Virginia traders in the area, 306.
12. Duncan D. Wallace, *South Carolina*, 33-44, 125-130.
13. It is interesting to note that the white man constructed his Georgia to Tennessee railroad over sections of this ancient trail from Keowee to the Over Hill Towns.
14. "Journal," *Early Travels in the Tennessee Country*, 192.
15. *History of the Dividing Line*, 298.
16. "Introduction" to Adair's *History*, IX.
17. Logan, 321-322; Sadie S. Patton, *The Story of Henderson County*, 37.
18. Logan, Chap. 12.
19. Milling, 268. See also Logan, 167-203.
20. Sadie S. Patton, *Sketches of Polk County*, 136.
21. Byrd, 246.
22. While the factor made reports and occasionally went to the fort, the Board appointed Ludovick Grant as reporter. His duty was to keep Charles Town informed of events taking place in the Cherokee country. He served in that capacity for many years and to his accounts the modern historian is indebted for much information.
23. For a brief biographical sketch of James Adair, see S. C. Williams's "Introduction" to Adair's *History*.
24. Mooney, 34.
25. His "Journal" is given in *Early Travels in the Tennessee Country*, 63-104.
26. Logan, Chap. XII. James Adair deplored the influx of unscrupulous traders into the Indian nations. See his *History*, 444-445.
27. Ludovick Grant wrote the account of the Keowee incident, asking that the traders present sign it with him as proof to the Board that the incredible event actually took place. For that account, see *Early Travels in the Tennessee Country*, footnote, 133.
28. *Early Travels in the Tennessee Country*, 136.
29. The picture shows the Cherokees stiff and unnatural in their English finery—and a bit frightened.
30. The terms of the treaty are given in *Early Travels in the Tennessee Country*, 138-143.
31. Ludovick Grant had earlier been given the task of arresting Priber, but had failed. On December 12, 1739, the Commons House of the Assembly of South Carolina ordered that Colonel Joseph Fox and two men be paid

of South Carolina ordered that Colonel Joseph Fox and two men be paid 402 pounds for "going to the Cherokees to fetch down Dr. Priber." *Journals of the Commons House of South Carolina,* II, 111.
32. Priber's reply was "We have a succession of agents to take up the work as fast as others leave. We never lose sight of a favorite point; nor are we bound by the strict rules of morality in the means when the end we pursue is laudable." Quoted by Sondley, I, 201. For Ludovick Grant's account of Priber's elaborate plans for an Indian confederacy, see Adair, footnote, 252-253. Antoine Bonnefoy, one of three Frenchmen captured in Ohio by the Cherokees and held as slaves in the home of an Over Hill chief from 1741 to 1742, recorded in the account of his experiences that Priber, visiting in the Indian home, asked the three Frenchmen to join his "society." He told them of his plans for an Indian empire and explained the system of government he proposed to put into operation in it. These rather full details tally with those given by Grant and Adair. Priber, in introducing himself to these Frenchmen, called himself Pierre Albert. See Bonnefoy's "Journal" in *Travels in the Tennessee Country,* 149-162.
33. Priber was a controversial figure to his contemporaries and he has remained so. Ludovick Grant wrote the account of his schemes and his arrest. So did Adair. Grant saw no good in the man, but Adair was charmed with the spy's personality and was challenged by his intellect. For a year—until the Indians got suspicious of the exchange of letters—he wrote to this German in the pay of France. A letter from Frederica, printed in the *South Carolina Gazette* of August 15, 1743, is gleeful over the arrest of Priber and points out the wickedness of his plans for his "Paradise." Yet the writer admits that the empire idea "has several flights full of invention" and charitably concludes, "It is a pity so much wit is applied to so bad a purpose." Adair, 253.

CHAPTER 5
Lightnings Flash and Thunders Roll

1. *History of the Dividing Line,* 246.
2. "Account," *Early Travels in the Tennessee Country,* 204-207.
3. Sondley, II, 514.
4. Milling, 281-282. See also Logan, 417-443.
5. Milling, 283-285.
6. Over a period of years letters of advice and protest had been sent to officials by these traders. On April 14, 1746, such communications were read in the House of Commons from Beamer, Grant, Dougherty, and Bunning. *Journal of the Commons House,* VI, 187-188. David H. Corkran gives a detailed account of the affair at Stecoe in an article, "The Unpleasantness at Stecoe, North Carolina," *N.C.H.R.,* XXXII (July, 1955), 358-375.
7. Governor Glenn, attended by a company of soldiers and some fifty civilians, made the trip to the capital of the Lower Towns. He bought several thousand acres of land on the Keowee River, refusing to accept the plot as a gift from the Cherokees. He remained in the Indian country while the fort was being built. It was a square structure, with

the plot as a gift from the Cherokees. He remained in the Indian country while the fort was being built. It was a square structure, with sides about two hundred feet in length and was constructed of earth and timbers. The fort itself was allowed to fall into decay so that in three years it was in ruins, although the barracks were still usable. Wallace, 171.
8. This treaty was signed on July 2, 1755. Under its terms the land was ceded to the king of England and for it the Cherokees received presents worth less than $350. David D. Wallace, *South Carolina*, 173.
9. deBrahm had been an engineer in the German Imperial Army. He was surveyor-general of Georgia in 1755, when South Carolina employed him to build adequate ramparts at Charles Town after the older ones had been destroyed by a hurricane. Wallace, 172.
10. *Early Travels in the Tennessee Country*, 187-194.
11. "Introduction," *Early Travels in the Tennessee Country*, 188.
12. Milling, 287.
13. Timberlake, *Memoirs*, 97-99.
14. Milling, 281-285.
15. This log structure was soon destroyed by the Cherokees. Wallace, 173.
16. R. D. W. Connor, *The Colonial and Revolutionary Periods*, 257. Virginia and South Carolina passed similar measures. Mismanagement characterized the trade with all Indians within these colonies, although Atkins singled out South Carolina's trade with the Cherokees for special criticism. He was given the task of unifying the trade. After a study of conditions, he reported to "the Right Honourable the Lords Commissioners For Trade and Plantations" [sic], submitting his "Plan of a general Direction and Management of the Indian Affairs throughout North America under one uniform Regulation of their Commerce, for retrieving and establishing the British Interest among the Indian nations, and thereby the future Security of our Colonies against the Designs of the French." [sic] The plan is signed Edmond Atkin. [sic]
17. Adair, *History*, 266.
18. Milling, 293; Connor, 280.
19. See his "Account," *Early Travels in the Tennessee Country*, 177-184.
20. Milling, 296-297; Wallace, 173-178. Wallace says there were 31 Cherokees in the delegation.
21. Wallace, *South Carolina, A Short History*, 171.
22. *Ibid*, 178-179; Milling, 296-297; Mooney, 4-42.
23. Milling, 298-310; Wallace, 179.
24. Milling, 302-303; Wallace, 179-180.
25. Milling, 303; Wallace, 180; Mooney, 42ff.
26. Milling, 304-305; Wallace, 180-182; Adair, 259-273.
27. See note 26.
28. Adair is accredited with being the first to write the name French with the Broad River west of the Blue Ridge, saying "It is natural for strangers to drink thereof, to quench thirst, gratify their curiosity, and have it to say they had drank [sic] of the French waters." *History*, 243. Sondley says the French had earlier called the river the Frank River. *Buncombe County*, II, 580.

CHAPTER 6
The Lull Between the Storms

1. *History of the Dividing Line,* 246.
2. Except for Byrd's estimate, the population figures are from Mooney, 31-34. Adair says that the small-pox epidemic of 1738 reduced the Cherokee population one half. *History,* 244.
3. Bartram says that before it was destroyed by Montgomery, Keowee extended six to eight miles along the river. The village was in ruins when he was there. *Travels in North and South Carolina,* 271.
4. For twenty-five years the Over Hill Towns had been the fertile soil for the seeds of French propaganda and in spite of Old Hopp's efforts, the Over Hill Cherokees became and remained strongly pro-French. It seems somewhat ironic, then, that of all the Cherokee towns, only these Over Hill villages should have been spared in the Cherokee War.
5. Timberlake, *Memoirs,* 26-56.
6. Timberlake has left one of the most valuable sources of information concerning the Cherokees during the late trading period. See his *Memoirs,* 57-103.
7. *Ibid.,* 115-148. Timberlake sacrificed his inherited estate and his small fortune to serve his colony and England. He received practically no recompense from either Virginia or the mother country and he died in England in poverty. *The Gentleman's Magazine* carried this notice of his death: "Died, September 30, 1765, Lieut. Henry Timberlake of the 42 Regiment. He came in with the Cherokee Indians, and attended them." XXXIV, 491. Quoted by S. C. Williams, who edited Timberlake's *Memoirs,* footnote, 175.
8. Mooney, 45-46.
9. Theodore Roosevelt, *The Winning of the West,* I, 187-188, 193 ff.; Felix Alley, *Random Thoughts and the Musings of a Mountaineer,* 302-303.
10. Tryon made a colorful military parade out of the trip from his "Palace" to the mountains of Western North Carolina. He was escorted by two regiments of militia, sixteen servants and aides, and two surveyors—altogether, some 100 persons. The two surveyors, with their Indian assistants, did most of the actual work after Tryon and the regiments had returned east. Carrying out the King's orders cost the colony the substantial sum of 1,490 pounds sterling, a sum that brought bitter complaints from the taxpayers, especially those in the "back country," where frontier conditions made money a rare commodity, indeed. Lefler and Newsome, 172.
11. Sondley, II, 514; Samuel A'C. Ashe, *A History of North Carolina,* I, 332-333.
12. John P. Arthur, *History of Watauga County,* 19. It was in such a herder's cabin that Boone is thought to have found shelter on some of his trips west of the Blue Ridge.
13. "Journal," *Early Travels in the Tennessee Country,* 193.
14. In 1771 the colony's population was estimated at 250,000. In the century preceding the Revolutionary War the population of North Carolina increased ninefold, making it the fourth most thickly populated colony. Lefler and Newsome, 71.

15. Ashe, I, 208-288; Sondley, I, 362-372; Lefler and Newsome, 71-81.
16. Lefler and Newsome, 77-78; Chalmers G. Davidson, *Piedmont Partisan*, 1-14; *Colonial Records*, IV, p. XXI.
17. On his vast stretch of land, Granville established a territorial system of land tenure. Settlers receiving grants paid annual quit-rents. These, they claimed, were exorbitant. The tract, which was subject neither to England nor to the colony, was a constant source of irritation to North Carolina. The settlers within it paid no taxes to the colony and the colony had no authority to deal with trouble arising between settlers over irregularities in land grants. There was much dishonesty in the dealings of Granville's agents in connection with both the settlers and Granville. When men crossed the Blue Ridge to make their homes in the lands to the west and learned that they were in North Carolina, they ignored the fact that they were in the Granville District, leasing their area from the Cherokees. E. M. Coulter, "The Granville District," J.S.H.P., XIII, 35-51; Alonzo T. Dill, *Tryon and His Palace*, 96-97.
18. "Spangenberg Diary," *Records of the Moravians*, I, 28-64; quotation, 43. The Spangenberg trip and the Moravian settlement that followed is presented by Adelaide Fries in her *Road to Salem*. The book is based upon the *Autobiography* of Anna Catherine Antes, who went to Bethabara in April, 1759, as the wife of the settlement's physician, Martin Kalberlahn. Her *Autobiography*, now in the Salem Moravian Archives, covers events in the first temporary stockaded village and in Salem from 1759 until 1803. While the Moravian settlement was a religion-centered, communal organization and not actually in Western North Carolina, the conditions these men and women found and the economic pattern of living they developed were repeated by settlers moving farther west to the foothills of the Blue Ridge and by those crossing the mountains to the valleys beyond.
19. "The Bethabara Diary." *Records of the Moravians*, 117-216, 227-238. The account of the journey of the "Brethern" from Pennsylvania to Wachovia is also given in *Travels in the American Colonies*, 327-356. See also John H. Clewell, *A History of Wachovia in North Carolina*, 4-18, and Fries, *Road to Salem*.
20. In that year, 1769, Boone went with a party that included Finley into Kentucky. He was asked by Finley to be the guide, since he knew the country. John Bakeless, *Daniel Boone*, 45-48; Arthur, *Watauga County*, 29-52; Roosevelt, I, 135-146.
21. Bakeless, 23.
22. Roosevelt, I, 166-175; Chap. VII; North Callahan, *Smoky Mountain Country*, 1-9; William E. Fitch, *The Battle of Alamance*, 42-55.
23. Roosevelt, I, 177-180.
24. *Ibid.*, 180-183; Lyman Draper, *King's Mountain and Its Heroes*, 418-422; Carl S. Driver, *John Sevier: Pioneer of the Old Southwest*.
25. Dill, 135; Davidson, Chap. III.
26. This act of violence, according to one account, gave the term "lynching" to the American language.
27. For accounts of the Battle of Alamance, see *Records of the Moravians*, I, 473-474, 450-476; R. D. W. Connor, *Rebuilding an Ancient Commonwealth*, I, 264-288; Lefler and Newsome, 171-178; Ashe, I, 340-342; Fitch, Chaps.

410 / Notes

I-II; William S. Powell, *The War of the Regulation;* Howard White, *The Battle of Alamance.*
28. Roosevelt, I, 183-185; Connor, I Chap. XIV.

CHAPTER 7
A New Flag for Western North Carolina

1. Lefler and Newsome, 191-192; Ashe, I, 437-459. For the document as written from memory see *Colonial Records,* IX, 1263-1265; *History Told By Contemporaries,* 99-100; *Mecklenburg in the Revolution,* 27-29; George W. Graham, *The Mecklenburg Declaration of Independence.*
2. On August 8, Governor Josiah Martin denounced the action of the people of Mecklenburg. For the *Resolves,* see *Colonial Records,* IX, 1282-1285; *History Told by Contemporaries,* 100-103; *Mecklenburg in the Revolution,* 34-41; Ashe, I, 450-453.
3. Lefler and Newsome, 197-198; 215-218.
4. These desperadoes increased in numbers as war entered the counties east of the Blue Ridge in 1780, and the mountains became hideouts for individuals and gangs. Davidson, Chap. V; Fries, *Road to Salem.*
5. Roosevelt, I, 249; Bakeless, 66-88; Stewart White, *Daniel Boone: Wilderness Scout,* 148-149. It was to make possible the migration to Transylvania that Boone and eight companions hacked out the Wilderness Trail. A few months later Henderson and his settlers actually took wagons over it. Bakeless, 93. The governors of both Virginia and North Carolina declared Henderson's treaty null and void. Connor, I, 295.
6. Roosevelt, I, 278-279. A print coming out of this attempt of the English to enlist Indians against the colonists shows an Indian presenting the scalps of white men to an English officer.
7. *Ibid.,* I, 281-282; Clarence W. Griffin, *History of Old Tryon and Rutherford Counties,* 34, 36.
8. Roosevelt, I, 283-294.
9. *Ibid.;* Ashe, I, 549-550; Samuel C. Williams, *The Lost State of Franklin,* 28.
10. Patton, *The Story of Henderson County,* 86-88.
11. Alley, *Random Thoughts,* 304.
12. The Department of Conservation and Development, cooperating with the State Department of Archives and History, has erected markers along the route taken by Rutherford and his army. The first is at Swannanoa Gap.
13. Connor, I, 406-407; Ashe, I, 547-553; Milling, 314-324; Griffin, 33-35.
14. Roosevelt says that Rutherford lost three men and that he killed twelve Indians. *Winning of the West,* I, 302. Ashe says that he also took nine prisoners. *History,* I, 547.
15. Ashe, I, 553; Ashe, "Rutherford's Expedition Against the Indians, 1776," *N.C.B.,* IV (December, 1904), 3-28. Moore's account of his mission is given in *Colonial Records,* X, 895-896.
16. This guerrilla band was led by Alexander Cameron, who had been deputy Indian agent.
17. Roosevelt, I, 302; Lefler and Newsome, 228.

18. Felix B. Alley, *Random Thoughts and Musings of a Mountaineer*, 305-306; Mooney, 53.
19. Mooney, 53; Sondley, I, 378 ff.
20. Sondley, I 378 ff.; Lefler and Newsome, 228; Archibald Henderson, "The Treaty of the Long Island," *N.C.H.R.*, III (January, 1931), 55-116.
21. Williams, *Lost State of Franklin*, 2.
22. Lefler and Newsome, 229.
23. *Ibid.*, 230-231; Griffin, 52; *Mecklenburg in the Revolution*, 53; Davidson, *Piedmont Partisan*, Chap. V.
24. Lefler and Newsome, 232-233.
25. *Ibid.*, 232-233; *Mecklenburg in the Revolution*, 54-56; Davidson, Chap. VI.
26. Lefler and Newsome, 233; Griffin, 52-58; Draper, 144-146.
27. Griffin, 54-56; Draper, 147-149; Lieutenant Anthony Allaire of Ferguson's forces recorded in his diary the movements and activities of that army through the land just east of the Blue Ridge. The *Diary* is given in Draper, *King's Mountain and Its Heroes*, 484-515.
28. Roosevelt, II, 242-254; Lefler and Newsome, 233; Griffin, 58-59; Draper, 169-174.
29. Roosevelt, II, 255-263; Griffin, 59-60; Draper, 175-187. Shepherd Dugger in his *War Trails of the Blue Ridge* gives a detailed account of the route of the mountain men. See Chaps. I-II.
30. For the detailed movements of both Ferguson's troops and those of the mountain men, see Draper, 199-222; Lefler and Newsome, 233-235.
31. Draper, 233-309; Driver, Chap. III; Davidson, 85-90; Ashe, I, 629-636; Connor, I, 355-358; Roosevelt, II, 272 ff. For the official report of the losses at this battle, see *Colonial Records*, XV, 163-165.
32. Lefler and Newsome, 235-238. During the entire Revolutionary War, men enlisted as volunteers in the forces furnished by the state to the Continental Line. Some were drafted. Others were members of local militia and saw service in their areas. In addition, men casually joined organized units for guerrilla warfare under one of the partisan officers dogging the British army. Still others joined to accomplish some specific objective. When that had been accomplished or the local campaign was over, they drifted back home. After the defeat at Camden, men straggled back to the "back country" and the mountains. McDowell's men made up such a group, and if Ferguson had not arrived, the men would have returned to their homes. In July, Isaac Shelby had led a band across the mountains to badger Ferguson's forces. Then they had returned home. Like the mountain men at the Battle of King's Mountain, most of these in the guerrilla bands were not, technically, in the army. Roosevelt, II, 248-251.

CHAPTER 8
East-West Tug-of-War

1. Arthur, *Watauga County*, 182; Dugger, 15.
2. The executions took place after a court martial, presided over by two men appointed as justices. Thirty-two men were condemned to death,

but after nine had been hanged, Colonel Shelby stopped the atrocities. The most prominent citizen losing his life was Colonel Ambrose Mills, a respected settler of Rutherford County. Draper, 330-343.
3. Roosevelt, II, 262-293; Griffin, 67-70.
4. Roosevelt, II, 295-323; Milling, 326 ff.; Mooney, 57-59; Driver, Chap. II.
5. Alley, 308-309; Mooney, 56-16, 75-76.
6. The Bonus Act, passed by the General Assemby in 1780, since it opened Cherokee land to veterans, made necessary the repeal of the Treaty of the Long Island of 1777. Lefler and Newsome, 241-242.
7. Roosevelt, II, 295-323. The Dumplin Creek Treaty is given in *State Records,* XXII, 649-650, also in *History Told by Contemporaries,* 72-73. See also Williams, *The Lost State of Franklin,* 75-86.
8. For the text of this treaty see *Indian Affairs: Laws and Treaties,* II, 8-11.
9. Ashe, I, 549-550; Lefler and Newsome, 259.
10. Roosevelt, II, 295-323; Williams, 165-171; Driver, Chap. II.
11. Williams, 207-212; Mooney, 60; Driver, John Sevier, Chap. II.
12. Lefler and Newsome, 95-97. It took from twelve to fifteen days to get from the Watauga Settlements to a meeting of the General Assembly at an eastern town. If the roads were in bad condition—and they frequently were—it took longer. Williams, 37. For a first-hand description of the roads in 1795, see John Brown's "Journal of Travels in 1795," edited by A. R. Newsome, *N.C.H.R.,* XI (October, 1934), 284-313.
13. Lefler and Newsome, 300-301.
14. *Ibid.,* 106-114; Davidson, *Piedmont Partisan,* Chap. III.
15. Williams, *The History of the Lost State of Franklin,* 268-272, Chap. XXXIII; Driver, Chap. I.
16. Lefler and Newsome, 218-221, 251-252; Ashe, II, 5-6; *Records of the Moravians,* II, 627-633; Griffin, 86. The basic issues in this east-west struggle are discussed by Connor in his *Rebuilding an Ancient Commonwealth, I, 469-474.*
17. Charles Beard and Mary Beard, *Basic History of the United States,* 179-181.
18. Williams, 18-25.
19. Lefler and Newsome, 258-259.
20. For Martin's letter of censure, see *State Records,* XXII, 642-647. See also Williams, 65-69.
21. The most detailed account of the stormy times in the struggle of the Washington District to become a state is given by Williams. See his *Lost State of Franklin,* Chaps. IV-XVI. See also Driver, Chap. V.
22. Williams, 193-204; Driver, Chap. V.
23. Williams, 193-204, 226-228, 119-121; Driver, Chap. V.
24. Driver, Chap. V.
25. The brief—and lost—state of Franklin, developing out of geographic conditions and local interests, makes a colorful, if stormy, chapter in the history of Western North Carolina. For other treatments of it, see Fitch, *The Origin, Rise, and Fall of the State of Franklin;* Connor, I, 408-412; Ashe, II 35-41, 51, 58-69.
26. Lefler and Newsome, 268-269.

CHAPTER 9
In Search of Beauty—An Interlude

1. George W. McCoy, "Wedgwood Used Western North Carolina Clay in Making Famous Ware," *Asheville Citizen-Times*, August 13, 1950; J. P. Brady, "Wedgwood Wrought His Genius in Clay From Macon County," *Asheville Citizen-Times*, October 20, 1956.
2. McCoy; Brady.
3. Louise B. Fisher, *An Eighteenth Century Garland*, 9-10.
4. *Ibid.*, 75; Charles Shull, *The Lure of Western North Carolina For the Explorer-Naturalists.*
5. Sondley, II, 522; *The Dictionary of American Biography*, II, 28.
6. The sections of his travel account dealing with Western North Carolina cover pages 263-302. This section furnished the Bartram material in this chapter. His papers and notebooks give 1775 as the year of his travels.
7. *Travels*, page 279.
8. Sondley, II, 519-522; *The Dictionary of American Biography*, XII, 591-592; Andre Michaux, "Travels," *Early Travels in the Tennessee Country*, 329-342.
9. Sondley, II, 519-522.
10. *Ibid.*, 522; Shull.

CHAPTER 10
With Their Goods and Chattels

1. Lefler and Newsome, 241-242.
2. *Ibid.*, 291. For the text of thest treaties, see *Indian Affairs*, 11, 29-33; 51-55.
3. Cordelia Camp, *Burke County Sketches*, 6.
4. Griffin, 7-8.
5. *Ibid.*, 42-45.
6. George H. Smathers, *The Story of Land Titles in Western North Carolina*, 10-15; 20-22; David L. Corbett, *The Formation of North Carolina Counties*, 11-17, 38-48; 188-192; 227-238.
7. Arthur, *Watauga County*, 19.
8. Jason B. Deyton, "The Toe River Valley to 1865," *N.C.H.R.*, XXIV (October, 1947), 428-438.
9. Sondley, I, 396-398, 420-421.
10. The grant given to Burton is given in Sondley, II, 838, and in Smathers, 42. For the grant to William Moore, see Smathers, 31-32, and for the one to Davidson, see Smathers, 9. Other early grants are given by Smathers, 42-43; 50-52.
11. Patton, *The Story of Henderson County*, 20-25, 27-32; Allen, Chap. 11.
12. Allen, *The Annals of Haywood County*, 35-39.
13. Sondley, I, 444-447.
14. *Ibid.*
15. "John Brown's Journal of Travel in 1795", in *N.C.H.R.*, Vol. XI, (October, 1934), 304.
16. *Ibid.*

414 / Notes

17. Patton, *Pages From the History of Speculation Land;* Patton, *Sketches of Polk County History,* 11-19; Arthur, *Western North Carolina,* 135-141.
18. Allen, *The Annals of Haywood County,* Chaps. II, VI.

CHAPTER 11
Weaving a Homespun Pattern of Living

1. Sondley, I, 398 ff., 428-441.
2. The pioneers were faced with the necessity of constructing their first homes in the shortest possible time, and they considered these structures temporary. The size of each house was determined not by the number of members in the family, but by the length of the logs to be used. Twenty-four feet made logs about as long as would insure uniformity of size and about as long as could easily be handled. However, many of the mountain cabins, perhaps most of the earliest ones, were not twenty-four feet long. Frances Johnston and Thomas T. Waterman, *The Early Architecture of North Carolina,* 3. See also Patton, *Henderson County,* 17-18; Arthur, *Western North Carolina,* 256-259, 263-264; Davidson, 6-7.
3. Alley, 257; Davidson, 6-7.
4. Alley, 260-271; Sondley, I, 427-430; Davidson, 6-7.
5. Williams, Chap. XXXIII; Arthur, *Western North Carolina,* Chap. XI; D. J. Whitener, *The History of Watauga County,* 29-41.
6. Griffin, 120, 144; Sondley, I, 481, II, 711-723.
7. Sondley, I, 398, 400.
8. Patton, *Henderson County,* 24.
9. Sondley, I, 402-404.
10. *Ibid.,* I, 339-400; Griffin, 52, 82, 141-143; Arthur, 284. John Brown's "Journal" in *N.C.H.R.,* vol. XI, 304. Used with permission.
11. Arthur, *Western North Carolina,* 284; Sondley, II, 497-500; Patton, *Henderson County,* 26-27; Guion G. Johnson, *Ante-Bellum North Carolina: A Social History,* 105-110; *John Brown's Journal.*
12. "Diary of a Journey of Moravians From Bethlehem, Pennsylvania, to Wachovia, North Carolina," *Travels in the American Colonies,* 350.
13. Whitener, 28-29; Arthur, *Western North Carolina,* 82-83.
14. Arthur, *op. cit.,* 232-235.
15. Sondley, II, 608-610.
16. *Ibid.,* II, 463; 600-606.
17. Francis Asbury, *Journal,* II, 481.
18. *Ibid.*
19. *Ibid.,* III, 91, 134. For the conditions of the roads, see John Brown's "Journal of Travels in 1795," *N.C.H.R.,* XI (October, 1934), 284-313.
20. Griffin, 2.
21. *Ibid.,* 149-150.
22. Asbury, II, 189.
23. Susan F. Cooper (ed.), *William West Skiles,* 10.
24. Lefter and Newsome, 250-251.
25. Griffin, 5, 584-587; Camp, 13-14.
26. George W. McCoy, *The First Presbyterian Church, Asheville, North Carolina,* 4-12.

27. Charles B. Williams, *A History of the Baptists in North Carolina*, 19-20.
28. Griffin, 587.
29. Williams, 100-107; Arthur, *Western North Carolina*, 223-226; Arthur, *Watauga County*, 71-77; 98-113.
30. Williams, 107; Sondley, II, 780-781.
31. Griffin, 590-592.
32. Asbury, II, 77.
33. Camp, 13-14.
34. Sondley, II, 676-685.
35. Patton, *Henderson County*, 27-32.
36. *Ibid. 1.*, 30; Sondley, II, 708; Johnson, *Ante Bellum North Carolina*, 370-402.
37. Asbury, *Journal*, II, 133.
38. Arthur, *Western North Carolina*, 421-423; Clement Dowd, *Zebulon Baird Vance*, 12.
39. Camp, 12.
40. Griffin, 151.
41. Sondley, II, 705-708; McCoy, 4-12.
42. When in 1776 the Watauga Settlement petitioned the General Assembly to be recognized as a part of North Carolina under the name of Washington District, the petition was signed by 463 settlers. Only ten of them had to use marks. See Williams, *The Lost State of Franklin*, Appendix B; *State Records*, XXII, 705-714.

CHAPTER 12
Boundaries and Western Leadership

1. North Carolina's commissioners were Christopher Gale, Edward Moseley, William Little, and John Lovick. The surveyors were Samuel Swann and Edward Moseley. At the place from which the Virginians turned back east, Byrd wrote: "Hereabouts from one of the Highest hills, we made the first Discovery of the Mountains, on the Northwest of our course ... They looked like Ranges of Blue clouds rising one above the other." [sic] *History of the Dividing Line*, 194. This early colonial survey is perhaps the best known one in American history due to Byrd's record of it. Written in an urbane, ironic style copied from eighteenth century English writers, it was the first writing produced in the colonies to have literary value. The mileage figures have been differently given. The one used here is from Lefler and Newsome, 66-67. See Connor, I, 5-9.
2. William K. Boyd, *The Federal Period*, 74-76.
3. Arthur, *Western North Carolina*, 37-38; Arthur, *Watauga County*, 117-121, John Strother, *Diary and Field Notes*, 1799.
4. The "Rainbow" dispute was not settled until 1914. Arthur, *Western North Carolina*, 48-49; *The Papers of Archibald D. Murphey*, II, 119; 190.
5. Lefler, *History of North Carolina*, II, 172-173; Lefler and Newsome, 149-152; Arthur, *Western North Carolina*, 28-32; Connor, I, 5-9; Wallace, Chap. XX. A detailed study of the North Carolina-South Carolina dispute over their common boundary is given by M. L. Skaggs in his *The North Carolina Boundary Disputes Involving Her Southern Line*, part I.
6. Skaggs, part II; Arthur, *Western North Carolina*, 32-37; Connor, I, 5-9; D.

R. Goodloe, "North Carolina and the Georgia Line," *N.C.B.*, no. 12, 1-22; *Papers of Archibald D. Murphey*, II, 189-190; E. M. Coulter, *Georgia: A Short History*, 223.
7. Arthur, *Western North Carolina*, 51-55. The text of this treaty settling this boundary is given in *Indian Affairs*, II, 72-73. For a history of the difficulties arising over the Meigs-Freeman line, involving a long series of law suits, see Smathers, *The History of Land Titles in Western North Carolina*, 59-132.
8. *The Formation of North Carolina Counties*, 11-17.
9. Lefler and Newsome, 294-297; Griffin, 155-162.
10. Ashe, II, 235; Mooney, 93-96.
11. Connor, I, 443-474; Lefler and Newsome, Chap. 20; Griffin, 167-168.
12. United States Census for 1790 and 1830.
13. These lists of slaves are among the McDowell family papers, now in possession of Miss Margaret Ligon of Asheville.
14. Lefler and Newsome, 298-302.
15. *Ibid.*, 303-304; In urging his program of internal improvements, Murphey admitted that "few men have the courage to impose taxes." *Papers of Archibald Murphey*, II, 179. In 1817 the state received from the western counties of Ashe, Burke, Rutherford, Wilkes, Buncombe, and Haywood a total of $4483.14 in taxes. Murphey, II, 171.
16. Lefler and Newsome, 308-311; Ashe, II, 200-201; Connor, I, 469-474.
17. Lefler and Newsome, 304-306; Griffin, 163-169. The census of 1850 showed that one third of all natives of North Carolina then living in the United States lived in states other than North Carolina. Some 400,000 had left the state. Connor, *Ante Bellum Builders of North Carolina*, 24.
18. Connor, *op. cit.*, 18, 24, 33-62; Connor, *Rebuilding an Ancient Commonwealth*, I, 475-495; Ashe, II, 246-249; Lefler, *History of North Carolina*, I, 309-315; Boyd, 91-100.
19. *The Papers of Archibald D. Murphey*, II, 189.
20. The "Memoir" is given in full in *The Papers of Archibald D. Murphey*, II, 103-195.
21. Murphey, "Report of the Committee on Public Education, December 19, 1816," *Papers of Archibald D. Murphey*, II, 49-56; *History of North Carolina Told by Contemporaries*, 164-168; Lefler, I, 315-319; Boyd, 101-104; M.C.S. Noble, *A History of the Public Schools of North Carolina*, 34-42. From 1790 to 1802 the General Assembly considered not one bill relating to education and the same can be said of it from 1804 to 1815. Connor, *Ante Bellum Builders*, 15.
22. Between 1776 and 1833, eighteen new counties were established in the piedmont and mountain sections of the state, and fifteen were established in the eastern section. Yet between 1790 and 1840 the population of the piedmont and mountain sections increased 156 per cent, while that of the eastern section increased 53 per cent. Connor, *op. cit.*, 29. For western legislators to get a bill passed creating a new county it was necessary for them to vote for a new eastern county; moreover, they were forced to have their new counties named for eastern leaders. Boyd, pp. 147-148. See also Boyd, 139-165; Lefler and Newsome, 307-311. For the Constitution of 1776, see *State Records*, XXIII, 980-984. It is also given in *History of North Carolina Told by Contemporaries*, 105-111.

Notes / 417

23. Lefler and Newsome, 332-336; The Constitution of 1776; Connor, *Ante Bellum Builders,* 25-26.
24. Ashe, II, 255-260; Lefler and Newsome, 316-317.
25. Griffin, 186-187.
26. Ashe, II, 277.
27. *Ibid.,* II, 290, 305.
28. *Ibid.,* II, 293-295; Lefler and Newsome, 317-318; Noble, *A History of the Public Schools,* chap. V.
30. Connor, *Ante Bellum Builders,* 66-95; Lefler and Newsome, 326-331; Ashe, II, 350-363; Sondley, II, 765-767.
31. Lefler and Newsome, 334-337.
32. *Ibid.;* Ashe, II, Chap. XXIII. For the voting returns by counties, see *North Carolina Manual, 1913,* 1010-1013.
33. Lefler and Newsome, 337-341; Connor, *Rebuilding an Ancient Commonwealth,* I, 518-536; Ashe, II, Chap. XXII.

CHAPTER 13
Gold in the Hills and on the Highways

1. Lefler and Newsome, 371-372; Griffin, 195. The name Dahlonega, site of the rich Georgia gold mines, is a corruption of the Cherokee word *tah lo ne ga,* meaning yellow or gold colored. Lanman. "Letters From the Alleghany Mountians," *Adventures in the Wilds of the United States,* I, 344. See also T. Conn Bryan, *The Gold Rush in Georgia.*
2. Lefler and Newsome, 371; Fletcher M. Green, "Gold Mining: A Forgotten Industry of Ante Bellum North Carolina," *N.C.H.R.,* XIV (January, 1937), 7. According to tradition, the lump of gold ore was used for two or three years by the Reed family as a doorstop. Then the father, John Reed, sold it, returning home with $3.50. See Bruce Roberts' *The Carolina Gold Rush.*
3. These counties, listed by state geologists, are sections of Montgomery, Anson, Mecklenburg, Cabarrus, Randolph, Rowan, Davidson, Burke, Union, Stanley, Catawba, Guilford, and Rutherford. Adjacent areas in South Carolina produced limited amounts, while mines in northern Georgia were heavy producers and played a decisive part in the history of Western North Carolina from 1815 to 1838. Griffin, 195.
4. Bryan, *op. cit.;* Green, 8-9.
5. *The North Carolina Spectator and Western Advertiser,* March 26, 1830. In Griffin, 205.
6. Green, 12.
7. *Ibid.,* 15-17.
8. Various issues of *The North Carolina Spectator,* quoted by Griffin, 204-205.
9. Green, 152; Lefler and Newsome, 371.
10. Green, 138; Lefler and Newsome, 372. See Bruce Roberts, *The Carolina Gold Rush.*
11. Green, 138, 152, Griffin, 204-207; Lefler and Newsome, 371-372.
12. Bechtler's advertisement in the *North Carolina Spectator* of August 27, 1831. It is given by Griffin, 197-198.
13. *Ibid.*

418 / Notes

14. *Ibid.*, 196-204; Green, 139-145.
15. Griffin, 201-202; Green, 142-145.
16. Green, 140; Lefler and Newsome, 372; Roberts, 30.
17. For contemporary descriptions of the gold mines, Bechtler's mint, and the gold country, see *History of North Carolina Told by Contemporaries*, 244-249.
18. Lefler and Newsome, 316-317; Sondley, II, 617-619.
19. Sondley, II, 609.
20. *Journal*, 111, 133.
21. Sondley, II, 609, 617-619.
22. *Ibid.*, II, 619-621. Wilma Dykeman gives a vivid description of these autumn drives in her book *The French Broad*, Chap. 9.
23. Sondley, II, 619.
24. *Ibid.*, II, 619-621.
25. *Ibid.*
26. Arthur, *Watauga County*, 114-115; Griffin, 163.
27. Arthur, *Western North Carolina*, 239-240.
28. Small scattered passages pertaining to the Turnpike appeared in this author's *Spire in the Mountains*, pages 26-27. They are used with the permission of the First Presbyterian Church of Asheville, copyright holder.

CHAPTER 14.
Light and Shade in the Mountains

1. Sondley, II, 626.
2. Lefler and Newsome, 107-110; Johnston and Waterman, *Early Architecture in North Carolina*, 3-8.
3. Such a farmstead has been reconstructed by moving buildings from various farms to a site in the Floyd Bottoms, bordering the Oconaluftee River between the village of Cherokee and Smokemont Camping Grounds in the Smokies. This project, called the Pioneer Farmstead, consists of a house and some dozen out-buildings, the barn being the only structure originally on the site. After the Civil War, the Floyd farm was a stand for drovers bringing their cattle over the road that William H. Thomas and his Cherokee Legion had constructed across the Smokies by way of Indian Gap. George McCoy, "Farmstead Depicts Early Days in Western North Carolina," *Asheville Citizen-Times*, August 30, 1953.
4. Kephart, *Our Southern Highlanders* (1913 edition), 110-125.
5. Beard and Beard, *History of the United States*, 168.
6. Griffin, 142; Arthur, *Western North Carolina*, 284.
7. Griffin, 130, 136; Sondley, 11, 617-619.
8. Sondley, II, 622.
9. *Ibid.*, II, 621-622; Griffin, 184-186.
10. Ashe, II, Chap. XXV; Sondley, II, 621-622.
11. See note 10.
12. Deyton, "Toe River Valley," 450-454. Except for minor changes, this manner of life persisted in the isolated coves for a century. See Kephart (1913 edition), chaps. XI-XII.
13. Of necessity people learned to set bones and to care for the sick. Many women became expert nurses, and all learned to gather healing herbs.

For a list of these, see Johnson, *Ante Bellum North Carolina,* 752-753, and Patton, *Henderson County,* 56-58. A list of diseases suffered by mountain people and the names of physicians practicing in Asheville from 1793 to 1885 are given by G. S. Tennent in his *Medicine in Buncombe County Down to 1885.*

14. Guion G. Johnson, *Ante-Bellum North Carolina,* 309-330.
15. The Plott family in the Plott Balsam area have for generations been renowned as hunters. They developed a breed of fine hunting dogs known as Plott hounds. Of all the many hunters, however, perhaps the best known was Big Tom Wilson, whose hunting domain was the Black Mountain range. It was Wilson who located the body of Dr. Elisha Mitchell. See Chapter XVII.
16. Kephart (1913 edition), 305-353; (1922 edition), Chap. V.
17. *Ibid.* (1913 edition), 40-41; Deyton, 454.
18. Connor, *Ante Bellum Builders,* 87-88; Ashe, II, 374-375.
19. "Report of the President and Directors of the Literary Fund, November, 1838," *Beginnings of Public Education in North Carolina,* 827-850, 893-912; Lefler and Newsome, 350-352.
20. Lefler and Newsome, 350-352. The School Law of 1839 is given in *History Told By Contemporaries,* 188-189.
21. Deyton, 448.
22. Arthur, *Western North Carolina,* 420-447; Boyd, 243-251; Ashe, II, 406-407; Deyton, 448-449; Johnson, 309-330.
23. See his "Letters on Public Education," *The Beginnings of Public Education in North Carolina,* 548-613.
24. M. S. C. Noble, *A History of the Public Schools in North Carolina,* Chap. VI; Lefler and Newsome, 351-352.
25. Lefler and Newsome, 363; Connor, 95-100.
26. Noble, 145-187.
27. *Ibid.,* 210-229.
28. Deyton, 449.

CHAPTER 15.

The Crack of Doom in the Mountains

1. In addition to the treaties so far mentioned, the Cherokees in Tennessee lost land through treaties with the federal government in 1804 and 1805. See *Indian Affairs,* II, 82-91. On March 22, 1816, the Cherokees sold their remaining land in South Carolina to that state for $5,000. Mooney, 84, 97.
2. An account of this historic meeting has been left by an unknown writer. The complete manuscript is quoted by W. C. Allen in his *Annals of Haywood County,* 44-46. Alley has quoted it from Allen in his *Random Thoughts,* 327-328. It is also given in John Parris, *The Cherokee Story,* 35-37, and in Glenn Tucker, *Tecumseh,* 212-213.
3. Among Junaluska's volunteers were Sequoyah and John Ross. Jackson had Cherokees from the Lower Towns in his forces when Junaluska and his warriors joined the campaign. He also had a small number of Creeks loyal to the Americans. Of these Creeks, 5 lost their lives and 11 were wounded in the battle. Of the Cherokees, 18 were killed and 36

wounded. Mooney gives the total number of Indians with Jackson as 500. Some writers have given the number as 600. Mooney lists the casualties among the Creeks as follows; 557 warriors killed; 253 more shot in the water as they attempted to escape; 300 prisoners taken, mostly women and children. Only 20 men escaped. Of the Americans, 26 were killed and 107 wounded. Mooney, 87-97; Ashe, II, 235; R. S. Cotterill, *The Southern Indians,* 176-190; Marion L. Starkey, *The Cherokee Nation,* 22-26; H. C. Wilburn, *Junaluska,* 7-8.

4. There was some opposition within the Cherokee nation to this reorganization and to the constitution. Among those opposing both was the influential chief, White Path. This leader distrusted the Americans and foretold catastrophe to the Cherokees if they adopted American institutions and forms of government. He gained a small following of nationalists or anti-Americans, known as Red Sticks. However, sentiment in the nation as a whole was against White Path and he was deposed. He lived to see his prophesies come to pass and he trudged west with his people. He did not reach the new land, for he died on the way. Mooney, 106-114; Milling, 341-343.

5. In 1839 Robert Strange published a novel based on the Cherokee removal and named it for Yonaguska. He spelled the name *Eoneguski*. This was the first piece of fiction dealing with a North Carolina subject written by a North Carolinian. Lefler and Newsome, 389; Lanman, "Letters From the Alleghany Mountains," 417-421.

6. Alley, 328-330; Mooney, 164-165. It is possible that Junaluska was never chosen a chief. The title may well have been attached to his name out of respect for his achievements. See Wilburn, *Junaluska.*

7. Parris, 46; Mooney, 112-114; 224-225; Milling, Chap. XVII.

8. Parris, 51-58; Milling, 342-343; Starkey, Chap. V; George E. Foster, *Se-Quo-yah: The American Cadmus,* Chaps. VIII-IX; Mooney, 106-135.

9. Mooney, 111-112; Parris, Chaps. VII-VIII.

10. Parris, Chaps. VII-VIII; Mooney, 111-112. John Eliot in New England translated parts of the Bible into an Indian language or dialect in 1653, but did not, of course, work out an Indian written language.

11. Mooney, 109-110; Starkey, 99.

12. Mooney, 83-84, 112-114; Starkey, 29-42.

13. R. S. Cotterill, *The Southern Indians,* 191-210. The text of this treaty is given in *Indian Affairs,* II, 140-144.

14. Mooney, 106. For the text of this treaty, see *Indian Affairs,* II, 177-181.

15. Mooney, 116-127; Starkey, 100-118; Cotterill, 211-230.

16. See Note 15.

17. Mooney, 120; Grant Foreman, *Indian Removal,* 233, 238. The Indian tenure of lands in Georgia had been a festering sore with that state since its cession of western lands to the federal government. Georgia lost much land through this cession and was eager to open land within its borders to white settlements. The federal government in 1802 agreed, therefore, to move all Georgia Indians west as soon as such a step could be taken peaceably. By the time its gold mines attracted wide attention, Georgia felt that the removal was long overdue and that the national government was grossly negligent in fulfilling its promise. The state also resented the federal government's handling of the Native Americans since it led these unwanted residents of Georgia to expect permanent

occupancy of the lands that had once been the Over Hill and Lower Towns section of their nation. See E. M. Coulter, *Georgia: A Short History*, 223-237.
18. Mooney, 125-126; Starkey, 53-59, 118-129; Foreman, 265-269. The Treaty of New Echota is given in *Indian Affairs*, II, 439-449.
19. Milling, 349. Foreman, 272, gives this statement made by General Wool, "The whole scene since I have been in this country has been nothing but a heartrending one."
20. The treatment of the Cherokees from 1815 to 1839 is a dark blot on the history of the white man's relation with the Native Americans. It has been the subject of much research by scholars and has been the theme of much writing. Its dramatic features made it the subject of the first piece of North Carolina fiction produced by a North Carolinian on a topic concerning his own state, and the conflict has come to life for 4,000,000 people who have viewed Kermit Hunter's drama, *Unto These Hills*, presented each summer at the Mountainside Theater at Cherokee. For a detailed account of the removal and of the chain of events leading up to it, see Grant Foreman's *Indian Removal*. See also Starkey, Chaps. XV-XVIII; Thomas Parker, *The Cherokee Indians*, Chaps. III-IV; Milling, 332-382.
21. Parris, 71-77; Mooney, 157; Hunter, *Unto These Hills;* Milling, 368-370.
22. See Note 21.
23. Through the efforts of Samuel E. Beck of Asheville, a trustee of the Cherokee Historical Association, and Robert B. Barker, a lawyer in Washington, D. C., and a native of Andrews, official documents concerning the Indian removal were located in the War Department in 1957, some 119 years after the events they describe transpired. These documents, in the form of letters giving official reports of army officers, contain the story of Tsali's role in Cherokee history. Copies of these letters, presented to Mr. Beck, are now in the Cherokee Museum at Cherokee. The account given in this chapter is based upon the letters of Lieutenant Smith and Captain Larned to Colonel Foster and upon Colonel Foster's report to his superior officer, all of which were forwarded to General Scott. General Scott, in turn, sent the letters, together with a brief note, to Brigadier-General R. Jones, Adjutant General of the United States.
24. While the account given by the American officers removes the aura of martyrdom from Tsali, it confirms the fact that through his death a thousand Cherokees were allowed to stay in the mountains of Western North Carolina. It also confirms the fact that the younger son was allowed to survive.
25. Thomas's ability and sincerity were felt not only by the Cherokees, who had accepted him as a member of their nation and the adopted son of their beloved chief, but also by white men coming into the Indian country. In his report to General Scott, Colonel Foster wrote: "I should do my feelings great injustice were I to omit to represent to you, and through you to the government—Mr. Wm. E.[sic] Thomas in the most favorable light and as an individual deserving the confidence and patronage of the Country—both for himself—and the Oconolufty[sic] Indians—on whom he appears to exercise unbounded influence for good purpose."

26. It was barely ten years after the forlorn group of Cherokees straggled down from the hills that Charles Lanman made his horseback tour through Western North Carolina. As a guest of Thomas, he spent several days at Qualla, where he had the opportunity of studying conditions in the new nation. He found the Cherokees a well organized governmental unit with a practically self-sufficient economy. They raised their food, grain, vegetables, and fruits on their small, allotted farms and owned herds of cattle and their farm animals. They manufactured their guns and their plows, axes, and other tools. The women wove the cloth that they fashioned into clothing. The people, he learned, were temperate, moral, responsible in their obligations, and faithful to their professed religion. They had their own courts and kept up their own roads. In fact, he found the Cherokees the "happiest community that I have yet met in this Southern country." *Letters From the Alleghany Mountains,* 407-409.
27. In 1910 the General Joseph Winston Chapter, D.A.R., erected a marker at the tomb of Junaluska and his wife. It carries the following inscription: "Here lie the bodies of the Cherokee Chief Junaluska and his wife, Nicie. Together with his warriors, he saved the life of Andrew Jackson at Horse Shoe Bend, and for his bravery and faithfulness, North Carolina made him a citizen and gave him lands in Graham County. He died November 20, 1858, aged more than one hundred years." The date of Junaluska's birth is not known, but H. C. Wilburn, a student of Cherokee history, states that it is unlikely that he attained the age generally ascribed to him. See his *Junaluska.*

CHAPTER 16

More Government for Western North Carolina

1. Lefler and Newsome, 334. By 1830 the piedmont and mountain counties had a population of 374,092 as compared with 363,896 in the eastern counties. Between 1830 and 1840 the piedmont population gained rapidly, greatly widening the difference between the sections.
2. Such treaties were also opening Cherokee lands in Tennessee to white settlements.
3. Dowd, *Zebulon Baird Vance,* 149.
4. Colonel Joab L. Moore served as deputy sheriff. He was responsible to Colonel James McKee, sheriff of Haywood County. C. D. Smith, *A Brief History of Macon County,* I.
5. Mrs. Lester Conley, "Macon County Was Created in 1828," *Asheville Citizen-Times,* March 26, 1950; *The State,* July 4, 1942, 1-2, 17-18; June 26, 1943, 19-23, 28.
6. "Indian Mound Deeded to Macon Residents," *Asheville Citizen-Times,* October 13, 1946.
7. C. D. Smith, *A Brief History of Macon County.*
8. In 1867 General Thomas Clingman became interested in mines in the present Mitchell County, especially the Sink Hole and the Clarissa, believing that they might profitably be worked. He based his faith in their output upon the fact that a slab taken from one of them showed marks made by metal tools. These tools, he felt, had been those of early

Spanish prospectors. Deyton, 428; *Selections From the Writings of Thomas L. Clingman,* 130-133.
9. Deyton, 432 ff.; *The State Magazine,* May 2, 1942, 1-2, 16-18.
10. Deyton, 442-443.
11. Patton, *Henderson County,* 54-55.
12. *Ibid.,* 63, 88-90.
13. *Journal,* 111, 237.
14. Patton, *op. cit.,* 85-96.
15. *Ibid.,* chap. 7.
16. *The Formation of North Carolina Counties,* 62-64; Mrs. C. W. Savage, "Cherokee Was Named for Indians," *Asheville Citizen-Times,* March 26, 1950; Margaret W. Freel, *Our Heritage; The People of Cherokee County,* Chaps. I-V.
17. *The Formation of North Carolina Counties,* 51-54; Fred G. Mahler, "Created Out of Burke and Wilkes, Caldwell Established in 1841," *Lenoir News-Topic,* October 25, 1934; "Forts and Stockades Protected Citizens of Caldwell Territory From Threatened Invasion of Indian Attacks," *Lenoir News-Topic,* September 9, 1941; *The State Magazine,* September 26, 1936, 12-15; January 31, 1942, 1-3, 18-22; May 20, 1944, 16-24.
18. *The Formation of North Carolina Counties,* 142-144; "Interesting Facts About McDowell County," *Asheville Citizen-Times,* November 27, 1936; "McDowell County is Described by Story on Radio," Radio speech by Paul J. Story and reported in *Asheville Citizen-Times,* November 27, 1936; *The State Magazine,* December 25, 1937, 23-28; July 19, 1941, 3-6, 24-25; April 15, 1944, 18-24.
19. Whitener, *History of Watauga County,* 36-37.
20. *Ibid.,* Arthur, *Watauga County,* 114-116; *The Formation of North Carolina Counties,* 220-223.
21. Lefler and Newsome, 334; Appendix B.
22. *The Formation of North Carolina Counties,* 144; George W. McCoy, "Madison County to Mark Its Centennial," *Asheville Citizen-Times,* January 14, 1951; *The State Magazine,* April 25, 1942, 1-2, 16-19.
23. Parris, 93-97.
24. *The Formation of North Carolina Counties,* 129-130; John Parrish and Clarence Griffin, *Historical Sketch of Jackson County;* Larry W. Mull, "Jackson County," *Asheville Citizen-Times,* March 26, 1950; *The State Magazine,* June 27, 1942, 1-2, 16-18; July 3, 1943, 16-21.
25. Patton, *Sketches of Polk County,* 25-27; Griffin, 231-233.
26. Patton, *op. cit.,* 27-31; Chap. 4; Griffin, 233-236.
27. *The Formation of North Carolina Counties,* 4-7; *The State Magazine,* September 5, 1942, 1-2, 19-20.
28. Patton, *Henderson County,* 103-116; *The Formation of North Carolina Counties,* 204-205; Ora L. Jones, "Transylvania County—What it Was and Is," *Asheville Citizen-Times,* January 7-March 24, 1917; *The State Magazine,* June 20, 1942, 1-2, 16-18; June 19, 1942, 16-21.
29. *The Formation of North Carolina Counties,* 63-64; Mrs. Robert Penland, "Clay County Makes Progress," *Asheville Citizen-Times,* March 26, 1950; *The State Magazine,* October 4, 1941, 5-6, 20.
30. *The Formation of North Carolina Counties,* 53; *The State Magazine,* June 14, 1952. The laws creating many of these counties and those adjusting their boundary lines are given by Smathers in his *History of Land Titles,* 133-142.

CHAPTER 17.
The Lure of the Mountains

1. The Reverend Mr. Skiles described the people coming to his first service in these words: "Men and women came straggling in, many on foot, some on horseback, the wife in sun-bonnet and straight, narrow gown, riding behind her husband. Here and there a woman was seen mounted on a steer, with a child or two in her arms, while the husband, walking beside them, goad in hand, guided the animal over the rough path...There were many more feet than shoes in the congregation." Cooper, *A Sketch of a Missionary Life,* 6-13.
2. A. S. Merrimon, "Journal, 1853-54," *N.C.H.R.,* VIII (July, 1931), 318-329.
3. This organization was given the name of Little Brittain [sic] Temperance Society, Auxiliary to the American Temperance Society. A constitution was formulated and a record made by the secretary, Henry M. Kerr. The group had 87 members. Griffin, 179-181.
4. Johnson, 88-89. In 1859 F. L. Wilson of the *North Carolina Standard,* Raleigh newspaper, visited Asheville and seemed surprised to find that the westerners, instead of being savages, were "intelligent, high-minded, hospitable, and civilized." Quoted by Johnson, 34.
5. Sondley, II, 621-624.
6. "Letters From the Alleghany Mountains," 408-413.
7. Patton, *Henderson County,* 96-97; Wilbur Zeigler and Ben Grosscup, *In The Heart of the Alleghanies,* 350-351; Edward R. Memminger, *An Historical Sketch of Flat Rock.*
8. Patton, *Flat Rock,* 96-99.
9. *Ibid.,* 216-217; Memminger, *op. cit.*
10. The rectory was built between 1832 and 1836 for the Reverend T. W. S. Mott and it later became known as the Diamond-in-the-Desert. From it, according to tradition, the first Confederate flag displayed in Western North Carolina waved. Shortly after 1850, the Reverend John Grimke Drayton came to Flat Rock as a resident at Ravenwood and was for many years rector at St. John-in-the-Wilderness. Patton, *op. cit.,* 200-213.
11. It is said that the Fletcher Church, completed in 1857, owed its organization to a meeting of estate owners held in the back parlor of the home of Alexander Blake, who gave the land for the edifice.
12. A. W. Long, "History of Transylvania County," *Asheville Citizen-Times,* May 8, 1941.
13. The names given to a few of these estates were: Mountain Lodge, home of the Charles Barings, who later built Highland Lake; Argyle, home of Judge Mitchell King; The Meadows, home of Daniel Blake of Fletcher; Rock Hill, home of C. C. Memminger and later the home of Carl Sandburg and called Connemara; The Castle, home of Count Joseph Marie Gabriel St. Xavier de Choiseul; Piedmont, the home of the Reverend Charles Cotesworth Pinckney; Beaumont, the home of Andrew Johnstone; Brookland, the home of Edmund Molyneaux; Glenroy, the home of Dr. Mitchell King; and Ravenwood, the home of the Reverend John Grimke Drayton. See Memminger, *Historical Sketch of Flat Rock* and Patton, *Flat Rock.*

14. In order to have a hotel, estate owners formed a company, each contributing $1000 toward the project. Henry Farmer, nephew of Mrs. Charles Baring, became the manager and a year later purchased the hotel. It was the first of the resort hotels for which Western North Carolina was in time to be famous. This hotel is still in operation under the name Woodfield Inn.
15. Sondley, II, 587-596, 609.
16. Charles Lanman, visiting Patton's hotel at Warm Springs, has left a vivid description of it and of the Painted Rock in his *Letters From the Alleghany Mountains,* 433-435.
17. Sondley, II, 609, 769.
18. Lanman, 427.
19. Sadie S. Patton, "Fame of Western North Carolina as Major Health Resort Dates From 18th Century," *The Asheville Citizen-Times,* March 26, 1950.
20. Sondley says that the grave of John Lyon, whose remains were moved from the churchyard of the First Presbyterian Church in Asheville to the newly opened Riverside Cemetery, was the first one there to have a stone. The marker was made possible by contributions sent by friends in Scotland. *Buncombe County,* II, 625-626, 715-719.
21. Sondley, Appendix M.
22. *Ibid.;* Charles A. Shull, "Fringed Bell: A New Name for Rare *Shortia*," *Asheville Citizen-Times,* March 26, 1950.
23. Sondley, II, 528-529.
24. Sondley traces the dispute between Clingman and Mitchell. See his *Buncombe County,* II, 529-565.
25. Mitchell, *Diary of a Geological Tour.* This was edited by Dr. Kemp P. Battle, who wrote the introduction.
26. Mitchell, 52.
27. Sondley, II, 532.
28. An account of the search written by Judge David Schenck, together with the story as told by Big Tom Wilson, appeared in the *Asheville Citizen* of November 20, 1887. A reprint appeared in the Anniversary issue of the *Citizen-Times,* March 26, 1950. See also Dykeman, Chap. V.
29. George W. McCoy, "Guyot: Greatest Explorer of Appalachian Mountains," *Asheville Citizen-Times,* June 18, 1950; Sondley II, 555; *Dictionary of American Biography,* VIII, 63-64.
30. Guyot, "Measurements of the Mountains of North Carolina." This information was given in a letter written to the editor of the *Asheville News* and printed in the issue of July 18, 1860. It is given in *The Writings of Thomas L. Clingman,* 138-147, and in Sondley, Appendix A. See also Guyot, "Notes on the Geography of the Mountain District of Western North Carolina." These notes, dated February 22, 1863, were found in 1929 in the library of the Coast and Geodetic Survey and were edited by Myron A. Avery and Kenneth Boardman in *N.C.H.R.,* XV (July, 1938), 251-290.

CHAPTER 18
Whigs in the Mountains

1. Lefler and Newsome, 328; William K. Boyd, *The Federal Period*, 166.
2. Deyton, 460.
3. Almost 22,000 of the 33,993 votes returned for Dudley came from the "back country" and the mountains. However, in addition to Yancey County, Ashe, Haywood, and Macon Counties returned majority votes for Richard Dobbs Spaight, the Democratic candidate. Hamilton, *Party Politics in North Carolina*, 39; Lefler and Newsome, 343.
4. Hamilton, *op. cit.*, 553-568; Lefler and Newsome, 343-345; Samuel A'C Ashe, *The History of North Carolina*, II, Chap. XXVI.
5. For the candidates these canvasses were strenuous, especially in the mountain section of the state with its wretched roads. In 1840, John Motley Morehead spent from March to August traveling by any means available to all parts of the state. The towns and villages greeted him with bands and parades and barbecues, arranged by the county party committees. These committees distributed the party's broadsides and newspapers to the assembled crowds. A vivid description of these meetings is given by Boyd, 266-270, 278-280, and by Hamilton, *op. cit.*, 553-568. The party platform in the 1840 election is given in Porter, *National Party Platforms*, Chap. 1.
6. Arthur, *Western North Carolina*, 359-363.
7. *Ibid.*, 367-368; Gilbert, *The Public Career of Thomas L. Clingman*, 36-40. Among other political figures in Western North Carolina choosing to settle their differences by dueling was Zebulon B. Vance. When he and David Coleman were campaigning for a seat in Congress and, as was customary, were traveling together, Coleman demanded an apology for a personal remark made by Vance. Vance refused, and preparations were made for a duel. Before the date set, Dr. J. F. E. Hardy of Asheville prevailed upon the men to settle their grievances in a more peaceful manner. Clement Dowd, *Zebulon B. Vance*, 37-38.
8. Griffin, 549-553.
9. Sondley, II, 711.
10. Clarence N. Griffin, *The Public Career of Thomas L. Clingman*, 549-550; Guion G. Johnson, *Ante-Bellum North Carolina*, 774-780.
11. Gilbert, 1-22.
12. *Ibid*, 24-99.
13. Dowd, 2-12.
14. *Ibid.*, 12. Vance's father, moved to the present Marshall when Zebulon was a child.
15. Given in Connor, *Ante Bellum Builders*, 135.
16. Griffin, 214.
17. Cecil K. Brown, *The State Highway System*, 3-19. In 1851 the General Assembly passed a bill appropriating $12,000 for a survey for a road from Salisbury to the place where the French Broad River enters Tennessee. The money was to come from Cherokee land sales and from the income from Cherokee land bonds. Too small a sum was realized from these sources to make the survey. Cecil K. Brown, *The State Highway System*, 97.

18. Deyton, 444. It was during this period that Judge Agustus C. Merrimon was finding travel over his circuit both disagreeable and time consuming. He could, if fortunate, get from Waynesville to Asheville between noon and bedtime, but when the weather was unfavorable, it took a full day to cover thirty miles. See his *Journal*.
19. Lefler and Newsome, 345-347; Cecil K. Brown, *A State Movement in Railroad Development,* Chaps. III-IV.
20. Agitation for state aid in railroad building began as early as 1833, and in that year and the following one, North Carolina issued no less than 10 charters to companies hoping to construct railroads. The state did not promise any of these companies aid. Brown, *op. cit.,* 27.
21. He expressed this view in his message to the General Assembly. Connor, *op. cit.,* 135.
22. Address delivered by Hayne in Charleston, October 22, 1835. *Proceedings* (Meetings connected with the Louisville, Cincinnati, Charleston Railroad,) part I.
23. *Ibid.*
24. *Ibid.,* part II.
25. Patton, *Henderson County,* 220-221; Wallace, 449.
26. The bill was written by W. S. Ashe, a Democrat, and the deciding vote in the Senate was cast for it by another Democrat, Calvin Graves. Brown, 63-69.
27. *Ibid.,* 90-91.
28. See his *Numbers of Carlton.*
29. Romulus S. Saunders, the Democrat defeated by John M. Morehead in the 1840 gubernatorial race, wrote a substitute bill for two pending bills concerning extension of the North Carolina Railroad. His bill provided for chartering two companies, one for an eastern extension and one for a western extension. It easily passed both houses of the Assembly. Brown, 98-99.
30. *Ibid.,* 104.
31. *Ibid.,* 101.
32. In the General Assembly William H. Thomas of Haywood County argued for the Ducktown route. B. E. Edney of Buncombe County and J. A. Fagg of Madison County argued for the French Broad River route. Brown, *op. cit.,* 140.
33. *Ibid.,* 127-128; Griffin, 239.
34. Arthur, *Western North Carolina,* 469-473; Brown, *op. cit.,* 142.
35. *The Asheville News,* February 24, 1859. Quoted by Brown, *op. cit.,* 141-142.
36. On June 2, 1859, the voters of Buncombe County voted to authorize the county to subscribe $125,000. Henderson County voters, at a special election, pledged the county to subscribe $100,000. Madison County voters authorized their county to subscribe $50,000. *The Asheville News,* August 11, 1859. Quoted by Brown, *op. cit.,* 142.
37. Brown, 143-145.
38. Lefler and Newsome, 362.
39. Brown, *The State Highway System,* 16-17. The *Raleigh Register* of February 28, 1849, carried an article discussing the cost, the income from, and the advantages of plank roads, "The Poor Man's Railroad." See *North Carolina History Told by Contemporaries,* 228-235.

40. Patton, *Henderson County*, 143; Sondley, II, 623-624.
41. Gilbert, 56.
42. Ashe, II, 486, 491, 503, 512-513.
43. Connor, *Rebuilding an Ancient Commonwealth*, II, 74-76; Porter, *National Party Platforms*, Chap. 5; Hamilton, *Party Politics*, 173-174; *Selections From the Writings of Thomas L. Clingman*, 355-356.

CHAPTER 19
War in the Land

1. Boyd, 296-329; Hamilton, *Party Politics in North Carolina*, 194-200.
2. Porter, Chap. 6.; Eaton, Clement, *A History of the Southern Confederacy*, 1-22.
3. R. D. W. Connor, *North Carolina*, 113.
4. Lefler and Newsome, 423.
5. Frontis W. Johnston, *The Papers of Zebulon Baird Vance*, "Introduction" XXXVI and XXXVII.
6. Lefler and Newsome, 422-423; Dowd, 62-64; Ashe, II, 536-546.
7. Dowd. The entire speech is given, 441 ff.
8. A full discussion of events leading up to the war is given in Lefler, *North Carolina*, II, Chap. XXVIII.
9. Hamilton, *North Carolina Since 1860*, 1-6; See Governor Ellis' letter to Leroy Pope Walker, Secretary of War, April 24, 1861, in *History Told By Contemporaries*, 290.
10. Griffin, *The History of Old Tryon and Rutherford Counties*, 249-250.
11. Sondley, II, 813-815; Walter Clark, "The Raising, Organization and Equipment of North Carolina Troops During the Civil War." *N.H.C., Bulletin* 23.
12. Dowd, 62-70; Sondley, II, 813; Johnston, *op. cit.*, XXXVIII.
13. Allen, *Haywood County*, 64.
14. Patton, *The Story of Henderson County*, 125.
15. Clarence N. Gilbert, *The Public Career of Thomas Lanier Clingman*, 100-107.
16. Manly Wade Wellman, *The Kingdom of Madison*, 81.
17. Ora L. Jones, "Transylvania County," *Asheville Citizen-Times*, February 24, 1917; Griffin, 251-252; Patton, *Henderson County*, 125.
18. Ora L. Jones "Transylvania County."
19. Sondley, II, 813-815; Griffin, 249-253; Patton, *Henderson County*, 125.
20. Sondley, II, 691.
21. The United States Census figures for 1860.
22. Alley states as typical his own family. His father joined the Confederate forces and his father's brother the Union forces. *Random Thoughts*, 2-3; See also Patton, *op. cit.* 127; Griffin, 249.
23. Deyton, 460; Whitener, *Watauga County*, 47; Jones, *op. cit.*
24. Dugger, *War Trails of the Blue Ridge*, 110-125.
25. Patton, *Henderson County*, 128; Patton, *Polk County*, 43-45.
26. Jones, *op. cit.*
27. Lefler and Newsome, 376-377.
28. Clark, "*The Raising of North Carolina Troops,*" *N.C.H.C. Bulletin*. In an address before the Association of the Maryland Line at Baltimore on February

23, 1885, Vance gave a summary of the goods brought into Wilmington by the Ad-Vance and other state owned blockade runners. See Dowd, 489-490.
29. North Carolina appointed Jonathan Worth as state salt commissioner. Eaton, 249. Nicholas W. Woodfin of Asheville was made an agent for the distribution of salt from the mines at Saltville, Virginia, to Western North Carolina. Hamilton, *op. cit.,* 49; Digges, George, *Historical Facts Concerning Buncombe County Government,* 206-207.
30. Lefler and Newsome, 437-439; Johnston, *op. cit.,* "Introduction" XLII-XLIII.
31. Clarence D. Douglas, *Conscription and the Writ of Habeas Corpus in North Carolina During the Civil War,* 5-35.
32. *The North Carolina Standard* for November 19, 1862, carried a letter from a farmer in Transylvania County telling of the desperate need for salt. Douglas, 5-39; With her husband and five sons in the Confederate army, Mrs. Lane, wife of Captain Lane, is said to have driven with a servant from her farm home in Henderson County to the salt mines in South Carolina to bring back a supply of the precious salt. Patton, *Henderson County,* 131.
33. Mooney, 168-172; Asheville and Wilkesboro were centers for collecting medicinal herbs and roots gathered by the women and children of the mountain region. Hamilton, *op. cit.,* 48.
34. Mooney, 168-172; Arthur, *Western North Carolina,* 609; George McCoy, "Trace of Old Thomas Road is Part of Farmstead Museum," *Asheville Times,* September 13, 1953.

CHAPTER 20
War Comes to the Hills

1. North Carolina banks suspended payments in specie in November, 1860. Both the State and the Confederacy issued treasury notes. These depreciated with alarming rapidity. By November, 1864, a State $100 bond was worth $7.50, and a Confederate bond of the same denomination was worth $4.00. As the value of the paper money fell, prices rose. In 1865 enough calico for a woman's dress cost $500. There was, of course, widespread speculation in spite of the efforts of a State Board appointed to set the prices of commodities every two months. Hamilton, *North Carolina Since 1860,* 46-55; Eaton, 239-240.
2. Eaton, 233-236; Lefler and Newsome, 443-444; Lefler, II, 520-521.
3. Ashe, II, 858-859; Arthur, *The History of Western North Carolina,* 603-604.
4. Many counties of the State had so many deserters before 1863 that the attention of officials was called to them. Wilkes County had "a whole regiment organized and under arms." Hamilton, *op. cit.,* 40. North Carolina during the conflict had 23,694 deserters. Other Confederate states had proportionate numbers. Eaton, 261, 271-279; Ashe, II, 775-776; Lefler and Newsome, 445-446.
5. Wellman, *The Kingdom of Madison,* 83-84; Ashe, II, 860; Arthur, *op. cit.,* 603; Dykeman, *The French Broad,* 96-98; See also Governor Vance's letter, Dowd, 74.
6. Ashe, II, 858-859; Arthur, *op. cit.,* 603-605.

7. Governor Vance insisted upon putting into practice the state's rights doctrine to which the Confederacy owed its being. Thus he held that the military power of the Confederacy must not interfere with the civil rights of citizens and the laws in operation in North Carolina. See his letter of November 11, 1862, to President Davis in which he makes these views clear. See also his letter of March 21, 1863, to Secretary Seddon in which he said he had ordered the State Militia to shoot the first man "who attempts to perpetrate a similar outrage without the authority of the marshall of that district." Dowd, 75, 81, 87. See also Lefler and Newsome, 445.
8. Lefler and Newsome, 443; Douglas, 5-39; Eaton, 278-279; Dowd, 78, 81.
9. *History Told by Contemporaries,* 295; Used with permission of the University of North Carolina Press.
10. Patton, *Henderson County*, 132; Patton, *Polk County*, 41; Jones, *Transylvania County*.
11. Patton, *Henderson County*, 127-128; Stephens, "Bushwhackers, Renegades, and Ruffians in the Western Mountains."
12. Stephens, *op. cit.;* Patton, *Henderson County*, 128; Hughes, *Hendersonville in Civil War Times*, 25-26; Patton, *Polk County*, 46.
13. Deyton, 465; Ashe, II, 860.
14. For Governor Vance's letter to Secretary Seddon, April 7, 1863, see Dowd, 82.
15. Van Noppen, *Stoneman's Last Raid*, 20; Dykeman, 117-118.
16. Ashe, II, 860.
17. Allen, 81-82.
18. Dugger, 126-133; In his *History of Western North Carolina*, 605-608, Arthur gives the details of this raid as told by the guide.
19. Dugger, Chap. III; Arthur, *History of Watauga County*, 174.
20. Dugger, Chap. III; Arthur, *op. cit.*, 174-176.
21. Sondley, II, 690; 692-694; Ashe, II, 1006-1007; Sondley, "The Battle of Asheville," *Asheville Citizen*, September 10, 1927.
22. Terror spread throughout the countryside as word came that Stoneman's troops were approaching. Emma Rankin, a private teacher in the home of Colonel Logan Carson of Pleasant Gardens, four miles from Marion, has left a description of what took place on that plantation. Silverware and jewelry were hastily buried. Clothes were hidden in slave quarters, and food was cached in unlikely places. The farm animals were driven to the wooded hills. Colonel Carson, at the urging of his family, sought personal safety in the hills, and the women were left to face the Union soldiers and carried out their part with bravery. See her *Stoneman's Raid*, also Hamilton, 36-38; and Lefler, II, 503-504.
23. Patton, *Polk County*, 45; Ashe, II, 994 ff; Chester S. Davis, "Stoneman's Raid into Northwest North Carolina," *Winston-Salem Journal and Sentinel*, October 4, 1953; Alfred M. Waddell, *The Last Year of the War in North Carolina*. See also Spencer, Cornelia Phillips, *The Last Ninety Days of the War*. The most complete account of this raid is given in Ina Van Noppen's *Stoneman's Last Raid*.
24. Allen, 83-85. An account of the surrender at Waynesville as written by Lieutenant Colonel William W. Stringfield of his *Memoirs* is given by Allen, 91-92.

CHAPTER 21
The Rebirth of a State

1. By May, 1865, thousands of North Carolina families were penniless. In some cases their homes had been stripped of furniture. Clothing consisted of badly worn garments. These people had no credit and no way of establishing credit. Randolph Shotwell, *The Shotwell Papers,* II, 215.
2. The General Assembly appropriated, during the four years of the war, $6,000,000 for relief work. When hostilities ceased, the State had on hands a six months' supply of food for 60,000 soldiers. All through the war the fare of both state and Confederate soldiers was simple and monotonous. During the final year, the meals consisted largely of corn bread and black-eyed peas, called by men "The Confederacy's Best Friend." At times sweet potatoes and sorghum varied the menus. Dowd, 489-490; Hamilton, *North Carolina Since 1860,* 48.
3. Prices of other food stuffs were in proportion. Between September, 1860, and March, 1865, the cost of eggs rose from 30 cents a dozen to $5.00 a dozen; corn from $1.00 a bushel to $30.00; and potatoes from $1.00 a bushel to $30.00. Hamilton, 46-48. The Pay of a Confederate soldier was $11.00 a month. As editor and owner of *The Asheville Citizen* in 1868-1869, Randolph Shotwell received as payment for subscriptions and job printing "wood, wheat, corn, apples, dried fruit, feathers, and rags." When he sold the paper and returned to Rutherfordton in 1869, he had the sum of $2.50 as his year's net profit. Shotwell, II, 310.
4. Out of the state's total white population of 629, 942, it furnished 124,000 men to the State and Confederate armies, that is, one out of every six persons in the State. Dowd, 465-470. More than 40,000 were killed in battle or died from disease. Thousands of others were maimed for life or suffered through the remainder of their lives from ailments connected to the war service. This appalling number does not include civilian deaths or incapacitating illnesses brought on by sufferings or privations of war. Lefler and Newsome, 448.
5. Griffin, 306, 314.
6. Tennent's letter, dated November 18, 1865, is among the McDowell family papers, now in possession of Miss Margaret Ligon of Asheville.
7. From every section of the state lawyers and other leading citizens wrote letters to President Johnson, describing conditions and making appeals for aid. Among them are letters from Western North Carolina, portions of which deal with court cases in the hopelessly war-torn Madison County and Yancey County. Several of these give details of the proceedings connected with the case of the death of Sheriff Ranson P. Merrill. "Letters of North Carolinians to Andrew Johnson." *N.C.H.R.,* XVIII (October, 1951), 507-516; XXIX (January, 1952), 115-117; 264-268.
8. Silas Weston, a Negro, and his family were shot by the Adair gang. Shotwell, II, 478-493. Columbus and Govan Adair, together with another member of their gang, were later hanged for this crime.
9. Ashe. 1016.
10. *Ibid.*
11. *History Told by Contemporaries,* 316-317; Lefler and Newsome, 453-455;

Hamilton, *Reconstruction in North Carolina.*, 106-147. See also Francis Butler Simkins, *A History of the South*, 255-257.
12. Lefler and Newsome, 459-460.
13. Benjamin S. Hedrick was a chemistry professor at the University. Responsibility for his dismissal from the faculty in 1856 was placed upon his colleagues. At a faculty meeting called by President David L. Swain, Hedrick was dismissed by a unanimous vote of the faculty members. He narrowly escaped mob violence in Salisbury and hastened to leave the state. Lefler and Newsome, 419.
14. Late in the war a peace meeting was held in Asheville. It was inspired, however, not by Holden, but by the desperate conditions prevailing in Western North Carolina. Patton, *Henderson County*, 127.
15. Ashe, II, 1023-1026; 1031-1036; Hamilton, *North Carolina Since 1860*, Chap. V.
16. Ashe, II, 1040-1060; Hamilton, *op. cit.*, 85-113; Hamilton, *Reconstruction in North Carolina*, 207-252. The Reconstruction Act is given in *History Told by Contemporaries*, 333-334.
17. Lefler and Newsome, 460.
18. *Ibid.*, 459-460; H. A. Herbert (ed.), *Why the Solid South*, 70-84; Connor, *Rebuilding an Ancient Commonwealth*, II, 293-299.
19. Ashe, II, 1064-1070; Hamilton, *North Carolina Since 1860*, Chap. VI. The text of the Constitution is given in *History Told by Contemporaries*, 336-340.
20. The Republican Party was formally organized in North Carolina on March 27, 1867, although for a year before that date, the word Republican had been applied to many citizens. Lefler and Newsome, 459.

CHAPTER 22
Long is the Night

1. Hamilton, *Reconstruction*, 207-252.
2. Griffin, *History of Old Tryon and Rutherford Counties*, 326; *History Told by Contemporaries*, 344-345.
3. The relief work done by the Freedman's Bureau for needy in North Carolina has not been generally known. Because of this aid, doubtless many of these people became members of the secret organization looked upon with favor by the Bureau and also became members of the Republican Party. See *History Told by Contemporaries*, 328-329; Lefler, II, 531-532; John Hope Franklin, *Reconstruction After the Civil War*, 36-39; Allen W. Trelease, *White Terror, Introduction*, XXIII-XXIV.
4. Simkins, *A History of the South*, 261-262.
5. The password is given in Dykeman, *The French Broad*, 121.
6. The symbol of a red string was chosen from the story of Rahab, who betrayed her country to the Israelites. She, with her family, was saved by the conquering Hebrews when they saw the red cord with which she had let their spies down over the walls of Jerusalem. Randolph Shotwell estimated that at least 250 of the educated, well-to-do citizens of Rutherford County and surrounding territory had not registered to vote. *Shotwell Papers*, II, 276 ff. This view is upheld in the excerpts given in *History Told by Contemporaries*, 318-321.

7. Franklin, *op. cit.*, 124-126; Ashe, II, 1108-1109; *History Told by Contemporaries*, 318-321; Hamilton, *Reconstruction*, 327-343.
8. Ashe, II, 1109; Hamilton, *Reconstruction*, Chap. VIII.
9. Whitener, Daniel J. *Prohibition in North Carolina*, 1-14; 50-51.
10. *Ibid.*, 53.
11. These churches were Round Hill and Liberty. They were probably destroyed by the Adair gang. Shotwell, II, 479.
12. Trelease, *op. cit.*, Note 1, 430; Franklin, *op. cit.*, 153 ff.
13. Mrs. T. J. Jarvis, "The Conditions That Led to the Ku Klux Klans," *N.C.B.*, I (April 10, 1902), 3-24; *History Told by Contemporaries*, 331-333; Ashe, II, 1061-1071; Hamilton, *Reconstruction*, Chap. XII. The North Carolina figures given are from Franklin, 157.
14. Griffin, *op. cit.*, 327-328; Shotwell, II, 355; On July 22, 1871, *The Rutherfordton Star* carried a summary of this event.
15. Griffin, *op. cit.*, 326-327; Hamilton, *Reconstruction*, 480-481; Shotwell, II, 421.
16. Lefler and Newsome, 470; Hamilton (ed.) "Prison Experiences of Randolph Shotwell," *N.C.H.R.*, II (April, 1925), 147-161; (July, 1925), 332-350; (October, 1925), 459-474. When Federal troops entered Rutherford County, citizens of Burnt Chimney drew up a set of resolutions protesting this action on the part of the National Government. The document was printed in *The Rutherfordton Star* of June 10, 1871. It is given in Griffin, 332-333. Shotwell was sentenced on the grounds of having participated in the raid on Justice. He was also fined $5,000.
17. Trelease, *op. cit.*, 209.
18. *Ibid.*, 292; Hamilton, *North Carolina Since the Civil War*, 149-153.
19. Trelease gives the names of the men on Holden's list. 217.
20. Lefler, II, 568-577; The excesses of the "Kirk-Holden War" acted as a boomerang to the leaders in state government and was a factor in the downfall of Governor Holden. At the same time, the anti-Ku Klux Klan laws it called forth brought the beginning of restored order to North Carolina. See *History Told by Contemporaries*, 341-344.
21. Charges upon which Holden was tried included: declaring martial law in the state, illegally arresting citizens in Alamance, Caswell, and Orange Counties, illegally recruiting soldiers, and refusing to honor writs of habeas corpus. Ashe, II, 1128-1131; Hamilton, *Reconstruction*, 537-558; *History Told By Contemporaries*, 341.
22. Lefler and Newsome, 448; 499.
23. *Ibid.*
24. Hamilton, *Reconstruction*, 201-206; Griffin, 336.
25. Cecil Brown, *A State Movement in Railroad Development*, 148-151.
26. *Ibid.*, 188-205.
27. *Ibid.*, 190.
28. *Ibid.*, 191-193.
29. Ashe, II, 1078.
30. *Ibid.*, 1104-1105; Brown, *op. cit.*, 193-196; Hamilton, *Reconstruction*, 427-451; Hamilton, *North Carolina Since 1860*, 120-127; Lefler II, 561-566.
31. Brown, *op. cit.* 195-196.

434 / Notes

32. *Ibid.*, 199-205; Hamilton, *Reconstruction*, 426-451. *The Report of the Commission to Investigate Charge of Fraud and Corruption Under Act of Assembly. Session 1871-72.*
33. Brown, *op. cit.*, 206-224.

CHAPTER 23
Dawn Breaks Over the Mountains

1. Griffin, 324; Hamilton, *North Carolina Since 1860*, 161-169; Arthur, *Watauga County*, 182; Shotwell, II, 421.
2. *Formation of North Carolina Counties*, 202-205; Arthur, *Western North Carolina*, 208-212; Smathers, *Land Titles*, 139-140; Guy Paul, Jr., "Swain County Emphasizing Its Scenic Attractions," *Asheville Citizen-Times*, March 26, 1950; *The State Magazine*, July 18, 1942, 1-2, 16-17.
3. *Formation of North Carolina Counties*, 107-108; Smathers, 135; Dorothy Childers, "Graham Emphasizes Lumbering," *Asheville Citizen-Times*, March 26, 1950; *The State Magazine*, July 11, 1942, 1-2, 17-18.
4. Even in reconstruction-torn Rutherford County a trend toward normal conditions was discernible by 1871. Academies were reopening by 1873. Mail service was resumed with some degree of regularity, and in 1874 the county's first textile plant was in operation. Griffin, 336-339.
5. Hamilton, *Reconstruction*, 642-643; Hamilton, *North Carolina Since 1860*. 188-189. The texts of many of these amendments are given in *History Told by Contemporaries*, 350-351.
6. Griffin 340; Hamilton, *North Carolina Since 1860*, 170-191; Dowd, 147.
7. *The Raleigh Sentinel* printed an account of the Bakersville rally. The crowd represented a wide territory. Fifty men from Yancey County swam their horses across swollen streams and rode over "the roughest, rockiest road in the United States" to see and hear Vance and Settle. Dowd, 149.
8. For Article IX of the Constitution of 1868, see *History Told by Contemporaries*, 333-340.
9. In North Carolina 38,649 white men and women and children over ten years of age could neither read not write. During the decade 1870-1880 illiteracy in the state increased. *History Told by Contemporaries*, 346; Lefler and Newsome, 503; Whitener, *Public Education in North Carolina During the Reconstruction*, 90.
10. M. C. S. Noble, *A History of the Public Schools in North Carolina*, 367. In 1870 only about one in ten of the state's children attended school. Whitener, 90.
11. Noble, 356; Hamilton, *Reconstruction*, 612-613; McIver's report for 1872 is given in *History Told by Contemporaries*, 345-347.
12. Lefler and Newsome, 503; Hamilton, *North Carolina Since 1860*, 359; Edgar W. Knight, "One Hundred Years of Public Education in North Carolina," *N.C.E.*, (February, 1936), 195.
13. Noble, 357-367; Lefler and Newsome, 502.
14. Noble, 367.
15. *Ibid.*, 357-358.

16. After the Educational Meeting at Raleigh, text books for the public schools were hastily written by North Carolina educators. The following year the publishing house of Sterling, Campbell, and Albright in Greensboro had a series called "Our Own" ready for distribution to the schools. Included in the set were a primer and readers, the work of Charles W. Smythe, two arithmetics by the Reverend S. Landers, and a *"Geography Reader For Dixie Children"* by Mrs. M. B. Moore. Wiley had earlier written text books, including the *North Carolina Reader*. William Bingham's *Latin Grammar* and *Caesar* were used as was Webster's *Blue Back Speller*. The new books were generously sprinkled with Confederate propaganda. Sterling and Campbell in their readers gave Bible verses in support of slavery, and the arithmetics presented problems with a war flavor. The most gleefully gory of these problem states, "If one Confederate soldier killed ninety Yankees, how many can ten Confederate soldiers kill?" Allison W. Honeycutt, "Text Book Development," *N.C.E.,* (February, 1936), 227-229, 261, 274; Noble, 237-238.
17. The Bible was frequently used as a text as was whatever almanac happened to be available. Noble, 325; *History Told by Contemporaries,* 345 ff.
18. At the end of the Reconstruction Period (1876) the school report listed 2,820 schools for white children with an enrollment of 119,083 pupils, less than half of the state's white children. The number of white teachers given was 2,108. Of these 613 were women. In the mountains the salary of teachers ranged from $16 to $25 per month, and many of the schools were in session only six weeks each year. Noble, 367-372.
19. *Ibid.,* 367.
20. Lefler and Newsome, 502; *History Told by Contemporaries,* 367ff.
21. Noble, 399-409; G. B. Phillips, "The Development of the Graded Schools," *N.C.E.,* (February, 1936), 211-212; Edgar W. Knight, "The Peabody Fund," *N.C.E.* (February, 1936), 206. In the face of pressing war needs, Wiley had succeeded on December 23, 1864, in getting a bill through the General Assembly, making the state's public school system a graded system. It also set up a six months' term. This law was never put into effect. Noble, 260.
22. Noble, 399-409.
23. Hamilton, *North Carolina Since 1860,* 349-350, 363-364.
24. *Ibid.,* 364-365; Noble, 428ff.; Knight, "One Hundred Years of Public Education in North Carolina," *N.C.E.* (February, 1936), 195-199.
25. Griffin, 338.
26. Camp, 12.
27. The Reverend Jesse Finley had opened the school at Lenoir in 1857. It had continued during the war.
28. James A. Hutchins, *Yancey Collegiate Institute at Burnsville;* Arthur, *Western North Carolina,* 424-447; Arthur, *Watauga County,* 243-264; "Private Schools of Asheville Gain Wide Recognition," *Asheville Citizen-Times,* March 26, 1950; "Old Judson College Building is Landmark," *Asheville Citizen-Times,* September 13, 1933.
29. Arthur, *Western North Carolina,* 430-439, 446-447; Arthur, *Watauga County,* Chap. XV; Bill Sharpe, *A New Geography,* 230-232.

30. Brown, *A State Movement in Railroad Building*, 223-225.
31. In her *Land of the Sky*, Christian Reid (Frances C. Fisher Tiernan) describes her ride in 1876 from the railroad terminal at Henry to Asheville. The "thirsty men and dusty women" traveled the distance in a coach drawn by "six fine white horses."
32. Lefler and Newsome, 486 ff.; C. R. Sumner, "Railroad Conquered the Blue Ridge," *Asheville Citizen-Times*, March 7, 1954.
33. Brown, 223-224.
34. Sondley, II, 630.
35. Sumner, *op. cit*. In 1881 H. Heaton Coleman, one of the assistant engineers, made a map of the Western North Carolina Railroad and gave the length of the tunnels through the Old Fort-Henry area as follows; Point—216 feet; Jarret's—125 feet; Lick Log—562 feet; McElroy—89 feet; High Ridge—451 feet; Burgin—252 feet; Swannanoa—1800 feet. The map was verified by J. W. Wilson.
36. Sondley, II, 631-632.
37. Brown, 226-230; Lefler and Newsome, 486-487.
38. Lefler and Newsome, 487; Arthur, *Western North Carolina*, 473-479.
39. Arthur, *op. cit.*, 473-479.
40. *Ibid.*, 479-484; Patton, *Henderson County*, 222-226; Hamilton, *North Carolina Since 1860*, Chap. XVIII.
41. Arthur, *op. cit.*, 482-484; Patton, *op. cit.*, 226.
42. In the counties just east of the Blue Ridge a multiplicity of characters was granted to companies during this period, and a confusing number of consolidations took place. Griffin, Chap. 25; John F. Stover, *The Railroads of the South*, Chaps. IX, XII-XIII.
43. Griffin, Chap. 25, and p. 361; Lefler and Newsome, 487.

SOURCES

For those interested in doing in-depth study of certain periods of the history of Western North Carolina, source material has been broken into three time areas.

MOUNTAINS AND MEN—TO 1781
THE NEW FRONTIERS—TO 1860
THE CIVIL WAR—RECONSTRUCTION DAYS

Explanations: To avoid repetitions, the following abbreviations are used:

D.U.P.	*Duke University Papers*
G.P.O.	Government Printing Office
J.S.H.P.	*James Sprunt Historical Publications*
N.C.B.	*North Carolina Booklet*
N.C.C. and D.	North Carolina Department of Conservation and Development
N.C.E.	*North Carolina Education*
N.C.H.C.	North Carolina Historical Commission
N.C.H.R.	*North Carolina Historical Review*
S.D.A. and H.	State Department of Archives and History

MOUNTAINS AND MEN—TO 1781

PRIMARY SOURCES

Colonial and State Records

Easterby, J. H. (ed.). *The Journal of the House of Assembly: Colonial Records of South Carolina.* 6 vols. Columbia, S. C., Historical Commission of South Carolina, 1951—1955.

McDowell, W. L. (ed.). *Journal of the Commissioners of the Indian Trade.* South Carolina Archives Department, 1955.

Saunders, W.L. (ed.). *Colonial Records of North Carolina.* 10 vols. Raleigh, State Printers, 1886-1890.

Personal Accounts, Records, Treaties, Letters

Avery, Myron, and Boardman, Kenneth. "Notes on the Geography of the Mountain District of Western North Carolina by Arnold Guyot," *N.C.H.R.,* XV (July, 1938).

Fries, Adelaide. (ed). *The Records of the Moravians in North Carolina, 1752-1822.* 8 vols. Raleigh, 1922-1954.

Graham, George W. *The Mecklenburg Declaration of Independence, May 20, and the Lives of its Signers.* New York, 1905.

Graham, Major William A. (ed.). *General Joseph Graham and his Papers on North Carolina Revolutionary History.* Raleigh, 1904.

Harriss, Frances Latham. (ed.). *History of North Carolina by John Lawson.* Richmond, 1952.

Henderson, Archibald. "The Treaty of the Long Island of the Holston, July, 1777," *N.C.H.R., III (January, 1931.)*

Indians of North Carolina—A Letter From the Secretary of Interior. Washington, G.P.O., 1915.

Jacobs, Wilbur R. (ed.). *A Plan for Imperial Indian Control by Edmund Atkins.* Columbia, S. C., 1954.

Kappler, Charles (ed.). *Indian Affairs: Laws and Treaties.* 2 vols. Washington, G.P.O., 1904.

Lefler, Hugh Talmadge. (ed.). *North Carolina History Told by Contemporaries.* Chapel Hill, 1948.

Mereness, Newton D. (ed.). *Travels Into the American Colonies.* New York, 1916.

Mooney, James. *Myths of the Cherokees. Nineteenth Annual Report of the Bureau of American Ethnology.* Washington, G.P.O., 1902.

Powell, William Stevens. *The Carolina Charter of 1663.* Raleigh, 1954.
Report of the DeSoto Commission. Washington, G.P.O., 1939.
Van Doren, Mark (ed.). *William Bartram's Travels Through North and South Carolina, Georgia, East and West of the Muscogules or Creek Confederacy, and the Country of the Choctaws.* New York, 1928.
Williams, Samuel C. (ed.). *James Adair's History of the American Indians.* Johnson City, Tenn., 1930.
_ _ _ _.(ed.). *Early Travels in the Tennessee Country, 1540-1800.* Johnson City, Tenn., 1928.

SECONDARY SOURCES

Alden, John R. *John Stuart and the Southern Colonial Frontier.* Ann Arbor, Mich., 1944.
Allen, W. C. *The Annals of Haywood County, North Carolina, 1808-1935.* Richmond, 1942.
Alley, Felix E. *The Random Thoughts and Musings of a Mountaineer.* Salisbury, N. C. 1941.
Arthur, John P. *A History of Watauga County.* Richmond, 1915.
_ _ _ _. *Western North Carolina: A History From 1730-1913.* Raleigh, 1914.
Ashe, Samuel A'Court. *A History of North Carolina.* 2 vols., Greensboro, 1908.
_ _ _ _. "Rutherford's Expedition Against the Indians in 1776." *N.C.B.*, IV (December, 1904).
Ayers, H. B. and Ashe, W. W. *The Southern Appalachian Mountains.* Washington, G.P.O., 1938.
Bakeless, John. *Daniel Boone.* New York, 1939.
Beard, Charles A., and Beard, Mary R. *A Basic History of the United States.* New York, 1944.
Bowman, Elizabeth. *Land of High Horizons.* Kingsport, Tenn., 1938.
Boyd, William K. "The Battle of King's Mountain." *N.C.B.*, VIII (1909).
Bryson, H. J. *The Story of the Geological Making of North Carolina.* Raleigh, S.D.A. and H., 1928.
Callahan, North. *Smoky Mountain Country.* Boston, 1952.
Cavarrubias, Miguel. *The Eagle, the Jaguar, and the Serpent.* New York, 1954.
Clewell, John H. *A History of Wachovia in North Carolina.* New York, 1902.
Connor, Robert D. W. *The History of North Carolina: The Colonial and Revolutionary Periods.* vol. 1.
_ _ _ _. *Rebuilding An Ancient Commonwealth.* Chicago, 1928.
Corkran, David H. "The Unpleasantness at Stecoa, in North Carolina." *N.C.H.R.*, XXXII (July, 1955).
Cotterill, R. S. *The Southern Indians.* Norman, Okla., 1954.
Coulter, E. Merton. "The Granville District." *J.S.H.P.* XIII, 1913.
Crittenden, Charles G. "Means of Transportation in North Carolina, 1763-1789." *N.C.H.R.* VIII (October, 1931.)
_ _ _ _ "Overland Travel and Transportation in North Carolina, 1763-1789." *N.C.H.R.* VIII (July, 1931)
Curtis, N. A. *The Woods and Timbers of North Carolina.* Raleigh, 1883.

Davidson, Chalmers G. *Piedmont Partisan: The Life and Times of William Lee Davidson.* Davidson, N. C., 1951.
Dickens, Roy. *The Pisgah Culture and Its Place in the History of the Southern Appalachians.* Unpublished thesis in the library of Warren Wilson College.
Dill, Alonzo T. *Governor Tryon and His Palace.* Chapel Hill, 1955.
Draper, Lyman. *King's Mountain and Its Heroes.* Cincinnati, 1954.
Driver, Carl S. *John Sevier: Pioneer of the Old Southwest.* Chapel Hill, 1923.
Dugger, Shepherd. *War Trails of the Blue Ridge.* Banner Elk, N. C., 1938.
Fitch, William E. *The Battle of Alamance.* Burlington, N.C. 1939.
_ _ _ _ *The Origin, Rise, and Fall of the State of Franklin, Under Her First and Only Governor, John Sevier.* Address before the New York Society of the Order of the Founders and Patriots of America, March 11, 1910.
Fitzgerald, Mary N. *The Cherokees.* Asheville, 1946.
Fries, Adelaide. *The Road to Salem.* Chapel Hill, 1944.
Gladwin, Harold S. *Men Out of Asia.* New York, 1947.
Gobbel, Luther L. *The Militia in North Carolina Colonial and Revolutionary Times.* D.U.P., Series XIII, 1919.
Griffin, James B. (ed.) *Archeology of Eastern United States.* Chicago, 1952.
Hamer, P. M. "Ft. Loudon in the Cherokee War, 1758-1761." *N.C.H.R.* II (October, 1925).
Harrell, I. M. "North Carolina Loyalists." *N.C.H.R.,* III (October, 1926.)
Henderson, Archibald. "The Treaty of the Long Island of Holston, July, 1777." *N.C.H.R.,* III (January, 1931.)
Henry, Thomas R. "Ice Age Man, the First American." *National Geographic Magazine,* CVIII (December, 1955).
Hoyt, William H. *The Mecklenburg Declaration of Independence.* New York, 1907.
Hunter, C. L. *Sketches of Western North Carolina, Historical and Biographical, Illustrating Principally the Revolutionary Period.* Raleigh, 1877.
Hunter, Kermit. *Horn in the West.* (Drama)
Kelsey, Harlan P. *The Unique Flora of the Great Smoky Mountains National Park.* Nashville, Tenn. No date.
Kephart, Horace. *Our Southern Highlanders.* New York, 1913.
King, Clyde. "Military Organization of North Carolina During and After the Revolution." *N.C.B.,* VIII (July, 1908)
King, Phillip B. and Stupka, Arthur. "The Great Smoky Mountains—Their Geology and Natural History." *Scientific Monthly,* LXXI (July, 1950).
Lefler, Hugh T., and Newsome, Albert R. *North Carolina,* Chapel Hill, 1963.
Lewis, Thomas M. N., and Kneberg, Madeline. *Hiwassee Island.* Knoxville, Tenn., 1946.
Logan, John A. *A History of the Upper Country of South Carolina.* Charleston, S. C. 1859.
Lord, Bill. *Nature Notes on the Blue Ridge Parkway.* Waynesboro, Va., 1955.
McCall, William A. *Cherokees and Pioneers.* Asheville, 1952.
McPherson, O. M. *Indians of North Carolina.* Washington, D. C., G.P.O., 1905.

Malone, Henry T. *Cherokees of the Old South: A People in Transition.* Athens, Ga., 1956.
Mecklenburg in the Revolution, 1740-1783. (In honor of the Sons of the American Revolution, 42 Congress, Charlotte, N. C., 1931.)
Milling, Chapman, Jr. *Red Carolinians.* Chapel Hill, 1940.
Morley, Margaret. *The Carolina Mountains.* Boston, 1913.
Myer, William E. *Indian Trails of the Southeast: 43 Annual Report of the Bureau of American Ethnology, 1924-1925.,* Washington, G.P.O.
Newsome, Albert Ray. "North Carolina and the Ratification of the Federal Constitution." *N.C.H.R.,* XVIII (October, 1940).
North Carolina and Its Resources. Raleigh, State Board of Agriculture, 1896.
Parker, Thomas. *The Cherokee Indians.* New York, 1907.
Parris, John. *The Cherokee Story.* Asheville, 1950.
____ *My Mountains, My People.* Asheville, 1957.
____ *These Storied Mountains.* Asheville, 1972.
Patton, Sadie Smathers. *Sketches of Polk County History.* Asheville, 1950.
____ *The Story of Henderson County.* Asheville, 1947.
Peattie, Roderick (ed.) *The Great Smokies and the Blue Ridge.* New York, 1943.
Powell, J. N. *Mound Builders: Twelfth Annual Report of the Bureau of American Ethnology.* Washington, D. C., G.P.O., 1891.
____ *Excavations in Caldwell, Burke, Wilkes, Haywood, Buncombe, and Henderson Counties, North Carolina: Twelfth Annual Report of the Bureau of American Ethnology, 1890-91.* Washington, D. C., G.P.O.
Powell, William Stevens. *The War of the Regulation and the Battle of Alamance, May 15, 1771.* Raleigh, S.D.A.H., 1949.
Pratt, Joseph H., and Boyer, Frederic Q. *Western North Carolina: Facts, Figures, Photographs.* Asheville, 1925.
Raper, C. L. *North Carolina: A Study in English Colonial Government.* New York, 1904.
____ "Social Life in Colonial North Carolina," *N.C.B.,* III (September, 1905)
Rights, Douglas L. *The American Indians in North Carolina.* Durham, N. C. D.U.P., 1947.
____ "The Trading Path to the Indians." *N.C.H.R.,* VIII (October, 1931.)
Roosevelt, Theodore. *The Winning of the West.* 4 vols. New York, 1897.
Setzler, Frank M., and Jennings, Jesse D. *Peachtree Mound and Village Site, Cherokee County, North Carolina: Bureau of American Ethnology, Bulletin 131.* Smithsonian Institution, Washington, D. C., G.P.O., 1941.
Shetrone, Henry Clude. *The Mound Builders.* Port Washington, New York, 1930.
Silverberg, Robert, *Mound Builders of Ancient America.* New York, 1967.
Smathers, George H. *The History of Land Titles in Western North Carolina.* Asheville, 1938.
Sondley, Foster Alexander. *The History of Buncombe County, North Carolina,* 2 vols. Asheville, 1922.

South, Stanley A. *Indians in North Carolina.* Raleigh, S.D.A.H. 1959.
Starkey, Marion L. *The Cherokee Nation.* New York, 1946.
Starr, Emmet. *A History of the Cherokee Nation.* Oklahoma City, 1921.
Stuckey, Jasper L., and Steel, Warren G. *The Geology and Mineral Resources of North Carolina.* Raleigh, 1953, N. C. C. and D.
Swanton, John R. *The Indians of the Southeastern United States.* Bureau of American Ethnology, *Bulletin 137.* Smithsonian Institution, Washington, G.P.O., 1946.
Truett, Randle B. *Trade and Travel Around the Southern Appalachians Before 1850.* Chapel Hill, 1935.
Van Noppen, John. J. and Ina W. *Daniel Boone: Backwoodsman.* Boone, N.C. 1966.
White, Howard. *The Battle of Alamance.* Burlington, N. C., No Date.
White, Stewart E. *Daniel Boone: Wilderness Scout.* New York, 1951.
Williams, Samuel C. *The History of the Lost State of Franklin.* Johnson City, Tenn., 1924.
Zeigler, W. G., and Grossup, Ben S. *In the Heart of the Alleghanies of Western North Carolina.* Raleigh, 1883.

NEWSPAPERS

Asheville Citizen. March 31, 1973.
Asheville Citizen-Times. March 26, 1950; July 25, 1950, August 23, 1953, August 30, 1953; Various issues, 1953-1954.

THE NEW FRONTIERS—TO 1860

PRIMARY SOURCES

State Records

Clark, Walter. (ed.). *The State Records of North Carolina.* 16 vols. Winston, Goldsboro, Charlotte, State Printers, 1895-1901. *Index.* 4 vols. Goldsboro, Charlotte, Raleigh, State Printers, 1909-1914.

Personal Accounts and Records, Treaties, Letters

Asbury, Francis. *Journal.* 3 vols. New York, 1852.
Byrd, William, *The History of the Dividing Line Betwixt Virginia and North Carolina.* N.C.H.C., Raleigh, 1929.
Caldwell, Joseph. *The Numbers of Carlton.* New York, 1828.
Corbitt, David L. (ed.). *The Formation of North Carolina Counties.* S.D.A. and H., Raleigh, 1950.

Fries, Adelaide. (ed.). *The Records of the Moravians in North Carolina, 1752-1822.* 8 vols. Raleigh, 1922-1954.

Hoyt, William H. (ed.). *The Papers of Archibald D. Murphey.* N.C.H.C., Raleigh, 1914.

Kappler, Charles. (ed.). *Indian Affairs: Laws and Treaties.* 2 vols. Washington, G.P.O., 1904.

Lanman, Charles. *Adventures in the Wilds of the United States and Bristish American Provinces.* Philadelphia, 1856.

Lefler, Hugh Talmadge. (ed.), *North Carolina History Told by Contemporaries.* Chapel Hill, 1934, 1948.

Mereness, Newton D. (ed.). *Travels Into the American Colonies.* New York, 1916.

Mitchell, Elisha. *Diary of a Geological Tour, 1827-1828.* J.S.H.P. Monograph 6, Chapel Hill, 1905.

Newsome, Albert Ray. (ed.). "John Brown's Journal of Travels in 1795," *N.C.H.R.,* XI (October, 1934).

_ _ _ _ (ed.). "The Journal of Augustus S. Merrimon, 1853-1854." *N.C.H.R.,* VIII (July, 1931).

Nichols, John. *Selections From the Speeches and Writings of Thomas Lanier Clingman.* Raleigh, 1877.

Reports Concerning the Cherokee Removal. Originals in the War Department, Washington. Copies in the Cherokee Museum, Cherokee, N. C.

Strother, John. *Diary and Field Notes, 1799.* Manuscript in the Brown Collection, S. D. A. and H.

Thomas, William Holland. *Explanations of the Rights of the North Carolina Cherokee Indians Submitted to the Attorney General of the United States.* Washington City, 1851.

Van Doren, Mark. (ed.). *William Bartram's Travels Through North and South Carolina, Georgia, East and West of the Muscogules or Creek Confederacy, and the Country of the Choctaws.* New York, 1928.

Williams, Samuel C. (ed.). *Early Travels in the Tennessee Country, 1540-1800.* Johnson City, Tenn., 1928.

SECONDARY SOURCES

Alden, John R. *John Stuart and the Southern Colonial Frontier.* Ann Arbor, Mich., 1944.

Allen W. C. *The Annals of Haywood County, North Carolina, 1808-1935.* Richmond, 1942.

Alley, Felix E. *The Random Thoughts and Musings of a Mountaineer.* Salisbury, N. C. 1941.

Arthur, John P. *A History of Watauga County.* Richmond, 1915.

_ _ _ _. *Western North Carolina: A History From 1730-1913.* Raleigh, 1914.

Ashe, Samuel A'Court. *A Biographical History of North Carolina From Colonial Times to the Present.* 8 vols. Greensboro, 1905.

_ _ _ _ *A History of North Carolina.* 2 vols. Greensboro, 1925.

Avery, Alphonso C. "Historical Homes of North Carolina: Pleasant Gardens and Quaker Meadows in Burke County." *N.C.B.,* IV (July, 1904.)

Beard, Charles A. and Beard, Mary R. *A Basic History of the United States.* New York, 1944.

Bowman, Elizabeth. *Land of High Horizons.* Kingsport, Tenn., 1938.

Boyd, William K. *The History of North Carolina: The Federal Period.* Chicago, 1919.

____. "The Literary Fund in North Carolina." *N.C.E.* II (February 1936).

Brown, Cecil K. *The State Highway System.* Chapel Hill, 1931

____. *A State Movement in Railroad Development.* Chapel Hill, 1928.

Bryan T. Conn. *The Gold Rush in Georgia.* A Reprint from the *Georgia Review.* IX (Winter, 1955).

Callahan, North. *Smoky Mountain Country.* Boston, 1952.

Camp, Cordelia. *David Lowry Swain: Governor and University President.* Asheville, 1963.

____. *Sketches of Burke County.* Morganton, N. C., 1954.

Chamberlain, Hope S. *Old Days in Chapel Hill.* Chapel Hill, 1926.

Clewell, John H. *A History of Wachovia in North Carolina.* New York, 1902.

Connor, Robert D. W. *Ante Bellum Builders of North Carolina.* Greensboro, 1923.

____. *Makers of North Carolina History.* Greensboro, 1923.

____. (ed.). *The Manual of North Carolina.* Raleigh, N.C.H.C., 1913.

____. *North Carolina: Rebuilding an Ancient Commonwealth.* Chicago, 1928.

Coon, Charles L. (ed.). *The Beginnings of Public Education in North Carolina: A Documentary History, 1770-1840.* Raleigh, N.C.H.C., 1908.

____. *North Carolina Schools and Academies, 1790-1840.* Raleigh, 1915.

Cooper, Susan. (ed.). *William West Skiles: A Sketch of a Missionary Life at Valle Crucis in Western North Carolina, 1842-1862.* New York, 1890.

Crittenden, Charles G. "Means of Transportation in North Carolina, 1763-1789." *N.C.H.R.,* VIII (October, 1931).

____. "Overland Travel and Transportation in North Carolina, 1763-1789." *N.C.H.R.,* VIII (July, 1931).

Coulter, E. M. *Georgia: A Short History.* Chapel Hill, 1947.

____. "The Granville District." *J.S.H.P.,* XIII (1913).

Crouch, John. *Historical Sketches of Wilkes County.* Wilkesboro, N. C., 1902.

Cushman, Rebecca. *Swing Your Mountain Gal.* Boston, 1933.

Davidson, Chalmers G. *Piedmont Partisan: The Life and Times of William Lee Davidson.* Davidson, N. C., 1951.

Deyton, Jason B. "The Toe River Valley to 1865." *N.C.H.R.,* XXIV (October, 1947).

Dictionary of American Biography. 21 vols. Edited by Allen Johnson. New York, 1928.

Dictionary of National Biography. 21 vols. Edited by Lester Stephens and Sidney Lee. New York, 1908.

Dowd, Clement. *Life of Zebulon B. Vance.* Charlotte, 1897.
Draper, Lyman. *King's Mountain and Its Heroes.* Cincinnati, 1954.
Driver, Carol S. *John Sevier: Pioneer of the Old Southwest.* Chapel Hill, 1923.
Dykeman, Wilma. *The French Broad* (Rivers of America Series). New York, 1955.
Dugger, Shepherd. *War Trails of the Blue Ridge.* Banner Elk, N. C., 1938.
Eaton, Allen H. *Handicrafts of the Southern Highlands.* New York, 1937. Part 1.
Erwin, Clyde A. "The Growth of Public Education in North Carolina." *N.C.E.* II (February, 1936.)
Finley, I. B. (ed.). *Sketches of Western Methodism.* Cincinnati, 1855.
Fisher, Louise B. *An Eighteenth Century Garland.* Williamsburg, 1951.
Fitch, William E. *The Origin, Rise, and Fall of the State of Franklin, Under Her First and Only Governor, John Sevier.* Address before the New York Society of the Order of the Founders and Patriots of America, March 11, 1910.
Fitzgerald, Mary N. *The Cherokees.* Asheville, 1946.
Foreman, Grant. *Indian Removal.* Norman, Okla., 1952.
____. *Sequoyah.* Norman, Okla., 1952.
Foster, George E. *Se-Quo-yah: The American Cadmus and Modern Moses.* Philadelphia, Office of Indian Rights Association, 1885.
Freel, Margaret W. *Our Heritage: The People of Cherokee County, North Carolina.* Asheville, 1956.
Fries, Adelaide. *The Road to Salem.* Chapel Hill, 1944.
Gilbert, Clarence N. *The Public Career of Thomas Lanier Clingman.* Manuscript Thesis at the University of North Carolina, 1946.
Goodloe, D. R. "North Carolina and the Georgia Line." *N.C.B.* III (April, 1904).
Green, Fletcher M. "Gold Mining: A Forgotten Industry of Ante Bellum North Carolina." *N.C.H.R.* (January, 1935; April 1937).
Griffin, Clarence W. *The History of Old Tryon and Rutherford Counties, 1730-1936.* Asheville, 1937.
____. *Western North Carolina Sketches.* Forest City, N. C., 1941.
____. *The History of Rutherford County, 1937-1951.* Asheville, 1951.
Hamilton, Joseph G. DeRoulhac. *Party Politics in North Carolina, 1835-1860.* J.S.H.P., Durham, 1916.
Hobbs, Samuel H. Jr. *North Carolina: Economic and Social.* Chapel Hill, 1936.
Hoffman, William S. "The Election of 1836 in North Carolina." *N.C.H.R.* XXXII (January, 1955).
Hunter, Kermit. *Unto These Hills: A Drama of the Cherokees.* Chapel Hill, 1950.
Johnson, Guion G. *Ante Bellum North Carolina: A Social History.* Chapel Hill, 1937.
____. "The Camp Meeting in Ante-Bellum North Carolina." *N.C.H.R.,* X (April, 1933).
____. "Revival Movements in Ante-Bellum North Carolina." *N.C.H.R.,* X (January, 1933).

Johnston, Frances B. and Waterman, Thomas T. *The Early Architecture of North Carolina: A Pictorial Study With an Architectural History.* Chapel Hill, 1941.

Kephart, Horace. *Our Southern Highlanders.* New York, 1913.

King, Clyde. "Military Organization in North Carolina During and After the Revolution." *N.C.B.,* VIII (July, 1908).

Knight, Edgar W. *Education in the United States.* Boston, 1951.

Lefler, Hugh Talmadge. *The History of North Carolina.* 4 vols. New York, 1956.

_ _ _ _ and Newsome, Albert Ray. *North Carolina.* Chapel Hill, 1954; 1963.

London, L. F. "The Representative Controversy in Colonial North Carolina." *N.C.H.R.,* XI (October, 1934).

McCall, William A. *Cherokees and Pioneers.* Asheville, 1952.

McCoy, George W. *The First Presbyterian Church, Asheville, North Carolina.* Asheville, 1951.

Mason, Robert L. *The Lure of the Great Smokies.* Boston, 1927.

Mooney, James. *Myths of the Cherokees. Nineteenth Annual Report of the Bureau of American Ethnology.* Washington D. C., G.P.O., 1902.

North Carolina and Its Resources. Raleigh, State Board of Agriculture, 1896.

Newsome, Albert Ray. "North Carolina and the Ratification of the Federal Constitution." *N.C.H.R.,* XVIII (October, 1940.)

_ _ _ _. "The Presidential Election of 1824 in North Carolina." *J.S.H.P.,* XXIII (1935).

Noble, Public Schools of North Carolina. Chapel Hill, 1930.

Nixon, J. R. "The German Settlers in Lincoln County and Western North Carolina." *J.S.H.P.,* XI (1912).

Parker, Mattie. *Money Problems of Early Tarheels.* Raleigh, S.D.A. and H., 1951.

Parris, John. *The Cherokee Story.* Asheville, 1950.

_ _ _ _. *My Mountains, My People.* Asheville, 1957.

_ _ _ _. *These Storied Mountains.* Asheville, 1972.

Parrish, John, Jr., and Griffin, Clarence W. "Historical Sketch of Jackson County, North Carolina." *North Carolina Historical and Genealogical Record.* I (1932).

Patton, Sadie Smathers. *A Condensed History of Flat Rock.* Asheville, 1961.

_ _ _ _. *Pages From the History of Speculation Lands.* Manuscript in Pack Memorial Library, Asheville.

_ _ _ _. *Sketches of Polk County History.* Asheville, 1950.

_ _ _ _. *The Story of Henderson County.* Asheville, 1947.

Peattie, Roderick D. *The Great Smokies and the Blue Ridge.* New York, 1943.

Price, R. E. *Rutherford County: Economic and Social.* Chapel Hill, 1918.

Proctor. A. M., and Leath, Mrs. Mary A. "School History Makers." *N.C.E.,* II (February 1936).

Roberts, Bruce. *The Carolina Gold Rush.* Charlotte, 1971.

Roosevelt, Theodore. *The Winning of the West.* 4 vols. New York, 1897. vol. II.

Royce, C. C. *Cessions of Land by Indian Tribes to the United States. First Annual Report of the United States Bureau of American Ethnology, 1879-1880.* Washington, D.C., G.P.O., 1880.
Sharpe, Bill. *A New Geography for North Carolina.* Raleigh, 1954.
Shull, Charles A. *The Lure of Western North Carolina for the Explorer-Naturalists.* (Paper read before the Western North Carolina Historical Association. Unpublished.)
Skaggs, M. L. *North Carolina Boundary Disputes Involving Her South-Lines.* Chapel Hill, 1941.
Smathers, George H. *The History of Land Titles in Western North Carolina.* Asheville, 1938.
Smith, C. D. *A Brief History of Macon County.* Franklin, N. C., 1891.
Smith, C. D., and Curtis, W. A. *A Brief History of Macon County, North Carolina, and the Topography of Macon County.* Franklin, N. C., 1921.
Sondley, Foster Alexander. *A History of Buncombe County, North Carolina* 2 vols. Asheville, 1930.
Starr, Emmet. *A History of the Cherokee Nation.* Oklahoma City, 1921.
Swanton, John R. *The Indians of the Southeastern United States.* Bureau of American Ethnology. *Bulletin 137.* Smithsonian Institution, Washington, D. C., G.P.O., 1946.
Tucker, Glenn. *Tecumseh: Vision of Glory.* New York, 1956.
_ _ _ _. *Zeb Vance: Champion of Personal Freedom.* New York, 1965.
Van Noppen, Ina W., and Van Noppen, John J. *Western North Carolina Since the Civil War.* Boone, N. C., 1973.
Wallace, Duncan D. *South Carolina: A Short History, 1520-1948.* Chapel Hill, 1951.
Wardell, Morris L. *A Political History of the Cherokee Nation, 1839-1907.* Norman, Oklahoma, 1938.
Wheeler, John H. *Historical Sketches of North Carolina From 1584-1851.* New York, 1925.
Whitener, Daniel J. *The History of Watauga County* (Souvenir of Watauga Centennial). Boone, N. C. 1949.
Wilburn, H. C. *Junaluska.* Asheville, 1951.
Williams, Charles B. *A History of the Baptists in North Carolina.* Raleigh, 1901.
Williams, Samuel C. *The History of the Lost State of Franklin.* Johnson City, Tenn., 1924.

Newspapers and Periodicals

Asheville Citizen-Times, March 26, 1950; various issues dating from January, 1917 to 1974.
Lenoir News-Topic, October 25, 1934; September 19, 1941.
The State Magazine. (various issues dating from September, 26, 1934 to 1970.)

THE CIVIL WAR—RECONSTRUCTION DAYS

PRIMARY SOURCES

State Records

Clark, Walter. (ed). *The State Records of North Carolina.* 16 vols. Winston, Goldsboro, Charlotte, State Printers, 1895-1901.

Personal Accounts and Records, Treaties, Letters

Corbitt, David L. (ed.) *The Formation of North Carolina Counties.* S.D.A. and H., Raleigh, 1950.
Hamilton, Joseph G. DeRoulhec. (ed.). *The Papers of William A. Graham.* Raleigh.
_ _ _ _ (ed.). "The Prison Experiences of Randolph Shotwell." *N.C.H.R.*, II (April, 1925; July, 1925; October, 1925).
_ _ _ _ (ed.). *The Shotwell Papers.* 3 vols. Raleigh, 1929.
Herbert, H. A. (ed.). *Why the Solid South.* Baltimore, 1890. Johnston, Frontis Withers. (ed.). *The Papers of Zebulon Baird Vance.* vol. I. S.D.A. and H., Raleigh, 1963.
Kappler, Charles, (ed.). *Indian Affairs: Laws and Treaties.* 2 vols. Washington, G.P.O., 1904.
Lefler, Hugh Talmadge. (ed.). *North Carolina History Told by Contemporaries.* Chapel Hill, 1934; 1948.
McPherson, Elizabeth G. (ed.). "Letters From North Carolinians to Andrew Johnson." *N.C.H.R.* XXVIII and XXIX (1951-1952).
Nichols, John (ed.). *Selections From the Speeches and Writings of Thomas Lanier Clingman.* Raleigh, 1877.
Porter, Kirk H. (ed.). *National Party Platforms.* New York, 1924.
Rankin, Emma. *Stoneman's Raid.* (In Memoriam), 1908. Pamphlet in Pack Memorial Library, Asheville.
Report of the Commission to Investigate Charges of Fraud and Corruption Under Act of Assembly, Session 1871-1872. Raleigh, 1872.
Spencer, Cornelia Phillips. *The Last Ninety Days of the War in North Carolina.* New York, 1866.
Tennent, Gilbert B. *Letter* to William W. McDowell of Asheville. (Among the McDowell Papers now in possession of Miss Margaret Ligon of Asheville.)

SECONDARY SOURCES

Allen, W. C. *The Annals of Haywood County, North Carolina, 1808-1935.* Richmond, 1942.
Alley, Felix E. *The Random Thoughts and Musings of a Mountaineer.* Salisbury, N. C., 1941.
Arthur, John P. *A History of Watauga County.* Richmond, 1915.
_ _ _ _. *Western North Carolina: A History From 1730-1913.* Raleigh, 1914.

Ashe, Samuel A'Court. *A Biographical History of North Carolina From Colonial Days to the Present.* 8 vols. Greensboro, 1905.
____. *A History of North Carolina.* 2 vols. Greensboro, 1925.
Bassett, John S. *Anti-Slavery Leaders in North Carolina.* Baltimore, 1889.
Beard, Charles A. and Beard, Mary R. *A Basic History of the United States.* New York, 1944.
Brown, Cecil K. *The State Highway System.* Chapel Hill, 1931.
____. *A State Movement in Railroad Development.* Chapel Hill, 1925.
Boyd, William K. "The Literary Fund in North Carolina." *N.C.E.,* II (February, 1936.)
Callahan, North. *Smoky Mountain Country.* Boston, 1952.
Camp, Cordelia. *Sketches of Burke County.* Morganton, N.C., 1963.
____. *Governor Vance.* Asheville, 1961.
____. *A Thought at Midnight.* Asheville, 1968. (Pamphlet)
Clark, Walter. "The Raising, Organization, and Equipment of North Carolina Troops During the Civil War." N.C.H.C., *Bulletin 23.*
Connor, Robert D. W. *Makers of North Carolina History.* Raleigh, 1923.
____. *North Carolina: Rebuilding an Ancient Commonwealth.* Chicago, 1928.
Crouch, John. *Historical Sketches of Wilkes County.* Wilkesboro, N. C., 1902.
Darris, Jonathan T. "Pardoning North Carolinians." *N.C.H.R.* XXIII (July, 1956).
Davidson, Allen. "Reminiscences of Western North Carolina." *N.C.H.R.* Address given November 7, 1890. *Lyceum* I (January, 1891).
Davis, J. H. "Reconstruction in Cleveland County." *D.U.P.* X (July, 1956).
Deyton, Jason B. "The Toe River Valley to 1865." *N.C.H.R.,* XXIV (October, 1947).
Digges, George A. Jr. *Historical Facts Concerning Buncombe County Government.* Asheville, 1937.
Douglas, Clarence B. "Conscription and the Writ of Habeas Corpus in North Carolina During the Civil War." *D.U.P.* Series XIV (1922).
Dowd, Clement. *Life of Zebulon B. Vance.* Charlotte, 1897.
Dugger, Shepherd. *War Trails of the Blue Ridge.* Banner Elk, N. C., 1938.
Dykeman, Wilma. *The French Broad.* (Rivers of America Series) New York, 1955.
Eaton, Clement. *A History of the Southern Confederacy.* New York, 1954.
Erwin, Clyde A. "The Growth of Public Education in North Carolina." *N.C.E.* II (February, 1936.)
Franklin, John Hope. *Reconstruction After the Civil War.* Chicago, 1961.
Freel, Margaret W. *Our Heritage: The People of Cherokee County, North Carolina.* Asheville, 1956.
Gilbert, Clarence N. *The Public Career of Thomas Lanier Clingman.* Thesis at the University of North Carolina, 1946.
Griffin, Clarence W. *The History of Old Tryon and Rutherford Counties, 1730-1936.* Asheville, 1937.
____. *The History of Rutherford County, 1937-1951.* Asheville, 1951.
____. *Western North Carolina Sketches.* Forest City, N. C., 1941.

Hamilton, Joseph G. DeRoulhac. *The History of North Carolina: North Carolina Since 1860.* Chicago, 1919.

_ _ _ _. *Party Politics in North Carolina, 1835-1860.* J.S.H.P. Durham, 1916.

_ _ _ _. *Reconstruction in North Carolina.* New York, 1914.

Hicks, John D. "The Farmers' Alliance in North Carolina." *N.C.H.R.* II (April, 1925).

Honeycutt, Allison W. "Text Book Development." *N.C.E.,* II (February, 1936.)

Hughes, N. Collin. *Hendersonville in Civil War Times.* Hendersonville, N. C., 1936.

Hunter, C. L. *Sketches of Western North Carolina: Historical and Biographical.* Raleigh, 1877.

Hutchins, James A. *A Sketch of Yancey Collegiate Institute at Burnsville.* Burnsville, N. C. 1951.

Hyman, M. L., Jr. "The Great Reconstructor." *N.C.H.R.,* XXIII (January, 1955).

Jarvis, M. W. "The Conditions that Led to the Ku Klux Klans." *N.C.B., I (April, 1902.)*

Johnson, Guion G. *Ante-Bellum North Carolina: A Social History.* Chapel Hill, 1935.

Jones, Ora L. "Transylvania County." *Citizen-Times,* February 24, 1917.

Knight, Edgar W. "One Hundred Years of Public Education in North Carolina." *N.C.E.* (February, 1936).

_ _ _ _. "The Peabody Fund." *N.C.E.* (February, 1936).

Lefler, Hugh Talmadge. *A History of North Carolina.* 4 vols. New York, 1956.

_ _ _ _ and Newsome, Albert Ray. *North Carolina: The History of a Southern State.* Chapel Hill, 1963.

McCoy, George W. *The First Presbyterian Church, Asheville, North Carolina.* Asheville, 1951.

Mead, Martha Norburn. *Asheville in the Land of the Sky.* Richmond, 1942.

Mooney, James. *Myths of the Cherokees; Nineteenth Annual Report of the Bureau of American Ethnology.* Washington, G.P.O. 1902.

Noble, N.C.S. *A History of the Public Schools of North Carolina.* Chapel Hill, 1930.

Olds, F. A. "The Development of North Carolina Railroads." *North Carolina Historical and Genealogical Record.* V, I (1932).

Patton, Sadie Smathers. *Sketches of Polk County History.* Asheville, 1950.

_ _ _ _. *The Story of Henderson County.* Asheville.

Price, R. E. *Rutherford County: Economic and Social.* Chapel Hill, 1918.

Reid, Christian (Frances B. Fisher Tiernan). "The Land of the Sky." A serial in *Appleton's Journal,* 1876.

Robinson, Blackwell P. (ed.). *The North Carolina Guide.* Chapel Hill, 1955.

Sheppard, Muriel E. *Cabins in the Laurel.* Chapel Hill, 1935.

Simkins, Francis Butler and Roland, Charles Pierce. *A History of the South.* New York, 1972 (Fourth Edition).

Smathers, George H. *The History of Land Titles in Western North Carolina.* Asheville, 1938.

Smith, C. D. *A Brief History of Macon County, North Carolina.* Franklin, N. C., 1921.

Sondley, Foster Alexander. *Asheville and Buncombe County.* Asheville, 1922.

____. *A History of Buncombe County, North Carolina,* 2 vols. Asheville, 1930.

Stephens, George Myers. *Bushwackers, Renegades, and Ruffians in the Western Mountains.* (Unpublished paper read before the Western North Carolina Historical Association.)

Stover, John F. *The Railroads of the South.* Chapel Hill, 1955.

Trelease, Allen W. *White Terror: The Ku Klux Klan Conspiracy and Southern Reconstruction.* New York, Evanston, London, 1971.

Tucker, Glenn. *Zeb Vance, Champion of Freedom.* Indianapolis, Kansas City, New York, 1965.

Van Noppen, Ina W. *Stoneman's Last Raid.* Boone, N. C., 1961.

____ and Van Noppen, John J. *Western North Carolina Since the Civil War.* Boone, N.C., 1973.

Waddell, Alfred M. *The Last Year of the War in North Carolina.* (Address given before the Association of the Army of Northern Virginia, Richmond, October 28, 1887).

Wellman, Manly Wade. *The Kingdom of Madison.* Chapel Hill, 1973.

Whitener, Daniel J. *The History of Watauga County.* (Souvenir of Watauga Centennial). Boone, N. C., 1949.

____. *Prohibition in North Carolina, 1715-1945.* Chapel Hill, 1945.

____. "Public Education in North Carolina During the Reconstruction." *Essays in Southern History.* (Presented to Joseph G. DeRoulhac Hamilton.) Chapel Hill, 1949.

NEWSPAPERS AND MAGAZINES

The Asheville Citizen-Times, March 26, 1950; Various issues from 1917-1970.
The Hendersonville Times-News, July 29, 1938.
The State Magazine. Various issues.
The Winston-Salem Journal and Sentinel, October 4, 1953.

INDEX

Abernethy, Robert, 390, 391
Academies, 180, 186-187, 204, 390-391
Act of Oblivion, 136
Act of Secession, 331; repeal, 361
Adair, James, 33, 61, 62, 72, 80, 84, 140
Adams, John Quincy, 306
Ad-Vance (blockade runner), 339
Alamance, battle of (1771), 101, 102-103, 108, 133, 155-156
Albemarle, 53, 54, 55, 79, 205
Alderman, Edwin A., 389
Alexander, John McKnitt, 108, 158
Alexander, Rachel, 159
Alleghany County, 9, 337, 349, 350, 391
Allen, Lawrence M., Lieutenant Colonel, 333, 345
Allen's Legion, 333, 345
American Foreign Mission Board, 247, 249
Amherst, Lord Jeffrey, 85
Amnesty Proclamation of 1865, 360
Andrews (town), 275
Animal Drives, 215-221
Apalachee Indians, 44
Appalachian Mountains, 1, 4, 9, 10, 11, 12, 13, 15, 16, 299, 304
Appomattox Courthouse, 356
Arch, John, 247
Arthur, Gabriel, 50-52, 56
Articles of Confederation, 134, 153
Articles of the Watauga Association, 103
Asbury, Reverend Daniel, 181
Asbury, Bishop Francis, 177-178, 179, 181-184, 185, 215, 269
Ashe County, 9, 15, 165, 181, 194, 261, 277, 278, 281, 297, 301, 337, 349, 359
Ashe, Governor Samuel, 163, 165
Asheville, 51, 160, 163-164, 165, 171, 175, 177, 182, 183, 186, 187, 198, 202, 215, 216, 220, 225, 263, 266, 288, 295, 297, 303, 312, 317, 319, 321, 323, 334, 342, 344, 353, 354, 355, 371, 374, 379, 384, 389, 393, 394, 396, 397, 399
Asheville, battle of, 353
Asheville News, The, 310, 322
Asheville Normal School, 391
Atkins, Edmund, 80
Attakullakulla (Cherokee chief), 68, 79, 82, 84, 86, 145-146, 147
Augusta (Ga.), 171, 220, 247, 295
Avery, Judge Waightstill, 125, 136, 164, 265, 351

Baird, Adolphus E., 279
Baird, Bedent, 160, 163, 175
Baird, Zebulon, 160, 163, 167, 175, 313
Bakersville, 283, 385
"Balds," 20-21
Balsam Mountains, 7, 398
Banner Elk (town), 371
Baring, Charles, 291
Bartlett, Lieutenant Colonel William C., 355
Bartram, William, 142-149, 150, 301
Beamer, James, 61, 75, 140
Beaufort (town), 199, 320
Bechtler, Augustus, 211, 212
Bechtler, Charles, 211
Bechtler, Christopher, 211, 212, 213
Bechtler, Christopher, Jr., 211
Bechtler Mint, 211-213, 287
Bedford's Mill, battle of, 116
Beech Mountain, battle of, 351
Bell, John, 328
Bennett, James, 319
Berkley, William, 48, 49
Best, William J., 397
Bethabara (town), 98, 174
Big Bethel, battle of, 332
Biggerstaff, Aaron, 371-372
Biggs, Asa, 329
Bingham, Major Harvey, 352
Bird Town (Cherokee village), 258
Black Mountains, 7, 299, 300, 301, 304, 305, 320, 321, 324
Blake, Alexander, 291
Blockade Runners, 339
Blount, John Gray, 265
Blount, Governor William (Tenn.), 137, 215
Blowing Rock (town), 354
Blue Ridge Mountains, 7, 12, 48, 74, 95, 96, 150, 161, 162, 164, 175, 186, 275, 321, 322, 335, 337, 351, 354, 367, 369, 379, 391, 393, 394, 396
Blue Ridge Railroad, 321, 322, 397
Board of Commissioners of Indian Affairs, 58, 59, 61, 62, 63, 66, 78
Boen (also spelled Bean), William, 100
Bonus Act (1782), 153
Boone (town), 96, 175, 276, 277, 337, 353, 354
Boone, Daniel, 51, 99, 109, 175, 180, 226, 277
Boudinot, Elias, 247
Bragg, Governor Thomas, 315, 375
Brahm, John William Gerard de, 13, 59, 76-77, 92-93, 140, 299
Brainard Indian School, 247, 249
Breckenridge, John C., 328
Brevard (town), 192, 282, 333
Brevard, Ephraim, 282
Bright, Samuel, 158, 175
Bright's Trail, 158, 175
Brittain, James, 272
Brooks, Judge George W., 375
Brown, David, 247
Brown, John, 163, 164, 171, 173
Bryson City, 381
Bryson, Daniel, Sr., 280
Bryson, Thaddeus D., 381
Buncombe County, 161-165, 175, 195, 198, 204, 215, 236, 263, 268, 269, 279, 285, 289, 299, 303, 315, 317, 321, 323, 332, 333, 335, 337, 355, 389
Buncombe Courthouse, See Asheville
Buncombe, Colonel Edward, 162
Buncombe Riflemen, 332
Buncombe Turnpike, 202-204, 215-220, 222, 223, 224, 225, 253, 262, 266, 270, 271, 288, 289, 293, 294, 295, 312, 314, 315, 324, 353, 377, 387
Bunning, Robert, 61, 75, 140
Bureau of Indian Affairs, 247
Burke County, 95, 155, 157, 159, 160, 162, 166, 171, 175, 178, 179, 180, 181, 182, 186, 208, 209, 261, 265, 274-275, 276, 283, 321, 391
Burningtown, 142
Burns, Captain Otway, 266

Burnsville, 266, 317, 344, 391
Burnt Chimney Academy, 390
Burnt Chimney Volunteers, 331-332
Burton, John, 160, 163, 172
Butler, Fort, 274, 275
Byrd, William, 60, 62, 73, 88, 190
Byrd, William III, 84, 99

Cabarrus County, 207
Caldwell County, 275-276, 283, 321
Caldwell, David, 197
Caldwell, Joseph, President of University, 236, 239, 240, 275, 316, 318, 320, 396
Calhoun (town), 283
Calhoun, John C., 299, 303
Camden (S. C.), 150
Camp Mast (raid of), 351-353
Camp Meeting Movement, 183-185
Camp Vance, 351
Campbell, Arthur, 127, 135
Campbell, David, 128
Campbell, John, Earl of Loudon, 77
Campbell, William, 116, 119
Canby, General Edward R. S., 362
Canton (town), 51, 161, 181
Cape Fear Mercury, The, 108
Cape Girardeau, 253
Carolina Gazette, The, 309
Carpenter, J. B., 273
Carson, John, 282
Carson, Samuel B., 309
Carter, John, 111
Carteret, George, Lord, 95
Cashiers (town), 293
Caswell, Fort, 331
Catalowhee (raid of), 217
Catawba Indians, 31, 79-80, 84, 95, 112, 191-192, 207, 265
Cathcart, William, 164, 265
Cession Act of 1783-4, 134, 135
Chambers, James, 161
Chambers, Samuel, 119
Champion, Captain James, 351-353
Chapman, Dr. Robert H., 355
Charles I, 52-53
Charles II, 53-54
Charleston (S. C.), 54, 56, 57, 58, 62, 65, 73, 77, 81, 93, 102, 103, 114, 115, 131, 132, 140, 141, 143, 146, 147, 149, 150, 155, 171
Charles Town, See Charleston
Charlotte (city), 95, 115, 120, 123, 150, 213, 320, 397
Cherokee County, 333, 336, 342, 346, 347, 350, 381
Cherokee Nation, domain, 30-33, 157; daily life, 33-41; trade with South Carolina, 56-69, 78-79; "Trail of Tears," 251-260; trails, 33-35; treaties, 69, 75-76, 86, 91, 109, 113-114, 127-128, 135, 153-154, 241-260, 262-263; wars, 64-65, 78-86, 95, 98, 109-114, 129, 155, 156
Cherokee Phoenix, The, 247, 250
Cherokee Village, 342
Cherokees (mention), 74, 75, 140, 141, 144, 145, 147, 152, 153, 154, 155, 156, 159, 171, 173, 190, 193, 207, 241-260, 262, 264, 265, 273, 277, 287, 291, 294
Chickasaw Indians, 31, 60, 129

Chicken, Colonel George, 63, 64, 66, 74
Chota (See Echota)
Christian, Colonel William, 111, 112, 113, 156
Clark, Governor Henry C., 334
Clay County, 9, 281-283
Clay, Henry, 249, 282
Clayton, Lambert, 164
Cleveland, Colonel Benjamin, 120, 156
Cleveland, Jeremiah (also spelled Cleaveland), 164
Clingman, Thomas Lanier, 299-302, 309, 311, 313, 317, 325, 329, 333, 396
Cloyd, Major Joseph, 155
Coffee, General John, 243
Co-fi-tash-e (Indian girl), 45, 46
Coleman, H. Heaton, 393, 394
Coleman, Colonel Thaddeus, 393, 394
Columbus (town), 281, 396
Confederacy, The, 331, 334, 335, 338, 339, 340, 341, 343, 345, 346, 347, 360, 361
Congaree, Fort, 60
Conscription Law of 1862, 340-341
Constitution of the United States, 137-138
Constitution of 1868 (state), 262-263, revised, 384-385
Constitutional Convention of 1868, 362-363
Constitutional Reform of 1835, 205-206
Continental Congress, 107, 108, 133, 134
Convention Act of 1861, 329
Cornwallis, Major General Charles, Lord, 114, 115, 120, 123-124, 194, 277
Council, Jordan, 220
Council, Jordan, Jr., 277
Council of Safety (N. C.), 111, 113
County Institutes, 389
Cowee (Cherokee town), 145
Cowee Mountains, 7, 141
Cox, General Jacob D., 360, 364
Coxe, Tench, 164
Cozby, Dr. James, 136
Crawford, William, 119
Creek Indians, 31, 75, 194, 242, 246
Crider, Fort, 275
Crown Point, Fort, 87
Cuming, Sir Alexander, 66-69, 70, 90, 92, 265, 299

Davenport, William, 158
Davidson County, 135
Davidson, Fort, 80, 155, 277
Davidson, John, 161
Davidson, General William Lee, 115
Davidson, Major William 159
Davidson, Samuel, 159
Davie, Governor William R., 115, 158
Davis, Jefferson, President of the Confederacy, 340, 346
Davis, Brigadier General William G., 158, 345
Deaver, Captain James, 349
Deaver, Colonel Reuben, 295
Deaver, William, 349
Declaration of Independence, 165
Defiance, Fort, 275
Delaware Indians, 31
Demere, Captain Paul, 81
Demere, Captain Raymond, 77
Democratic Party, 325-328, 340, 361, 375, 384, 385, 386

454 / Index

Deserters (Civil War), 344-345, 347, 348-349
DeSoto, Hernando, 13, 43-47, 207, 241, 265
Dinwiddie, Governor Robert (Va.), 74
Distribution of Surplus Act, 237
Doak, Reverend Samuel, 119, 314
Dobson (town), 155
Dog-trot houses, 222-223
Dougherty, Cornelius, 61, 75
Douglas, Stephen Arnold, 328
Drake, Sir Francis, 48
Drowning Bear (See Yonaguska)
Drummond, William, 55
Dudley, Edward B., 307
Duquesne, Fort, 87

East La Porte (town), 280
Eastern Band of Cherokees, 254-258
Echoee (town, also spelled Etchoe), 83, 85
Echota (town, also spelled Etchota), 31, 79, 89, 113, 127, 129
Edney, General Baylus E., 349
Edney, Samuel, 161, 183
Edneyville, 225
Educational Association of North Carolina, 240
Elizabeth I, 48
Ellis, David, 351
Ellis, Judge (later Governor) John W., 280, 331, 332, 361
Emancipation Proclamation, 365
Estatoe (Cherokee town), 282
Everett, Edward, 249
Excavations of Indian Mounds, 26-28

Fairchild, Ebenezer, 158
Farmer, Henry T., 291
Farmers' Alliance, 389-390
Farmsteads, 223-224
Fayetteville, 205, 312, 389
Federal Arsenal, 331, 338
Ferguson, Colonel Patrick, 115, 116, 118, 120, 123, 157, 194, 280
Fiftoe of Keowee (Cherokee), 82
Finley (also spelled Findley), 99
Finley School for Boys, 391
Fisher, Allen, 280
Fisk University, 365
Flat Rock (community), 271, 288-294
Fletcher (community), 291
Forests, 16-20
Forster (also spelled Foster), Thomas, 163
Forster, William, 159, 178
Forster (also spelled Foster), William III, 186-187
Foster Trading Station, 280
Foster, Colonel William S., 255
Fothergill, Dr. John, 142, 143
Fox, Colonel Joseph, 70
Franklin (town), 112, 264, 265
Franklin, Governor Jesse, 264
Franklin, "State" of, 128, 135-136
Frasier, John, 150-151
Fredericka (Ga.), 71
Freedman's Bureau, 365-367, 368, 371
Fremont, John Charles, 329, 361
French-Broad Railroad, 396-397
French and Indian War, 80-87
Frontenac, Fort, 87
Frontier Lite, 166-173
Furber, Robert, 142

Gaston, William, 205
Gates, General Horatio, 115
Gau-ax-u-le (Cherokee town), 42, 47
Geology of the Mountains, 8-13

George II, 68, 80
George III, 90, 141, 190
George, Ephraim, 164
Georgia (state), 212, 220, 241, 250, 251, 252
Georgia-North Carolina Boundary Dispute, (See "Walton War")
Gilbert Town, 116, 157
Gillem, Brigadier General Alvan C., 354
Gillespie, Matthew, 268
Gist, Nathaniel, 246
Glenn, Governor James (S. C.), 61, 74, 75
Gold Mining, 207-211
Goldsboro, 320
Gooch, John, 161
Government Mint (Charlotte), 213, 33.
Gowdy's Trading Post, 60
Graham County, 381
Graham, William A., 375, 381
Grandfather Mountain, 11, 150, 299, 301, 305
Grant, Lieutenant Colonel James, 84, 85-86, 88, 110, 112, 140
Grant, Ludovick, 61, 67, 75, 140
Grant, President Ulysses S., 375
Granville Tract, 91, 95-96, 98, 152, 153, 157, 158
Gray, Asa, 297, 298
Great Migration, 251-252
Great Smoky Mountains, 7, 18, 191
Great Tellico (Cherokee town), 63, 70, 89
Greenville (S. C.), 215, 216, 225, 253, 269, 289
Griffiths, Thomas, 140, 141-142
Gudger, William, 159
Guilford Academy, 197
Guilford Courthouse (battle of), 124, 155
Guyot, Arnold Henry, 303-304
Gwynn, Walter, 321

Haile, John, 111
Hall, Reverend James, 180
Hambright, Frederick, 120
Hamilton, Captain James, 337
Hampton, Christopher, 293
Hampton Institute, 365
Hampton, Wade, 293
Harris, James H., 368
Hastings, Colonel Theopholus, 58
Hayge, Charite, 58
Hayne, Robert Y., 319
Haywood County, 15, 154, 161, 165, 195, 256, 261, 263, 279, 285, 311, 332-333, 342, 350, 355, 387
Haywood, John, 165
Heath Grant, The, 52-53
Heath, Sir Robert, 52-53
Helper, Hinton Rowan, 336
Henderson County, 161, 215, 265, 266-272, 279, 280, 281, 282, 285, 289, 323, 333, 337, 348, 349, 376, 391
Henderson County Guards, 332-333
Henderson, Judge Leonard, 271
Henderson Purchase, 109
Henderson, Richard, 109
Hendersonville, 272, 323, 332-333, 397
Henry, Robert, 163, 164, 186, 191, 295
Heroes of America (See Red Strings)
Hickory (town), 96
Hickory Nut Gap, 74, 269, 305, 317, 354, 355
Hicks, Charles, 246
Highland Messenger, The, 309
Hillsboro (also spelled Hillsborough), 115, 130, 137, 138, 197, 311
Hodges, Thomas, 158
Holden, William H., 325, 360, 361, 362, 363, 368, (later Governor) 374-376, 378, 384

Holstein, Stephen, 74
Holtzclaw, Henry, 301
Holtzclaw, James, 157
Home Guards, 344
Hopewell Treaty, 128
Horse Shoe Bend (battle of), 194, 242-243, 250, 260, 342
Horton, Nathan, 158
Hot Springs, 215, 216, 295, 345
Howard, Benjamin, 99
Howard, Captain Thomas, 111, 281
Hughes, Barnard, 75
Hume, Robert, 291
Hunter, Colonel Archibald R. S., 274
Hyams, George McQueen, 298
Hyde, Edward, 55

Immigration 1759-1771, 92-95
Impeachment of Governor Holden, 375-376, 384
Impending Crisis, The, 336
Indian Road Gap, 342
Indian Territory (now Oklahoma), 253, 254
Inflation (1863-1871), 356-357
Innkeepers, 218-220
Iroquois Indians, 29, 32
Isaac, James, 351

Jackson, General Andrew, later President, 194, 203-204, 242-243, 245, 250-251, 279, 306
Jackson County, 15, 192, 280, 285, 333, 337, 342, 380
James I, 48
Jamestown, 48
Jefferson (town), 165, 312
Jefferson, Thomas, 142
Jewel Hill (now Walnut), 279
Johnson, President Andrew, 349, 360, 362
Johnson, Fort, 331
Johnson, Hugh, 271
Johnson, John, 272
Johnson, Governor Robert (S. C.), 69, 88
Johnston, General Joseph E., 354
Johnston, William J., 340
Joliet, Louis, 64
Jonesboro (town, Tenn.), 322
Joree (Cherokee town), 67
Judaculla Rock, 40, 279
Judd's Friend (See Ostenaco)
Judson College, 391
Junaluska (Cherokee leader), 194, 242-245, 250-251, 258-260, 381

Kansas-Nebraska Bill, 326
Keith, Lieutenant Colonel, James A., 345, 346
Keith, Sir William, 69
Kennedy, Captain Quentin, 84
Kentucky, 216, 220
Keowee (Cherokee town), 63, 67, 74, 75, 81, 83, 85, 143, 144, 147
Killian, David, 160, 178, 183
Kilpatrick, Reverend Joseph D., 180
King, Mitchell, 272, 291, 319
King's Mountain (battle of), 120-123, 136, 156, 157, 160, 265, 272, 275, 277
Kirby, Colonel Isaac M., 353
Kirk, Colonel George W., 346, 349-351, 354, 358, 374-375
"Kirk-Holden War," 374-375, 379
Kirk, John, 129
Kirk's Raids, 346, 349-351
Know-Nothing Party, 326-327
Knox, John, 179

Knoxville (Tenn.), 153, 175, 182, 215, 353
Ku Klux Klan, 370-375, 384

Lacey, William, 120
Lanman, Charles, 287, 295, 304-305
Larned, Captain C. H., 256
LaSalle, Robert, Sieur de, 64
Latimer, George, 164
Latimer, James, 164
Lederer, John, 49
Lee, General Charles, 114
Lee, General Robert E., 332, 355
Lee School for Boys, 391
Lenoir (town), 275, 399
Lenoir, General William, 275
Letters from the Alleghany Mountains (by Lanman), 305
Lexington (battle of), 107
Library Association, The, 240
Life in the Coves, 227-235
Lincoln, President Abraham, 329, 331, 336, 360
Lincoln, General Benjamin, 115
Lincoln County, 120, 196
Lincolnton, 225
Lindsey, Fort, 256
Linville Mountain, 150
Literary Fund, The, 203, 236, 237, 239, 276, 387
Littlefield, General Milton S., 368, 378, 379
Logan, George W., 327, 367, 373
Logan, Robert, 273
Loudon, Fort, 59, 76-77, 79-84, 246
Love, James R., 295
Love, Colonel Robert R., 161, 165, 191, 195, 280, 350, 355
Love, General Thomas, 161, 165
Lovingood, George W., 275
Lovingood, Hiram, 274-275
Lowney (Cherokee), 254-255
Loyalists, 108, 109, 110, 113, 114, 115, 116, 123, 125, 156, 157, 277
Ludwell, Governor Philip (under Proprietors), 55
Lyon, John, 297
Lyttleton, Governor William (S.C.), 81, 82

McDowell, Colonel Charles, 116ff., 282
McDowell County, 116, 276-277, 283
McDowell, General Joseph, 191
McDowell, Mayor Joseph, 115, 276-277
McDowell, Silas, 163
McDowell, Captain William W., 332, 357, 376
McElroy, Brigadier General John W., 344, 346
McFadden, Fort, 155
McGaughey, Fort, 155
McIver, Alexander, 387, 389
McPeters, Jonathan, 161

Macon County, 9, 112, 263-265, 273, 279, 311, 342, 349, 373, 380, 389
Macon, Nathaniel, 263
Madison County, 278-279, 285, 314, 321, 323, 333, 336, 337, 345, 349, 358
Marietta-Georgia Railroad, 397
Marion (town), 277, 354
Marion, Francis, 277
Marquette, Jacques, 64
Marshall (town), 220, 279, 345, 358, 374
Marshall, Judge John, 251, 279

456 / Index

Mars Hill (town), 391
Mars Hill College, 391
Martin, Governor Alexander, 135
Martin, Adjutant General James Green, 331, 339, 354, 355
Martin, Brigadier General Joseph, 107, 127, 156
Martin, Robert, 161
Matthews, Maurice, 56
Matthews, Major Mussendine, 191
Mebane, James, 191
Mecklenburg Council of Safety, 107
Mecklenburg County, 130
Mecklenburg Declaration of Independence, 108
Mecklenburg Resolves, 108
Meigs-Freeman Line, 165, 193, 241, 262, 280
Memminger, C. G., 293
Merrill, Ransom P., 358
Merrimon, Judge Augustus S., 285, 345-346, 375, 379
Michaux, Andre, 150, 151, 235, 298, 301
Michaux, Francois Andre, 150
Middleton, Colonel Thomas, 84, 143
Military "Exercises," 173
Miller, Benjamin, 180
Miller, William, 158
Mills, Dr. Columbus, 281, 349
Mills, Marvil, 284
Mills, William, 160-161, 172-173, 181
Mims, Fort, 242
Minerals, 13-15
Mitchell County, 162, 281, 282-283, 337, 349, 385, 389
Mitchell, Elisha, 203, 282, 300-303
Montcalm, Louis Joseph, Marquis de, 87
Montgomery, Colonel Archibald, 83-84, 85, 86, 88, 110, 113
Moore, Fort, 58
Moore, James, 56, 58
Moore, Captain William, 112, 113, 161, 173, 259
Moore's Creek Bridge (battle of), 114
Moravians, 249
Morehead, Governor John Motley, 315, 317, 318, 320, 321
Morgan, Colonel Gideon, 243
Morgan, Thomas, 294
Morganton, 96, 136, 150, 161, 171, 178, 186, 192, 220, 225, 263, 265, 276, 315, 317, 323, 324, 343, 351, 354, 377, 378, 379
Morris, John, 161
Morris, Robert, 161, 277
Morristown (See Asheville)
Mount Mitchell, 5, 7, 18, 299-300
Mountain Animals, 21-23
Mountain Birds, 24
Mountain Flora, 15, 16, 18-21
Moytoy (Cherokee Chief), 67, 68
Muckleroy, Samuel, 58
Murphey, Archibald D., 191, 197-198, 199, 200, 201, 202, 204, 237, 240, 274
Murphey Improvement Program, 197-201
Murphy (town), 112, 274, 344, 350, 396, 397
Muster Day, 173, 230

Nantahala Mountains, 249, 263
Nantahala Tunrpike, 312, 317
Nash, Judge Frederick, 275
Nashville (Tenn.), 136, 150, 253
Native Americans (see Cherokee Nation)
Needham, James, 50-52, 56, 64
Neill, James, 282
Nelson, David, 161

New Bern, 320
New Echota (Ga.) 243, 247, 251
Newport (Tenn.), 127, 217
Newton Academy, 180, 186-187, 204
Newton, Reverend George, 180, 186-187
Nicholson, Governor Francis (S. C.), 62
Nikwassi (Cherokee town), 31, 46, 47, 66, 83, 84, 85, 89, 145, 264, 265
Normal Schools, 389-399
North Carolina Common School Journal (later, *N. C. Journal of Education*), 240
North Carolina Gazette, The, 108
North Carolina-South Carolina Boundary Dispute, 191
North Carolina Spectator and Western Advertiser, The, 309
North Carolina Standard, The, 325, 360, 361
North Carolina Temperance Societies, 285
Numbers of Carlton, The (by Joseph Caldwell), 320

Oak Hill Academy, 390
Oconostota (Cherokee Chief), 82, 83, 109
Old Field Schools, 185-186, 187, 313
Old Fort (See also Fort Davidson), 110, 317, 378, 379, 393, 398
Old Hopp (Cherokee Chief), 75, 78, 79, 86, 89
Old Tassel (Cherokee Chief), 127, 129, 246
Olmsted, Dennison, 203, 301
Ostenaco (Cherokee Chief), 79, 81, 82, 84, 89, 90, 141
Overmountain Men (march of), 116-120
Outliers (See also Deserters), 337, 344-345, 347-349

Paint Rock, The, 215, 295, 323, 331, 378
Palmer, Brigadier General William J., 353, 354
Pardo, Juan, 47-48
Party Newspapers, 309-311
Patton Hotel, 294-295
Patton, James, 159, 163
Patton, James W., 294, 295
Patton, John, 159
Patton, John E., 295, 305, 314
Patton, Robert, 159
Patton, William, 302
Payne, John Howard, 250
Peace Conferences (Civil War), 329
Peachtree Mound (See also Gau-ax-a-le), 42
Pearis, Richard, 1
Pendley, William, 158
Pennsylvania Road, The, 95, 96, 98, 130, 131, 157, 174-175, 211
Philadelphia Mint, The, 208, 209, 213
Pioneer Education, 185-188
Pioneer Life, 166-173
Pitcairn, Major John, 107
Plank Roads, 324-325
Poinsett, Joel, 319
Political Rallies, 308-309
Polk County, 180, 272, 278-281, 287, 337, 349, 371
Polk, Thomas, 107
Posey, Humphrey, 181
Priber, Christian, 69-72
Prince George, Fort, 60, 75, 81, 82, 83, 86, 141, 144
Provincial Congress of North Carolina, The, 107, 110, 111
Provisional Constitution of the Confederacy, 331
Public School Laws, 237-240

Quaker Meadows, 120, 282
Qualla Trading Post, 256
Quallatown (Cherokee village), 342

Raids (local during Civil War), 345, 346
Railroads, Eastern, 318-320
Railroads, Western, plans for, 318-323; see also Western North Carolina Railroads
Raleigh (city), 205, 208, 309, 312, 361, 363, 373, 378
Raleigh Sentinel, The, 375
Raleigh, Sir Walter, 48
Reconstruction Acts (1867), 262, 364
Red Strings, the, 367, 384
Regulator Movement, 101-103, 108, 133, 155-156, 196
Reid, Governor David S., 325
Religious Denominations, 179-185; 390-391
Renegade Gangs (See also Deserters and Outliers), 346-349, 359
Republican Party, 326, 328, 362, 367, 368, 369, 375, 384
Revenue Laws, 369-370
Revolutionary War, 106-124, 277
Reynolds, Henry, 294
Richardson, Jesse, 181
Ridge, John, 251
Ridges (Tsali's son), 254-255
"Rip Van Winkle State," 195, 203, 206
Roads (See also Plank Roads), 130-131, 173-178, 315-317, 376
Roan Mountain, 150, 151, 175, 299, 305
Robbinsville, 258, 381
Robertson, Charles, 111
Robertson, James, 101, 129, 175, 265
Rock Formations, 8-11
Rosman (town), 282
Ross, John, 244, 245-246, 249-251, 253
Rough and Ready Guards, 332
Round Hill Academy, 390
Rowan County, 155, 157
Russell, George, 111
Rutherford College, 391
Rutherford County, 91, 111, 116, 154, 156, 157, 158, 159, 160, 162, 166, 171, 175, 178, 179, 180, 181, 182, 186, 195, 199, 208, 212, 256, 261, 269, 272, 276, 281, 287, 288, 309, 315, 317, 321, 322, 323, 324, 333, 335, 367, 371, 372, 373, 390
Rutherford, General Griffith, 111-112, 113, 114, 115, 155, 157
Rutherford Riflemen, The, 332
Rutherford Star, The, 273
Rutherford's Cherokee Campaign (1776), 112-113, 280
Rutherfordton, 155, 171, 178, 211, 213, 220, 225, 288, 372, 373, 385, 397

St. John-in-the-Wilderness (Episcopal church), 291
St. Xavier, Joseph Gabriel, Count de Choiseul, 293
Salem (town), 225
Salisbury (town), 317, 320, 321, 323, 346, 354, 359, 375, 377, 396, 397
Saluda, 161, 398
Saluda Gap, 215, 217, 269
Saluda Old Town (Cherokee), 75
Sargent, Dr. Charles S., 298
Schermerhorn, Reverend J. F., 251
Schneider, Martin, 38
Schofield, General John, 360, 364
School, Law of 1873, 387
Schools, private, 185-188, 229, 232, 236-240, 390-391; public, 387-389
Shuyucha (Cherokee), 111
Scott, Fort, 257
Scott, General Winfield, 252, 254-256
Seddon, James A., Secretary of War of the Confederacy, 346, 347, 349
Sequoyah (author of the Cherokee Syllabary), 245-249
Settle, Thomas, 385-387
Sevier, John, 101, 106, 111 116ff., 125, 127, 128, 129, 135, 136, 137
Sevier, Robert, 125
Sevierville (Tenn.), 127, 342
Sharpe, Alexander, 158
Sharpe, John, 58
Sharpe, William, 158
Shelby, Colonel Evan, 109
Shelby, Isaac, 106, 116, 117, 120
Sherman, General William T., 354
Shoffner Act, 273
Shook, Jacob, 183
Short, Dr. Charles W., 297
Shortia, search for, 297-299
Shotwell, Randolph, 371-372
Sickles, General David E., 362
Sitton, Phillip, 268
Skiles, Reverend W. W., 284
Sloan, Major Benjamin, 334
Smith, Second Lieutenant A. J., 255, 256
Smith, James McConnel, 195
Smith, Captain John, 48, 53
Smith, Phillip, 163, 178
Smithsonian Institution, 304
Smoky Mountains, 254, 255, 299, 380, 381
Snowbird Reservation, 258
South Carolina Gazette and Country Journal, 108
Southern Railway Company, 397
Spangenberg, Bishop A. G., 96-98, 99, 181, 277
Sparta (town), 281, 389
Sparta Academy, 391
Stagecoaches, 225-226, 377
Stamp Act, The, 107
Stekoa (Cherokee town on site of present Whittier), 75, 113, 257
Stephen, Colonel Adam, 84, 89
Stills, 223-224, 232-233
Stokes, Montford, 191
Stoneman, General George, 353-354, 377
Stoneman's Raid, 353-355
Stringfield, Lieutenant Colonel William W., 344, 349, 350, 355
Strother, Fort, 242
Strother, John, 191
Stuart, Captain John, 80, 83, 146
Sulphur Springs Hotel, 295, 305
Sumter, Fort, 329, 331
Surry County, 120, 155-156, 278, 311, 349
Suspension of Habeas Corpus, 346ff.
Swain County, 15, 147, 380-381
Swain, David Lowry, President of University and later Governor, 204-206, 236, 239, 240, 307, 311, 314, 380
Swain, George, 159-160, 163
Swanton, Dr. John R., 41, 46
Swepson, George W., 378, 379
Swepson-Littlefield Scandal, 377-379
Sycamore Shoals, 116
Sylva (town), 192, 280

Table Rock, 150
Tahlequah (Okla.), 249
Tassee (Cherokee town), 85

Tate, Samuel, 378
Taylor, John Louis, 204
Teachers' Associations, 240
Tecumseh (Indian Chief), 242, 245,
Tennent, Gilbert B., 357-358, 376
Tennessee, 216, 220, 225, 241-242, 247, 261, 265, 266, 278, 279, 281, 323
Thatcher, Daniel, 179
Thomas Legion, The, 342, 345, 350, 355
Thomas, Robert, 349
Thomas, William Holland, 241-242, 244, 255-258, 287, 342, 355
Ticonderoga, Fort, 87
Timberlake, Henry, 38, 78, 89-90, 140
Tipton, Colonel John, 135-136, 137
Toe River Valley, 158
Tories, See Loyalists
Toulouse, Fort, 65, 71, 81
Tourgee, Albion W., 367
Trail of Tears, 253-254
Transylvania Company, 109
Transylvania County, 192, 193, 281-282, 333, 335, 337, 348, 389
Transylvania Railroad, 399
Tryon (town), 111
Tryon County, 156, 157
Tryon, Royal Governor William, 91, 92, 103, 155
Tsali (Cherokee, also called Old Charley), 254-256, 380
Tucker's Barn, 275
Turner, James C., 321
Turner, Josiah, 375
Tweed, Elisha J., 358

Unaka Mountain Range, 7, 12, 191
"Underground Railroads," 337, 351
Unicoi Mountain Range, 5, 7
Union League, The, 367-369, 371, 384
University of North Carolina (Chapel Hill), 187, 197, 236, 239, 301, 311, 314, 376, 389

Valle Crucis (village), 284, 352
Van Buren, President Martin, 252
Vance-Carson Duel, 309
Vance, Colonel David, 159, 191, 220
Vance, Brigadier General Robert Brank, 342, 347
Vance, Governor Zebulon Baird, 186, 309, 313-316, 329, 331, 332, 339, 340, 341, 345, 346, 347, 349, 359, 361, 385-386, 398, 399
Vann, Joseph, 250
Vaughn, Colonel John C., 371

Wachovia, 98
Waddell, Colonel Hugh, 84, 103
Wake County, 175
Walker, Felix, 256, 257
Walker's Settlement, 99
"Walton War," 189, 192-193
War of 1812, 194-195
Ward, Nancy, 110
Warm Springs (See Hot Springs)
Washington College, 314
Washington County (now in Tenn.), 111, 116, 128, 130, 135, 137
Washington, President George, 142, 369

Watauga Association (Articles of), 103-105, 190
Watauga County, 13, 74, 100, 137, 158, 277-278, 279, 283, 301, 315, 321, 337, 349, 350
Watauga Settlements, 99-106, 110, 113, 114, 129-130, 135, 158, 159, 166, 175, 265, 277, 283
Wayne, General Anthony, 165
Waynesville, 112, 161, 165, 171, 258, 263, 295, 317, 321, 323, 344, 350, 355, 396
Weatherford, Billy, 242-243, 244
Weaver, John, 159
Weaverville College, 391
Webster (town), 280
Webster, Daniel, 249
Wedgwood, Josiah, 140
Weidner, Heinrich, 155
Welch, James, 256
Wesley, John, 179
West, William, 349
Western North Carolina Railroad (See also Railroads), 323-324, 377-379, 391-394, 397
Western Star of Liberty, The, 309
Whatogo (Cherokee town), 145, 149
Whig Party, 306ff., 325, 326, 327, 328, 329, 360, 381
Whiskey Rebellion, 224
White, John, 48
White Sulphur Springs, 295; battle of, 355
Whittaker, James, 181
Whittier (town), 127
Wilderness Road, 175, 220
Wiley, Dr. Calvin Henderson, 239-240, 315
Wilkes County, 120, 157, 166, 171, 178, 180, 181, 182, 186, 261, 275, 277, 278, 359
Wilkes, John, 157
Wilkesboro, 180, 275, 301, 312, 342
Williams, James, 120
Williams, Colonel Joseph, 115
Williamsburg, 74, 90
Williamson, Major (later Colonel) Andrew, 111, 112, 113
Wilmington, 124, 199
Wilson, Major James W., 392, 393, 394
Wilson, "Big Tom," 302, 303
Winston, Major Joseph, 120, 156
Wiseman, William, 158
Wolfe, General James, 87
Womack, Jacob, 111
Wood, General Abraham, 50, 52, 56, 73
Woodfin, Nicholas W., 286, 323, 379
Woodward, Henry, 49-50, 56, 92
Wool, General John E., 252
Worchester, Reverend S. A., 247, 249, 250
Worth, Governor Jonathan, 361, 362
Wright, Gideon, 155
Wrosetacatow (Cherokee Chief), 63

Yadkin Valley, 51, 74, 83, 86, 96
Yancey, Bartlett, 266
Yancey Collegiate Institute, 391
Yancey County, 265-267, 277, 279, 283, 285, 297, 302, 303, 317, 337, 349
Yeargin, Reverend Andrew, 181
Yellow Mountain, 150, 175
Yonaguska (Cherokee Leader), 244, 256, 257
Yorktown, 123, 124

ABOUT THE AUTHOR

ORA BLACKMUN was a native of Southern Minnesota, but moved to Fayetteville, Arkansas as a teenager. Blackmun earned her Bachelor's and Master's degrees from the University of Arkansas. She did further graduate work at the University of Chicago and at the University of Southern California. She was an associate professor in the English Department of the University of Central Arkansas at Conway. She later moved to Asheville, NC, where she taught at the University of North Carolina Asheville.

This book was designed by Spencer Qualls. The type face is Bembo, a classical Roman design of the 16th century, set by Trade Typesetters, Inc., Greensboro, North Carolina. Printed and bound by Publication Press, Inc. and Graphic Arts Finishing Company, Baltimore, Maryland. Color printing is by Gilbert Printing Company, Asheville, North Carolina.

Other Books Published and/or Distributed by

APPALACHIAN CONSORTIUM PRESS

Boone, North Carolina 28607

"... *a right good People*," by Harold Warren
Artisans/Appalachia/USA, text and photographs by David Gaynes
Arts and Crafts of the Cherokee, by Rodney L. Leftwich
Bibliography of Southern Appalachia, edited by Charlotte T. Ross
Bits of Mountain Speech, by Paul M. Fink
Down to Earth — People of Appalachia, text and photographs by Kenneth Murray
Laurel Leaves, an occasional journal of the Appalachian Consortium
Mountain Measure (hardcover and paper editions), by Francis Pledger Hulme with photographs by Robert Amberg
Music of the Blue Ridge (LP Recording), by Bob Harman and the Blue Ridge Descendants
'Round the Mountains, by Ruth Camblos and Virginia Winger
Symposium on Trout Habitat Research and Management Proceedings
Tall Tales from Old Smoky (hardcover and paper editions), by C. Hodge Mathes
The Birth of Forestry in America (hardcover and paper editions), by Carl Alwin Schenck
The Good Life Almanac, edited by Ruth Smalley
The Southern Appalachian Heritage
The Wataugans, by Dr. J. Max Dixon
Toward 1984: The Future of Appalachia, Southern Appalachian Regional Conference Proceedings
Voices from the Hills (hardcover and paper editions), edited by Robert J. Higgs and Ambrose N. Manning
Western North Carolina Since the Civil War (hardcover and paper editions), by Drs. Ina W. and John J. Van Noppen

DESCRIPTIVE CATALOG AVAILABLE

www.ingramcontent.com/pod-product-compliance
Lightning Source LLC
Chambersburg PA
CBHW071309150426
43191CB00007B/553